Regional Australia and The Great War

In this book, Philip Payton provides a vivid insight into the experiences of regional Australia during the Great War of 1914–18. He depicts the homefront experience, interweaving it with the battlefront to show how closely connected each was with the other. He draws an intimate portrait of Australia at war, from the lives (and deaths) of local soldiers—all volunteers—in the trenches far from home to the myriad reactions and activities of those in a community struggling to grasp the enormity of the situation in which it found itself.

The book shows how community cohesion was fractured by the Conscription debate, as the war dragged on. And it shows how those volunteer soldiers fared in each of the great battles in which the Australians participated—from Gallipoli to the Western Front and the heady days of 1918.

Philip Payton spent part of his early childhood in South Perth, Western Australia, and later attended the University of Adelaide where he was awarded a doctorate for his thesis on 'The Cornish in South Australia'. He later served in the Royal Navy, and was Senior Lecturer in History at the Royal Naval College, Greenwich, from 1989 to 1991. Subsequently, he served in the Royal Naval Reserve, rising to the rank of Commander. In 1991 Philip joined the University of Exeter as Director of the Institute of Cornish Studies, and was promoted Professor in 2000. A frequent visitor to Australia, in 2007 he was Visiting Fellow in the Humanities Research Centre at the Australian National University. He is a past president of the British Australian Studies Association, and edited the Association's journal *Australian Studies*, negotiating its relaunch as an on-line publication under the aegis of the National Library of Australia. He has published widely on Cornish and Australian themes.

Other books by Philip Payton published by University of Exeter Press

A.L. Rowse and Cornwall: A paradoxical patriot (2005)
Making Moonta: The invention of 'Australia's Little Cornwall' (2007)
John Betjeman and Cornwall: 'The Celebrated Cornish Nationalist' (2010)

Regional Australia and The Great War

'The Boys from Old Kio'

PHILIP PAYTON

UNIVERSITY
of
EXETER
PRESS

Paperback cover images The image on the front cover is the frontispiece of *The Anzac Book* (1915), from a drawing by Trooper W. Otho Hewett of the Light Horse. A souvenir postcard from 1919 is reproduced on the back cover.

First published in 2012 by
University of Exeter Press
Reed Hall, Streatham Drive
Exeter EX4 4QR
UK

www.exeterpress.co.uk

British Library Cataloguing in Publication Data
A catalogue record for this book is available from the British Library

Hardback ISBN 978 0 85989 872 0
Paperback ISBN 978 0 85989 873 7

Typeset in Perpetua 11.5/13 by Carnegie Book Production, Lancaster
Printed in Great Britain by CPI Anthony Rowe, Chippenham

Contents

List of Illustrations   vii

Preface   xiii

1   'A different war': The regional experience   1

2   'To make Australia's name glorious': Kio goes to war   13

3   'Our motto is "dig on, dig ever"': Gallipoli   45

4   'Mothers, Manliness and Moonta': The Somme   79

5   'I'm fed up with England now': Blighty   111

6   'Not only Germany's war; it's Rome's war too': Conscription   139

7   'Doing their best for the Empire': Australia Triumphant   163

8   'Returning with the scars of deadly conflict': Aftermath   195

Epilogue: 'The Hub of the Universe?'   219

Notes   223

Index   244

*For all the people, past and present,
of northern Yorke Peninsula,
South Australia*

Illustrations

Chapter 1.   A different war

Map 1. Northern Yorke Peninsula, South Australia   xviii

Map 2. Gallipoli: Anzac Cove and environs.
      Drawn by András Bereznay   5

Map 3. The Western Front 1916–18   8

Chapter 2.   Kio goes to War

1.   Moonta township on the eve of the Great War   14

2.   The heart of 'Old Kio' – Moonta Mines   15

3.   Wallaroo in the early twentieth century   16

4.   Kadina, the third of the northern Yorke Peninsula mining towns   17

5.   The Wallaroo mine, c.1914   19

6.   H. Lipson Hancock (1867–1935)   28

7.   The young women of the Wallaroo Mines Girls Club   31

8.   South Australian recruits during initial training at Mitcham, near Adelaide   32

9.   Officers of the 10th Battalion, Australian Imperial Force, at Mena Camp in Egypt   33

10.   The personal effects of Lieutenant Kenneth Grant Jacob   34

11.   Reinforcement Sappers for the Australian Tunnelling Companies await embarkation at Port Melbourne, Victoria   37

12.   Richard 'Lee' Leopard Pomeroy and William 'Will' Albert Pomeroy   42

Chapter 3. Gallipoli

13. Letter from Sarah Jane Elphick of Wallaroo to the Base
Records Office in Melbourne   51

14. Australians wait behind Quinn's Post, Gallipoli, 29 May 1915   52

15. The women of the Adelaide Cheer-Up Society   58

16. The Salvation Army barracks at Wallaroo   61

17. Sergeant Roy Percival Pollard   62

18. 'Australia Day' parade, Moonta, 30 July 1915   64

19. Australian and Turkish dead lie together on a trench parapet
at Lone Pine, Gallipoli   67

20. Australian graves at Shrapnel Gully, Gallipoli   69

21. The Roach brothers from Moonta   74

Chapter 4. The Somme

22. Leonard John Harvey, self-styled 'Kio boy'   81

23. John Verran, Labor Premier (1910–12) of South Australia   82

24. Letter from the military authorities (the Base Records Office
in Melbourne) to Isabella Rose   86

25. Isabella Rose's response to the Base Records Office   88

26. Anxious moments for the Australians before 'hopping the
bags' at Fromelles on 19 July 1916   95

27. Letter from Mary Ann Quintrell to the Base Records Office   98

28. Private Clarence Rhody Swan Hoffman, one of the Kio boys
who fell at Fromelles   99

29. Australian dead at Fromelles   100

30. Jubilant Australians sport the German caps and *pickelhaube*
spiked helmets captured at Pozières   103

31. Richard Daw from Moonta   105

32. Australian stretcher-bearers   108

Chapter 5. Blighty

33. Australian soldiers in camp at Weymouth in Dorset, England   114

34. Switch Trench, on the Somme   121

35. The military hospital at Keswick, near Adelaide   124

36. The Mayoress of Exeter greets Australian troops as their train
pauses at Exeter Queen Street station in Devon, England   127

37. 'English wives' and their babies, bound for Australia in the
    SS Borda in 1919 — 130

38. A group of Australian soldiers enjoy picnic refreshments
    during a YMCA outing in London in 1918 — 133

Chapter 6.   Conscription

39. The visit of the Recruiting Train to Wallaroo Mines on
    30 March 1916 — 140

40. Patriotic carnival at Kadina in 1916 — 141

41. War work – miners deep underground on northern Yorke
    Peninsula, c.1916 — 142

42. War work – toiling in the heat of the smelting works at
    Wallaroo — 142

43. The children of the Beginners' Department enjoy their
    tea-treat at Moonta Mines — 145

44. Robert Stanley ('R.S.' or 'Bob') Richards — 150

45. Trade unionists of the Amalgamated Miners of Australia in
    the Labor Day parade at Moonta in 1914 — 157

46. The jetty at Wallaroo — 158

Chapter 7.   Australia Triumphant

47. Robert Learmond, local grocer and Mayor of Moonta — 165

48. The makeshift battlefield grave of Ernest Elmer 'Snowy'
    Reynolds — 171

49. Australian Tunnellers work by candlelight beneath Flanders'
    fields, 1917 — 172

50. Australian soldiers fix bayonets in the forward area trenches
    near Zonnebeke, in the Ypres sector, September 1917 — 179

51. Seymour Jacka Thomas, from Moonta, 10th Battalion A.I.F. — 180

52. An 18-pounder gun of the Australian Field Artillery dug in
    among the ruins of an old factory near Zonnebeke, Ypres
    sector, October 1917 — 182

53. Sapper William James Perry, 1st Reinforcements, No. 5
    Tunnelling Company, from Cross Roads near Moonta — 183

54. Gassed Australians await medical attention at the dressing
    station at White Chateau, near Villers-Bretonneux — 185

55. Sergeant-Major Richard Ritter — 186

56. Australians collect German dead for burial in the aftermath of
the battle for Amiens   189

57. Sergeant William J. Mitchell of Hardingdale farm, near Kadina   190

58. The elaborate cross marking William J. Mitchell's grave   191

59. Australian infantry in action at Mont St Quentin,
1 September 1918   192

60. Hundreds of people gather outside the Institute at Wallaroo
on 11 November 1918, waiting for news of the Armistice   193

Chapter 8.   Aftermath

61. The flags of the victorious Allies decorate the Wallaroo Mines
Methodist Sunday school tea-treat, late 1918   196

62. Australian soldiers line the decks of a troopship as it docks at
Outer Harbour, Port Adelaide, in 1919   198

63. Anxious relations await their returning loved ones   199

64. Thirty-three Allied Prisoners of War at Stendal POW camp
in Germany   203

65. The unveiling of Moonta's War Memorial, 27 November 1920   208

66. Peace Procession at Moonta, probably on 'Peace Day',
Saturday 19 July 1919   211

67. Salvaged material collected for sale at the Wallaroo mine,
following closure in November 1923   214

68. Oswald Pryor's cartoon 'Scatterin' The Bal' (dismantling the
mine)   215

69. The cementation works at the Moonta mine   217

70. Stacking wheat at Moonta railway station, c.1930s   218

Epilogue

71. The 'Cousin Jacks' who took Thomas Wood underground at
the Moonta Extended Mine, c.1930–31   221

Illustration acknowledgements

Images from the author's collection: 2, 3, 4, 5, 16, 23, 14, 42, 44, 46.

Courtesy National Trust of South Australia: Moonta Branch: 1, 6, 12, 18, 21, 28, 45, 47, 55, 65, 68, 69, 70, 71; Kadina Branch: 57, 58; Wallaroo Branch: 60.

Courtesy State Library of South Australia: 7 (Image B54851); 8 (Image B41848); 15 (Image SRG6/34/6); 35 (Image B26285/87); 40 (Image PRG280/1/39/51); 43 (Image PRG1185/7/12); 61 (Image B55081); 62 (Image PRG280/1/22/114); 66 (Image B45891).

Courtesy Australian War Memorial: 9 (Image P02321.005); 11 (Image PB0664); 14 (Image G01011); 17 (Image DA11359); 19 (Image AO2025); 20 (Image PO1337.005); 26 (Image A03042); 30 (Image EZ01325); 32 (Image E04946.1); 33 (Image PO3236.319); 34 (Image E00575); 36 (Image A00768); 37 (Image D00935); 38 (Image H01203); 48 (Image J00013); 49 (Image E04621); 50 (Image E01402); 51 (Image P05120.002); 52 (Image E01209); 53 (Image DA14531); 54 (Image E04852); 56 (Image A01925); 59 (Image E03139); 63 (Image H11576); 64 (Image PO6889.009).

Courtesy National Archives of Australia: 10, 13, 24, 25, 27.

Courtesy Carol Howard, Adelaide, South Australia: 22.

Reproduced from Fridolin Solleder (ed.), *Vier Jahre Westfront: Geschichte des Regiments List R.I.R.16* (Munich: Verlag Max Schick, 1932): 29.

Courtesy Lillian James, Moonta, South Australia, 31.

Courtesy Keith Bailey, Kadina, South Australia, 39, 67.

Map 3 is reproduced by permission of Cambridge University Press, from *The Anzac Illusion* by E.M. Andrews (1994)

Preface

'All books of non-fiction are to a degree autobiographical'. It is hard to disagree with the opinion of Paul Fussell, expressed in his volume *The Great War and Modern Memory*, first published in 1975, and all of us who write non-fiction – especially history and biography – must surely acknowledge the autobiographical strands in our work.

I was not born until after the Second World War, in the 1950s, but my grandfather – who lived with us when I was a small child – had fought in the Great War, and I was aware of its shadow. My grandfather talked rarely about his experiences, and then only incidentally – the inscrutability of the French peasantry, for instance, 'you never knew what they were thinking' – but far more eloquent were the few artefacts that lay about the house. Two fearsome knobkerries, relics of hand-to-hand fighting and trench warfare, hung beside the basement door (to assist in the repulse of burglars, I wondered), and in one dark cupboard lurked the malevolent *pickelhaube* – taken from a dead German, I surmised. To handle the spiked helmet was to be transported to the Somme mud, and to achieve a chilling intimacy with the unfortunate individual to whom it had once belonged, and whose remains – for all I knew – still lay undiscovered or unrecognised in the earth of distant battlefields. Even today, I recall the hardened polished leather and its metal trim, together with the regimental badge and, of course, the evil spike itself.

Aged eight, I was in Grade Four at primary school in South Perth in Western Australia, immersed in *Social Studies through Activities*, a volume designed to introduce inquisitive young minds to history, geography and what was called 'citizenship'. Here my classmates and I learned the significance of Anzac Day. 'April 25th is Anzac Day', announced *Social Studies*: 'On that day every year schools and shops and offices are closed while people pay honour to those who died in World War I (1914–18) and World War II (1939–1945), and later wars'. There were commemorative church services, it added, while 'soldiers march through the streets, and men and women, and boys and girls, gather at war memorials and place flowers upon them'. The very first Anzac Day, it was explained, was 25 April 1915, when 'thousands of Australian and New Zealand soldiers, who were ever afterwards known as Anzacs', went ashore in 'the half light of dawn' at Gallipoli. In 'spite of terrible rifle and machine-gun fire', the narrative continued, 'our men drove the Turks back' and 'won for themselves a narrow strip of land'.

Then there was the story of saintly Private Simpson, the 'man with the donkey', who, unarmed, saved the life of many a poor wounded soldier but who was himself cut down, 'shot through the heart by a sniper'. We pupils were encouraged to give 'lecturettes' to our classmates, and were asked to describe what it was like going ashore at Anzac Cove. We were invited to imagine that we were injured soldiers, rescued by Private Simpson, and were instructed solemnly to write letters to our imaginary mothers. 'My Dear Mother', we were to begin, 'I am lucky to be able to write you this letter. A few days ago I was lying badly wounded near Shrapnel Gully when . . .'. In this way, we were drawn, individually and collectively, into the Anzac myth – based as it was on the exploits of the Australian and New Zealand Army Corps – and for those few hours that we studied Gallipoli and Private Simpson we lived the experience for ourselves, in the way that young children do.

Years later, a postgraduate student at the University of Adelaide, I encountered the numerous glowing reviews of Bill Gammage's newly published volume, *The Broken Years: Australian Soldiers in the Great War*. Like others, I was attracted by its 'democratic' approach – its reliance upon the testaments of those who had fought and suffered in the war – and was quick to read the book itself. Ever since, for me, it has remained a favourite and a yardstick, surviving the furious fads and fashions of historiographical debate that have attended the Great War and the Anzac tradition. More than a decade later, now on the staff of the Royal Naval College, Greenwich, *The Broken Years* was always to hand, as in seminars and lectures we analysed the experiences and lessons of amphibious warfare, with Gallipoli as the inevitable case study.

In the Royal Navy, things have the habit of moving sooner or later from the theoretical to the practical, from the classroom to operations at sea. Thus it was in early 2003 that I found myself, a Naval Reservist, 'recalled to active service' on the battlestaff of the Commander Amphibious Task Group in his flagship, the aircraft carrier *HMS Ark Royal*. Tasked with putting ashore elements of 3 Commando Brigade in the opening moves of the Iraq War, we revisited again the lessons of Gallipoli and amphibious warfare. And, appropriately, the frigate *HMAS Anzac*, part of Australia's contribution to the coalition, had been assigned to provide naval gunfire support for our assault on the El Faw peninsula, operating alongside three British warships in clearing the way for the Royal Marines to land ashore. *HMAS Kanimbla*, an amphibious transport ship, was likewise in the thick of it, seemingly everywhere as she conducted numerous boardings of suspicious vessels, including the timely interception of Iraqi minelayers.

Four years later, in April 2007, I arrived in Canberra to take up a Visiting Fellowship in the Humanities Research Centre at the Australian National University. An invitation for my wife Dee and I to march in the national Anzac Day parade was gladly accepted, an event that seemed somehow to round off my lengthy association — as I saw it — with the Anzac tradition. But again serendipity intervened, for, in finding my office at the ANU, I noticed that the name on the door immediately opposite was 'Professor Bill Gammage'. That Bill, now retired, was an Adjunct Professor at the ANU was news that had somehow passed me by. But we swiftly established a firm friendship, my interest in Australia and the Great War rekindled anew. Further serendipity beckoned, for a visit in May of that year to South Australia's northern Yorke Peninsula to participate in the biennial 'Kernewek Lowender' Cornish festival, led to my introduction to the internationally significant archival work conducted by Liz Coole and the late Jim Harbison, along with their team of volunteers, at the former Moonta School of Mines. Now a National Trust museum and research centre, the Moonta School of Mines had amassed important collections of archival material relating to the region, including the Great War. Back in Canberra, the idea for a regional study of Australia and the Great War quickly took shape — what was the experience of war like for one particular region? could one reconstruct the intimacy of the relationship between battlefront and homefront by concentrating on such a region? — with Bill Gammage's seal of approval for the project a powerful incentive. Two subsequent visits to northern Yorke Peninsula, both in 2009, allowed further research at Moonta, not least in the files of local newspapers, not yet available on line. And two years on, this book is the result of a lifetime's interest and nearly half a decade of research and writing.

* * *

A great many individuals and organisations have helped me in the production of this book, and it is impossible to name them all. My grandfather, the late Cecil Williams, unwittingly lent a hand all those years ago, and my classmates and teachers at Kensington School — together with the educationalists in the Western Australian state government — all deserve due acknowledgement, as I am sure do countless others who have assisted one way or another over the years.

My wife Deidre — Dee — deserves especial mention, as always, for her constant love and support. Like me, a Naval Reservist, Dee was enormously supportive of my recall in 2003, and subsequently accompanied me on all my research visits to Australia, including my time at the Australian National

University, assisting in numerous ways. At the ANU, Bill Gammage proved inspirational but I am also grateful to many others in the Humanities Research Centre and wider University community in Canberra, including Leena Messina — the Centre's indefatigable administrator — my fellow Visiting Fellows, Helena Hammond and Toby Haggith, and Bruce Bennett and Matthew Spriggs. At the National Trust of South Australia, Moonta Branch, I am overwhelming indebted to Liz Coole who, with the late Jim Harbison, put at my disposal the vast quantity of archival material deposited at the School of Mines. I was made extremely welcome on each of my visits, and none of my requests or questions proved too awkward or tiresome, with Liz and her team anxious to share their own research findings and to assist in every way possible. Stephen Stock, the Secretary of the Moonta Branch, was likewise extremely helpful, not least in his permission to use material from the archival collection and to reproduce photographs. Lillian James, Graham Hancock, and both the Kadina and Wallaroo Branches of the National Trust of South Australia — especially Nick Woods, Jean Hutchings and Jeanette Ireland — likewise assisted in the identification of appropriate illustrations for this book.

Carol Howard and Beth Scott deserve especial thanks for their ready permission to allow me to draw extensively from the letters and diaries of their late father, Lance-Corporal Signaller Leonard John Harvey, which has enhanced this volume immeasurably. In Australia, Brigadier Tony Gill, David and Kay Gill, Ros and Neil Paterson, Paul and Kathryn Thomas, and other friends all helped in various ways, as did fellow historians Geoffrey Blainey, David Dunstan, Paula Dunstan, Jillian Durance, Ed Jaggard, John McQuilton, Peter Pedersen, Aaron Pegram, Robin Prior, Keir Reeves, Bruce Scates and Peter Stanley. In the United Kingdom, I am similarly indebted to my colleagues at the University of Exeter — especially Catriona Pennell at the Cornwall Campus and Richard Toye and Martin Thomas at Streatham — as well as to Carl Bridge at the Menzies Centre for Australian Studies, King's College London, and Jenny McLeod at the University of Hull. I am also grateful to my third-year Australian History students, especially Emma Bennett (with her twin enthusiasm for Cornwall and Australia), whose energetic seminar discussions of the Great War and the Anzac myth offered numerous stimulating insights. Beyond the academic world, my sister Jackie, with characteristic generosity, gave me her copy of *The Broken Years*, and fellow Reservist Mark Prout (of the Territorial Army) likewise assisted with the timely gift of other important volumes.

Numerous other institutions have helped in various ways. The Australian War Memorial, the National Archives of Australia, and the State Library of South Australia have been unfailing in their assistance, and I am greatly indebted to them for permission to use material in their respective collections, and especially for permission to reproduce photographs. In 2008 I presented preliminary ideas for this book at the biennial conference of the British Australian Studies Association at Royal Holloway College, University of London, and in 2009 the History Trust of South Australia (now 'History SA') invited me to speak on 'Old Kio' at its annual conference at Kadina.

And finally, of course, I am especially indebted to University of Exeter Press – to Simon Baker and Helen Gannon, and the UEP readers – whose invaluable advice and assistance have added so much to this book, and with whom, as ever, it has been such a pleasure to work.

Philip Payton
Bodmin, Cornwall
26 January 2012
Australia Day

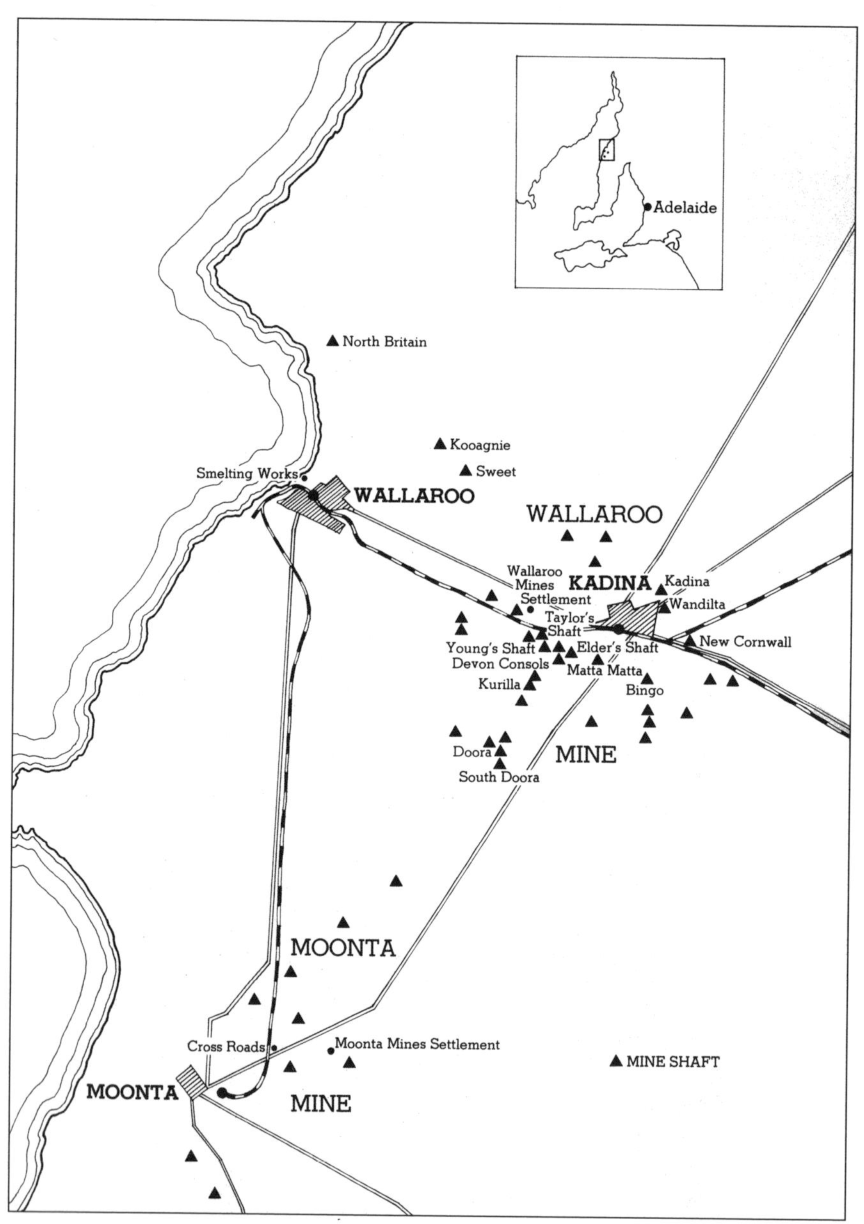

Map 1.   Northern Yorke Peninsula, South Australia.

CHAPTER ONE

'A different war'

The regional experience

For many years there was a photo of three soldiers hanging in the passage of the Quintrell cottage on Moonta Mines. These soldiers were my grandmother's brothers. There were also two medals for each of the soldiers. These had been sent to their mother (my great-grandmother) Mary Ann Quintrell. These medals were the British War Medal and the Victory Medal. There were also three Commemorative Plaques sent to Mary Ann – one for each of her sons who died in the war. The old cottage is gone now. Sadly so are the photos and medals. I have two of the plaques. The third was found by some work-men clearing the site of the cottage.[1]

So wrote Brian Cooper in September 2003, in a short account of the three Quintrell brothers – Clarence, John and Richard – who lost their lives in the Great War of 1914–18, compiled for family and friends to ensure that 'the stories of Clarrie, Jack and Dick . . . should never be entirely forgotten'. As Cooper explained, when he was young he 'would often walk with my grandmother from her home on Moonta Mines to the town of Moonta which was only about a mile away'. Sometimes, he added, 'we would look at the names of her three brothers inscribed on the war memorial in the grounds of the Moonta Memorial Park Bowling Club. She did tell me a little about them', he said, but it was not until much later that he began to unravel the details of a complex and tragic tale.[2]

'Circles of mourning'

Although the small boy who gazed so intently upon the war memorial might not have realised it, at countless similar sites across Australia and far beyond, others were likewise engaged in what were everyday acts of commemoration. From the Shetlands to New Zealand, passers-by would stop briefly to read again the names of relations, friends and neighbours, and in the ubiquitous memorial halls that sprang up across the towns and villages of the Empire, remembrance was re-enacted daily in the whist-drives, amateur dramatics, jumble sales, dances, public meetings and the like that marked the rhythm of community life. Here was a universal experience, shared by countless millions across the globe whose lives had been touched by the Great War, and yet whose remembrance was often intensely personal and intensely local – rooted in particular places, each with its peculiar associations and its own sense of what the war had been like and what it had meant for individuals and communities. Here were intimacies shared – within families and neighbourhoods and further afield across localities – and particular places wove their own stories of how they had suffered together, and had endured. In this way, regional identities were renegotiated – sometimes reinforced, sometimes contested, sometimes both – by the experiences of war.

Brian Cooper appreciated, as he grew older, that part of the Quintrell family tragedy in the Great War was the experiences of the three brothers on the battlefield, and the means by which they had lost their lives. But, as Cooper also understood, equally significant were the experiences of those on the Australian homefront, not least those of Mary Ann Quintrell herself, the boys' mother. Again, hers was a universal story – mothers on all sides of the conflict suffered prolonged and multiple agonies during the war, from the constant gnawing fear of not knowing what was happening on the battlefields so far away, to the awful debilitating shock of bad news when it arrived on the doorstep. Perhaps Mary Ann Quintrell suffered more than most. But hers was an experience that was repeated time and again across France, Russia, Germany, Turkey and all the other belligerent powers, as well as the Dominions of the British Empire, replicated endlessly in innumerable discrete communities as individuals learned the tragic fate of loved-ones in distant lands. Here again was a universal experience but one that had, at its core, dimensions that were always intensely personal and intensely local, above all rooted in place.

Indeed, the complex interplay of the personal and the local created those 'circles of mourning', as Annette Becker has described them, where the greater the losses sustained by families in a particular locality, the wider the community implications and the greater the social dislocation that resulted.[3] Mary Ann Quintrell lived within such a circle, and each time she was the recipient of bad news, so the circle became more intricate, drawing in the clergymen who bore the ill tidings, the off-spring who provided solace, the neighbours who rallied round, the journalists and editors who found the right words for their newspaper articles, and the politicians who insisted upon proper remembrance. Yet she was but one of the bereaved in a community where loss was commonplace, and as more and more names were added to the lists of those killed, missing, captured, wounded or ill, so increasing numbers of individuals were caught up in ever more complex circles of mourning.

Born in Cornwall c.1844, Mary Ann Datson (as she was before marriage) came to South Australia when three years old, settling eventually at Moonta Mines in the copper-mining region of northern Yorke Peninsula, where she met her husband, Stephen Quintrell. Together, they had thirteen children, but, by the end of the Great War, Mary Ann was a widow with only six surviving offspring. As Cooper observed, her first two daughters lived long lives. Her third died when a teenager, and a fourth suffered life-long disability as a result of childhood illness. Of her first four sons, only one survived infancy, the others were buried in Moonta cemetery with the hundreds of other babies who perished in the periodic epidemics that swept the Mines settlements. Of the adult sons, as we have seen, three died in the Great War. Added to this loss was the death of Mary Ann's brother in a mining accident. Yet, despite this apparent narrative of unrelieved misery, Mary Ann remained stoic in the face of adversity, and throughout her life retained undiminished a fierce and patriotic pride in the ultimate sacrifice of her boys, Clarence, John and Richard. She lived to be 90.[4]

Competing myths, 'myriad meanings'

Mary Ann Quintrell's reaction to the loss of her three sons alerts us to the complexities (and contradictions) of human responses to the experience of war, especially the Great War.[5] Much of English-language literature — academic as well as popular — has depicted the Great War as senseless slaughter. Young innocents, so the story goes, naïve in their misplaced patriotic fervour, were sent to their deaths by incompetent generals and self-serving politicians, leading swiftly to despondency and disillusion on the battlefield as well as the homefront, and to an enduring legacy of loss and hopelessness which shaped popular memory of the war, especially in Britain.[6] In 1934, for example, Daphne du Maurier, then an up and coming young biographer and novelist, detected in contemporary England a 'bitterness and a fresh realisation of terrible futility' and, catching the national mood of the moment, described a 'world grown old and weary with fighting', a 'universal catastrophe that seemed to be changing the face of the earth'. Peace, 'with its promises unfulfilled', had, she thought, brought only 'bewilderment' to a people who were now 'too tired, too utterly worn in mind and body'.[7]

It was a powerful imagining, shared by many, and helped shape the attitude of a generation of writers. 'The war was beyond the capacity of generals and statesmen alike',[8] announced A.J.P. Taylor in his book *The First World War*, first published in 1963, describing a collective madness where millions of men writhed to no purpose in vast landscapes of mud, all the while subjected to uninterrupted bombardment by terrifying ordnance of huge destructive force. Although more recent scholarship from the pens of battle analysts such as Gary Sheffield and William Philpott has done much to refute such a view, restoring agency to the generals who ran the war and to the men who fought and won (or lost) it, it nonetheless remains a powerful myth, again – especially in Britain.[9]

In Australia, as in New Zealand and Canada, as Mark Sheftall has argued in his *Altered Memories of the Great War*, there were (and are) different myths. In Britain, he says, in the aftermath of the Great War, the emphasis was on 'the human, material, social and spiritual cost of the conflict'.[10] But in Australia and the other Dominions, by contrast, the war, 'for all its carnage and discord, had confirmed the potential and the destiny of these – no longer colonies – nations'. Here they had proved themselves as 'healthy young countries, isolated from the ills of the Old World ... as the uncorrupted heirs of British supremacy'.[11] This, of course, found its ultimate expression in the Anzac myth, crafted initially by the war correspondent C.E.W. Bean and given lasting voice in his *The Official History of Australia in the War of 1914–18*, published in Sydney in 1929. Here the Australian nation was born on the heights of Gallipoli, and received its full baptism of fire at Pozières on the Somme. Tall and bronzed, their survival skills honed in the unforgiving Outback, the Australians were natural warriors. The Anzac soldier, as Joan Beaumont put it, was 'a superb fighter, something of a larrikin, instinctively egalitarian, distrustful of authority, endlessly resourceful, dryly humorous and above all, loyal to his mates'.[12] Or so the myth insisted.

Inevitably, the Anzac myth has been deconstructed. From K.S. Inglis' seminal article, 'The Anzac Tradition', published in 1965, and E.M. Andrews' persuasive *The Anzac Illusion* of 1993, to Jenny MacLeod's *Reconsidering Gallipoli* (2004) and Chris Pugsley's recent military (and New Zealand) perspective in his *The Anzac Experience*, writers have probed the origin and nature of the myth.[13] Some feminists, like Patricia Grimshaw, have objected to the very notion of men 'giving birth', while Robin Gerster has challenged what he and other sceptics have termed the 'heroic theme' in Australian war writing, dismissing it as mere chimera.[14] As this millennium unfolds, the debate continues, its vigour undiminished. John Hirst, for example, tackling the deconstructionists head-on, has sharply criticised the view of 'literary critics, semioticians and linguists' that 'it was only journalistic hype which made the Australians into good soldiers'. As he points out, at Gallipoli, 'though under fire while defenceless in open rowing boats, though having to wade ashore, though lacking the direction of officers, though facing unknown and unexpected cliffs ... the Australians did dislodge the Turks and establish a bridgehead'. In Hirst's estimation, then, it is self-evident that 'our soldiers have a deserved reputation for valour and resource'. [15] And so the debate goes on.

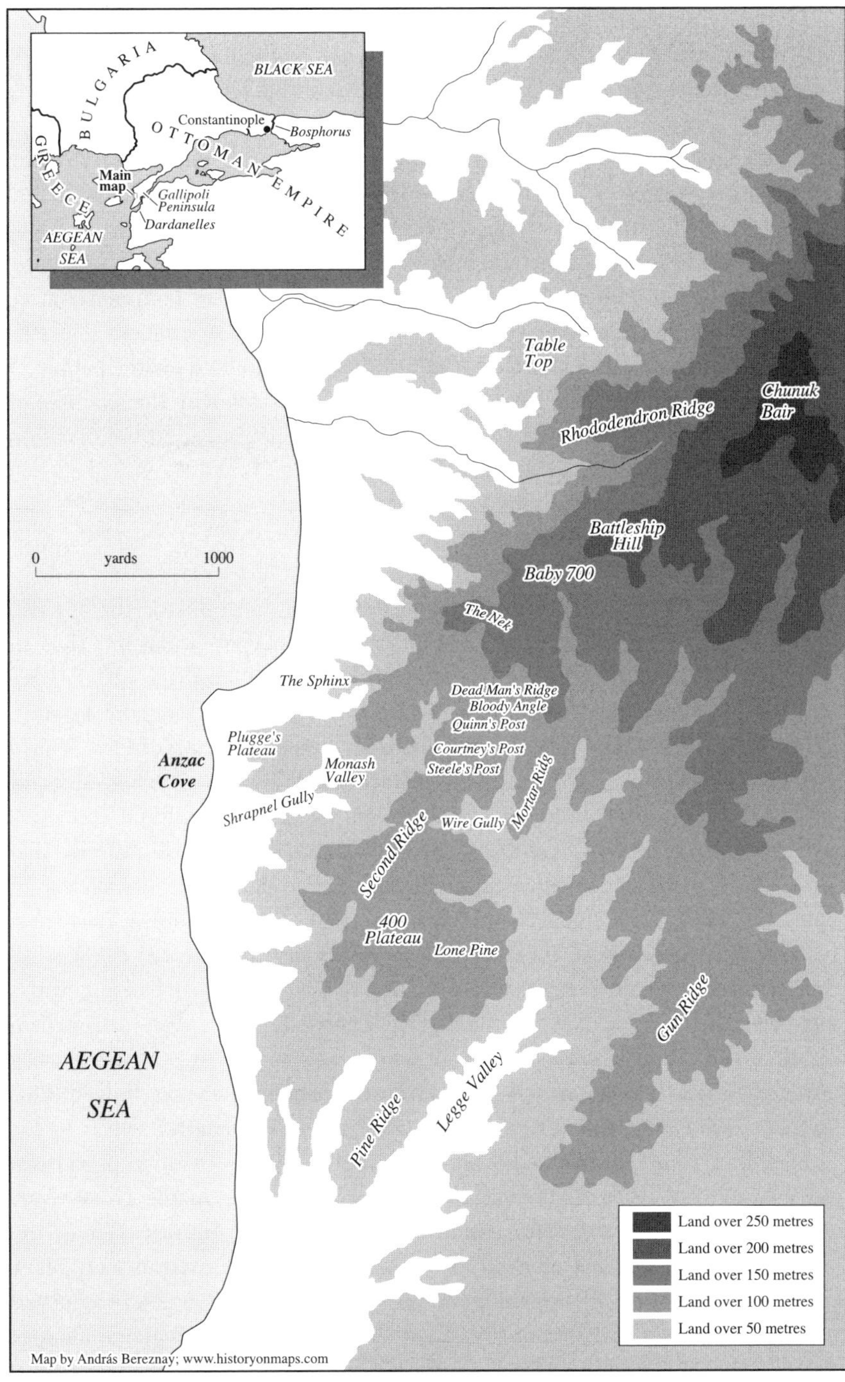

Map 2. Gallipoli: Anzac Cove and environs.

Martin Crotty, meanwhile, has acknowledged what was and remains an essential truth; that the 'Anzac experience, which began at Gallipoli, is the centrepiece of collective memory in Australia'. As he has explained, 'Australia's experience of war, particularly World War I, has assumed a quasi-religious status in Australian collective memory', enacted each year in Anzac Day commemorations across the nation.[16] But while indisputably national in spirit, Anzac Day from the first had a strong regional flavour. After the war, local branches of the recently formed Returned Sailors' and Soldiers' Imperial League of Australia took the lead in organising commemorative events, including Anzac Day, investing them with local significance. 'Anzac Day mirrored the myriad meanings the war had come to hold for the people of the North East [of Victoria]', argues John McQuilton, offering the example of rural Victoria to show how in the 1920s local personalities used the occasion to articulate regional anxieties and aspirations.[17]

Empire, nation and region

Paradoxically, in their preoccupation with the Anzac myth, historians – critics and apologists alike – have been complicit in its perpetuation and thus in the elaboration of Australia's collective memory. Bill Gammage's *The Broken Years*, first published in 1974, 'was instrumental in revivifying the legend', according to Joan Beaumont, part of the 'democratic tradition of First World War historiography' in Australia, which alighted upon the experiences of ordinary men (and sometimes women), so important in moulding collective memory.[18] In his book, Gammage exposed the illusions of Empire that rallied Australians to Britain's cause. But he never doubted the sincerity of their opinions or the strength of their emotions, acknowledging that most Australians in 1914 saw themselves as integral to an Imperial 'British World'. This was no false consciousness, as Australian radical mythology has sometimes suggested. Instead, as Neville Meaney has argued: 'Australian nationalism was not "thwarted"' by this Imperial sentiment: 'rather, it was based on a local patriotism which saw itself as part of a pan-Britishness'. Indeed, this 'Britishness was probably stronger in Australia than in Britain itself'.[19]

For Mary Ann Quintrell, this blend of Imperial and Australian patriotism underpinned her pride in the sacrifice of her three sons in the Great War, a tragic pride she shared with countless other bereaved mothers across the continent. But, born in Cornwall and the widow of a Cornish miner, Mary Ann – who had lived all her adult life on Moonta Mines – was also exposed to another kind of local patriotism, an adherence to a strong regional identity forged in the copper-mining communities of northern Yorke Peninsula.[20] For, in addition to its entwinement of Imperial and national sentiment, Australian identity also possessed a significant regional component. Regional identities were to play an important role in the Great War, as we shall see in this book, and much of the collective memory of the war in Australia – then and now – was formed and expressed at regional community level. This was true in the 1920s, as John McQuilton has shown, but it was still true nearly ninety years later. In July 2008 the dramatic news of the discovery in France of a mass grave containing the remains of soldiers killed in the battle of Fromelles reverberated across Australia.[21] It was a story that caught national headlines. But, as descendants of the fallen struggled to learn more about the fate of their family members of long ago, so it was the regional press that became the principal forum for the outpouring of memory renewed.

Brian Cooper, for example, wrote to the *Yorke Peninsula Country Times* to tell again the story of Mary Ann Quintrell and her three boys, and to speculate whether Richard Quintrell was one of those whose remains had been uncovered at Fromelles.[22] As Cooper reflected, the successive deaths of the three Quintrell boys had been a series of unimaginably severe shocks for their poor mother, each reported widely in the Peninsula press at the time. And now, nine decades later, powerful memories of those traumatic events were readily stirred in the community, with the families of those who fought (and sometimes died) anxious to recall the melancholy links between their locality and the battlefields of the Great War. To the story of the Quintrell brothers, for example, was added that of Clarence Hoffman, another Moonta boy who had fallen at Fromelles, told now with vigour and passion by his descendants, Maggie Schwann and Lyn Barker.[23]

This book, then, responds to this continuing sense of intimacy between regional Australia and the Great War. As Michael McKernan hinted in his *The Australian People and the Great War*, and as John McQuilton subsequently made plain in his *Rural Australia and the Great War: From Tarrawingee to Tangambalanga*, the conflict in regional Australia was in several respects 'a different war' to that experienced in the metropolitan cities.[24] Pressure to enlist was often higher in regional communities, especially those with a distinctive local identity where conspicuous contribution to the war effort was a matter of collective civic pride. Similarly, the Conscription controversy – whether or not Australia should introduce Conscription to its armed forces – was often highly regional in character, reflecting the mix of distinctive ethno-religious identities and strongly-voiced concerns about retaining sufficient reservoirs of local labour to support the continuance of farming, mining and other strategic regional industries. Paradoxically, those regional communities where pressure to enlist had been high, could also be those where opposition to Conscription was most intense.

However, as John McQuilton has noted, most of the literature of the Great War has drawn on metropolitan sources, with a general assumption that the war in regional Australia merely reflected the war in the cities. Even Bobbie

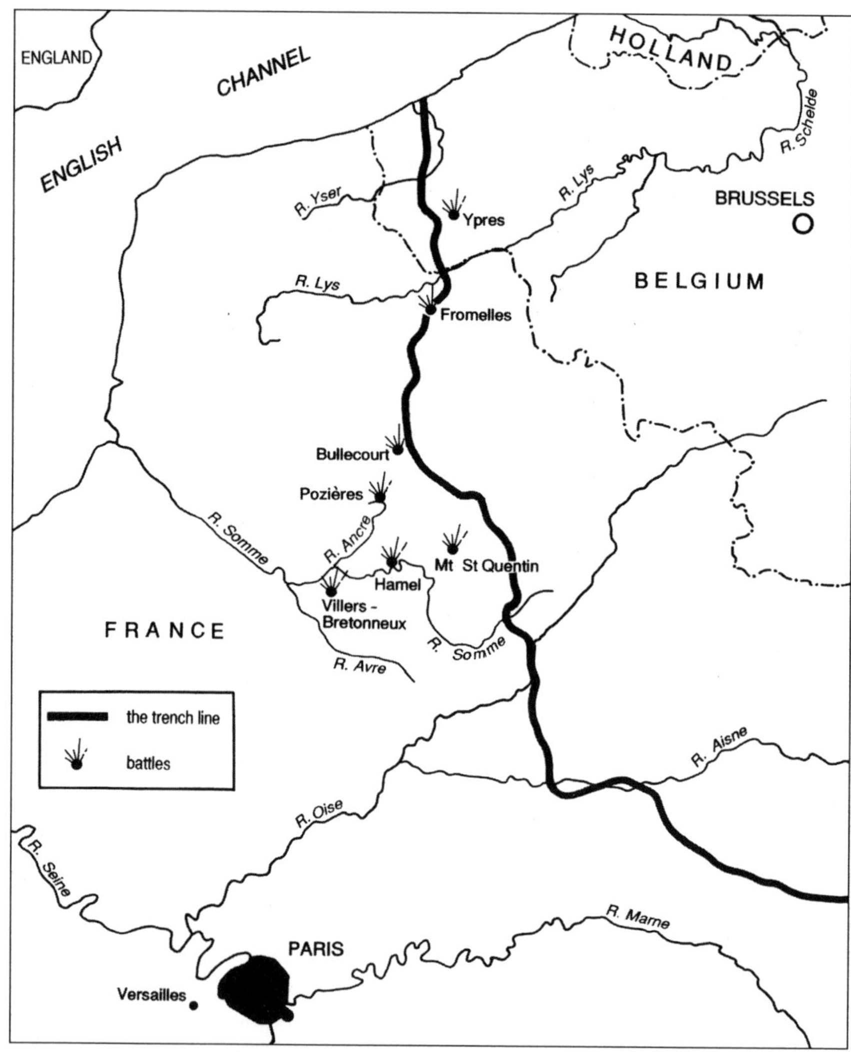

Map 3.   The Western Front.
A simplified composite map of the Western Front trench line 1916—18
showing principal battles in which the Australians were involved.

Oliver's *War and Peace in Western Australia* was largely metropolitan in focus, despite its central argument that Western Australia in the early twentieth century was an essentially heterogeneous society.[25] There were exceptions to this metropolitan bias, in the studies of New South Wales, Tasmania and Queensland by Raymond Evans, Marilyn Lake and others, who, as Evans put it, exposed a patchwork of different societies 'riven by class, ethnic and ideological divisions'.[26] But in his book *Rural Australia and the Great War*,

John McQuilton set out to offer an emphatic corrective to this over-riding metropolitan bias. Acknowledging that rural Australia was an extremely 'broad canvas', as he put it, he decided to take 'one rural region' as his exemplar, the North Eastern area of Victoria, a mixed mining, agricultural and pastoral district with a similarly mixed population of Anglicans, Cornish Methodists, Catholics, a sizeable minority of Germans, and other groups.[27] In so doing, he was able to capture the texture of wartime rural Australia, furnishing a case study which provided insights into the experience of rural Australia as a whole but also painted a vivid picture of the impact of the Great War in one specific region.

This book takes up where McQuilton has left off. Like McQuilton's study, it selects one region – the northern Yorke Peninsula of South Australia – as its case study. It argues that the locality's experience in the Great War was in some respects typical of regional Australia generally but that in others it was highly distinctive, reflecting its particular cultural, economic and political make-up. Both semi-urban (the copper-mining heartland of Moonta-Wallaroo-Kadina) and agricultural/rural, with wheat-lands stretching down towards the southern tip of the Peninsula and eastwards to Barunga Gap at its neck, the district owed much of its distinctiveness to the settlement of Cornish families in the nineteenth century. Moonta – or 'Kio' as it was known locally – was the self-proclaimed hub of the locality, a status to which neighbouring settlements usually acquiesced, albeit grudgingly. Copper mining and smelting emerged as an important strategic activity during the Great War, adding a further dimension to a Conscription debate already dominated by tension between the locality's dominant Methodist and Labor affiliations.

Like McQuilton's study, this book explores these and other tensions, examining the roles of local politicians, trade unionists, women's groups, journalists, religious leaders and others in their responses to issues generated by the Great War. It also allows the examination of more generic questions, so often exhibited graphically at regional level. We can observe at close quarters the nature of wartime civil society, especially a community solidarity that found itself increasingly under stress as the war went on. There was also the enduring gulf between metropolis and region – between town and country – and the key role in this regional setting of extended family and kin networks in shaping local reactions to the war. Here again the role of women (matriarchs especially) was significant, not least in sustaining (and sometimes challenging) community commitment to the war, and in 'keeping the home fires burning', to use the contemporary euphemism. There were also religious, ethnic and class tensions, again more pronounced as the war dragged on, and which again had strong regional implications.[28] Likewise, regional focus allows close-quarters analysis of the aftermath of war, from the problems and dislocations of repatriation, the trauma of economic change, and the politics of discontent, to the culture of remembrance and the creation of a returned servicemen identity.

Battlefront and homefront

However, in a marked departure from John McQuilton's approach, this book also places centre-stage the symbiotic relationship between military activity at 'the front' and the reactions of the community 'back home', drawing especially upon local newspaper reports to examine how that relationship between battlefront and homefront was mediated by the press over time. Entirely volunteer-manned, Australian military units in the Great War retained strong links with the districts in which they raised or from which they recruited. Unlike the British army where, as the war progressed, Irishmen might find themselves posted to Scottish regiments to fill gaps, or Lancashire men to Yorkshire battalions, the Australians continued to place new recruits in units with strong regional connections. This contributed to the sense of solidarity in such units – exemplified in Edgar Rule's *Jacka's Mob*, a short memoir published in 1933 of the 14th Battalion (raised in Victoria in 1914) – and provided a strong contrast to the increasing homogeneity that appeared often to characterise British military units.[29]

Australians were aware of regional diversity within the British World. They lumped English units together pejoratively as 'chooms' ('chums') – a collective parody of the Midlands-cum-North country accents they detected and thought amusing – but admired the distinctive qualities of the 'Jocks' (especially the Highlanders), glad to claim affinity and common cause with them and their independent, feisty ways.[30] They also admired the Welsh – 'the Welsh are great fighters',[31] wrote one Australian soldier in September 1916 – and likewise they identified with New Zealanders and Canadians, and sometimes South Africans and even Americans. But they were also alive to intra-Australian diversity, perpetuated in the regional composition of Australian military units. In this they were akin to the British 'Pals' battalions – the 'Accrington Pals', 'Sheffield Pals' and so on – part of the hastily recruited Kitchener's Army in which, atypically and unlike the majority of British regiments, 'real pals, often from a single village, a single street, a single factory or sports club, stuck together'.[32] In these locally raised battalions, there was 'some element of the civilian community structure … bringing together neighbours, workmates or friends, officered by prominent local men'.[33] But the Pals battalions suffered inordinately on the Somme, and were unable to sustain their local recruiting base thereafter, while in much of the rest of Kitchener's Army 'county affiliation was, even from the outset, little respected'.[34]

By contrast, the identification of Australian units with geographical localities was, broadly speaking, perpetuated throughout the war, with new recruits posted to battalions in which there were already friends, relations, and neighbours. In this way, as we shall see, individual soldiers sought out the company of those they had known at home – or even strangers who hailed from neighbouring localities with whom they could claim affinity or kinship. They trained together in Australia, and in Egypt, England and France, living together in camps such as those at Weymouth and on Salisbury Plain, going on leave together, and fighting and sometimes dying together in battles from Gallipoli to the great clashes of the Western Front. They tended the graves of the fallen, whom perhaps they had known since childhood, and wrote letters of condolence to bereaved parents whose faces they could picture and whose precincts they knew.

This was as true for the 'boys from old Kio' – those from northern Yorke Peninsula – as it was for those from other parts of regional Australia, and their tight-knit existence at the battlefront was reflected at length in the pages of the several regional newspapers. Most soldiers would write home as frequently as they could, their letters – with surprisingly candid (and seemingly only lightly censored) accounts of bloody actions and eagerly awaited news of other local boys at the front – often finding their way into the newspapers. Here the juxtaposition of war news, especially as conveyed in those vivid letters home, with reports of community events and attitudes, created that peculiar sense of intimacy between the war and regional Australia as experienced on Yorke Peninsula.

Here, then, in this book, the soldiers at the front are as much part of the narrative as the men and women at home. In an echo of the democratic approach deployed by Bill Gammage in *The Broken Years*, the soldiers also speak for themselves – in extracts from those newspapers and also from other sources, such as memoirs, private letters and diaries. Details of their military lives (and deaths) are further provided in official service records in the National Archives of Australia and the Australian Red Cross Society Wounded and Missing Enquiry Bureau files. Such records often include intimate correspondence with families, regional organisations (such a local branches of friendly societies) and other regional actors, including ministers of religion. These records afford further insights into the relationship between soldiers at the front and the communities from which they sprang, as well as allowing their personal (and often poignant, even tragic) experiences to be investigated in full. Considered alongside other sources, these records allow soldiers' lives (and deaths) to be reconstructed in remarkable and revealing depth. We know these soldiers' occupations before they enlisted, their religious affiliations, their parents' addresses, their height and weight on joining-up, as well as complete details of their military service – theatres of deployment, illnesses, wounds, offences and punishments, when they were killed or when they returned home to Australia. Complications, such as illegitimate children and their entitlement to the war medals of those killed in action, are commonplace. Often it is possible to trace the same groups of characters – soldiers at the front, families and friends at home – throughout the years of conflict, elaborating their individual and collective stories against the changing backdrop of the war. Likewise, the richness of documentary evidence allows a considerable degree of intricate cross-referencing, with the same events or series of events viewed and re-told from several standpoints.

This book, then, builds upon strong historiographical trends already established in the study of Australia and the Great War – notably the work of John McQuilton and Bill Gammage – but also breaks new ground in offering for the first time an integrated consideration of the war on both 'fronts': the battlefield half-a-world away and the homefront in regional Australia. It combines chronological and thematic approaches, beginning with consideration of the dramatic initial consequences of the declaration of war – the temporary cessation of mining on Yorke Peninsula consequent upon the closure of its principal (German) market – and ends with the traumatic aftermath of the war, including the final abandonment of copper mining in 1923 and the region's re-alignment as an overwhelmingly agricultural district.

Between these twin events, the progress of the war and its impact on the regional community are examined in detail, from the 'Empire enthusiasm' of the early days to the jaded war-weariness of later years – with the impact of mounting casualty lists, disillusion with England, the Conscription issue (including the scapegoating of South Australia's German community), and the bitterness caused by ever widening ideological divisions within the community. To this is added the significance of regional identity and local pride of place – the feats of 'the boys of old Kio' on the field of battle, the significance of visits by soldiers on leave or convalescence to Britain (including Cornwall), the intense friendship and solidarity shown by 'Peninsularites' to one another in the trenches and elsewhere overseas, the tireless devotion of bodies at home such as the Moonta Patriotic Committee, and the significance of 'farewell' and 'welcome home' celebrations, not least the political posturing of local worthies who attended such events. This is the story of regional Australia but the constant backdrop is, of course, the war itself – from Egypt and Gallipoli to France and Flanders, punctuated by events such as the dawn landing, Fromelles, Pozières, Bullecourt, Messines, Third Ypres, and the fast-moving, heady days of 1918.

CHAPTER TWO

'To make Australia's name glorious'

Kio goes to war

In the later years of Queen Victoria's reign, an old and battered signpost stood at the northern outskirts of Moonta, the celebrated copper-mining town on South Australia's Yorke Peninsula. 'Kio' it proclaimed in its rudimentary simplicity, pointing northwards through a landscape of make-shift cottages, mine stacks and spoil heaps towards the adjoining township, Kadina, less than a dozen miles distant.[1] Visitors from afar would search in vain in their maps and atlases for this elusive Kio, and the local 'Peninsularites' would smile in amusement at their confusion. For here was another 'Cousin Jack joke' – integral to the Cornish humour that Moonta and northern Yorke Peninsula had made their own – designed, as were so many, to take in the 'foreigner' while asserting the strength and exclusivity of regional identity.[2]

'Don't you know Moonta is Kio?'

'Kio' announced the road-sign, erected hurriedly and cheaply years before, its modest purpose nothing more than setting the traveller in the right direction for Kadina, some ten miles away. But if this intention was not immediately obvious to the bemused visitor, then the locals had given the sign new meaning, investing it with a powerful and enduring sense of place. It was not until the late 1960s that the local authority, spurred on by the success of Oswald Pryor's eponymous book, and seeking to nurture a sense of 'difference' in the interests of heritage tourism, erected its signboard 'Welcome to Moonta – Australia's Little Cornwall' at the northern boundary of the town.[3] Yet three-quarters of a century earlier, 'Kio' – or 'Kio', as it was interpreted by all and sundry – had provided exactly that distinctive identity; not in support of an incipient tourism but in celebration of Moonta's industrial prowess and global claim to fame. Moonta had already insisted upon its special niche in the Cornish transnational world, that pantheon of places across the globe to which emigrant Cousin Jacks and Cousin Jennys

1.   Moonta township on the eve of the Great War.

had ventured, proclaiming itself 'hub of the universe' and boasting that 'if you haven't been to Moonta, you haven't travelled'.[4] But in so readily adopting 'Kio', a nickname universally understood by locals and yet so bewilderingly inexplicable to outsiders, Moonta had established for itself a vibrant mechanism of community solidarity, and for its citizens an important badge of allegiance and 'belonging'.

Writing in July 1945, an anonymous contributor to the local *People's Weekly* newspaper, published at Moonta, recalled the days 'About 1900' when he had completed his apprenticeship (as a baker) in Adelaide. He had secured a position at Moonta, he explained, and, being a city slicker, he looked forward to the opportunity 'to show these country boys a thing or two'. He duly travelled up from the metropolis, and when the train had left Wallaroo, the third of the Peninsula mining towns, he went out onto the verandah at the end of his carriage to savour the last leg of the journey to Moonta. He was joined shortly by 'a strong looking youth' who, after the usual exchange of pleasantries, asked in the Cornish idiom characteristic of the Peninsula: 'Where are ee going – to Kio?'. 'No, I'm going to Moonta', was the inevitable reply, responded to gleefully by the triumphant youth. 'Gus home', he cried, 'thee es going up long to Kio. Don't you know Moonta is Kio? Well, 'tis'. He then asked inquiringly, 'What are ee goin' to do?', and, when told that the newly qualified baker was about to work for Trenerry Bros, the youth scored again, explaining how the surname should be pronounced properly in the Cornish way (Tre-nerry; not Tren-erry) . As the newcomer reflected, he had been trumped twice by 'the Moonta boy, which was only a forerunner of a good many more at Moonta boys' hands'.[5]

Noticeable here was the Cornish inheritance – accent and dialect, as well as Cousin Jack humour. But there was also an unmistakeable self-confidence in regional identity, forged on the Peninsula, a local pride which insisted that the presumptuous outsider be taken down a peg or two. It was a self-confident identity expressed persistently in myriad, and sometimes unlikely, ways. In August 1899, for example, a 'Kio Cycle Works' was opened in Ryan Street, Moonta, its proprietor soon manufacturing his own 'Kio' range of bicycles, well able to compete locally with expensive imports from Britain and North America.[6] Thirty years later, in 1929, another local named his motorboat 'Kio' (he had a second vessel, 'Miss Moonta'), to show, as he explained later, that 'I am not ashamed of the old place'.[7] When local families moved to other districts, they took their 'Kio' allegiances with them, not a few 'sticking together' in the clannish manner of which Moonta folk were often accused. In the 1890s and early 1900s many had left the Peninsula mining towns for the rapidly developing goldfields of Western Australia. In March 1906, for example, it was reported from Boulder City, in the heart of the goldfields, that there was to be a glittering double wedding at the local Wesleyan church, no fewer than 'three of the four happy principals' able to 'claim Kio as their "homeland"'.[8] Likewise, in May 1907 the *People's Weekly* duly noted the

2. The heart of 'Old Kio' – Moonta Mines – home to many of those from northern Yorke Peninsula who volunteered for service in the Australian Imperial Force during the Great War.

goldfields wedding of Mary Elsie Tregear, 'for some years resident in Kio', and just two months later yet another marriage in Western Australia was recorded between a couple 'popularly known in the little hamlet of Kio, and the adjacent villages'.[9] It was an identification that endured. One family gave the name 'Kio' to a succession of pet dogs, a tradition still going strong in the early twenty-first century.[10] In 2008 a 'retired Mineralogist from Tasmania' visited the National Trust museum at Moonta Mines, on the old mineral lease area east of the township, and mentioned in passing that 'many years ago' his family had had a holiday shack named 'Kio' at nearby Moonta Bay.[11]

As Oswald Pryor showed, Moonta's claim to be 'Australia's Little Cornwall' carried, despite its apparent exclusivity, a certain ambiguity.[12] When it suited local interests, 'Little Cornwall' expanded unobtrusively but persuasively to include all three Peninsula towns — Wallaroo, Kadina and Moonta — and their hinterlands, expressive now not so much of an erstwhile intimacy with Cornwall itself but redolent of an assertive Australian regional identity. So it was with 'Kio' — or at least to a degree. At home on the Peninsula, boundaries were observed — sometimes jealously, even aggressively — but when in 'foreign parts' 'Peninsularites' from the three towns were apt to claim common cause. In Western Australia, for example, there were appeals in the press to 'Kio and Kadinaites', the running together of the two place-names aided by a certain alliteration which made Moonta and Kadina seem happy bedfellows — as indeed they were; sometimes.[13] In times of tension and conflict, this wider sense of solidarity usually prevailed, as in the great miners' strikes of 1864 and 1874 when workers from the two principal mines in the district — the Moonta and the Wallaroo — had acted in concert in pursuit of their aims.[14]

3.   Wallaroo in the early twentieth century — the names above the shops betray the town's Welsh and Cornish origins.

4. Kadina, the third of the northern Yorke Peninsula mining towns.

Later, as we shall see, this wider sense of kinship extended to the battlefields of the Great War, where the 'boys from old Kio' were keen to acknowledge and embrace other Peninsularites as close cousins.[15]

As Pryor made plain, northern Yorke Peninsula owed its distinctiveness in large part to its Cornish origins. Following major discoveries of copper in 1859 and 1861, in what was then arid, isolated frontier country, far removed from the areas of farming and 'close settlement', large numbers of Cornish mineworkers and their families were enticed to the new workings. Some were already in South Australia, at the Burra Burra and Kapunda mines, and others were recruited from neighbouring Victoria and, of course, from Cornwall itself. Indeed, Cornwall remained a source of skilled labour for the Moonta, Wallaroo, and scores of smaller Peninsula mines, until the mid-1880s, the steady stream of 'new blood' keeping alive the district's reputation as being 'more Cornish than Cornwall itself'.[16] By the mid-1870s, the population of the district already exceeded 20,000 souls, some three-fifths of these dwelling in Moonta or the adjoining Moonta Mines settlement. These Cornish immigrants brought their culture with them — everything from traditional Cornish fare (including the inevitable Cornish pasty) and sports (notably Cornish wrestling) to a wide range of musical activities. Methodists of various hues — Wesleyans, Bible Christians, Primitive Methodists — the Cornish also stamped their ethno-religious identity on the Peninsula: the characteristic Methodist chapels that dominated the skylines of the three towns but also an array of beliefs, attitudes and assumptions that coloured daily life, especially the 'self-help' ethos and a commitment to 'mutual improvement'. In the 1891 census, an astonishing 80 per cent of the population of northern Yorke Peninsula were recorded as Methodist.[17] Masonic lodges and friendly societies were also vehicles for mutual improvement, and likewise encouraged a sense of community solidarity. Geographically distant from the colonial capital of Adelaide, some 100 miles away, northern Yorke Peninsula – with 'Kio' at its heart – was decidedly its own place.

In population size, northern Yorke Peninsula was second only to Adelaide. In economic terms, it was crucial to the economic well-being of the colony, the mighty copper mines of Moonta and Wallaroo of international reputation and significance. Here the Cornish inheritance was also noticeable, from the tribute and tutwork system of employment and remuneration – where part of the entrepreneurial function was provided by the miners themselves – to the terminology, technology and general organisation of the mines, which were run on Cornish principles.[18] There was likewise a strong sense of ethno-occupational solidarity, the workers here – as elsewhere – deploying the myth of Cousin Jack, the insistence that the Cornish were innately the best hard-rock miners in the world. This solidarity was also evident within the local trade union, eventually a branch of the Amalgamated Miners Association of Australia, and in the political Labor movement that emerged in its wake. The Peninsula gave South Australia its first Labor Premier – John Verran, in 1910–12 – and became an important centre of the United Labor Party, although its local branches were only informally affiliated to the ULP structure in Adelaide. In this, as in other areas, the Peninsula guarded its independence. In the Federation referendum of 1898, for example, the Peninsula voted in favour of the forthcoming federation of the Australian colonies, despite ULP policy which was against.[19]

'Cultivation is transforming that which was a desert and scrubby waste'

By the early 1900s, the Cousin Jack identity of northern Yorke Peninsula owed less to the gradually fading links with Cornwall and more to the strong sense of place cultivated in Moonta and environs. At the mines, the lengthy career of Captain Henry Richard Hancock, who as General Superintendent had intentionally run Moonta and Wallaroo as Cornish mines, had given way in 1898 to the entirely different managerial regime of his son and successor, H. Lipson Hancock. In a bid to modernise the mines, Lipson Hancock moved the main focus of the operations from Moonta to Wallaroo (the latter by now the more profitable of the two), at the same time replacing many of the old Cornish beam-engines and engine-houses with new power-plants, driven by electricity. In this way, new investment and bold developmental plans ushered

5.   The Wallaroo mine, c.1914, by now the principal working on the northern
Yorke Peninsula copper-mining field.

in a revitalised period of prosperity at the Peninsula mines – and in the
Peninsula towns – in the first decade of the twentieth century.[20]

Similarly, by 1900 the Peninsula's economy had also diversified, mining
complemented now by an important agricultural industry that had gradually
transformed the locality since the first European attempts to tame the
wilderness in the 1860s. As Jan Lokan has shown, although it was enhanced
remuneration for their skills that had enticed many Cornish miners to
South Australia in the first place, not a few hoped for new self-improvement
opportunities in the colony, especially the chance to exchange the pick for
the plough – to become independent farmers, owning their own land and
working for themselves.[21] This aspiration was assisted by Strangways Act
of 1868, which followed the South Australian government's announcement
in the previous year that it was to make available for selection by farmers
three million acres of frontier mallee land. Northern Yorke Peninsula was
part of this 'mallee' country, so-called because of the dense mallee scrub
that dominated an otherwise featureless landscape. It also lay just beyond
'Goyder's Line', a line drawn on the map of South Australia in 1865 by George
Goyder, the Surveyor General, to mark the southern limit of the drought then
being endured by the colony's agriculturalists. In time, Goyder's Line came

to be seen as the boundary between land that could be cultivated and turned successfully into good farming country, and that which could not.[22] Moonta and environs, just north of the line, was perilously close to the latter; marginal country where would-be farmers would struggle to wrest a living from the arid, unpromising soil. But this not deter those anxious to acquire property, and in July 1870 the Adelaide *Observer* could note with satisfaction that Green's Plains, near Kadina, was 'gradually being occupied for agricultural purposes. There are thousands of acres of good arable land which are yet destined to blush with the fresh verdure of cereal crops'. As the newspaper put it: 'Farmers are struggling manfully to supplant mallee scrub with cornfields'.[23] Moreover, northern Yorke Peninsula had the advantage of a coastline, and Wallaroo – already an important port, serving the nearby copper-smelting works – was to develop swiftly as a major outlet for local agricultural produce.

In 1872 the Strangways Act was improved and updated, and this combined with a series of excellent harvests in the early 1870s to increase the clamour for more land to be made available and for land laws to be further liberalised. In May 1873, for example, an editorial in the *Yorke's Peninsula Advertiser* articulated local agitation for greater agricultural expansion in the district.[24] Twelve months later a petition from Peninsula miners calling on the government to open-up more land was presented to the Parliament in Adelaide, and in June 1876 the Peninsula press could report that 'land in the vicinity is being taken up ... and cultivation is transforming that which was but a desert and scrubby waste'.[25] By January 1878 no less than one third of the entire area of Yorke Peninsula was in use for either farming or grazing, the region's wheat output amounting to one million bushels per annum, worth £250,000.[26] Nonetheless, many of the locality's small farmers found it difficult to make ends meet, and not a few went under in the 1880s and 1890s, their plight made worse by periodic droughts.[27] Yet those who could hang on, acquiring the properties of their less fortunate neighbours at low prices, were able to benefit from later improvements in agricultural machinery and technology (not least the introduction of superphosphates manufactured as a by-product at the Wallaroo smelters), together with the return of wetter winters and brighter economic conditions. In this way, by the early twentieth century northern Yorke Peninsula had become established as a major wheat-producing district, 'Kio boys' spread now across a new farming landscape that ranged from the southern reaches of the Peninsula to the Hummocks hills at its neck, the latter its natural geographic boundary.

This, then, was Kio in 1914: Moonta, the self-appointed heart of the northern Yorke Peninsula mining district, and its hinterland – not only the sister townships of Kadina and Wallaroo but also the golden wheat-fields that stretched now for miles in every direction. Moreover, by 1914, on the eve of the Great War, the vibrant community spirit and sense of belonging that had long exemplified 'Kio' and the wider Peninsula had matured into a robust regional identity. It was an identity that was recognised widely in South Australia and beyond, the Peninsula perceived as somehow 'different', especially in the eyes of metropolitan Adelaide.[28] Yet in other respects northern Yorke Peninsula in 1914 was perhaps also 'typical' of regional Australia. Its mixed mining and farming economy was mirrored many times over across the continent, not least in neighbouring Victoria, and its maritime location was shared with a good many other places, large and small, around the Australian littoral. To that extent, northern Yorke Peninsula was an integral part of the rich mosaic of places and identities that comprised regional Australia, at once both 'different' and 'typical'. For those who cared to see, the Peninsula shed comparative light on the Australian regional experience in general, and yet it also offered insights into what was in so many ways a singular community, worthy of being understood for its own sake, as May Vivienne appreciated in her pen-picture of the locality that appeared in her *Sunny South Australia* in 1908. As she observed, 'the people living there have a very high opinion of themselves'.[29] The Peninsula was certainly not unique in its singularity – the Barossa valley in South Australia, with its German-Lutheran communities and an economy increasingly dominated by wine production, was at least as distinctive – but it did occupy a particular place in the Australian consciousness, and indeed in the wider 'British world' and on the global stage.[30]

'The primitive Boer, untouched … by European civilisation'

Notwithstanding the opposition of the Labor movement as a whole to Federation, northern Yorke Peninsula – a Labor stronghold – had welcomed the coming together of the Australian colonies in 1901 to form the new Commonwealth. However, this reflected not so much a regional penchant for nation-building, an incipient Australian nationalism that now demanded institutional expression, but rather a simple, pragmatic insistence that Federation would be good for the region's copper industry.[31] Nonetheless, the outbreak of the Boer War on the eve of Federation had revealed an emergent Australian patriotism, on Yorke Peninsula as elsewhere in South Australia, a belief that Australia's importance and status within the British Empire was enhanced by lending the mother country a timely hand in its hour of need. That Australian light horsemen could match the bush skills of the wily Boers, who had so often confounded British troops unused and unsuited to their terrain, was a particular source of national pride.[32] Here was a suggestion of soldiery superiority, especially when compared to the supposedly lacklustre British who had suffered embarrassing reverses during the course of the war, that anticipated the Anzac myth of Gallipoli in 1915.

In all, Australia had sent some 16,000 horsemen (plus horses) to support the Empire in its campaign against the Boers in 1899–1902. Of these, some 1,169 were raised in South Australia, of whom fifty-nine were to lose their lives during the conflict. In marked contrast to Britain, there was little 'pro-Boer' sentiment in South Australia (even the Radical Premier, Charles Cameron Kingston, supported the war), and the Lutheran church – which might have echoed Germany's support for the Boers' struggle – was diplomatically silent on the matter. Yet there were members of the United Labor Party who expressed unease over the war. Likewise, the military execution by the British in 1902 of Harry 'Breaker' Morant (a soldier in the South Australian Mounted Rifles and later the irregular Bush Veldt Carbineers), who was found guilty of murdering Boer prisoners, caused anxiety among those who imagined that he had been made an example of to help placate international condemnation of British 'atrocities'. There was also the matter of Australia's own embarrassment, when three hundred Australian soldiers in South Africa mutinied in response to a string of offensive remarks from a British general.[33] And for those who fought and survived there were the inevitable scars – mental as well as physical – that reflected the reality of warfare and its effect on the individual. There were also those, even at this very early stage, who began to question Australia's role in defence of Empire – on moral grounds as much as to do with the occasional clash of British attitudes and Australian sensitivities:

> I killed a man at Graspan;
>   My first and, God! My last;
> Harder to dodge than my bullet is
>   The look that his dead eyes cast.
> If the Empire asks for me later on
>   It'll ask for me in vain
> Before I reach for my bandolier
>   To fire on a man again.[34]

On northern Yorke Peninsula, the departure of local boys for South Africa in 1899 prompted a public display of Empire loyalism which masked any doubts or dissent that may have existed in the community, even among ULP supporters. Letters from the front found their ways into the press, the *People's Weekly*, for example, publishing the sentimental musings of one Kio boy far from home, who in quiet moments found that his 'mind wandered back to dear old Moonta on a Saturday evening' where, in his imagination, he 'could see George Street, with the bands playing, and the thousands of people moving up and down'.[35] The *People's Weekly*, in marshalling its justification for the war and supporting Australian participation, quoted at length from the recent proceedings in Cornwall of the Ponsanooth Mutual Improvement Society. These illustrated, it said, that disenfranchised Uitlanders in the Boer Republics – including many emigrant Cornish miners – had received rough treatment at the hands of 'the primitive Boer, untouched as he was by the influence of European civilisation'.[36]

In addition to Australia's duty to support the Empire in its efforts to extend the rule of British law, and all that that implied, there was also – the newspaper suggested – a Peninsula dimension to the conflict which would touch the hearts of many locals. Here, it was intimated, the community's natural sympathy for the plight of Cornish emigrants in South Africa gave the war a particular immediacy and relevance. Likewise, when it was insinuated in the British press that the Cornish had shown great cowardice in their flight from Johannesburg, and that 'the Cousin Jack miners trampled women and children underfoot', the *People's Weekly* could note that such reports were 'resented locally by Cornishmen', and protest that the Duke of Cornwall's Light Infantry had displayed great courage on the field of battle during the war.[37] Nurturing regional as well as Australian national sentiment, the paper had voiced its support of Empire. But in doing so it had dismissed British criticism of Cornish behaviour in South Africa, interpreting this scathing assessment of the Cornish as an affront to the Peninsula's own regional identity. Such were the paradoxes and complexities of identity formation on early twentieth-century Yorke Peninsula, and in the newly-federated Australia generally.

Australia had entered the Boer War as six self-governing British colonies; it emerged from the peace as a federated Dominion, the Commonwealth of Australia – not yet fully independent but now a unified country with its own constitution and its own flag to fly. But, like other parts of the Empire, Australia was still dependent on Britain for its foreign policy and its defence. Sometimes there were strikingly differing perspectives – Britain had largely welcomed, and indeed assisted, Japan's rising power in the Pacific region, while Australia looked askance at this new version of the 'yellow peril'. But, more generally, there was a sense of shared Imperial interest between Britain and Australia. This was especially so with regard to German imperial designs in the south-west Pacific, not least in New Guinea where the German protectorate (annexed in 1884) shared a border with Papua, the British territory inherited by Australia in 1906. Australians felt that, should some calamity ever befall the mother country, then Germany – already in their backyard – would move ruthlessly and swiftly to add Australia to its imperial possessions. Likewise, Australians were acutely aware that to keep the Germans – and perhaps French, Japanese, even Russians – at bay in their part of the world, they were reliant upon the might of the Royal Navy. They observed with a mixture of alarm and satisfaction the naval arms race between Britain and Germany – alarm, because it demonstrated German maritime ambition and capability; satisfaction, because Britain acted decisively to maintain its superiority. And Australia sought to do its bit too. In July 1911 the Royal Australian Navy came formally into being, and a series of modern, expensive warships was ordered from British yards. When the new battlecruiser *HMAS Australia* arrived with her escorts in Australian waters in 1913, she seemed more than a match for the threatening German East Asiatic Cruiser Squadron, based at Tsingtao in China, and signalled to Japanese military observers Australia's determination to bolster the Empire's naval presence in the Pacific.[38]

'Britain – Australia – Moonta'

Nervousness about German intentions in the south-west Pacific was tempered by an admiration for German technology and innovation, an attitude which survived almost to the eve of war. On Yorke Peninsula, as elsewhere in Australia, news of German ingenuity continued to impress, as in October 1913 when the *Yorke's Peninsula Advertiser* displayed undisguised wonder at a new 'German method of converting fish unsuitable for food' into 'valuable products, such as grease, glue, fertilizer, and meal for fowls'. Likewise, there was local acclaim for the 'German inventor, Grimmeisen', said 'to have found a method for using wireless waves . . . for lighting up distant lamps'.[39] However, this almost universal applause for German industrial capability had begun to wane during the naval arms race, when those hitherto much admired German qualities of efficiency and high craftsmanship were seen increasingly as a direct threat to the Empire's well-being, through economic and military competition. But if that sneaking regard lingered a little longer on Yorke Peninsula, then this reflected the intimate relationship that existed between its copper-mining industry and the continued expansion of German industrial capacity. As Marnie Haig-Muir has observed, by 1914 'several large German firms virtually controlled Australia's base metal industries'.[40] The Moonta and Wallaroo mines had remained in Australian ownership but German manipulation of their output had ensured that, by the outbreak of war, the lion's share of the Peninsula's production went to supply German industry.[41] This accounted, perhaps, for that lingering regard – and for the fact that the exquisitely detailed models of mineral processing plant displayed in the laboratories at the Moonta School of Mines were made in Germany; not Britain or America.[42] It also accounted for the acute embarrassment, often felt but rarely expressed, that arose after the outbreak of hostilities, the knowledge that the copper mines of northern Yorke Peninsula had played no small part in the growth of German industrial prowess and military muscle. Moreover, it accounted for the severe economic disruption experienced on the Peninsula at the moment war was declared.

As elsewhere, Peninsula residents had seen the war coming, and were braced for what increasingly seemed inevitable. In 1911 an Australia-wide compulsory cadet-training scheme was brought in, designed to introduce boys between the ages of 12 and 18 to the military skills that they might need one day to defend the Empire.[43] In January 1914, as the international situation continued to deteriorate, advertisements in the Peninsula press reminded parents that boys who would reach the age of 14 during the year must register them for military training before the end of February. Failure to comply would be to invite a £10 fine.[44] Such activities created a general atmosphere of preparedness for war, and in July and August of 1914 Australians watched with a mixture of anxiety and anticipation as the countdown to conflict gathered pace. The German invasion of Belgium on 4 August, in the face of British and French determination to defend Belgium's neutrality and independence, seemed the final act in the rapid unfolding of events that led to war. Britain declared war on Germany, and, for Australia and the rest of the British Empire, the Great War had begun.

Australia moved swiftly to counter the German threat on its doorstep. The Royal Australian Navy captured or detained more than forty enemy merchant ships in the first weeks of the war, and on 7 September *HMAS Australia* led an attack on the port of Rabaul in German New Guinea, home of a strategically important German wireless station. The German island of Naura, with its own communications facilities, was also captured, and the Australians went on to take the rest of German New Guinea and adjoining Bougainville. Then, on 9 November, the lightcruiser *HMAS Sydney* encountered the German raider *Emden* near the Cocos Islands. Pulverised and driven aground in shallow waters, the *Emden* was soon knocked out by the *Sydney's* superior gunnery.[45] In a matter of weeks, the Australians had removed the immediate threat to their security, opening sea-lanes for the convoying of troops abroad, and had captured swathes of German territory. For Australia, it was an auspicious opening to the war.

Australian public opinion was buoyed by news of these actions, redoubling the wave of excitement it had displayed at the outbreak of war in August. In contrast to the complex, cautious and often mixed responses that met the declaration of war in Britain, in Australia there was widespread enthusiasm and approval.[46] Strategic interests as well as bonds of kinship and affection tied Australia and Britain, and membership of the British Empire was a source of national pride. Even more than in the Boer War, there was a sense that lending Britain a hand in its hour of need enhanced Australia's place within the Empire. Moreover, here was a chance, as one Peninsula newspaper argued, for the young nation to 'make Australia's name glorious'.[47] This was not merely a question of demonstrating martial prowess, or even loyalty to Empire, but was also about national pride in defending freedom against tyranny. It was a war of Good against Evil. The Methodist *Australian Christian Commonwealth* magazine, published in Adelaide but read widely on Yorke Peninsula (John Verran was a subscriber), explained it thus: 'Every soldier we send [to war] goes out in defence of great moral principles, and to check a braggart power that is prepared to trample every principle of ... righteousness under foot'.[48]

On Yorke Peninsula, Ephraim Major jun., mayoral candidate in Moonta in November 1914, articulated the complementary strands of loyalty and identity felt by most local people. His personal motto, he explained, was 'BRITAIN – AUSTRALIA – MOONTA', a meld of the Imperial, national, and regional sentiment that most Peninsula folk experienced and understood instinctively. Most locals were also prepared to embrace the new stereotypical depictions of Germans by now commonplace in the regional press. No longer to be admired for scientific aptitude or inventiveness, the 'Hun' was now the epitome of barbarism. Indeed: 'To anyone who knows modern Germany, the accounts of German brutalities in the present war cannot cause the smallest surprise'.[49] Australian missionaries had been 'shockingly treated' by the Germans in New Ireland (in the south-west Pacific), it was alleged, evidence that 'If Germany were to win Australia would probably suffer most', and that, therefore, it was 'the palpable duty of all Australians to assist the Motherland in this terrific struggle'.[50] Should there be any doubt about the matter, the *Yorke's Peninsula Advertiser* spelt it out, adopting for itself the mantle of moral spokesman for the region:

> The world stands horrified as it beholds how completely thorough-going the German can be in connection with oppression; and how utterly and callously abandoned he can become to barbarism in his murder of the innocent, his spoliation of the beautiful, and his desecration of the revered. With little provocation he tears the Belgian babe from its mother's breast and shoots it before her eyes. Out of mere destructive wantonness he levels the centuries old and richly historic cathedral to the ground, after breaking in upon its peaceful precincts and spoiling its treasures of art and religion.[51]

'Our fellow German colonists'

A willingness to repeat uncritically the more lurid propaganda stories from Europe combined with genuine disbelief at the ruthlessness and destructive force of the German war machine to precipitate such moral outrage in the press. But, early in the war, there was little sense that this righteous indignation should be turned against 'our fellow German colonists'[52] on the Peninsula and in South Australia generally. In 1914 there were still German-language newspapers and German-speaking schools in the Barossa Valley and in Adelaide Hills settlements such as Hahndorf. But, as the *Australian Christian Commonwealth* opined, these German settlers 'have laboured with us to develop these fair lands, they have proven themselves loyal and noble citizens of our Commonwealth, their blood is mingled with ours'.[53] Indeed, over several generations, many had been dispersed around the state, becoming entirely anglophone and adopting British-Australian idiom and mannerisms, as well as intermarrying with people of other origins. Several of these had found their way to northern Yorke Peninsula, some working in the mining industry, distinguished only by their German surnames – Fuss, Beythien, Goerecke, Mannheim, and so on.[54] Hans Rieken, and others like him on the Peninsula, joined the Australian Imperial Force without embarrassment or hindrance (he went on to serve at Gallipoli, where he was wounded), the only restriction to enlistment announced in August 1914 being applied to 'persons not of substantially European origin'.[55] Of course, notwithstanding the initial engagements in the Pacific, Australia's 'personal' enemy early in the war was 'Johnny Turk'. It was only after Australian troops has seen action – and suffered heavy losses – on the Western Front in 1916 that the 'Hun' became the real focus of deep hatred and uncompromising hostility. Only then, for example, did Edgar Degenhardt, a bank clerk in Moonta, decide that it was politic to change his name to Edgar Russell, despite being 'a natural born British subject'.[56]

But there were gleeful reports in the *Kadina and Wallaroo Times* in January 1915 expressing satisfaction at the 'copper famine' now being suffered by Germany. Exports from northern Yorke Peninsula to Germany had been halted abruptly on the outbreak of war, and as a result, it was alleged, the German munitions industry was now desperately short of the metal.[57] In Peninsula eyes, this good news helped to ameliorate the discomfort felt locally about the pre-war supply of South Australian copper to Germany. It also made up for the distress experienced when, in August 1914, the Wallaroo and Moonta Mining and Smelting Company had decided that it had no alternative but to cease production immediately. As H. Lipson Hancock, the general manager, put it rather delicately: 'in consequence of the outbreak of war in Europe, and the inability of the contractors to take delivery of our copper, it has become imperative to at once curtail operations'.[58] The pumps at the mines would be kept going, he added, to prevent the underground workings from flooding, and at the Moonta cementation works 'leaching liquors' would continue to be applied so that the treatment process employed in recycling mine wastes could be restarted when required. But otherwise the mines were suddenly idle, with some 2,000 men thrown out of work, and thousands more jobs in the region put at risk. It was a situation that could not be allowed to

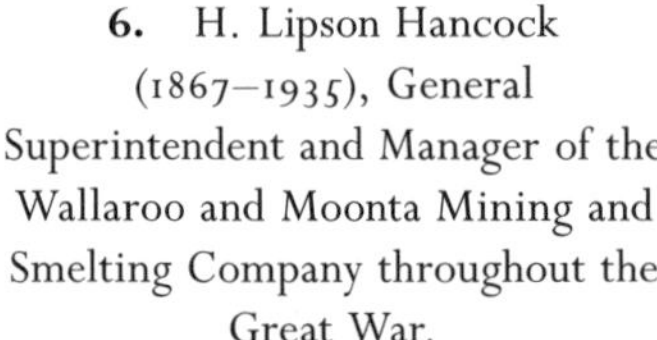

6. H. Lipson Hancock (1867–1935), General Superintendent and Manager of the Wallaroo and Moonta Mining and Smelting Company throughout the Great War.

endure, not least because metal mines throughout Australia found themselves in similar positions.

Billy Hughes, shortly to become Prime Minister of Australia but in late 1914 Attorney-General in the federal Labor government, intervened to ensure permanent national control over what were vital strategic metals.[59] This included the formation of an association of principal copper producers, designed to co-ordinate the sale of all copper surplus to Australian needs to Britain to support the manufacture of munitions. Among other measures was the acquisition of the hitherto German-owned Port Kembla copper smelting works in New South Wales. On northern Yorke Peninsula, these developments were followed closely, not least by members of the Amalgamated Miners' Association who had been obliged to agree that, when production was resumed, ten percent of wages would be held back for the duration of the war, to be paid out in full on cessation of hostilities. There was talk of an extension to twenty percent should things become even more difficult, and when the British government (keen to procure copper from wherever it could, at the lowest possible prices) announced that it could not give preference to Australian produce, the sense of anxiety grew. In fact, as Keith Bailey has shown, after the initial dislocation, the speedy return to work engineered by the federal government ushered in a period of hectic production and renewed prosperity in the Peninsula mines.[60]

By the end of November 1914, the *Yorke's Peninsula Advertiser* could note that, although the region was 'seriously affected on the outbreak of war by the closing of the Mines', the 'successful financial negotiations' arranged by the government had 'permitted and enabled our mining industry to resume and assist in our support'. The mine company itself had demonstrated its 'patriotic feelings in so actively dealing with the serious situation and restarting work', while the 'employees too assisted in the situation by willing co-operation'.[61] It was an analysis that portrayed a determination by all parties to compromise in the interests of the war effort – a benign picture of employers and employees working together hand in glove, and of a grateful region indebted to a wise government for enabling it to 'do its bit' in support of the mother country. In many ways, it was an accurate assessment, at least in the short term. The years 1915–18 were boom times in the Peninsula mines, with the comparatively high wages paid to the mineworkers percolating through into the local economy, which prospered as a result, despite the drought that affected its rural hinterland from 1914. However, as the miners' trade union recognised, the surge in demand for Australian copper also meant unprecedented returns for shareholders, especially as the international price of copper rose dramatically, and with it came an uneasy sense that investors were profiting unduly from the war.

'A "red hot Labour centre"'

Hughes' especially generous treatment of corporate interests in the mining industry had raised eyebrows in the Labor movement throughout Australia.[62] In August 1914, on the outbreak of war, the Adelaide *Register* had remarked reassuringly that: 'Although politically a "red hot Labour [*sic*] centre", the Yorke's Peninsula mines have been remarkably free of labour troubles'.[63] After the bitter and damaging strike of 1891–92, there had indeed been a long period of relative industrial harmony on the Peninsula, the Amalgamated Miners' Association using its influence to good effect in securing various advantageous agreements in return for co-operation with the company's modernisation plans at the mines.[64] However, beneath the veneer of continued co-operation in the national interest, there was after the events of late 1914 a renewed suspicion of the Wallaroo and Moonta Mining and Smelting Company that would eventually manifest itself in the complex disputes of 1916–17, when Labor issues would become inextricably entwined in wider conflicts involving Conscription (to the armed forces), religion and ethnicity (see Chapter Six). For the moment, however, there seemed only goodwill and consensus, a general desire for the Peninsula's mining industry to prosper in service of the British Empire.

The mines back in full production, the greater part of the region's copper output was now purchased by the British government, with smaller amounts going to the Indian and Australian authorities for their respective needs. In 1915 a contract was secured, with the blessing and assistance of the British government, for the supply of almost all the region's output to Kynoch Ltd, the ammunition manufacturer in Birmingham, England.[65] This laid the foundation for the mines' wartime prosperity, and strengthened the belief locally that the Peninsula's economy was now contributing directly and significantly to the war effort.[66] The ten percent wage retention was soon abandoned (and back-pay refunded in full), and there was even an attempt (not entirely successful) to convert the machinery workshop at the Wallaroo mine for manufacture of high explosive shrapnel shells.[67] At the same time, modernisation of the mines continued apace, with shafts sunk ever deeper and new machinery installed. As before, most of this new investment was concentrated on the Wallaroo mine, now the principal focus of the Peninsula's copper output.

The redoubling of effort in the mines was mirrored more generally in the community, where new organisations such as the 'Moonta Patriotic Committee' and, later, the 'Moonta Mines Soldiers' Aid League' were formed to articulate patriotic opinion as well as to offer moral and practical support for those enlisting in the forces. The Patriotic Fund was launched in the Council Chamber, the mayor presiding, and with representatives appointed from Moonta, Moonta Mines, North Moonta and neighbouring Cross Roads, as well as from outlying settlements on Yorke Peninsula such as Agery, Penang, Arthurton, Cunliffe, and Tiparra.[68] Kadina and Wallaroo formed their own committees, likewise extending representation to nearby settlements in their vicinity. Being councillors and other local dignitaries, these representatives were necessarily almost all men, and, not unnaturally, thought immediately of the Yorke's Peninsula Football Association as that organisation most likely to offer its facilities in support of the Patriotic Fund's proposed activities. However, if this appeared a decidedly masculine approach to the business of mobilising the homefront, then gender balance was restored through the activities of the 'Belgian Relief Fund'. At its local committee meeting in early November 1914, for example, held at the Moonta Institute, there was said to be 'a good attendance of ladies', who secured donations of cash and clothing to be sent to alleviate the suffering in Belgium.[69] Women, they made clear, had every bit as important a role to play as men in rallying the community. Indeed, it was implied, their womanly instincts were tailor-made for the supply of comforts to distressed civilians, as well as serving men, in distant lands, their sympathies humanitarian rather than martial. Women were also good at getting things done. They organised a fund-raising concert at Weetulta, a small agricultural settlement on the Peninsula, and arranged for the 'Wallaroo Mines Dramatic Company' to perform a popular play before a full house at Moonta Mines, the proceeds going to the local Belgium Relief Fund.[70]

7.   The young women of the Wallaroo Mines Girls Club,
ready to do their bit in the Great War.

'Recruiting … is proceeding satisfactorily'

Community enthusiasm was also evident in those young (and not so young) men coming forward to join the forces. 'Recruiting in connection with the [Australian] Expeditionary Force is proceeding satisfactorily', reported the *Yorke's Peninsula Advertiser* in December 1914.[71] Several 'well-known in Moonta', as the *People's Weekly* had put it the September, were already enlisted: 'Messrs O. Davey, R. Shields, T. Kindail, D.G. Shaw, J. Merrifield, Ross, John, and Kenneth Grant Jacob, and the Rev G.W. Shepley. Messrs H.S. Holthouse (son of our local postmaster) and W.L. Rowett'. [72] It was a modest list, the first of the crop, a mere drop in the ocean – but it was a start. Locals were proud, but hoped for more. Yet they had not even an inkling of what would befall these few in the months and years ahead.

William Rowett got no further than Egypt, where he was found to be suffering from choroiditis, an inflammation of the eye that caused blurred vision and could lead to blindness.[73] He was sent back to Adelaide, where he was discharged from the army in February 1916 – with a disability pension. James Merrifield, born at Wallaroo, was a rising star, already promoted corporal by the time he arrived in Egypt, from where he wrote home to say that he and Lieutenant Davey wished all at Moonta a Merry Christmas: 'You might mention this in the People's Weekly'.[74] He fought at Gallipoli, where he was 'wounded in action, seriously', with a gunshot wound to the knee. He recovered, and was later promoted Captain. But he was a day late joining

8.   South Australian recruits during initial training at Mitcham, near Adelaide.

the Overseas Training Brigade on Salisbury Plain, in England, on 23 August 1918. He was found guilty at Court Martial of being Absent Without Leave, and was Reprimanded. A few months later, the war was over, and he went home to Australia.[75]

Oliver Davey, already thirty-seven years old when he enlisted, was a mining surveyor from Moonta Mines. Now a Lieutenant in the militia, he had served in the 3rd Light Horse in the Boer War. He too fought at Gallipoli where, as a Medical Board explained later, 'on 29 May ... he was blown up by a mine explosion'.[76] In fact, as Davey himself was to explain, he had been placed in charge of a party of Australian miners at Quinn's Post, the most dangerous and exposed of all the Anzac positions, just yards from the Turkish lines. On several occasions they had successfully undermined the Turkish trenches, setting off charges to spectacular effect. But, he said, on 29 May 'the Turks got in first and blew up the Australian miners' tunnel'.[77] As a result of his injuries, his 'right knee was very swollen and he was unable to walk'. Evacuated to Malta, and then to the Royal Free Hospital in Grays Inn Road, London, Davey underwent an operation for the removal of a dislocated cartilage. 'He is unable to walk up or down an incline without the knee giving way', reported the Medical Board, and he 'is also shaky and nervous and suffering from insomnia'. He was posted back to Australia for light duties, and served as Recruiting Officer at Kadina in early 1916, before rejoining his regiment at Tel-el-Kebir in Egypt in June of that year. From there he was sent to France but his knee was no better and was he removed to England and 'struck off strength' in October 1917, before being repatriated to Australia. He applied for an incapacity pension in 1918 but was 'Rejected on the grounds that claimant is not incapacitated for earning a living'.[78]

Ross Jacob, one of the several Jacob brothers of Kadina, went as part of the 'famous 10th' – the 10th Battalion A.I.F. – to Gallipoli where he too was wounded. He recovered in hospital in Manchester before rejoining his regiment, and thereafter climbed steadily through the ranks.[79] His was a glittering rise to prominence, and in February 1917 – still a Major – he was granted temporary command of the 10th Battalion. He was subsequently promoted Lieutenant-Colonel and his command confirmed, and from there was posted to England to take charge of the 3rd Training Battalion. He returned to the 'famous 10th' as commanding officer in April 1918 but things were not right. Soon he was in hospital with influenza (the epidemic that killed millions as the war eventually drew to a close), and was in low spirits. He wrote to his Brigade Commander, explaining that: 'I am the eldest of five brothers who have served or are serving in the A.I.F., I have had 3 years and 9 months service and have only been absent from duty twice, once wounded and once sick'. He continued: 'Two of my brothers have been rendered permanently unfit for any work and have been discharged'. A third brother,

9.   Officers of the 10th Battalion, Australian Imperial Force, at Mena Camp in Egypt on Christmas Day 1914 (not 1915, as the photograph suggests). On the far right is Captain Ross Blyth Jacob of Kadina, who later rose to command the 'famous 10th'.

he added, 'was badly wounded and taken prisoner in April 1917 and is now in Germany'. Kenneth Grant, his fourth brother, had been in the A.I.F. since August 1914, serving in the 12th Battalion (where he was now a Lieutenant). Back in Kadina, their father struggled to run his property on his own, and as 'only two of us remain who have not been rendered unfit', Jacob was anxious to return to Australian as soon as possible 'to assist in its management'. Besides, he explained, he had just been discharged from hospital 'and feel that my health is not good enough to allow me to carry out the duties of a Battalion commander in the Field'. H.G. Bennett, the Divisional Brigadier-General, was inclined to be sympathetic, and recommended to his superior that Jacob be released. Major-General Harold 'Hookey' Walker, who had earned the respect of the Australians at Gallipoli, thought likewise, and replied on 30 May 1918 that 'I have to advise you [Bennett] that his younger brother Lieut. K.G. JACOB 12th Battalion was today killed in action. It is considered that this is an additional reason why the application of Lieut-Colonel Jacob for return to Australia be approved'.[80]

It was true. Ross Jacob's brother, Kenneth Grant Jacob, had been killed near Hazebrouck on the very day that 'Hookey' Walker had been considering

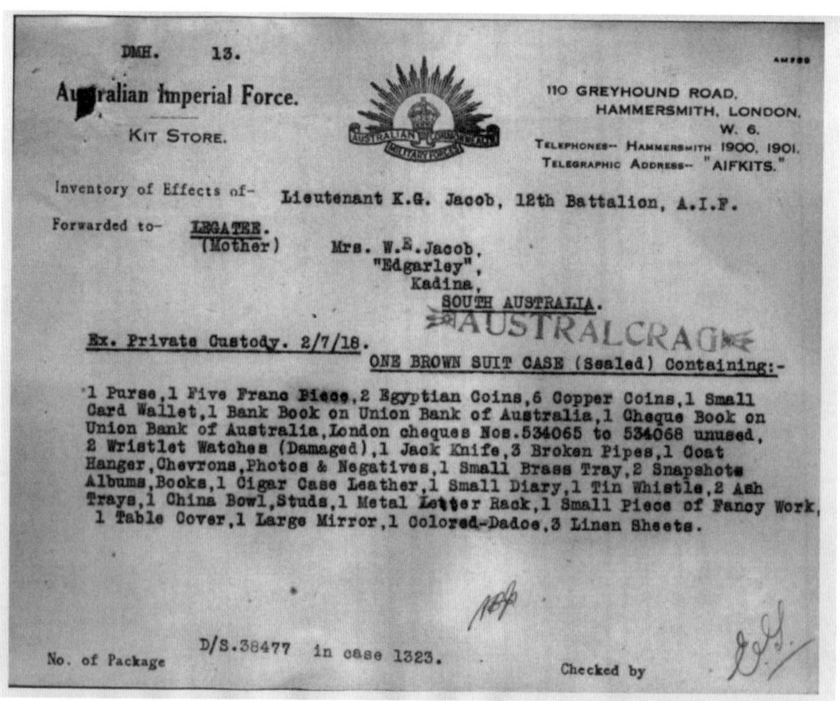

10.   The personal effects of Lieutenant Kenneth Grant Jacob, killed in action in Flanders on 30 May 1918, sent home to his mother in Kadina.

his brother's discharge request. Kenneth, as the *People's Weekly* had noted, joined up at the same time as Ross. He too went to Gallipoli, where he promptly went down with enteric fever. He recovered well in hospital, although on release it was noted that 'he still suffers from nightmares and his heart is irritable', and in early 1916 was posted to France. There, in a freak accident on the parade ground at Etaples (the troop training and concentration centre), he stumbled, fell awkwardly, and damaged the semilunar cartilage in his right knee, occasioning an operation and a lengthy spell of convalescence. Eventually, he rejoined his unit, the 12th Battalion A.I.F., in which he served until 30 May 1918 when he was killed in action in Flanders, just inside the French border, where the Australians had only recently checked Ludendorff's great advance, the famous 'spring offensive'. His personal effects were sent back to his mother in Kadina: three suit cases and a kit bag in the steamship *Australcrag* – comprising items such as his bank books, a cigar case, an 'Old Time Revolver (unloaded and NOT government property)', a pair of gum boots, and an illustrated book of Australia. Following on the *Coo-ee* was a parcel containing one wrist-watch and strap (damaged), one leather cigarette case, one muffler, one metal flask, one wallet, and several letters. Such was the detritus of war – or, alternatively, the treasured mementos of a loved-one buried in a far-off land.[81]

'Moonta is well represented'

There were, of course, those who survived unscathed. H.S. Holthouse, the postmaster's son, served all the way through from the first landings at Gallipoli until the war's end, returning at last to South Australia where, years later in May 1967, he was able to write to the army to request his Anzac badge – having been at Anzac Cove on that fateful first day.[82] In August 1914, none of this could have been imagined or foreseen by readers of the Peninsula press, and for the next few months at least a certain naivety, even innocence, prevailed. Publicly, through the regional press and the utterances of civic leaders, the able-bodied were exhorted to enlist as their patriotic duty. Privately, as Bill Gammage has observed, there was any number of reasons why men came forward.[83] Some, indeed, were motivated by patriotic considerations – whether for Empire, Australia or region; or all three – and others by the prospect of adventure. Quite what that adventure might be, varied from person to person. For some, the prospect of war itself seemed exciting. Few had served in the Boer War, and those able to give first hand accounts of the realities of modern warfare were remarkably rare. Adventure for many meant the ability to travel abroad. Those born in the British Isles looked forward to a free trip 'home', and even for the Australian-born there was the attraction of seeing the mother country for themselves – especially for those on the Peninsula, where Cornwall exerted an especial allure. Still others might be looking to escape a boring job, or a boring marriage, or from the consequences of some recent misdemeanour. There was also peer pressure – wanting to be part of the gang, and not to look cowardly in front of the girls. The uniform itself had a certain appeal, especially for the opposite sex.

And there were those who were never quite sure why they, or others, were joining up. It was an uncertainty caught by C.J. Dennis, the South Australian poet whose *Songs of a Sentimental Bloke* was published in October 1915 (when the agony of Gallipoli was at its height) and was an instant success, striking a chord with soldiers and civilians alike. Dennis was popular on Yorke Peninsula, as he was elsewhere, and was a friend and admirer of Oswald Pryor, 'grass captain' at the Moonta mine cementation works but by then also a budding cartoonist and local historian. *The Moods of Ginger Mick*, a sequel to the *Songs*, was published shortly after and proved equally popular, detailing the adventures of its eponymous anti-hero:

> Wot price ole Ginger Mick? 'E's done a break –
>   Gone to the flamin' war to stoush the foe.
> Wus it for glory, or a woman's sake?
>   Ar, arst me somethin' easy! I dunno.
> 'Is Kharki clobber set 'im off a treat,
> That's all I know; 'is motive's got me beat.[84]

At official levels, there was recognition that the mines of northern Yorke Peninsula would be the source of much needed mining and mining engineering skills. Routine tasks of entrenchment and fortification could make good use of such abilities but, as the war developed, so more specialist undertakings were envisaged for those with mining backgrounds. At Gallipoli, tunnels were dug under enemy positions and filled with explosives, which were then detonated with startling effect. Later, tunnelling and counter-tunnelling, with the intention of setting off huge explosions beneath enemy positions, became part of the anatomy of warfare on the Western Front, and one to which Australian forces made an important contribution.[85] As the *Kadina and Wallaroo Times* reported, for officers there were now positions available for those with underground experience in mining engineering and mining surveying, while for NCOs (non-commissioned officers) and sappers (privates in engineering regiments) there were openings for shift bosses, tunnellers, carpenters and blacksmiths.[86] There were indeed local miners, and those in allied trades, keen to apply their professional skills in a military context. Charles Bodinner, from Cross Roads, near Moonta, for example, a railwayman, joined up initially in the Army Medical Corps was but soon re-categorised as a sapper in the Australian Tunnelling Corps (alas, he was killed in an air raid in France in

11. Reinforcement Sappers for the Australian Tunnelling Companies await embarkation at Port Melbourne, Victoria. Among their number (extreme right, partly obscured, holding kitbag drawstring) is Sapper Percy Sutton from Wallaroo.

October 1918, less than a fortnight before the Armistice).[87] The brothers Stan and Percy Quintrell, also Cross Roads boys, both miners (and Methodists), likewise joined the Tunnelling Corps, serving in France and returning home in 1919.[88] Needless to say, there was also a sense that miners, irrespective of what particular skills they might bring to the battlefield, were inherently well qualified as soldiers. Mining was a dangerous, arduous, often frightening occupation, and the miner had to live on his wits, relying on physical strength as well as his own ingenuity, and having to deal effectively with calamities such as rock falls or premature explosions where colleagues might be badly injured. Such experiences stood the miner in good stead for life at the front.

Certainly, Kio boys continued to come forward. 'Moonta is well represented', observed the *People's Weekly* on 12 December 1914, noting the recent enlistment of Percy Brokenshire (whose brother Bill would shortly be the first Moonta soldier to die in the war), William and Lee Pomeroy, Charles Anderson, and others.[89] Soon, after the formalities of enlistment and periods of basic training in camp near Adelaide were completed, the newly joined soldiers returned to the Peninsula for their private and public farewells. It is difficult to know what happened behind closed doors – the tears from mothers and wives, perhaps, the stiffening advice from fathers and uncles – but the public 'Soldiers' Farewells' (as the press dubbed them) were often grand occasions. In February 1915, for example, Percy Brokenshire and Charles Anderson were sent off in considerable style at a 'smoke social' in the Moonta Mines Recreation Pavilion. The Moonta Mines Male Voice Choir provided appropriate musical entertainment, and Ephraim Major – the newly elected mayor – opined that, as Australian Light Horsemen, the two guests would be sure to 'uphold the best traditions of British soldiers'.[90]

He also introduced the three 'M's, as he put it. This was his advice to new recruits, a simple litany that over the years, as Major settled into his role as spokesman for the community, would develop as a well-remembered catch-cry in the locality. As he presented Troopers Brokenshire and Anderson each with 'a case containing military brushes and comb', he 'sought their continuous remembrance of the three "M"s, which might well stand for Manliness – keep to the right; Mother – her last word is still with me; and Moonta – they expect the best'.[91] Here, in addition to the much-trumpeted patriotic duty, was a new set of moral imperatives, one intended to instil personal discipline and responsibility, and demanding particular qualities. 'Soldiers' Farewells' were occasions to wish departing servicemen Godspeed. But they were also opportunities for the soldiers to be told what the community expected of them – or rather, what the community's representatives, already warming to their roles as arbiters of community opinion in wartime, expected. A few weeks later Ephraim Major addressed another 'Soldiers Farewell', when 'eight soldiers had returned from camp to spend a few days with their parents and friends, prior to leaving for the front'. Proffering his usual advice, Major added pointedly that he hoped they would 'return home better men for the experiences which they would have to encounter'.[92]

In practice, of course, it was difficult for individual soldiers to live up to such high expectations. Australians troops soon earned a reputation for their healthy disregard for discipline, especially the formal discipline of the parade ground and the training camp – such as the saluting of officers – and were adept at granting themselves unofficial leave.[93] Percy Brokenshire was particularly prone to the latter. In 1915 he found himself sick in hospital in Fishponds, a suburb of Bristol, in England, and it was probably there that he met his wife-to-be Ethel Comley, who lived at Bathbridge in the same district. Perhaps it was over zealous courtship that led subsequently to Brokenshire being absent without leave for five days from camp at Weymouth, for which he paid with 168 hours' detention and a fine of thirteen days' pay. At any rate, it was a habit that, once acquired, he found difficult to shed. At Etaples he was detained and fined twice for similar offences, and later in France on active service was again punished on three separate occasions. But Percy Brokenshire was a good soldier. He was promoted lance-corporal in June 1917, then made up to full corporal, and became a sergeant in July 1918. In 1919 he returned safely to Australia, with his English bride and young child.[94]

Meanwhile, Charles Anderson, Percy's pal (they both came from Caroline Street, in Moonta), had made it to Gallipoli, where he received a severe leg wound in August 1915. After a spell in hospital in Egypt he was sent home as unfit for further service. He later settled at Ardrossan, on southern Yorke Peninsula, and lived until 1990.[95]

As the soldiers departed for the front, there was the anxious wait for news. Ships took several weeks to reach the Middle East or Europe, during which time one would not expect to hear anything, and thereafter the exigencies of service life might well get in the way of letter-writing. Added to that were the vagaries of the postal system itself. For all the military efficiency of the postal service, there were so many imponderables that could intervene to prevent or delay correspondence reaching its intended recipients in Australia. As one Peninsula newspaper reflected, the 'silence was becoming unbearable'.[96] Rumours abounded. In January 1915 one prescient rumour that reached Peninsula ears insisted that Australian troops in Cairo were about to be attacked by the Turks.[97] In fact, the Turks attacked along the Suez Canal – the Empire's lifeline – on 3 February. But before the Australians could be deployed, the ill-conceived assault had already been repulsed, not least through spirited action by New Zealand and Indian troops. People at home on the Peninsula would have to wait a few months yet before receiving substantive news of Kio boys in action. In the meantime, they were eager for any other news, however meagre, that might shed light on the activities of Peninsula folk in distant theatres.

In September 1914, for example, it had been reported that Herbert Wood, son of John Wood, bricklayer at Hamley Flat (Moonta Mines), had rejoined his old regiment, the Scots Guards. He had left Moonta seven years previously, serving in the British Army for three years, and then settling in London where he married, and subsequently joined the police force. However, on the outbreak of war, he had re-enlisted in the Scots Guards. He was, said the *People's Weekly*, a 'strapping young fellow of 6 feet and 2 inches', and as a guardsman had already done duty at Buckingham Palace, parading in his red jacket, bearskin, and highly-polished boots. But now he had been deployed to the Continent as part of the British Expeditionary Force, and, as the newspaper explained: 'Naturally his father is anxiously awaiting news of how he has fared in the various engagements in which his regiment has been engaged'.[98] In fact, the Scots Guards had participated in the First Battle of Ypres in Belgium in 19–31 October 1914, experiencing the full brunt of modern industrial warfare. The regiment's 2nd Battalion lost some 500 men in the struggle, more than fifty percent of its complement. The 1st Battalion suffered equally as badly, losing 344 men killed, wounded, missing or taken prisoner on 29 October, and a further 125 men two days later.[99] It was not until January of the following year that John Wood heard that his son had fallen 'into the hands of the enemy, and is now detained as a prisoner by the Germans in Hanover'.[100] It was not, of course, exactly the news that he had wanted to hear (although glad his son was alive) – nor, indeed, was it at all like the much anticipated tales of glory that the wider community had been encouraged to expect. Likewise, when, in early January 1915, a letter arrived at Moonta from Private Richard 'Dick' Shields, serving with the first Australian Expeditionary Force in Egypt, it was a trifle irksome to find that it contained nothing more uplifting than news that poor Shields was in hospital at Alexandria suffering from appendicitis.[101]

'The Empire swings to the common cause'

Publicly, there was little dismay expressed at such isolated reversals and disappointments, and when news filtered through to the Peninsula of the riotous behaviour of Australian troops in Egypt in March and April of 1915, locals were happy to believe that – as Donald Dowling of Kadina, serving with the 4th Field Ambulance at Heliopolis, insisted – 'the New Zealanders have been the rowdiest right through'.[102] In those early days, before the experiences at Gallipoli had forged a common Anzac bond, the Australians were all too happy to blame their misdemeanours on the New Zealanders (and *vice versa*), not least as uninformed observers sometimes found it difficult to distinguish between the two nationalities. Unchecked by the British Military Police, who were at a loss how to deal with the impetuous and unruly Australians, things went from bad to worse. On Good Friday, 2 April, 1915, some Australian and New Zealand units had heard that, at last, they were to be sent to the front. Weeks of pent-up frustration, boredom, and anxiety were released in one great paroxysm of destructive energy, when soldiers from those units ran amok in the Wasser, the red light district of Cairo. There were, as Bill Gammage has noted, 'long standing grievances against the bad drink and diseased women sold in the area'.[103] In the mayhem, several prostitutes were thrown off balconies, local men beaten up, their property smashed or burned, and several houses were gutted. It did not show the Australians in a good light. But, like Donald Dowling, most were quick to point the finger at their antipodean cousins. Fred Carthew, a West Australian serving in Egypt, considered that the 'New Zealanders took a very important part' in the disturbances: 'in fact they started most of the trouble, but it is the poor old Aussie that has to take all the blame, and it seems to be their fate to get more blame than they deserve'.[104]

This was the view put to readers of the *Kadina and Wallaroo Times*, courtesy of Donald Dowling. Some subscribers might have 'heard awful tales of the behaviour of our troops here', he admitted: 'But they seem to be mostly baseless'. Besides, he continued, the Egyptians probably deserved it. Confident in his Imperial superiority, Dowling reported that Cairo was 'nothing but stinks, yelling, and disease-ridden niggers'. At least he thought they were 'niggers': 'some are niggers; a good many seem to be all colors [*sic*], varying from white to black. Some are absolutely black, and some almost look like Europeans, or at least Australians'. But if their racial composition was perplexing, there was no doubt at all about the manners and hygiene of the Egyptians. 'Talking about the natives', he added, 'I believe they are the dirtiest people I have seen, and I hope I will never see anyone dirtier'. A medical man, he was horrified to find that 'Egyptians have many dread diseases among them. Venereal disease seems to taint 80 to 90 per cent of them, and shows up in some appalling forms. I saw a poor beggar with no nose at all, just a hole above his mouth'. Moreover, their 'habits are absolutely filthy and disgusting. They don't worry about going to sanitary conveniences … the gutter or the side of the road is good enough for them, and such a thing as modesty does not enter into their reckoning at all'.[105]

Far from being embarrassed by such a vitriolic torrent, the *Kadina and Wallaroo Times* found it editorially advantageous to print Dowling's observations at length. They confirmed Australians in their racial and moral superiority, part of the great British Imperial people, and helped to assuage any lingering discomfort that readers might have felt about Australian behaviour in Egypt. Similarly, when it became known that 'undesirables' — those persistently guilty of the most heinous disciplinary offences, or lacking moral fibre, or suffering from chronic venereal disease, or in other ways unfit to wear the King's uniform — were being sent home in disgrace, the newspapers made the best of this disappointing news. William Pomeroy, who had been bade farewell in the previous December, was now back on the Peninsula, having been one of those soldiers selected to act as escorts to the undesirables shipped to Australia. He attended a 'welcome home' evening at the Moonta Athletic Club in early June 1915, where, the *People's Weekly* reported, he was 'congratulated … on his having been selected by the military authorities for such an important duty', and was further 'congratulated … on the important duties entrusted to him'. Indeed, such was the esteem in which he was held, that Pomeroy was presented with a case of pipes. Somewhat overwhelmed, Pomeroy in his reply protested that he 'was not much of a speaker'. Nonetheless, he held his audience spellbound for over an hour, the listeners paying 'close attention' — especially when he 'spoke at length on the definition of the word "undesirable"'. Thoughtfully, the *People's Weekly* spared its readers those unpleasant details. But they were left in no doubt as to the superior qualities of William Pomeroy, the Moonta boy.[106] Undesirables, it was inferred, were from elsewhere: Peninsula recruits were made of sterner, nobler stuff.

In the seemingly long wait for real action, the regional press had papered

12.   Richard 'Lee' Leopard Pomeroy and William 'Will' Albert Pomeroy.
The two brothers, from Moonta, served with distinction throughout the Great War
in the 1st Machine Gun Battalion, their exploits followed with keen interest in
the Yorke Peninsula press.

adroitly over cracks as they had appeared. Moonta and environs had continued to assert their presumed regional superiority, and the papers had been rock solid in their very public display of Empire loyalism. Against the sustained articulation of such rhetoric, it is difficult to gauge the extent to which there were dissenting voices in the community, and when and how such dissent was voiced. Later, in the heated debates over Conscription, the regional press became the platform for often vociferous exchanges concerning the conduct of the war. But in the period August 1914 to April 1915, from the outbreak of war to the Gallipoli landings, alternative opinions seemed almost non-existent, at least in the public domain. This was not an experience restricted to northern Yorke Peninsula, or indeed to South Australia generally, and was replicated time and again across regional Australia. In north-eastern Victoria, for example, the *Corryong Courier* noted confidently that: 'The call of Empire has brought all into line. Class, creed and faction are swept aside by the common wave of enthusiasm with which the Empire swings to the common cause'.[107] It was the same in rural Moyarra, in the South Gippsland region of Victoria where, as Jillian Durrance has argued, 'It was a matter of duty and loyalty to the motherland to assist in her hour of need and that's how the Moyarra men would have seen it'.[108] Across in Western Australia, where, as on Yorke Peninsula, the Conscription crisis of 1916 and 1917 would expose bitter divisions, the early months of war also appeared to offer consensus in the cause of Empire – in the capital Perth, and in regions as disparate as Albany in the south-west and the Kalgoorlie-Coolgardie-Boulder mining district in the interior. Newspapers with varying ideological or political affiliations – from the socialist *Westralian Worker* to the conservative *Western Mail* – echoed the *West Australian's* view that in 'a moment political factions have become obliterated, the tumult of partisans' voices stilled, and a united nation stands prepared to do it duty'.[109]

Both 'different' and 'typical', the mixed mining and farming region of northern Yorke Peninsula had reacted to the outbreak of the Great War in a manner that seemed true to type. In line with opinion expressed throughout Australia, there was almost unanimous agreement that here was an opportunity, in helping the motherland, to prove the loyalty and worth of the new nation and to bolster Australia's standing within the British Empire. Yet regional considerations remained important – not only the difficult situation in which the copper industry had found itself but also the distinctive, self-confident regional identity that Kio embodied. Ephraim Major had caught this mood, with his appeal to 'Britain-Australia-Moonta', and with his insistence on the three 'M's where Moonta 'expect[s] the best'. Men came forward to enlist, as they did elsewhere in Australia, and the community mobilised to do its bit in support of the war effort, activities that created roles for both men and women. Most importantly, regional newspapers – already flourishing and widely read on the Peninsula, with deeply entrenched roles as opinion-shapers — had now adopted the mantle of arbiters and interpreters of war news, and as guardians of the new consensus. Civic leaders, too, saw it as their responsibility to encourage enlistment, to support the homefront efforts of bodies such as the 'Moonta Patriotic League', and to maintain morale. In so doing, they enhanced their own standing as pillars of the local community and as loyal citizens of the Empire and Australia. As politicians or public figures, such enhancement could only serve to further their own interests and ambitious, their patriotic outpourings inviting popularity, approval and applause. But for the soldiers who went to war, there could be no telling yet what would become of them, and what they would encounter half-a-world away on 25 April 1915 and in the months and years thereafter.

CHAPTER THREE

'Our motto is "dig on, dig ever"'
Gallipoli

Desperate for positive news of Kio boys in action, the Yorke Peninsula press – and its avid readers, the local populace – had waited anxiously for the redeployment of Australian forces from Egypt into theatres of battle. The massive build-up of troops in the Middle East was seen as evidence that something big was afoot in that part of the world, and, as 1914 turned to 1915, Yorke Peninsula – like the rest of Australia – held its breath.[1] But, strangely, the first news of hostilities came not from those distant lands but from much closer to home – from Broken Hill, the silver-lead mining town just across the border in outback New South Wales, where there were strong community links with Moonta, Kadina and Wallaroo.

'A frightful tragedy at Broken Hill'

Indeed, for many, Broken Hill was almost an outpost of northern Yorke Peninsula, such were the ties of kinship and affinity, with a constant movement to and fro between the two regions. South Broken Hill had its own suburb of 'Moonta Town', and hotel names such as 'The South Australian' and 'The Duke of Cornwall' were more than a clue to the district's cultural origins. 'Har ee goin ome Xmas?' was the question on the lips of many ex-Peninsularites at Broken Hill in December 1893, according to the Moonta *People's Weekly*, with the paper opining that there was no other town in Australia where the seasonal exodus was so great, 'and on this occasion there is quite the usual number leaving for the well-remembered sights of Kadina, Moonta and Wallaroo'.[2] Silver-lead had been discovered at Broken Hill a decade earlier, in 1883, and the district had developed swiftly thereafter, a magnet for miners from across Australia, especially from northern Yorke Peninsula. In 1888 one observer could note that Broken Hill 'geographically belongs to New South Wales but commercially to South Australia'.[3] Big mines, such as the Block 10 (run by John Warren, formerly captain of the

Hamley mine at Moonta) and Broken Hill Proprietary (where Richard Piper, previously at the Wallaroo mine, was underground captain), were often in the managerial hands of experienced Peninsula men. The foundation of the Cornish Association of Broken Hill in March 1892 also spoke volumes about the district's character, as the *Burra Record* (published in South Australia) noted proudly: 'in a large mining field like Broken Hill . . . it is not surprising to find the Cornish element is so predominant'.[4]

Nor was it surprising, given this intimacy, to find that that at least one 'Moonta boy'[5] was among those aboard the special train chartered to take passengers from Broken Hill to nearby Silverton for the miners' union New Year's Day picnic in January 1915. As the *People's Weekly* explained, this Moonta boy was Frank White, one of the many enticed from Yorke Peninsula to the silver-lead fields of Broken Hill in the years before the Great War. The miners' excursion was an annual event, and on this occasion the train conveyed more than a thousand holidaymakers, including women and children, in forty open mineral trucks. It was, as the *People's Weekly* remarked, 'one of the longest and most crowded picnic trains that have ever left Broken Hill'. The passengers were in carnival mood, until about two miles into the journey when, without warning, two 'Turks' – flying the Turkish national flag – fired on the train. Killing three of the travellers and wounding several more, the Turks then fled to a quartz outcrop to the north of the town, where they were surrounded by local police and militia and promptly shot dead. As the *People's Weekly* put it, relishing the detail, the 'perpetrators lay riddled with bullets'.[6]

Frank White, the Moonta boy, was in one of those railway trucks and, as he explained in a letter his parents, two of those killed were in wagons immediately ahead of him, while those wounded were in ones behind. He wrote:

> I was sitting in one of the open trucks watching the two men shooting – not realising, of course, that they were firing bullets. When our truck was directly opposite them (only about 30 yards away) I saw one of the Turks fire in the air. The other fired point blank at our carriage. I then thought it was time to duck. Just then a shot hit our truck, and the bullets flew all ways for a second or two.[7]

'The sight was dreadful in the truck behind', added White: 'One woman . . . tried to shield her baby and was shot in the mouth. The baby was covered in blood. In this truck the blood was something terrible. It seemed like a slaughter house'. A man following the train on a bicycle was also shot down and killed, said White, and in Broken Hill itself, he reported, everyone 'seemed to be running to and fro carrying guns, and the whole town had the appearance of a military camp'. It was as if the war had suddenly arrived in Australia, visiting random violence and terror on the unsuspecting and the innocent: 'The town is still upset, and Lord help the man who opens his mouth too much'.[8]

The two Turks, it turned out, were Mullah Abdullah – a local camel-driver turned Muslim *mullah*, originally from Baluchistan, whose ritual slaughter of sheep had run foul of the local health authorities – and Gool Mahomet, an Afghan who had served in the Turkish army before returning to Broken Hill in 1912 to work in the mines. Together, it seems, the two men had decided on a suicide mission, motivated – as Brian Kennedy has put it – by 'a mixture of religious zeal, resentment at past slights, and loyalty to the [Turkish] Sultan'.[9] For the *People's Weekly*, however, they were merely 'desperate Turks', and the paper published Frank White's letter in full, anxious to report the 'frightful tragedy at Broken Hill', bringing news of the terrible incident into homes across the Peninsula. It was a story calculated to shock and to fascinate, horrifying those who had not imagined 'war' breaking out on their doorstep.[10] Individuals on Yorke Peninsula felt as touched by the event as did those at Broken Hill – Frank White's parents lost no time in handing their son's letter over to the press, and, in the absence of news 'from the front', the *People's Weekly* was more than happy to report the awful details.

The newspaper also reported the aftermath – a 'fresh development as a sequel to Friday's happenings', as it put it – the rounding up of 'alien enemies resident in Broken Hill' by the local militia. The swoop led to the arrest of eleven aliens – six Austrians, four Germans, and one Turk – and at the large Central mine the management asked all such aliens to 'stand down for the time being'.[11] In contrast to earlier, more generous estimations of the positive contributions of German settlers in Australia, this evidenced a hardening of attitudes. But, once the initial outrage had subsided, the general response appeared remarkably restrained. Public figures in Broken Hill were at pains to emphasise that Afghan cameleers were a familiar and loyal element of local society, and that a great many Indian Muslims were at that very moment serving in the armed forces of the British Empire.[12]

Moreover, given the whiff of ethno-religious antagonism detected in the Broken Hill shooting, there was surprisingly little evidence of heightened Islamophobia in the community. In Egypt, Australian soldiers had displayed their usual contempt for 'the natives'. But many, remarkably, had shown considerable respect for the antiquity of Egyptian culture. More than a few had behaved as though they were tourists, visiting the pyramids and other famous sites. Private Cliff Green wrote from Egypt to his father at East Moonta, for example, explaining that he had 'visited some of the fine historic buildings, which were equal to anything ... seen in Adelaide', while among those 'ancient sights' he was 'privileged to see was a tomb 700 years old ... the outside being worked in gold'.[13] Another visited Cairo Museum, 'a wonderful place' with 'marvellous things', including the mummies of the pharaohs Rameses I and V.[14] Mosques, and by extension, Islam, were likewise treated with due deference as part of an ancient heritage, with 'the Mosque of a thousand lights' at Cairo deemed 'a beautiful sight' by one Moonta soldier.[15] At home, although the tone of anti-enemy rhetoric grew ever more intemperate, religious animosity was rarely part of the vituperative repertoire, notwithstanding the familiar tensions between Catholics and Protestants. Appeals to God for help against the 'un-Christian' regimes of Germany and Austria-Hungary were commonplace. But overt hostility to Islam or other religions was unusual – one rare example being a sermon delivered at Moonta Methodist church in September 1915, by which time the scale of Australian losses at the hands of the Turks had become clear. 'Christian arms had protected Luther', thundered the minister, 'had put down slavery in America, Mahdism in the Soudan, and was now driving Mohamedanism [*sic*], with its lust and massacres, out of Europe'.[16] Yet there was no particular desire to drive Islam out of Australia, and the Afghan camel drivers continued to ply the Outback routes, much as they had done before.

'Floods of glory'

The Broken Hill incident had acted as a warning and as a distraction – a warning that the war might indeed intrude on the homefront in violent and unexpected ways, and a distraction that caught the wrapt attention of those impatient for news of actions abroad. Meanwhile, however, behind the apparent inactivity, there was indeed something big afoot overseas. In fact, the impending attack on the Dardenelles by Allied troops – Australian, New Zealand, Indian, British, French – turned out to be one of the worst kept military secrets of the Great War. In a bold (or reckless) attempt to open a second front and force Turkey out of the war, the Allies intended to strike the Ottoman Empire at its heart. The plan, enthusiastically endorsed by Winston Churchill as First Lord of the Admiralty, was to force the straits of the Dardenelles, the strategically significant stretch of water linking the Mediterranean to the Black Sea. Churchill calculated that the sudden appearance of Royal Navy (and French) warships so close to Constantinople would intimidate – or batter – the Turks into early surrender. Obsolescent battleships would be quite capable of this simple task, it was thought, and were deployed accordingly, leaving modern dreadnoughts available elsewhere for potentially more arduous duties.

On 19 February 1915 the naval operation commenced. It was immediately obvious, however, that Turkish resolve and capability had been seriously underestimated. Concealed Turkish batteries on either side of the straits concentrated their considerable firepower on the British and French warships, and newly-laid minefields took a terrible toll.[17] On 18 March no less than a third of the Allied force was sunk or disabled to a greater or lesser degree, and the operation was hastily abandoned – or rather it was modified. In the original plan, the successful forcing of the Dardenelles by the Allied warships would be the prelude to a land operation, with massed troops going ashore to occupy the territory subdued by the British and French navies. Now the plan was reversed, with the Allied armies directed to conduct an amphibious landing on the Gallipoli peninsula, designed to overwhelm the Turkish defences and thus open the Dardenelles for the safe passage of Allied shipping. Meanwhile, of course, the naval operation had alerted the Turks to the Allies' intentions, and the huge build-up of Allied troops and naval vessels on and around the Mediterranean islands of Lemnos and Mudros was further evidence of what was planned. Allied units had completed their training in Egypt, and had been conveyed to the islands in readiness for the imminent assault. These units included the South Australians (Kio boys among them) of the 'famous 10th' Battalion – part of 3rd Brigade, 1st Australian Division – who on 1 March had been taken by rail from their camps in Egypt to the port of Alexandria for the journey to Lemnos.[18] Together, the combined Mediterranean Expeditionary Force, as it was known, comprised some 70,000 men, including the 20,000 Australians in the two Divisions of the Australian and New Zealand Army Corps (ANZAC), ready now for the attack on Gallipoli.

The long-expected amphibious assault came on the morning of 25 April 1915. The Australians and New Zealanders landed at what soon became known as Anzac Cove, while the British and Indians came ashore at Cape Helles, at the southern tip of the Gallipoli peninsula, with the French attacking both Cape Helles and the Asian side of the Dardenelles. The British journalist, Ellis Ashmead-Bartlett, observed the Anzac landing from a Royal Navy warship offshore.[19] His dramatic account of the assault was the first to reach Australia, appearing in newspapers on 8 May. 'The Australians ... rose to the occasion', he wrote: 'Not waiting for orders, or for the boats to reach the beach, they sprang into the sea, and, forming a sort of rough line, rushed the enemy trenches'. The Australians 'were happy because they knew that they had been tried for the first time and not been found wanting ... There has been no finer feat in this war than this sudden landing in the dark and the storming of the heights'.[20]

It was news that galvanised Australia. Yorke Peninsula papers were anxious now for their own share of the story (and glory), to give local colour to the extraordinary happenings, to sing the praises of local boys and their daring feats of arms. The *Yorke's Peninsula Advertiser* had already divined that something momentous had occurred, reporting on 7 May 1915 that there were now 'Australians in Action'. It eagerly anticipated the 'splendid heroism displayed by "Our Boys"' and the 'floods of glory' that would inevitably accrue.[21] In the days and weeks ahead, there were further insights into Australian exploits, snippets seized upon greedily by the local press. Australia was 'knocking at the gates of the Ottoman Empire', insisted the *Yorke's Peninsula Advertiser*.[22] The *Kadina and Wallaroo Times* reached for even grander phrases: 'To-day the British Empire is one vast unity', it reported, 'inspired by one ideal, and resolved to fight for the one supreme issue'.[23]

'Now reported wounded not missing'

Alas, the first substantive news to reach Yorke Peninsula was not the eye-witness letters so impatiently awaited; many in any case not yet written, and those that were, still weeks away from delivery. Instead, telegrams started to arrive, ones and twos at first, and then a steady stream, informing unfortunate relations and friends of the wounded, missing and fallen. Private Les Barlow, whose parents had lived near the old Hamley mine on Moonta Mines, and whose sister and brothers still resided at Cross Roads, just outside Moonta on the Kadina road, was reported in the *People's Weekly* on 15 May as wounded 'in the Dardenelles engagement'.[24] In fact, he had been hit in the left shoulder by rifle-fire, and was evacuated from Anzac Cove to the safety of Egypt. It was there, in hospital in Alexandria, in an unfortunate irony, that he received news of the death of his father back in South Australia. Ironically too, his own letter home was one of the first of those to arrive on Yorke Peninsula. Writing to his uncle (W.H. Harvey) at Moonta Mines, he explained that he had been hit by a shrapnel bullet, which on impact had turned at the shoulder blade, travelling down to his ribs. 'When I got hit', he said, 'it was if someone gave me a knock on the arm and ribs with a sledge hammer, followed by a burning sensation and numbness'. The *People's Weekly*, publishing the extracts, was also pleased to report that Barlow had 'referred to the attack of the Australians as a great exploit, in which they were as cool under shrapnel as on parade'.[25] Rejoining his unit (the 10th) at Gallipoli, Barlow soon went down with a bad case of diarrhoea, and was again evacuated to hospital, this time on the island of Mudros. He recovered well; too well, because there he contracted the dreaded 'V.D.G.', as it was inscribed on his service documents, a dose of gonorrhoea which once again confined him to hospital. Eventually, Les Barlow found himself in France, where he was twice wounded – in August 1916 and again in April 1917 – before being repatriated to Australia and discharged as medically unfit in November 1917.[26]

Less fortunate was Lance Corporal Arthur Elphick of Wallaroo. Shot in the buttocks at Gallipoli, he was evacuated in HM Hospital Ship *Gascon*, where he died of his wounds on 6 May and was subsequently buried at sea. The tragic news was conveyed to his widowed mother, Sarah Jane Elphick, by the Roman Catholic priest at Wallaroo, Father Blake. Flags flew at half-mast in the town,

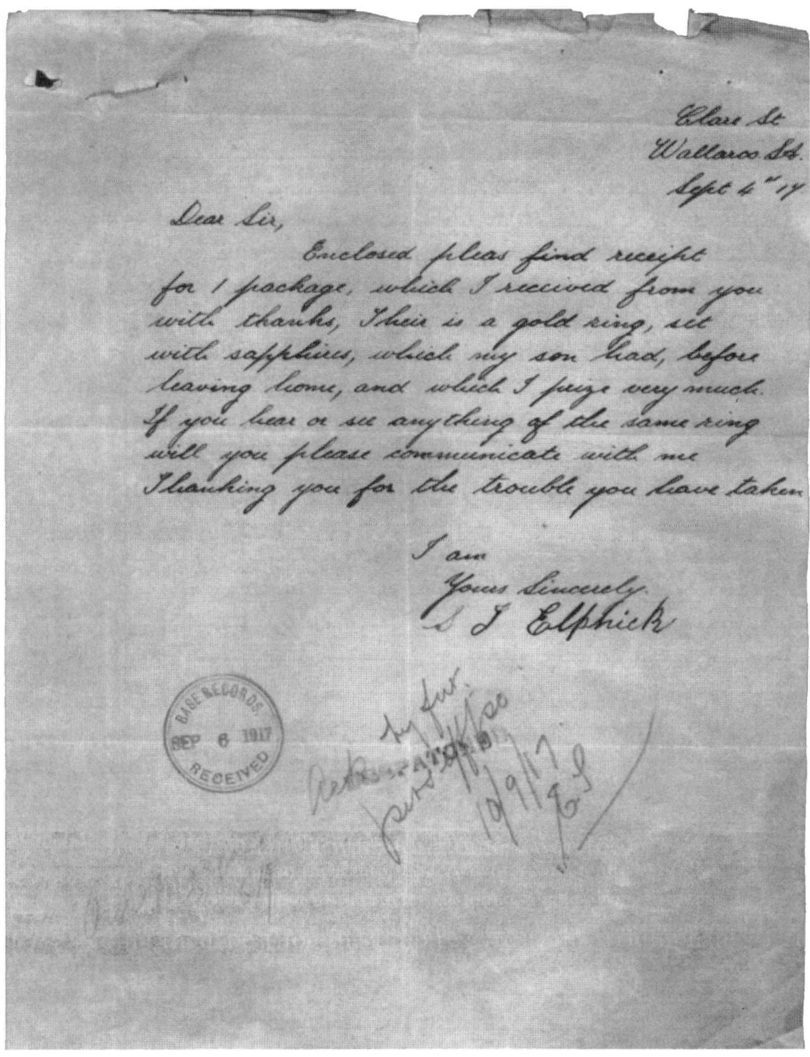

13.   The letter from Sarah Jane Elphick of Wallaroo to the Base Records Office in Melbourne, inquiring about the 'gold ring, set with sapphires' that she had given to her late son Arthur, who died of his wounds during evacuation from Gallipoli, 6 May 1915, and was buried at sea.

and the mayor (Mr Price) called to express his sympathy. Thirty-two years of age, Elphick was of 'fine physique' (his documents showed that he was 5 ft 9 ins tall, weighing 156 lbs, when he enlisted) and 'popular locally', as the *People's Weekly* put it.[27] He had served in the militia, where he had earned a reputation as a fine marksman, and years before he had volunteered to join the

Australian contingent in the Boer War. But his mother then had begged him to stay at home, and, reluctantly, he had deferred to her wishes. This time, however, she had consented to his departure, and with a heavy heart gave her blessing for her son to go off to the Great War, and, as we know, to his death. Elphick's personal belongings – 'Disc; Wristwatch and strap, 2 knives, Military book, Notebook, fountain pen' – were duly sent home to Sarah Jane, arriving in the September in the troopship *Ayrshire*. She opened the package, signed for the contents, and then wrote a sad letter to the military authorities. 'Enclosed pleas [*sic*] find receipt for 1 package, which I received with thanks', she began. She went on: 'Their [*sic*] is a gold ring, set with sapphires, which my son had, before leaving home, and which I prize very much. If you hear or see anything of the same ring will you please communicate with me. Thanking you for the trouble you have taken'.[28] Whatever had happened to Arthur Elphick's gold ring we can only surmise, but it is unlikely to have been committed to the deep with its owner.

Other telegrams arrived. 'News was received here during the week that several Moonta men have been wounded while fighting in the Dardenelles', reported the *People's Weekly* on 19 June.[29] Lieutenant Davey had been wounded in the knee (see p. 32), it was explained, but there was no news yet of the injuries sustained by Privates Melville Pethick (who, it later transpired, had been slightly wounded in the face and back, and was suffering from shellshock[30]) or Joe Cock. A week later, and what was already the forty-third casualty list from Gallipoli was published, and again it carried the names of

14.   Australians wait behind Quinn's Post, Gallipoli, 29 May 1915, a fortnight after Lance-Sergeant David Ballantyne (from Wallaroo) was killed there.

local boys. Among these was Lance-Sergeant David Ballantyne, who hailed from Scotland but for the past two years had been living at Wallaroo, working on the jetty extension at that port.[31] He had been killed in action on 15 May at the notoriously dangerous Quinn's Post, the most forward and exposed of the Anzac positions at Gallipoli, situated only a few feet from the Turkish lines.[32] A marginal note on his service documents recorded that Ballantyne was 'Buried near trench at the side of Quinn's Post by Rev G. Green'. Another scribble said that he lay in an 'Isolated grave date 15-5-15. In next Gully under Plugg[e]'s Right side of Road from beach'.[33] Perhaps the two annotations were recording the same spot, perhaps not. Men were often buried where they fell, and sometimes in the confusion of battle their graves were swiftly lost sight of, their locations incorrectly or vaguely remembered.

Back on Yorke Peninsula, of course, there was little sense of this muddle and uncertainty, with the minutiae of service documentation kept away from civilian scrutiny, and the release of information regarding the fate of loved ones carefully managed through the Base Records Office in Melbourne. Nonetheless, the entire community could share in the awful predicament that afflicted the family of Private Harry Cecil Brown, 'another Wallaroo boy', who was reported missing in the same casualty list.[34] All too often, missing meant that the unfortunate soldier had been destroyed by shellfire, his remains unrecognisable, or that his body had been interred by the enemy, or perhaps still lay where he had fallen in inaccessible no-man's land. For the family back home, half-a-world away, by contrast, missing was a source of lingering hope, that perhaps the soldier had been taken prisoner, alive and well, or was at that very moment recovering in a frantically busy field hospital that had not had time to inform the chain of command of his whereabouts. Sometimes families had to wait years to find out what had really happened; sometimes they never did. But for the Brown family, and for the town of Wallaroo, there was relief all round when it was discovered shortly after that he was 'now reported wounded not missing', and that his injuries had been light enough for him to have returned to his unit by the end of May. Yet, as we see with hindsight, his recovery merely put off the evil day, the celebration at home illusory, for Harry Brown was later seriously wounded in France in 1917, and was killed in action there in August 1918.[35]

'All the boys from old Kio are still alive and doing well'

Bad news continued to arrive. Lee Bray Nankivell, for example, a former Cross Roads resident who had joined up in Sydney (where his mother and father now lived), was reported killed in action on 14 May, and buried near where he fell in Shrapnel Gully, about 400 yards south-east of Anzac Cove.[36] The *People's Weekly* felt it only right to 'tender the sympathy of their many friends at Moonta to Mr and Mrs Elias Nankivell', Lee's grieving parents.[37] But there was brighter news too, for by now the long-anticipated missives from the front were beginning to arrive at last. In mid-July, for example, the parents of Private Fred Raymond were overjoyed to receive a letter from their son, penned in up-beat mood. 'All the boys from old Kio are still alive and doing well at the front', said Fred, optimistically: 'We send our regards to all our Moonta friends and trust that all is going well in the dear old town'.[38] Among those in the frontline trenches alongside him, he added, were William Brokenshire and Richard ('Dick') Shields, both Moonta boys. Unfortunately, all this excitement was tempered somewhat when a day or two later Fred's parents received a telegram to the effect that their son was now in hospital at Ghezireh in Egypt suffering from phthisis ('miners' complaint', as it was known on northern Yorke Peninsula), a respiratory disease which turned out to be a debilitating attack of bronchitis from which Fred Raymond never really recovered. Eventually, he was shipped back to Australia, where on 17 April 1916 he was discharged as 'Medically unfit (Not due to Misconduct)', although, curiously, on the same day he was sentenced by Court Martial to ninety days' detention for an unspecified misdemeanour.[39]

For now, however, it was enough to know that sons, husbands, fathers, were alive and well, and to hear something from the front. Private Richard ('Lee') Pomeroy, for example, serving with his brother William in the 1st Machine Gun Battalion, wrote home to his parents at Moonta Mines to provide a glimpse of life at Gallipoli. 'We are still living in the trenches', he explained, 'but our biggest difficulty is to get water to wash our clothes'. There was also the matter of the Turks: 'Of course, as you may imagine, we have had many narrow escapes, but have not "stopped anything" of any consequence so far'. Reassuringly, he added that 'We have plenty of good food to eat'.[40] Pomeroy went on to survive the war, although wounded in Flanders in September 1917; he reached the rank of Sergeant and was awarded the Belgian Croix de Guerre in 1919.[41]

Among the letters now arriving home was a sprinkling from those who had been there on that momentous day, 25 April, when the assault at Gallipoli had begun. Private Leigh Treweek Lennell, for example, had written to his mother at Moonta Mines on 28 May, a little over a month after the dawn landing. His recollection of the event remained vivid, especially the moment when the silence of their stealthy approach was broken suddenly by the eruption of Turkish guns. 'We had a great shock when landing', he admitted: 'I was sitting on deck viewing our position when the enemy commenced firing shrapnel shells on us'. He continued: 'Our boat capsised. It was awful to see many of the poor fellows who were picked off while quite unable to defend themselves. Our party landed safely, however, and went straight into the trenches, and are still there'.[42] Corporal Roy Pickering, another of the original Anzacs, wrote in similar vein to friends at Moonta. He was, he explained, in the 10th Battalion, itself part of the 3rd Brigade, and comprised six Companies from South Australia, six from Western Australia, four from Queensland, and two from Tasmania. Reprinted in the *Yorke's Peninsula Advertiser* on 9 July, it was the first and most complete public statement by a local witness of the dawn landing at Anzac Cove on 25 April 1915.[43]

'I must have said my prayers a dozen times'

Training together, Pickering said, the Brigade had for nine weeks practised the art of amphibious warfare on Lemnos, units and individuals learning their respective roles in the assault and, most especially, acquiring the discipline of 'landing in complete silence'. At 11 a.m. on 24 April he embarked in *HMS Prince of Wales*, which set sail at 1 p.m. next morning in concert, he estimated, with some dozen or so major warships, about twenty torpedo boats, and over one hundred transports. He continued:

> At about midnight, Saturday, we were given a good hot meal, marched up on deck (no lights), and then put into the lifeboats – each man knowing where to go. We then had a little steam pinnace to tow three or four boats each … everything was nice and quiet and you could hardly hear the throb of the engine of the pinnace. We were about 50 yards from the shore, when there was … a rifle shot that was the signal and in about five minutes a thousand rifles and machine guns were pouring lead at us as fast as they could. The sailor in our boat was hit but you can't frighten the English navy men, and our boat load got out of the water with bullets spitting all around us and waded ashore up to our necks. Twice I fell over going ashore but I seemed to miss the bullets alright.[44]

Once ashore, he added, his unit took cover under some ridges, where they removed their packs and fixed bayonets. 'Then the order came to charge', he said, 'and we went like wild men at those Turks yelling at the tops of our voices'. At that point the beach was only some 12 ft wide, with the shore rising up at a gradient of approximately 1-in-15, with the Turks entrenched about half way up that hill. Maddened by the loss of friends and colleagues on the beach below, Pickering continued, the Australians dislodged the Turks from their defences and forced them further up the hillside. 'There were two Turks left in a trench I passed', he said, 'but our chaps soon finished them with bayonets. You would have thought the Australians had been soldiers all their lives to see how cool they took it, no fear in them at all'. In total, he said, they drove the Turks back over three hills before the Australians were ordered to halt and began entrenching: 'We had not long been there before they put a few big guns around us on our left flank and infiladed us with shrapnel and what with rifle fire, machine guns and artillery it was terrible, they were knocking our chaps out in dozens yet we would not give in'. Pickering recalled the appalling spectacle of seeing 'your comrades falling one by one and laying about all over the battlefield . . . I stayed there to about 5 p.m. without getting hit, only a bullet striking the heel of my boot and doing no damage. I must have said my prayers a dozen times'. They began retiring from this exposed position just after 5pm, stealing away in twos, back to the relative safety of the firing line established by the reinforcements coming ashore. But 'I had not been there more than five minutes', exclaimed Pickering, 'when I got a bullet clean through my hand so that finished me for a while'. He was also hit in the shoulder and head. Much to his chagrin he was evacuated to Alexandria and then Cairo, where in hospital he was able to pen his letter. 'Our men have got a footing now and the Turks will never shift them', he predicted, 'before long our troops will be marching into Constantinople'.[45]

Here at last was the real news that people at home had waited for. It made a welcome change, of course, from the depressing lists of casualties and those seemingly endless telegrams. But more than that, for those whose loved ones had fallen, here was vindication of their courage and determination, of the selfless way they had laid down their lives for 'old Kio' and for Britain and the Empire. They had also proved themselves as Australians, displaying extraordinary coolness under fire and showing contempt for danger, qualities that would now be thought typically Australian. Australians were to be considered natural soldiers, as Pickering observed, and those that returned would be treated as heroes, revered as fathers of the young Australian nation. The Anzac myth was already in the making, as it was elsewhere in Australia. Pickering may have known what he was doing, with his way with words, penning his letter in such a manner that it would so easily find its way into the press. The *Yorke's Peninsula Advertiser* certainly knew what it was up to. Here was a compelling antidote to doubt, uncertainty, rumour, speculation, depression, a rousing first-hand description of what had actually happened (as readers were encouraged to imagine it), an account to stiffen resolve and encourage pride in the community.

The 'third hill' that Corporal Pickering and his mates had reached and briefly held was perhaps Gun Ridge, as it became known, or simply 'Third Ridge' as it was explained to the party of scouts (of which Pickering may have been a member) embarked in the *Prince of Wales*. 'When you get out of the boat, go like hell for Third Ridge',[46] was the order given to these men, and they did just that. Exactly as Pickering had described, a handful of Australians made it to Third – or Gun – Ridge, where opposition was negligible at first, until the Turks began to outflank them with heavy enfilading fire, forcing withdrawal.[47] Pickering claimed to have held on until 5pm but he may already have fallen back towards 400 Plateau, which was caught by artillery brought up to Gun Ridge by the Turks, causing the carnage Pickering described. The brief foray to Gun Ridge, and the penetration beyond by a plucky few who glimpsed the blue waters of the straits beyond, the ultimate objective of the assault, was the furthest point reached by the Australians during the Gallipoli campaign.

In many ways the attack had been a triumph, the troops coming ashore under fire and scaling the heights, with innumerable individual displays of initiative, courage and determination, the Australians demonstrating an élan for which they would be renowned throughout the war. But already the action was moving towards stalemate. The Anzac assault had captured less than a third of the ground the military planners had sought, and in pushing on too fast, too far in the opening hours, pockets of men had become isolated, their positions unknown, adding to the general confusion of the landing. Although 27,000 Australian troops had come ashore by 1 May, they lacked the military resources – especially heavy artillery – to break out of the tactically disadvantageous situation in which they found themselves, hemmed in amongst the bleak hills above the beaches. Strategically, the mission had failed already, and Lieutenant-General Sir William Birdwood, the Anzac commander, began to wonder whether immediate evacuation might be the best option. He was famously rebuffed by his commanding officer, General Sir Ian Hamilton, safely at sea with his staff in *HMS Queen Elizabeth*, who reassured him that 'You have got through the difficult business, now you only have to dig, dig, dig, until you are safe'.[48]

'Australia's name high in the annals of fame'

Corporal Roy Pickering, for all the splash he had caused in the local press, never made it back home to Australia. Like many Dardenelles veterans, having survived the rigours of Gallipoli, he was posted to France, where in the summer of 1916 he fell in the attack on Pozières.[49] Luckier was Henry Charles Banfield, a Private in the 10th Battalion who, like Pickering, had also landed on 25 April. Born at Moonta, Henry Banfield was almost forty-four years old when he joined-up in 1914, a comparatively old man (his hair was already grey) among the sea of youngsters coming forward. He was too a widower, his wife Olive (an East Moonta girl) having died some time before, their son Albert now cared for in the Salvation Army Home at Mount Barker in the Adelaide Hills. After initial training at Morphetville, near Adelaide, Banfield had sailed with his unit in the troopship *Clan MacGillivray*, bound for Egypt via Colombo and Aden. There was the further training at Mena camp, near the pyramids, and on Lemnos, before the short voyage to Gallipoli and the dawn landing. Safely ashore, Banfield fought constantly for about fifteen hours, he

15.   The women of the Adelaide Cheer-Up Society who had so impressed Private
Henry Banfield on his return from Gallipoli.

reckoned later, before being hit in the back, buttocks and thigh during the
battle for Second Ridge. Stretcher-bearers came to his rescue and carried him
to the beach, from where he was evacuated to Alexandria. Assessed as never
being likely to be fit again for active duty, he was repatriated to Australia in
the transport *Ballarat*, and formally discharged on 11 May 1916.[50]

Henry Banfield was impressed by the enthusiastic reception he and other
returning servicemen received from the Cheer-Up Society in Adelaide, the
morale-boosting women's organisation that offered support and encouragement
to members of the armed forces.[51] He was left in no doubt by the scale of this
welcome that he was a hero. But this newfound status, flattering as it was,
brought in its wake responsibilities and obligations, as Banfield was to learn.
A confident performer — as a member of the Salvation Army he was used to
engaging his audiences passionately and enthusiastically with telling anecdotes
and penetrating insights — he was soon to find himself much in demand as
speaker at functions across Yorke Peninsula and beyond. People were eager
to hear what it was like at Gallipoli, and to learn first hand the exploits of
Kio boys, with the press as ever anxious for thrilling snippets of news to pass
on to its readership. But more than that, Banfield found himself at the heart
of both fund-raising and recruiting campaigns. As a 'Salvo' he spoke with a

moral authority and religious conviction that could not fail to impress, and as a silver-haired as well as silver-tongued father figure he talked reassuringly and persuasively to the youngsters thinking of joining-up. Yet, despite his age, he was just a Private soldier, as the new recruits would themselves become on enlisting, and could speak to them man-to-man, rather than in the patronising tones of a 'brass hat' used to talking down to 'other ranks'. He made an ideal 'recruiting sergeant'.

On the eve of Henry Banfield's return, Ephraim Major – Moonta's mayor – had let it be known that he was worried about the falling levels of recruitment in the locality. He chose his words carefully, and was reported accordingly. 'Although the young men of Moonta were not coming forward very readily', noted the *Yorke's Peninsula Advertiser*, the mayor 'was of the opinion they were giving the matter serious consideration. No councillor nor any townsman would allow it to be said the young men lacked courage or patriotism'.[52] A week later and Banfield, hailed as 'an old Moonta boy', had been engaged to address a local meeting of the State Recruiting Campaign, where he duly 'appealed to the young men to enlist, and take part in this fight for righteousness'.[53] He also addressed a packed meeting at the Moonta Institute, where a collection in aid of the Cheer-Up Society raised £5 5s. The mayor, who chaired the gathering, explained to the assembled townsfolk that he had met Henry Banfield from the train on the day he had arrived home, and had asked him there and then to speak at the Institute. He was, he said, 'pleased to see so many present on so short notice to do honour to one who had been wounded in the defence of the Empire'.[54] Councillor Sweeney, who shared the stage with Major and Banfield, was keen to add his voice to the accolades showered upon the returning hero, declaring that 'the landing of the famous 10th on Gallipoli Peninsula on April 25 was the most glorious [military action] in British history to date'. Moreover, he reminded everyone present, 'Pte Banfield had participated in that historic event, and took part in the charge which has written in blood Australia's name high in the annals of fame'.[55]

At last, it was Henry Banfield's turn to speak, and the 'audience rose en masse and cheered lustily'. It was a consummate performance. Like others before him, who had written home from Egypt, Banfield spoke reverentially of 'the famous pyramids' while in the same breath condemning Cairo as 'one of the worst and most sinful [cities] in the world'. Their prejudices confirmed, his listeners were 'kept . . . in good humour', it was reported, as he 'related many amusing incidents that took place' during his time in Egypt. He also explained how on Lemnos he had met Private Richard Shields, from Moonta, and how they had sailed together to Gallipoli in the same ship. Tactfully, he added that although Dick Shields 'had the name of being a hard citizen', he had 'found him a very good fellow'.[56] Shields, it seems, enjoyed a reputation as a likeable larrikin, perhaps rather disapproved of in Salvation Army circles but popular among his peers, especially those in (khaki) uniform. He also had a way with words, writing to Ephraim Major (of all people) to explain that he had had the 'misfortune, or should he say luck' to miss the dawn landing. Suffering from a 'crook foot', as he put it, he had been left behind on board to guard the officers' baggage. But he had seen the action from the ship, and 'reckoned it was hell itself . . . I felt sorry for our boys, but on they went as if they were rushing for a pint of beer'.[57]

It was not quite Banfield's language, with the emphasis on booze rather than Empire, but it was light-hearted and down to earth in a way that Banfield might have appreciated. Like others who had experienced the dawn landing, Banfield had acquired an undying admiration for his 'mates', those with whom he had trained in Egypt and on Lemnos, and who had stormed ashore so bravely at Gallipoli, fighting furiously and yet standing by him when he was wounded. He recalled the opening moments of the amphibious assault at Anzac Cove, telling what was now an increasingly familiar story, but which the audience was anxious to hear again:

> All lights were out and silence reigned supreme. About 3 or 4 o'clock in the morning, when the moon went down, a rush was made for the shore; but before the men could get into the small boats to effect the landing the enemy discovered their presence and commenced a heavy fire on them. Many men were either killed or wounded . . . one boat [was] capsised by a shell. On nearing the shore the men jumped out into the water to their armpits in depth, and dashed on to the beach . . . One man undid another's pack, dropped it on the beach, and, with a yell, they charged up a steep hill with bayonets fixed amidst a murderous hail of shot and shell, which the enemy hurled upon them.[58]

So swift was the advance, said Banfield, that he reckoned 'there were numerous speed records broken that morning':

> The Australians ran for all they were worth, but the Turks ran faster, crying 'Allah' as they went. The orders given to the 10th was to land and hold the hill at all costs. Men fell in all directions, but the remainder rushed on, driving the enemy before them. Not content with taking the first hill they pushed on to the second, which was steeper than the first. They bayoneted the Turks out of the trenches, and subsequently dug themselves in on the second hill.[59]

Banfield was also keen to dispel a few myths that were circulating in the community. It had been rumoured, for example, that the men had gone ashore without ammunition. This was simply not true, insisted Banfield, who

16.   The impressive Salvation Army barracks at Wallaroo, testament to the influence and moral authority of the 'Salvos' on northern Yorke Peninsula before and during the Great War.

explained that each soldier had been given 250 rounds before the assault. It was true, however, that their magazines were not charged as they stormed the heights, 'but the bayonet was good enough for them just then'. He had also heard it said that socks knitted or purchased by civilians to be sent to the troops were being sold in the camps and at the front. This was another story without foundation, for the socks were handed out free, although, he conceded, a 'few unscrupulous men have sold a few pairs for drink, nothing more'.[60] In all, Henry Banfield had spoken for two hours at the Institute, holding his audience spellbound throughout. But still people wanted more, and on subsequent Sundays Banfield attracted large congregations when he conducted the services at the Salvation Army barracks at Moonta Mines.[61] Evidently, his reputation as an effective communicator spread far and wide – two months later he was returning from a fortnight's tour of Eyre Peninsula, where he had raised some £50 for the Cheer-Up Society and the Wounded Soldiers' Fund.[62]

'Where are the Boys of Australia Tonight?'

It is difficult to gauge the extent to which Henry Banfield's efforts affected the recruiting and fund-raising climates on northern Yorke Peninsula. It was, perhaps, easier to persuade individuals to put their hands into their pockets to

17. Sergeant Roy Percival Pollard, photographed shortly after his 'farewell' at the Moonta Mines Methodist Sunday school in early September 1915. He was later badly wounded and repatriated to Australia in 1917. His brother Lloyd damaged his spine while stretcher bearing under fire, and died in agony in hospital in Adelaide.

support the boys at the front, than it was to get them to join up. Nonetheless, men continued to come forward – together with a sprinkling of women, such as Nurse R. Williams of Wallaroo who 'has volunteered for active service in Red Cross work at the front'[63] – and, as the community recovered from the shock of the initial spate of bad-news telegrams and became more accustomed to the regular posting of casualty lists, so resistance to enlistment softened. Indeed, there was a redoubling of patriotic rhetoric on the lips of civic leaders. The mayor of Wallaroo, W. Price, put himself forward as an example to his townsfolk, but when he failed the army's medical examination he returned to the district unbowed, offering 'to serve in any other capacity if required'.[64]

Supporting activities of varying types continued unabated. There was a 'Wallaroo Mines Gallipoli Fair' to raise funds for the troops at the front, and in the July a garden fete was held at Agery in aid of wounded soldiers returning home. Twelve young girls performed a maypole dance 'tastefully dressed in red, white and blue', and an 'enthusiastic auction sale' raised £3 for a hand-made quilt and gratifying sums for half a ton of chaff, poultry, flowers, bacon, and a cigar.[65] In the same month, H. Lipson Hancock – general manager of the Wallaroo and Moonta Mining and Smelting Company – had topped the Moonta list of gifts to the South Australian Soldiers Fund with an exceptionally generous donation of £33 6s. 8d. which, of course, was made public in the press. A few months later the Moonta railway staff clubbed together to contribute £1 15s. 6d. to the same fund, the station porters Temby and Lathlean giving two shillings each from their modest wages, as the *People's Weekly* reported gratefully.[66]

Soldiers leaving for the front continued to be 'farewelled', as before. In early September there was a 'pleasing ceremony' at Moonta Mines Methodist Sunday school to say good-by to Sergeant Roy Pollard, 'an old scholar', who was presented with a pocket Testament and Bible. Likewise, in the Council Chamber at Kadina there was a 'public gathering to say a few words of farewell' to four local recruits destined for the war, with the mayor (Paul Roach) presiding over an audience of some thirty impressionable members of the Kadina Young Men's Club. Bert Grummet was given a wristwatch by an appreciative Moonta Tennis Club when he joined up, and Private Leigh Rogers received a periscope at his send-off at the Cross Roads Lecture Hall, outside Moonta. Increasingly, periscopes – manufactured locally from scraps of metal by hands skilled in the mines workshops – were the preferred farewell gifts, enormously useful for both defensive and offensive purposes in trench warfare.[67] The Cross Roads send-off, indeed, seemed an especially elaborate affair, with musical entertainment ('Where are the Boys of Australia Tonight?', sung with feeling by Miss Maddaford), and 'a descriptive and stirring address' by the Hon. John Verran, the former Labor Premier of South Australia, known for his florid and charismatic if somewhat voluble and pompous style. Tongue-in-cheek, the *People's Weekly* observed that Verran's speech 'was worthy of being fully reported, but, unfortunately, our correspondent is not a shorthand writer'.[68]

The co-option of the Kadina Young Men's Club, like the vigorous display of the Agery maypole girls, indicated the extent to which children and adolescents had become enmeshed in the community's homefront activities. At Moonta High School, for example, children were engaged in the making of 'billy-cans' for soldiers at the front, an activity encouraged by the South Australian Children's Patriotic Fund which awarded war service medals (with bars, as appropriate) in recognition of individual achievement in pursuit of the war effort.[69] Extremely useful for carrying water, brewing tea, boiling food, and any number of other functions, the billy-can was a much-prized component of any soldier's personal kit. At any rate, when Frederick Teo received his billy-can in Cairo in time for Christmas 1915, he was delighted. He wrote appreciatively to young Ilene Andrewartha, at Moonta, to thank her for her kindness:

My Dear Friend Ilene,

Just a few lines to let you know that I received your Xmas billy with thanks and I can assure you it was beautiful. There was a lot of fun when the chaps got their billys to see who had the best. Most of them were looking for a mouth organ. I was pleased with my billy as there were lots of things I was greatly in need of. I also thank you very much for sending me the compliments of the season, which I hope you will accept from me. I again thank you for the Xmas gifts. – I remain your sincere friend,

Gunner F. Teo,
Cairo, 5 January 1916.[70]

For children such as Ilene Andrewartha, it was thrilling to receive a personal letter from a soldier at the front, to have a friend of their very own in those almost unimaginably strange and far-away lands. It was yet another mechanism by which a sense of intimacy was established between the home and battle fronts, and the means by which even children were encouraged to think that they were doing their bit. It seems unlikely, however, that Teo, a bachelor in his mid-thirties, and Ilene kept in touch. Two days after penning his few lines, Teo went Absent Without Leave (AWOL) until 8 January, when at summary trial he was fined one day's pay and sentenced to three days' punishment routine. A month later, he was in hospital in Egypt with suspected mild heart trouble. Repatriated to Australia, he was discharged as medically unfit, only to rejoin the army in 1917 when, perhaps, standards had been relaxed in the increasingly difficult struggle to find new recruits.

18. 'Australia Day' parade, Moonta, 30 July 1915 – the artillery piece on the right appears to be the 'Joffre, Quick Firing Gun' mentioned in local newspaper reports.

Teo went on to serve in France and, despite two further AWOL episodes, was promoted to sergeant before returning home safely to Australia in 1919.[71]

Maypole dancing and billy-can making were fun. At the so-called 'Australia Day' celebrations on 30 July 1915, a fund-raising campaign co-ordinated across the country to assist sick and wounded soldiers, children played a prominent part.[72] In a procession at Moonta, for example, they wore patriotic fancy-dress, carefully run-up by their mothers and grandmothers, and rode on floats or accompanied displays such as the 'Joffre, Quick Firing Gun'.[73] Despite the militaristic overtones, this was also a fun event, conducted in carnival mood and enjoyed by all. But, as many parents now realised, the good-cause humour disguised a deeper reality, that some of the youthful participants had already lost – or would shortly lose – brothers or fathers, and that even those menfolk who came home eventually would be changed by the experience of war. There were, therefore, more sombre occasions, to which children were also exposed, such as the memorial service for fallen soldiers held at Moonta Methodist church in September 1915. The pulpit was swathed in the Union Flag, the choir sang Tennyson's 'Crossing the Bar', and organist J.H. 'Johnnie' Thomas – composer of Moonta's famous 'Cornish carols' – gave a rendition of the 'Dead March in Saul'. 'We are gathered to lay wreaths, metaphorically at least', said the minister, 'on the graves where our brave soldiers lie sleeping at Gallipoli, who nobly gave themselves in sacrifice for King and country, justice and righteousness'. He continued, solemnly: 'Though war is such a dire evil, yea the most fearful scourge that can come on a country, yet there are occasions when it is justified in defence of hearths and homes'.[74]

Lone Pine

Behind the clichés there was a heartfelt sincerity, a new rhetoric which gradually grew louder alongside the continued patriotic outpourings of local politicians and press, a sense that war was now not glorious but 'evil', 'fearful', a 'scourge'. Yet this war was also righteous, and its reverses and losses had to be born with quiet dignity and forbearance in the full knowledge that the cause was just: 'Those who tell us that war has no justification, and that Christians ought never to engage in it, are forgetful of the sacred scripture'.[75] This was a changing public mood, a subtle shift from the excitement and exuberance of late 1914 to the subdued and dutiful steadfastness that had become apparent across Australia by the antipodean spring of 1915. It was felt keenly on Yorke Peninsula, as it was elsewhere, and at Moonta was precipitated largely, as we shall see, by the death of Private William Brokenshire at the battle of Lone Pine on 6 August 1915.

In the three months or so since the dawn landing, the stalemate at Gallipoli had been characterised by determined Turkish attempts to throw the Anzacs and Allies back into the sea, while the Australians and other Empire forces had made equally dogged efforts to hold their positions and gain ground. The main Turkish attempt had occurred on 19 May, when early in the morning thousands of Ottoman troops rose suddenly from their trenches and poured along Wire Gully in the direction of Second Ridge and 400 Plateau. But the Australians were waiting for them, and in a spirited defence they stopped the Turks in their tracks. By 5 a.m. it was all but over, the Turks having suffered some 10,000 casualties, their bodies strewn in great heaps across the battlefield. Lee Pomeroy described what it was like to experience the full-fury of the Turkish assault. 'We were attacked on the 19th May', he wrote to his father at Moonta, 'and being my first time under fire, I was excited. I was blazing away through the loophole as hard as I could with my rifle ... when I felt a sharp sting on the top of my head'. On closer inspection, he found a neat hole in his cap and a new parting in his hair that had included a slight graze to the skin: 'Had it been slightly lower I should not be writing this'.[76] Despite the ferocity and strength of the Turkish onslaught, the Anzacs had held their positions, although at some places, notably Quinn's Post, it had been a close run thing. At Courtney's Post, another of the Australian defensive positions, seven Turks did break through. But they had not reckoned with Lance-Corporal Albert Jacka, who crept up behind them, leaping into their midst, bayoneting five and shooting the other two.[77] For this action, Jacka received the Victoria Cross. A forestry worker from Wedderburn in Victoria, Jacka was of Cornish descent — as the *People's Weekly* at Moonta was quick to spot. 'The first V.C. to come to Australia', it announced proudly, 'was won by ... [a] Cornishman in the person of Lance-Corporal Jacka'.[78]

News of other actions also found its way back to the Yorke Peninsula press. Alf Martyn, from Wallaroo, in a letter dated 29 June and written on a bit of cardboard salvaged from a spent ammunition box, observed laconically: 'The Turks have not driven us back into the sea, although they claimed to have done it twice. We get very lively here at times'.[79] Dick Shields, writing to Richard Cowling, mine captain at Moonta, quipped in typical fashion that 'shooting Turks agreed with him'. He also noted that his colleague Joe Weatherill, 'an old Moonta man', had been Mentioned in Dispatches for conspicuous bravery.[80] In fact, Weatherill had earlier won the Distinguished Conduct Medal for his exploits on 25 April, the day of the dawn landing. The *London Gazette* explained the circumstances of the award: 'During operation near Gaba Tepe [south of Anzac Cove] for exceptionally good work in scouting and in an attack resulting in the capture of two of the enemy's guns'.[81] Intriguingly, Dick Shields, from his vantage point at sea, had himself observed the fall of Gaba Tepe gun emplacement that morning, the action in which Weatherill had won his DCM. Much decorated, Joseph Weatherill

19.   In the aftermath of battle, Australian and Turkish dead lie together on a trench parapet at Lone Pine, Gallipoli.

was to end the Great War as a Warrant Officer, and was commissioned in the Second.

Thomas Bowden wrote to his sister at Cross Roads on 2 August 1915, in what turned out to be the build-up to Lone Pine, describing an action on the night of 31 July, 'when we took a row of Turkish trenches'. As he explained, the attack began with an artillery barrage – it was 'a pretty sight to see the naval guns blowing portions of Achi Baba [hill fortress] up into the air' – followed by rapid rifle fire which sent the Turks scurrying from their positions as the Australians advanced. He added that 'things are quiet just now', yet in only a few days time he and other Anzac forces would be in the midst of the last great Allied attempt at breakthrough at Gallipoli.[82]

General Hamilton's ambitious plan included a major thrust to capture the heights of the Sari Bair ridge, defended in strength by the Turks, and part of the operation was a series of diversions or feints, designed to throw the enemy off guard and to entice Turkish reinforcements away from the area of the main assault. One of these feints was the attack at Lone Pine.

Described as a battle of 'incomparable savagery', 'an epic of savagery and sacrifice', Lone Pine entered the Australian imagination as perhaps the most hideous of all the Gallipoli experiences.[83] Yet it was also an Australian victory, for when the last of the Turkish counterattacks had petered out by 10

August, the Anzacs still held the ground they had won. Surprise was part of this success, throwing the Turks off-guard in the way Hamilton had hoped. But there had also been careful preparation beforehand, with an underground trench system created under no-man's-land to allow the attackers to approach the Turkish lines unnoticed until the last minute. The Turkish positions were likewise complex, roofed over with a mass of timber, and with a maze of galleries and passages beneath. An Allied artillery barrage commenced at 4.30 on the afternoon of 6 August, designed to distract the attention of the Turkish defenders, as the Australians massed silently in their tunnels ready for their assault at 6pm. Precisely on time, the Anzacs emerged from their hiding places and penetrated the enemy positions according to plan. There then followed two days solid of vicious, largely subterranean, hand-to-hand fighting, much of it conducted in darkness in the covered Turkish trenches, a desperate frenzy of bayonets and bombings, of throttling and kicking and gouging. Seven Victoria Crosses were won by Australians during this struggle. Three were awarded to men born in rural Victoria 'of Cornish stock'[84] (as Les Carlyon has put it) – William Symons, Frederick Tubb, William Dunstan – but this time the *People's Weekly* did not notice them. Instead, it was transfixed by the death of William Brokenshire, killed in action on the first evening of the battle.

There had been a steady stream of casualties since 25 April – with news of the dead, wounded, missing, and sick – but, at Moonta at least, the loss of 'Bill' or 'Billy' Brokenshire (as he was known to his friends) struck a particular nerve. There had been Moonta soldiers among those injured, of course, and the death of Lee Bray Nankivell, a former Cross Roads boy, had been reported with due solemnity in the press. But, as the local newspapers noted, Private Brokenshire 'was the first soldier from Moonta who had been killed in action'.[85] It fell to the mayor, Ephraim Major, to visit Brokenshire's mother, Kate, in Caroline Street, where he was handed a series of letters that showed just how active Billy had been in the trenches in recent weeks and months. The next Council meeting observed five minutes' silence in honour of Brokenshire's memory. A death notice appeared in the following week's *People's Weekly* – '"FOR KING AND COUNTRY". BROKENSHIRE – On the 6th August, William James, third son of Catherine and the late N.G. Brokenshire; killed in action at the Dardenelles'.[86] Brokenshire had been almost twenty-seven years old when he joined up in December 1914. A blacksmith at the mines, he was a familiar figure on the streets of Moonta, and on the news of his death a wave of sympathy for his mother swept the township, for Kate had lost both her husband and her daughter during that same year.[87]

At Gallipoli, William Brokenshire had been no less popular among the Kio boys. For several weeks after Lone Pine, letters written home referred sadly to his death; some, like that from Roy Perkins, noted merely that

20.   There is an almost spectral quality to this photograph of Australian graves at
Shrapnel Gully, Gallipoli, taken in 1915 as casualties mounted.

'W. Brokenshire was killed', while others felt able to elaborate. 'I suppose you
have heard that one Moonta boy has been killed in this battle [Lone Pine]',
wrote Joseph Keen to his parents at East Moonta: 'William Brokenshire
died a noble death'.[88] Later, Trooper Jake Roach, another Moonta soldier,
wrote home to say that 'I saw poor old Billy Brokenshire's grave yesterday'.
Brokenshire had been interred the day after he had fallen, at a spot recorded
in his documents as Victoria Gully, about half-a-mile south-east of Anzac
Cove, near the 10th Battalion HQ.[89] 'He is buried in the same grave with
four others from the 10th', continued Jake Roach, 'Old Dick Shields is looking
after it'.[90]

William Brokenshire's brother, Percy, also serving at Gallipoli, did not
learn of Billy's death until a fortnight or so after the news had reached
Moonta. As Percy observed in a letter to his mother, Kate: 'When Roy
Perkins met me on the beach [at Anzac Cove] on September 15 and told
me what had happened, although having learned to expect anything on the
battlefield, it sort of struck me dumb'. Perkins had gone on to recount the
circumstances of Billy's death, and, perhaps in kindness or possibly accurately,
had told Percy that his brother had been killed instantly. 'When I saw a poor
fellow ... with one leg blown off and the other hanging, and dying slowly,
and begging a man standing by to shoot him', wrote Percy to his mother, 'I
could not but thank God that poor old Bill did not suffer'. He continued: 'On
August 6 there was a general advance from one end of the Australian lines
to the other. We were all in it, but the third brigade of infantry, with Bill's

battalion with them, charged at about 5pm ... and as they were advancing a shell dropped between him and two others, killing the three of them'. He concluded: 'That is how it was related to me'. Percy had also heard 'that old Dick Shields cried like a child when he learned the sad news', and that 'Dick was making a cross and carving his name, where he came from, and the date on which he was killed. This he intended placing over the grave. I would like to see Dick, if only to shake hands with him for the kindness of his heart'. Dick, tending his mate's grave, had also been told that Billy had been killed instantly, although his version advised that 'Poor Bill Brokenshire got a shrapnel bullet right through his heart on the night of the big attack'. As Dick mused: 'I am sorry for his mother'.[91]

Back at Moonta, William Brokenshire's pitifully few personal belongings arrived home eventually, the only notable items being 'two stone curios', presumably archaeological relics (authentic or otherwise) acquired in Cairo, further evidence of Australian fascination with ancient Egypt. Kate Brokenshire, meanwhile, as next of kin, was granted a modest pension (£13 per annum, dated from 7 August 1915). Years later she was careful to apply for her Memorial Scroll, in honour of William, and, with a painful pride that did not diminish with time, she liked to remind people that 'I had a son killed in the Lone Pine Battle'.[92]

'I regret to be the bearer of bad news'

Leigh Treweek Lennell, who had earlier written home describing the dawn landing, was another Moonta casualty at Lone Pine – although he lived to tell the tale. Back in June, Lennell had received a face injury in fighting near Gapa Tepe but, after prompt attention by the field ambulance, was soon back at his post. At Lone Pine he fared less well. On 7 August, the second day of the battle, he was struck down in the midst of the slaughter. 'Nearly all my mates were killed',[93] he recalled later, and at first he was left for dead, reported killed in action.[94] But he was alive and, discovered among the heaped bodies, was removed from the battlefield and evacuated to Malta in the hospital ship *Dunluce Castle*. On route to the island he underwent surgery, and his shattered right arm (incorrectly recorded as 'left' in initial reports) was removed. Lennell's mother, relieved that he been found among the living, wired the Base Records Office in Melbourne for more news: 'MOTHER SENDS GREETINGS. ANXIOUS WELFARE. LOVE MRS E. LENNELL MOONTA MINES'.[95] But it was not until she received a letter from the Revd H. Pennerley Dodd, Wesleyan Chaplain at Malta, that the details became clear. 'I regret to be the bearer of bad news', wrote Dodd, 'and yet it might be worse'. As he explained, 'I came across your son ... in the hospital here this evening. He had just landed [at Malta], and I am sorry to say that he had to lose his right arm. It was amputated to save his life . . . and the Drs removed it on the boat whilst he was coming to this island'. Skilled at his job, Dodd also offered words of support for Lennell's mother: 'Strange to say, he is in no great pain, but is most cheerful. I promised to drop you a line and it seemed to be a comfort to him . . . I will certainly do all that I can to assist him in any way possible'.[96]

Shortly after, Leigh Lennell was sent to England for recuperation. His mother was keen to know when he might return to Australia, and whether he would have to disembark at Sydney, where he had first enlisted. Joseph C. Treweek (her brother) wrote to the Base Records Office on her behalf. 'What his mother would like to know is', he explained, 'will he have to go to Sydney to get his discharge?' He added that the 'poor boy has lost his right arm', and emphasised that Mrs Lennell was very anxious to meet her son from the ship when it docked in Port Adelaide. Treweek received a prompt but terse reply: 'there is no information that this soldier is returning to Australia . . . If Private Lennell wishes to disembark at Adelaide it will be necessary to obtain permission from the Military Commandant, Keswick Barracks, Adelaide'. Eventually, Leigh Lennell did return safely to Australia (see p. 119), obtaining his formal discharge on 18 July 1916, when he was granted a pension of £3 per fortnight.[97]

Another inmate of St George's military hospital at Malta was Signaller Cuttris, who was suffering from an unspecified sickness, probably chronic diarrhoea or dysentery, which was by then rife at Gallipoli. As he explained in a letter that was to appear in the *Yorke's Peninsula Advertiser*, 'if a fellow does three months in the trenches its pulls him into a low state, especially when he has to sleep with all his gear on, with 250 rounds of cartridges around his waste and over his shoulder'. It was even more difficult to go into action in such a reduced condition. But this is what Cuttris and many others like him had had to do in Hamilton's big push in early August. Attached to the (dismounted) Otago Mounted Rifles, New Zealanders, Cuttris participated in the main thrust to capture the heights of Chunuk Bair and the summit of Koja Chemen Tepe beyond. Unlike the feint at Lone Pine, the objectives were not achieved – but not for want of trying. 'Well, we had to sweep Turks off . . . two ridges and hold the second ridge', wrote Cuttris, and as the New Zealanders attacked, the Turks 'started yelling "Allah! Allah!" and some other gibberish. Such a row you never heard'. This was countered by 'cheer after cheer from all directions as trench after trench was taken by the colonials'. But it was still not enough to achieve the breakthrough that Hamilton had planned, and, as Cuttris added, it was soon back to the stalemate routine of trench warfare. 'I received the cake, socks and towel', he wrote appreciatively, the 'socks came just in time, as we had not had a change of socks for four days and my feet were very sore'.[98]

'The weather is becoming very cold here'

The failure of Hamilton's big push effectively marked the end of the Gallipoli adventure. Weakened by heavy losses in combat and the debilitating effects of disease, the Anzac and Allied forces were in no position to face the approaching winter, let alone mount a renewed offensive. In October 1915 the *Kadina and Wallaroo Times* had heard it whispered in official circles that withdrawal was now a serious option, and as early as 21 August Roy Perkins had worried in a letter from the front that the 'days are getting very short and the nights very cold here. I don't know when winter sets in and the snow falls on the hills. It will be very hard for us all then'.[99] Private Thomas Pedler thought likewise, writing to his cousin at East Moonta: 'The weather is becoming very cold here ... We are told it snows here in winter, but as yet none has fallen'.[100]

In the aftermath of Lone Pine and the big push, life had returned, as Signaller Cuttris observed, to the business of day-to-day survival. 'Wherever you look now you find a network of trenches and entanglements', wrote Private Frank Harwood to his brother Harry at Kadina, 'especially in front of us where the Turks are'. In this environment, warfare had acquired an individual, almost personal dimension. 'The first Turk, to my knowledge, that I got was early this morning', said Frank Harwood: 'He was walking leisurely down a traverse with a shovel on his shoulder, and he went down at the first shot'. As he explained: 'We were watching the place pretty closely, and had the range down to an inch'. Harwood was sniping from a concealed observation post, he said: 'The two loopholes are covered with green bushes, and I think must be hard to detect. We have scarcely had any bullets our way, and we have been shooting five or six days out of our hole ... potting at these Turks' heads as they poke them up'.[101] Harwood's good luck continued. He survived Gallipoli unscathed, and served thereafter in France, returning at last to Australia in 1919.[102] Aircraft also introduced a new dimension to trench warfare, as Roy Perkins reported. 'We have a German airman', he explained, who dropped bombs over the Anzac lines, together with 'another new thing they use which we call darts. They go right through a man if they hit him'. When the hum of a plane was heard, the soldiers looked up sharply, searching for the insignia on the wings: 'If he has crosses it's look out for bombs or darts. If he has rings we recognise him as one of ours and it is for the Turks to look out then'.[103]

Dick Shields, the likeable larrikin who had tended Bill Brokenshire's grave, also provided insights into the nature of trench warfare, written for the benefit of friends back home. 'I have been exceedingly lucky so far not to have sustained even a scar with a bullet or shell', he wrote to W. Stocker of Moonta: 'The nearest I have got to it ... was due to an 18lb shell which knocked my dugout in and buried me, but I got only a few scratches – nothing to talk about'. He was now in charge of a bomb throwing party, he said, and there 'is plenty of shell fighting around here, but we take no notice of it'.[104] Jake Roach, writing shortly after Lone Pine, also admitted to being 'right in the thick of it', and explained that he had recently put the finishing touches to his shrapnel-proof dugout, which he had christened 'Beaumont House', complete with nameplate. 'I would just like you to look up our gully and see some of the dug-outs our lads have made for themselves', he wrote to his mother: 'I will just give you the names of some of them. "Savoy House", "St Clair", "Pension Rita", "The Wassa", "Sphinx Hotel", "The Home for Shrapnel" . . . We are all of us pretty good under the circumstances and as for myself I am quite at home'. Water was still a problem, however, and Roach claimed that he had not had a proper wash since leaving Lemnos. Situated three miles inland they were not allowed to go to the beach, he said, although 'We have been promised a swim tomorrow, so those that are picked to go will enjoy it'. They made their own fun, he intimated, and one popular pastime was baiting the Poms: 'A British Tommy said to me the other day, "Say, chum, have you any of them there Kangaroo feathers? I'm saving them oop"'.[105] They also tried to make the best of foodstuffs that arrived in their parcels. 'I am cook at present', explained Alf Martyn to his parents at North Yelta, Cross Roads, 'and attempted a plum duff last Sunday. There was not a crumb of it left either, even if it was my first attempt'. Men had saved their precious daily rum ration to contribute to the pudding, so Alf took it as an endorsement of his culinary skills when he was asked to make another plum duff the following Sunday.[106]

Socks continued to be a subject of keen concern. 'Kio boys here are well, including Will [Pomeroy] and Joe Weatherill', wrote Lee Pomeroy to his father. This was his twenty-seventh week in the trenches, he noted, 'and I have enjoyed good health and have nothing to complain of. I get plenty of socks'.[107] Corporal John Dunstan Woon, from Wallaroo, was likewise grateful for such mercies, writing to Mrs Wearne at Moonta Mines to note that the 'socks you so kindly sent have arrived', and to thank her profusely 'for your kindness to a soldier in need of socks'.[108] The near obsession with socks reflected the widespread anxiety that feet be kept clean and healthy and free from pain and sores, so important for mobility and agility in the trenches. But it was also symptomatic of a wider yearning for home comforts, for a sense of well-being and security. Despite the brave face put on things by the likes of Jake Roach and Lee Pomeroy, many of the men had now been in the trenches for months, and it was beginning to take its toll. Roy Perkins, for example, complained that he had been in the firing line for eight weeks continuously, and 'would be very glad when the war was over'.[109] He was sustained, he confessed, by the letters from his sister, and was grateful for the copies of the

21.   The Roach brothers from Moonta – *left to right:* Doug, Jake and Jim.
Jake was celebrated as the first Moonta boy to enlist, and participated in the dawn
landing at Gallipoli. Jim later fought in Flanders, where he won the Military Medal.
Doug, alas, was fatally wounded in action on 4 July 1918. Clara, their mother –
hitherto a staunch supporter of the homefront war effort – appeared to suffer a
nervous breakdown after her son's death.

People's Weekly she sent over regularly, with their welcome news from home. Jake Roach also noted the importance of the local newspapers. 'Don't forget to send "Weeklys" and "K & W Times"', he wrote to his mother, 'as I always get them'.[110]

Having played such a vital role in bringing the conflict to the homefront, in mediating and interpreting the war for its civilian readership, and acting as a voice for patriotic opinion and for enlistment and fund-raising, the Yorke Peninsula press was now performing an increasingly significant role abroad – that of psychological support for troops in the trenches. The arrival of newspapers on Gallipoli was, in its way, a method for transporting the community vividly and directly into the lives of soldiers at the front. The multiplicity of incidental news – farming prices, weddings and funerals, sporting results – reported in the pages of local papers was a source of comfort, although, in its familiarity, it could sometimes be the cause of heightened angst and longing, the desire to go home. In such cases, the psychological sword, as it were, was double-edged. 'I wouldn't mind if I could get down to Moonta now and again of a weekend', wrote Private Davies, only partly tongue-in-cheek: 'It would be an appreciable change'. Indeed, he said, the 'sooner this war is over the better it will be for everyone, that is what I think about it'.[111] Even the redoubtable Jake Roach admitted that: 'When I get back! I often think of the time, and wonder when it will be. Somehow I think I will return whole-skinned because I am too lucky to get hurt'.[112] His hunch was right, as it happened, although it would not be until 1919 that Roach was finally demobilised in Australia.[113] Sometimes there was a yearning for something more tangible and distinctive from home, to complement the letters and newspapers, something to give – quite literally – a taste of life on Yorke Peninsula, the flavour of old Kio. 'A Cornish pasty wouldn't go bad by way of a change', wrote Private Harry Chappel to his parents at Moonta Mines, together with 'a good feed of yeast buns'.[114] It was a sentiment shared by Dick Shields, who reported that he and his Moonta pals, dreaming of the delights of home, 'would like some of Stocker's pasties over here'.[115]

By now, with Hamilton's big push having come to little, and winter already approaching, there was an increasing war-weariness at Gallipoli. Corporal 'Masher' Thomas, from Wallaroo, reported to the *People's Weekly* that 'I have seen some big fine men waste away here, and at the finish sent to hospital'.[116] Even the physically and mentally robust, such as Jake Roach, recognised that the campaign had ground to a halt, and that there was little they could do – collectively or individually – to make a difference to the situation in which they found themselves. In an ironic if unwitting echo of Hamilton's directive to his subordinate, General Birdwood, all those months ago, Roach observed with an air of resignation that: 'Our motto is now "Dig on, Dig ever"'.[117]

'Why don't they volunteer?'

Yet, beneath this veneer of resignation, was a sense of fury – that, despite all the sacrifices since 25 April, all the privations and the spent efforts, the loss of life and mutilation and sickness, the Anzacs had not quite brought it off. There had been strategic and tactical errors, and the Anzacs were aware of this. But there was a sense that, if only they had had more resources – especially manpower – then they would have dislodged the Turks from the Gallipoli peninsula, opening the Dardenelles, and even now be marching on Constantinople to effect the destruction of the Ottoman Empire. In their frustration, the Anzacs turned on their kinfolk at home who had hesitated to join them in the trenches. Here was another unintended consequence of those newspapers sent out to them. 'When I look at our Australian papers', said Jake Roach, 'and see photos of the hundreds of boys and men that are watching football matches, &c, it fills me with disgust'. 'Why don't they volunteer?', he asked rhetorically: 'I wouldn't be in Australia now dressed in "civvies" for all the tea in China. If the Empire had a few thousand more men in France and Gallipoli like the Australians I reckon they would make short work of the Germans and Turks'.[118]

It was a commonly held view in the trenches. Percy Brokenshire, who had lost his brother Bill at Lone Pine, felt his frustration and anger deeply. 'The sooner this war is over the better for everybody in the world', he declared. But, he added, vehemently, the 'chaps who don't enlist are more than cowards, and you can tell them from me'.[119] Alf Martyn, from Cross Roads, reckoned that there were 250 eligible young men in that vicinity, 'well able to do their bit', but he knew of only four of them out there at Gallipoli. 'It's a very small average, isn't it?' he asked pointedly. He continued, ironically: 'But, I suppose, they all wear patriotic badges in their hats – as all true Australians should!'.[120] Likewise, Harry Chappel inquired with feeling: 'why don't the young chaps enlist – it's their duty to do so ... there are hundreds of chaps there who could and should be over here doing their share of the work'. Indeed, if the war was to be won decisively, then they would have to join up: 'I think every available man will be wanted before a settling day comes'.[121]

As these soldiers knew, their comments would more than likely find their way into the Yorke Peninsula newspapers, completing the symbiotic relationship between home and battle fronts that the papers had helped to create, but also bolstering the recruiting agenda that still held sway in the region's press. It was a paradoxical situation. The Anzacs, complicit in the making of their own myth, believed the Australians to be superior to other Allied and Empire troops – hence the insistence that a few thousand more of them would tip the balance in the war – but those who had hesitated to join them were somehow less than Australian. Those who remained at home, basking in the reflected glory of their countrymen in uniform were, for all their patriotic posturing (those 'badges in their hats'), cowards, and had not yet earned the right to share in the newly-crafted Australian nationhood. The men at the battlefront were interested not in glory itself but rather in getting the job done, of doing the right thing by their mates – especially the fallen – and bringing the war to a successful conclusion as soon as possible.

A further paradox was that, in emphasising their Australian-ness, the Anzacs from Yorke Peninsula prized their enhanced status within the Empire, while at the same time asserting the continuing salience of old Kio in their make-up. Of course, bonds of family and friendship and common origin underpinned this sense of regional identity. That they fought together in the same units further strengthened these bonds, sharing triumphs and sorrows, and looking out together for letters and newspapers and newcomers from home. They shared the same dreams – of Cornish pasties and saffron buns, and of going home to Yorke Peninsula some day not too distant – and carried in their minds' eyes the well remembered sights of Kadina, Moonta and Wallaroo.

'Turks are big fine men'

In this world of paradoxes, there was also the changing regard for the Turk as enemy and adversary. In the immediate aftermath of the dawn landing, before exhilaration had given way to stalemate, there was a sense that the Turks would inevitably crumble in the face of Australian prowess. Private J.W. Gill wrote home to Moonta from Anzac Cove shortly after the landing: 'Johnny Turk will never forget it. He felt the Australian bayonet then, and he has shown a great disinclination to face it ever since'.[122] It was a view that was modified over time, as the Australians came to admire the stoicism and determination of 'Johnny Turk'. After the experience of Lone Pine, Joseph Keen, writing to his parents at East Moonta, could admit that the 'Turks are big fine men, and they are very good trench fighters'. And yet, 'once they are forced out of their trenches and the bayonet is introduced they are finished'. The Turks had had plenty of experience of warfare, he admitted, but, in facing the Australians, 'they have struck more than their match this time'.[123]

However, as the Australians well knew, despite their best efforts they had not dislodged 'Johnny Turk' from Gallipoli. 'Masher' Thomas, from Wallaroo, had more than a sneaking regard for his opponents. He had witnessed the 'plenty of dead Turks lying about between the trenches' after Lone Pine, marvelling at the courage of those who had stood their ground and perished, and had participated in the lively 'bomb competitions that take place' between the equally game Anzacs and Turks. He also considered that 'John Turk is a fair fighter'. He recounted how on one occasion 'one of our fellows got wounded taking a trench', and became separated from his mates. The poor chap fell into the hands of the enemy, said Masher, but the 'Turks bound his wounds up, and helped him over their trench, and sent him back to our lines. Of course, I have heard different tales about the Turk, but I am only speaking of him as we know him around our position'.[124]

Grudgingly sometimes, but more often with open admiration, the Australians recognised that the Turks could not be ejected from their positions, and that there would be no triumphal entry into Constantinople. By the end of November, as blizzards swept Gallipoli, withdrawal had become inevitable. Gradually, troops were spirited away under the noses of the Turks, leaving a core of 20,000 to cover the final two nights of the evacuation, the 18 and 19 December 1915. Eventually, the last of the troops was away, and, as the *Kadina and Wallaroo Times* observed as the news was wired to Australia, all this had been achieved without loss and without the Turks realising what was happening.[125] It was undoubtedly the most successful part of the Dardenelles campaign. But, unlike those heroic stories of the dawn landing, reported in detail in the regional press, it would be a good while yet before tales of the great escape from Gallipoli were found their proper place in local lore.

CHAPTER FOUR

'Mothers, Manliness and Moonta'
The Somme

In 1916 the centre of action for Australian forces shifted decisively to France. For all its far-reaching consequences, Gallipoli was a relatively modest adventure compared with the vast, hugely destructive industrial warfare that was about to embroil the Australians on the Western Front. But, in the immediate aftermath of the Gallipoli evacuation, there was little hint of the severe tests that the Anzacs would face in just a few months time. To begin with, for the average soldier it was by no means clear that the focus would move inevitably to France. The defeat – for that is what it was – at Gallipoli had left the Middle East dangerously exposed, and, as Australian units regrouped and retrained in Egypt in the aftermath of the evacuation, it appeared to many that their task would be the defence of the Suez Canal and other strategic points vital to Imperial interests in the region.

In fact, their principal role in Egypt was the assimilation and training of new recruits from Australia and New Zealand. On northern Yorke Peninsula, as elsewhere in Australia, recruitment had remained strong as the Gallipoli saga had unfolded. There were occasional peaks and troughs, and soldiers at the front, frustrated at their inability to bring the war to a swift conclusion, railed at the shirkers who hesitated to join them. But for the moment, the steady stream of volunteers continued. Candidates from all over the Peninsula and beyond presented themselves for medical examination at the Local Centre at Kadina during the early months of 1916. They came from Wallaroo, Kadina, Wallaroo Mines, Moonta, and other places in the immediate vicinity – from Tickera and Bute, Maitland and Barunga – as well as from much further afield, such as Cowell and West Coast on Eyre Peninsula, and distant Fowlers Bay on the Nullarbor.[1] Some were turned away, disappointed at not making the medical grade, but others went on to enlist, such as those farewelled at the Moonta Mines Recreation Grounds pavilion in April 1916.[2]

'Play the game, and make a name for Moonta'

Among the departing soldiers honoured on that memorable – and fateful – occasion were Leonard Harvey, Jack Pyatt, Reuben 'Charlie' Rose, Fred Davey, Peter Sampson, William Shorter, Richard 'Dick' Trembath, William 'Len' Trembath, Gilbert Oats, William 'Billy' Abbott, Lloyd Pollard, and Eustice 'Glynn' Pethick, all local boys, most of whom had known each other since early childhood. As ever, none could tell then what fate held in store for these young men, although, in a little more than a year, most were already maimed or dead, their experiences on the battlefield a surreal contrast with the rhetoric and lofty sentiments of their send-off that evening at Moonta Mines. Leonard Harvey survived the war, bequeathing to posterity a vivid diary and a rich collection of letters sent home from England and from France and Belgium, providing searing insights into the trauma of the battlefield. As he tells us, he was in action with his battalion, the 43rd, in Flanders on 31 July 1917, the first day of the Third Battle of Ypres. So too were those newly enlisted Kio boys with whom he had gone on to serve – Pyatt, Sampson, Shorter, the two Trembaths, Oats and Abbott – each one becoming a casualty on that terrible day.[3] Of the others who had said farewell at Moonta Mines in April 1916, Fred Davey served in the 11th Field Ambulance, and returned home unscathed to Australia in 1919. Charlie Rose died heroically in August 1918 and was posthumously awarded the Military Medal. Lloyd Pollard damaged his spine while stretcher-bearing under fire, and died a lingering and painful death in hospital. Glynn Pethick was lucky enough to escape with only a bout of trench foot, along with several punishments for absence without leave, before demobilisation in Australia at the war's end.[4]

But none of this could have been foreseen by Revd H.A. 'Harry' Gunter, minister at Moonta Mines Methodist church, who had spoken at the pavilion at Moonta Mines when Leonard Harvey and his ill-fated mates were given their fond farewell, although he knew then that 'they would quit themselves like men, play the game, and make a name for Moonta'.[5] By now Harry Gunter had become a familiar figure at such events. Earlier, during March of 1916, he had chaired a 'Soldiers' Welcome and Send-off' at the same pavilion, organised by the Moonta Mines Soldiers' Aid League. Here he delivered 'an interesting and forceful address', as it was adjudged by one journalist present at the proceedings, setting the tone for an evening 'of a most enthusiastic character'. 'God Bless Our Splendid Men' sang the audience, as Mrs Gunter, the minister's wife, handed out a 'sleeping outfit' to each of the departing soldiers, with Gunter himself presenting them with the now obligatory periscopes.[6] A week later, and Harry Gunter was again in action at the pavilion, farewelling another group of new recruits, equipping them with

22. Leonard John Harvey, self-styled 'Kio boy' and author of a series of letters and diary entries that shed important light on the experiences of soldiers from northern Yorke Peninsula on the Western Front and in England during the war years. Leonard Harvey survived the war, returning home to South Australia in 1919 where he lived until his death sixty years later in March 1979.

their sleeping outfits and periscopes, together with balaclavas, socks, mittens, and other necessities, including 'a little Testament, suitably inscribed'.[7]

That Harry Gunter was a minister of religion added greatly to his authority. There were politicians who spoke at these events – William Cowling, the current Mayor of Moonta, and the ubiquitous Councillor Sweeney, along with other local personalities – but as sacrifice became an ever stronger theme, so the religious dimension of the send-offs became correspondingly more important. That God was on their side was a considerable comfort, even inspiration, for soldiers heading for the battlefield, while for those left at home there was knowledge that their loved-ones were in His care. When the casualty telegrams arrived, the Revd Gunter and others like him were on hand to offer solace and support, and to tell the bereaved that the fallen had not given their lives in vain, that they had died in a just cause. In a community in which religion remained an important element of everyday life, locals looked to the clergy for guidance as well as succour, and ministers such as Revd Gunter found themselves regarded as important opinion-formers and leaders. Their views counted among those who needed to be shown the way in matters secular as well as theological, especially among those who needed help in making sense of an increasingly complex international situation.

In Methodism, local preachers could be every bit as important as ordained clergy in fulfilling such roles, and were likewise familiar figures of authority.

23. John Verran, erstwhile Labor Premier (1910–12) of South Australia and virulent anti-German. Later, during the Conscription crisis, Verran followed the example of Billy Hughes, abandoning the Labor Party and arguing for the introduction of Conscription in Australia. After the war, Verran moved further to the political Right, seeking to engage returned servicemen in a 'new brotherhood' that would 'stand together and dictate their demands to Australia'.

In time – during the Conscription crisis (see Chapter Six) – it was an authority that would tested, and sometimes found wanting. But in the opening months of 1916, the Methodist local preachers of northern Yorke Peninsula discovered that their existing influence within the community had extended seamlessly to their opinions about the war, and, as the conflict moved to its new phase in France, so their views about the changing nature of the contest were sought eagerly. Foremost among these local preachers was the Hon. John Verran, only recently Premier of South Australia, a politician as well as preacher who insisted that religion and politics were intimately entwined. 'Religion is citizenship', he declared, 'and the relationship between religion and politics is very close'. Indeed, he added: 'When we come to justice and righteousness and truth these are great elementary principles of religion which affect the base of our manhood. Religion is not a question of going to heaven. It is a question of living and making the world better for having been in it'.[8]

It was an opinion that translated easily into fervid support for the Allied cause in the Great War, and, not surprisingly, Verran often found himself on the rostrum alongside Gunter, Cowling and the others, wishing departing soldiers all the best for what lay ahead, and extolling others to join up too. Already well known for his robust language and charismatic style, Verran always 'delivered a characteristic address, which aroused considerable enthusiasm', or so it was reported in the local press.[9] He made much of self-sacrifice – of the men who volunteered, and of the mothers at home who readily sent their sons and husbands to fight for King and Country. On one such occasion, turning suddenly in mid speech to confront a new recruit, Verran looked the young lad in the eye. Fixing the youth with his gaze, he implored him 'to put aside sickly sentiment and destroy as many Germans as he possibly could', predicting that 'the last German he would see in his travels would be a dead one'.[10] Verran spoke as a man of religion as well as a politician, yet his audience saw no moral dilemma in his opinion– the Germans had proved themselves beyond the pale of Christian civilisation, while the Allies had received God's sanction in their quest to save the world from German aggression. To his credit, perhaps, Verran spoke with equal zest when his youngest son Fred departed for the front in April 1916. 'The young soldier', the *People's Weekly* observed, 'was also presented with a periscope and a parcel of trench comforts, including a New Testament'.[11] But having entered the Pay Corps, Fred Verran transferred shortly to the 16th (later 15th) Field Ambulance, serving in England and in France, where he devoted his efforts to saving lives, both Allied and enemy, before returning home safely to Australia on 6 August 1919.[12]

Like John Verran, William Henry Hayes was a man of some standing in the community. A mine captain at Moonta, he was also an active Methodist local preacher and Sunday school superintendent, earning a reputation as an earnest theologian. One 'new chum', who at the beginning of the twentieth century had gone to work at the mine, recalled wryly that he first went 'underground at Moonta Mines in [the] charge of the underground manager, Captain Hayes. He was a local preacher', explained the newcomer, 'and on the strength of my father being a parson, we spent most of the time sitting in a stope [excavation] while he told me of sermons he had read, sermons he had heard, and (mostly) sermons he had preached'.[13] Like Gunter and Verran, W.H. Hayes found himself in demand as a speaker at farewell send-offs. At Cross Roads in April 1916, for example, he dealt with 'German diplomacy, militarism, and ambitions' in a speech thought to be 'masterly' by all who heard it, and in which he 'emphatically denounced their [German] depravity, treachery and frightfulness'. He also delivered an important 'message to Moonta mothers', noting that, in the estimation of all who had met the new recruits, 'local boys were conspicuous in their noble bearing and exemplary in conduct'.[14] Not only were the Germans confirmed in their beastliness, but Kio boys were revealed as the very epitome of Empire soldiery. It was a reputation, Hayes explained, of which every Moonta mother had a right to be very proud.

Henry Lipson Hancock, general manager of the Wallaroo and Moonta Mining and Smelting Company, was a staunch patron of the Moonta Mines

Methodist Church, as well as local preacher, and likewise a pillar of the Yorke Peninsula community. He too spoke with authority, and, as President of the Moonta Mines Soldiers' League, often participated in the send-offs, his presence on such occasions seen as tacit approval by the mining company of their employees' decisions to join the colours. Mrs Hancock, his wife, would also be on hand, to give out fountain pens to the departing soldiers on behalf of the Moonta Mines Methodist Sunday school.[15] In the antipodean autumn of 1916 the honeymoon period between the mining company and the local trade unionists was, more or less, still intact. Robert Stanley Richards, a former miner who worked now as moulder and carpenter in the Wallaroo smelting works, was a budding union activist and aspiring United Labor Party politician, as well as Methodist local preacher. Before long, he would be mouthpiece of the radical left, opposing Conscription and bitterly attacking both John Verran and the mining company. But for now he was happy to share the rostrum with H. Lipson Hancock and the others, as he did at Cross Roads in April 1916, and to echo their patriotic rhetoric, emphasising 'the freedom and liberty prevailing under protection of the British flag', and pointing an accusing finger at 'certain naturalised subjects [Germans]' who in South Australia had abused the privileges that citizenship had conferred. Poor Mrs Fuss, who was busy distributing 'campaign comforts' to the new soldiers as Richards spoke, may have blushed at that point, but perhaps she, like others, was deemed to have married into a family of 'good Germans'.[16]

Goodbye Charlie Rose

As John Verran and W.H. Hayes both understood, the image of local mothers tearfully bidding farewell to their loved-ones, and then returning home quietly to wait anxiously but patiently for news from the battlefield, was emotionally powerful and resonated throughout the community. Not surprisingly, then, it was an image deployed frequently by civic and religious leaders during that flurry of departures in early 1916, designed to stiffen resolve and to imbue an enhanced sense of duty and responsibility in those young recruits leaving for the front. Ephraim Major, the erstwhile mayor of Moonta, had in early 1915 coined the three 'M's, as he called them, (see p. 38), and a year later they had become commonplace, with frequent appeals to 'Mothers, Manliness and Moonta' as a code of conduct by which the soldiers might live. When Reuben 'Charlie' Rose was farewelled by the Moonta Mines Male Voice Choir in April 1916, he told assembled well-wishers that he intended to stick to these sentiments through thick and thin, whatever the future had in store for him.[17] He was not alone. When Lance-Sergeant William 'Len' Trembath was invalided home in June 1918, he explained at his welcoming reception that he 'had been given three "M"s when he left Moonta for the front' in April 1916, and these watch-words, he said, 'he had never forgotten and endeavoured to live up to', even when he was badly wounded at the Third Battle of Ypres. Touchingly, he added that: 'Mother had particularly appealed' to him. He was, he confessed, 'more than delighted to return home to her'.[18]

For those gathered to greet Len Trembath as he returned to Moonta, there could be no doubt that strict adherence to the three 'M's accounted, at least in part, for his winning the Military Medal in action at Armentières on 5 February 1917. Len's mother, Emily Dunstan, had received a letter from none other than Major-General Monash himself, commander of the 3rd Australian Division, informing her of her son's heroism. Monash explained that Len, then a Lance-Corporal, had been in charge of a Lewis machine gun. About 7pm in the evening, after dark but in full moonlight, scouts had gone forward into no-man's land. Unfortunately, they were spotted by the Germans, who opened-up with machine-gun fire, wounding one of the scouts. Trembath, sensing what had happened, said Monash (quoting from the official citation), 'engaged the enemy's gun from over the parapet' with his own Lewis gun, 'he himself being exposed to heavy fire, thus enabling the wounded man to be brought back'. Moreover, not only had Len Trembath 'succeeded in silencing the enemy gun', added Monash, but, handing over his weapon to colleagues, had 'crawled out to the front of our wire' to help carry the wounded scout back to the Australian lines.[19]

Charlie Rose was made of similar stuff. Farewelled at the Moonta Mines pavilion on the same occasion as Len Trembath, Charlie Rose was likewise feted by the Moonta Mines Male Voice Choir (of which he had been a founding member) at the Druid's Hall in Moonta, and by the East Moonta Football Club (of which he was formerly secretary) at the Rechabite Hall. He had worked in both the Moonta and Wallaroo mines, and was secretary of the South Moonta Methodist Church Sunday school, as well as a member of its choir.[20] Popular as well as active in the community, Private Rose – as he had now become – was, it was reported, greeted by 'torrents of applause' whenever he spoke prior to his departure.[21] His mother, Isabella, a Scotswoman who had married a Cornish miner, Reuben Rose, was now a widow, her husband having been killed in the Moonta mine in 1905. She had also lost her eldest son, Ernest, in a mining accident, electrocuted at the Ivanhoe mine at Boulder in Western Australia in June 1911.[22] Not surprisingly, when Charlie was deployed overseas – first to camp in England (see p. 134) and then to France – she treasured the letters that he wrote home. Whenever one arrived, she would raise the Australian flag on a makeshift pole at her cottage at East Moonta, a signal to her female neighbours that she had put the kettle on and that they should call round to hear Charlie's latest news over a cup of tea.[23]

A member of the 43rd Battalion, Charlie Rose was spared the fate of many of his pals at Third Ypres but succumbed the following year, killed in action on 26 August 1918, on the eve of the successful battle for Mont St Quentin. He was buried near where he fell, at the village of Rancourt, about six miles north-north-west of Péronne on the Bapaume road. The tragic news was tempered, perhaps, by the announcement that he had been awarded the Military Medal posthumously, for his part in a spectacularly successful action near Hamel on 8 August 1918, the day Ludendorff – the German commander – dubbed 'der schwarze Tag' (the black day) of the German army, sensing that the war had finally and irrevocably turned against Germany.[24] Charlie Rose's part in that turning point was explained in a letter to Isabella, his mother, from the Base Records Office in Melbourne. Charlie had been decorated, it said, 'For bravery and devotion to duty'. Specifically: 'On the 8th August, 1918, during operations east of Hamel his section in attacking an enemy field gun was held up by machine gun fire. Lance Corporal Rose rushed his Lewis gun to a flank and engaged the enemy machine gun at close range completely silencing it and enabling his section to capture the field gun'.[25] The letter went on, further eulogising Charlie Rose's contribution to that great day: 'I

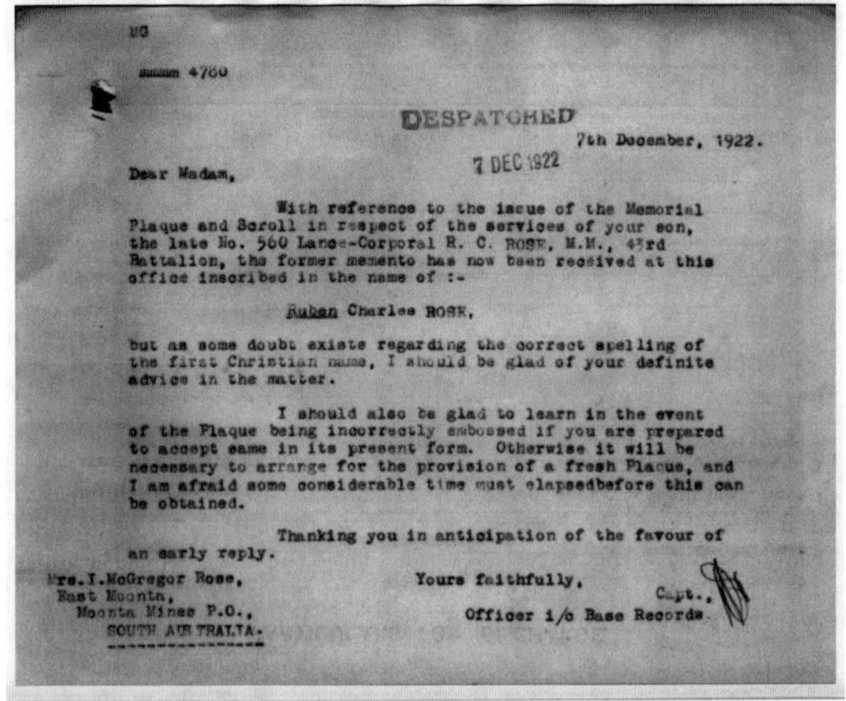

MG

4780

DESPATCHED

7th December, 1922.

7 DEC 1922

Dear Madam,

     With reference to the issue of the Memorial Plaque and Scroll in respect of the services of your son, the late No. 560 Lance-Corporal R. C. ROSE, M.M., 43rd Battalion, the former memento has now been received at this office inscribed in the name of :-

     Ruben Charles ROSE,

but as some doubt exists regarding the correct spelling of the first Christian name, I should be glad of your definite advice in the matter.

     I should also be glad to learn in the event of the Plaque being incorrectly embossed if you are prepared to accept same in its present form. Otherwise it will be necessary to arrange for the provision of a fresh Plaque, and I am afraid some considerable time must elapsedbefore this can be obtained.

     Thanking you in anticipation of the favour of an early reply.

Mrs.I.McGregor Rose,   Yours faithfully,
East Moonta,
Moonta Mines P.O.,   Capt.,
SOUTH AUSTRALIA.   Officer i/c Base Records

24. The disingenuous letter from the military authorities (the Base Records Office in Melbourne) explaining to Isabella Rose that a mistake *may* have been made in the inscription of her late son's name on his Memorial Plaque.

am also to ask you to accept his [His Majesty The King's] sympathy in the loss which, not only you, but the Australian Army has sustained by the death of Lance Corporal Rose'. Indeed, his 'magnificent conduct on the field of battle has helped to earn for our Australian soldiers a fame which will endure as long as memory lasts'.[26]

It was an accolade designed to lift the heart of any bereaved mother. It was unfortunate, then, when the same Base Records Office wrote to Isabella in December 1922 to suggest that a mistake might have been made in the inscription of her son's Memorial Plaque. Although Charlie's service records had shown consistently that his first name was 'Reuben', the letter explained (disingenuously) that the plaque had been inscribed 'Ruben Charles Rose', and that 'as some doubt exists regarding the correct spelling of the first Christian name, I should be glad of your definite advice in the matter'. Deviously, the letter also enquired whether, if 'incorrectly embossed if you are prepared to accept same', adding that 'Otherwise ... I am afraid some considerable time must elapse' before another one might be provided. Daunted by the prospect of indefinite delay, Isabella replied sadly: 'I have to advise that correct spelling of the first Christian Surname [*sic*] is (Reuben) not Ruben ... But I am prepared to except [*sic*] same in its present form'.[27]

There was a hint of resignation here, perhaps. But, if so, it could hardly detract from that mother's pride Isabella had expressed so vividly four years earlier when composing her son's death notice for the local newspapers, a verse which extolled Charlie Rose's moral superiority over those shirkers who would never join up unless enlistment was forced upon them:

> So died a boy, so rests a man,
>   A boy in years,
>   A man in deeds;
> He questioned not, when war again;
> The call to arms of men meant him.
>   He pondered not
>   Nor waited till
> A nation's scheme included him.[28]

For grieving relations, such public testaments were a source of comfort, the sentimental doggerel a necessary component of this cathartic process. But Len Trembath and Peter Sampson, who had joined up with Charlie Rose and had both been invalided home with war wounds, expressed themselves more simply and more straightforwardly, perhaps more effectively: 'Killed in action on the 26th August 1918, Private R.C. Rose, 43rd Battalion. "A noble life sacrificed, / Ere it had begun"'.[29] Likewise, Jack Pyatt, another of that group who had enlisted together, wrote tenderly to Isabella Rose after

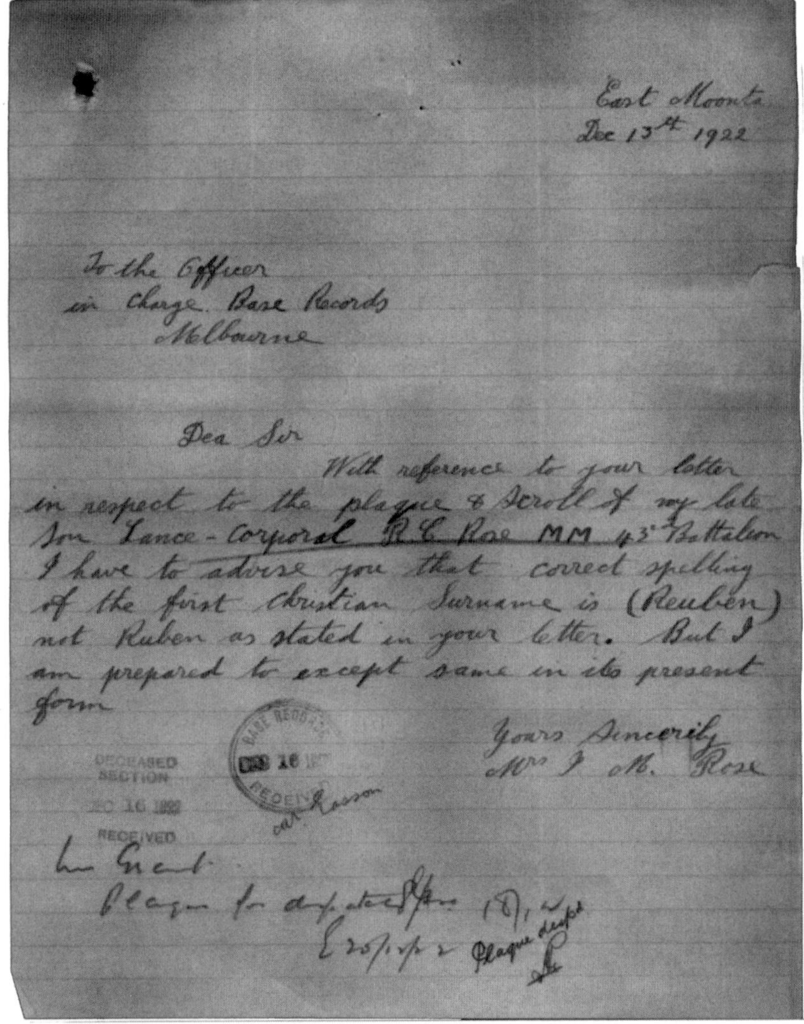

25.   Isabella Rose's response to the Base Records Office, admitting her willingness to accept the Memorial Plaque of her late son, Reuben Charles Rose MM, even though his first Christian name had been spelled wrongly.

Charlie's death. 'It is with deep regret that I re-open the wound', he said, 'which I know must cause you all such acute pain and grief; yet I could not let the occasion pass without saying a few words of praise and express my admiration for your son, whom I greatly respected'. Indeed, he added: 'Poor Charley, we were much more closely attached than a good many brothers. He was admired by the whole Battalion ... and was in every attack up until his death'. And so, Jack Pyatt concluded: 'Dear Mrs Rose, I beg you to feel that all my heartfelt sympathy is with you in this your hour of trial and grief and pain. He has gone, but will never be forgotten'.[30] A few months later, in February 1919, Charlie Rose's former workmates at the Devon concentrating plant at the Wallaroo mine presented Isabella with a large framed photograph of her son, 'suitably inscribed', a mark of their sympathy and respect.[31]

'Ready to have a go at the Germans'

But all this lay in the future. In the early months of 1916, as the new recruits left northern Yorke Peninsula, the period of consolidation and training continued in Egypt. Private Albert Cross, from Moonta Mines, wrote home in the February from Aerodrome Camp, Heliopolis, to explain that he had already 'been in Egypt about three months now, and have seen just about all the sights there are to be seen here; so things are getting a bit stale. We want a change of scenery'. He was glad, he said, that recruiting was continuing apace. 'I see that they are enlisting in Moonta', he observed, but complained that the rate was still too slow: 'It would not do for us all to be hanging back. There are a lot at Moonta Mines I would like to see over this way'. Training had intensified, he added: 'Well, they are drilling us fairly hard now; they are getting us ready to have a go at the Germans'. The Turkish threat to the Suez Canal remained acute – the Australians were 'well prepared to meet the Turks' – but increasingly now the talk was of moving to the European theatre of war. 'They say that for certain some of us will be in Flanders in April', he reported, 'so by the time you get this letter I shall either be out of Egypt or just about to leave. I would like to have a look at France'. The troops themselves, he said, 'are all spoiling for a fight', and 'the boys here will give a good account of themselves when they meet the Germans'.[32]

As he had anticipated, Albert Cross did indeed have his chance to 'have a go at the Germans' and to see France. He found himself, as did thousands of his colleagues, on the Somme in July 1916, and was wounded in action on 16 August in the desperate battle for Mouquet Farm – 'Mucky Farm' or 'Moo-cow Farm' to the Australians – in the aftermath of the infamous struggle for Pozières. Suffering from shell shock as well as the effects of his wounds, he was never quite the same again. In rest camp at Boulogne later that year, he was several times Absent Without Leave, on one occasion being 'arrested by Camp M.[ilitary] Police at 11.30 p.m. in a private house in Rue de la Paix', and on another spectacularly 'Breaking out of camp'. He managed to scald his foot badly (his Commanding Officer testifying that it was not a self-inflicted wound), and spent several months in hospital in England, eventually being returned to Australia in July 1918 suffering from 'Hip Disease', a result of the injuries sustained two years previously at Mouquet Farm.[33]

Signaller Fred Willard, from Yelta, near Moonta, was another of those Australians who fought on the Somme, where he was killed in action at Pozières on 6 August 1916. Remarkably, among those effects sent home to his grieving parents was a notebook, which recorded his experiences in the months before his death.[34] Herein was another insight into that period of preparation in Egypt, before the transfer to France, extracts from which were published posthumously in the *People's Weekly*. 1 ANZAC Corps – comprising now the 1st and 2nd Australian Divisions, together with the New Zealand Division – had left Egypt for France on 13 March 1916, leaving the remaining Australian units to take over defence of the Canal line, a gruelling three-day march across the desert from Tel-el-Kebir. Stupidly, unit commanders decided that this should be an endurance test, conducted in full kit. Fred Willard described the consequences. 'We were marching on an average of 15 miles a day', he recorded, 'and on some of these days, after going 9 or 10 miles, many of the boys would drop out for want of water, while numbers were so exhausted they could not go another step'. Each night they camped at about 8 p.m., he said, 'and hours after you would see these poor boys who had fallen out coming in in twos and threes and fall down exhausted'. Most of those in Willard's unit 'stood the strain' but the '4th Brigade got lost in the desert, and had to go 20 miles with one bottle of water, and out of 3,000 men only 600 of them got to camp'. Eventually, they were found by a party of New Zealanders that had been sent to look for them. The disoriented Australians had 'black, swollen tongues', wrote Willard in his makeshift diary, and some 'went mad with the heat; eight died, and one officer', it was rumoured, 'shot himself'. As Fred Willard concluded: 'We have been in Egypt now four months, and most of us are utterly sick of it'.[35] They need not have worried. Their training in Egypt was soon completed, and the 4th Division, followed shortly by the 5th, was shipped to France in time to prepare for the forthcoming Somme offensive.

The Somme

Lee and Will Pomeroy, from Moonta Mines, were among the Kio boys arriving in France in early 1916. Like others despatched from Egypt, they landed at Marseilles, whence they made the long journey to the north-east of the country by rail. 'We were travelling from some 50 hours in the train', they wrote to their parents, 'and have seen some of the best scenery in the world'. They passed very near Paris, they added, 'so you will notice that we have seen some well-known places'. Now they were 'not very far from the front – close enough, in fact, to hear the big guns and to see some shots fired at the aeroplanes. We are billeted in farm houses', they added, 'which are very nice and warm, and are very different from the sandy desert of Egypt'. They had just endured a gruelling route march, they reported, but at least it 'gave us an opportunity to see this pretty country'. Indeed, so enamoured were they of this delightful place that 'We would not mind coming back here to work after the war'.[36]

This enchantment with rural France was by no means uncommon. The contrast with Egypt was overwhelming, and for most Australians this was their first exposure to continental Europe, and to a landscape and lifestyle that to antipodean eyes seemed timelessly picturesque. Sergeant George Vercoe was another of those who waxed lyrical about what he found there. Writing to his parents at Moonta, he explained how at the weekend he gone for 'a long walk in the country. That is what I like best in this country – the walks all about are glorious'. There was, he said, 'the nice white undulating road with lovely big green trees on both sides ... thousands of lovely little yellow buttercups, with their beautiful satin petals, peeping up amongst the green sward'. There were 'cornfields and the beautiful red poppies, or perhaps a field of lucerne with its heliotrope flowers, and then the red poppies all mixed in'. He searched for the rights words to convey the wonder of it all but, modestly, thought his vocabulary too limited. 'Our walk was more beautiful than that', he insisted, 'and for me to do it justice I should have to have a much better power of description'.[37]

At one of the villages encountered during his foray, George Vercoe came across 'such a lovely villa with the most beautiful rose garden I have ever seen. Of course, there was a little madam attending to her roses, so we said "Bon Soir, madam" (meaning [*sic*] "Good afternoon, madam"). She returned our greeting, and then we talked to her about her fine roses, so she gave us "un rosa and panse" each'. Next, Vercoe explained, he went to a small café in search of food. Inside, 'was a big crowd of fellows ... indulging egg omelettes ... cooked on a kind of spirit stove by three women'. There was one 'old lady bossing the show, one man doing odd jobs, and three small girls assisting, and the whole lot were chattering like a lot of [Australian] magpies'. Each table was 'occupied with French folk drinking beer, wine &c', but Vercoe and his pal managed to squeeze in, purchasing some black coffee and bread and butter, and taking the opportunity to improve their French by chatting to the locals. Eventually, they walked back to camp in the twilight, 'satisfied with the afternoon's outing'.[38]

George Vercoe penned his letter on 5 July 1916, just a few days into the Somme offensive. Even as he wrote, extolling the beauty and peace of the French countryside and the appealing simplicity of the French peasantry, he knew that the all-engulfing war was close at hand. Perhaps he realised then that the beauty and peace and simplicity of the Somme country faced imminent destruction, its charming villages soon to be obliterated, although he could not know that the ubiquitous red poppy would one day soon be the enduring symbol for the sacrifice of the Great War. He wrote to his parents, with perhaps a touch of irony: 'I suppose you are all excited over this big offensive which the Allies have commenced with such splendid results'. As he explained: 'We are all hoping that the weather continues good, so that we can still push ahead'. But Sergeant Vercoe, sensitive observer of life that he was, was no warmonger. 'It is costing us very dear though', he admitted: 'The train-loads of wounded that come down every day are appalling, yet often we envy these fellows who have done their bit and now taste the well-earned fruits of rest'. There was also the slightly unsettling lecture, which he had been required to attend, delivered by a Scottish officer, whose portents of the war as testing ground for the new Australian nation gave Vercoe and his colleagues ample food for thought:

> Then speaking about [how] Britain allows her colonies to work out their own salvation or otherwise, he stirred me by these words — 'Remember, you lads from Australia, you have been given a great and glorious country. You are a northern people in a southern country; so be careful what you make of it — it will either be d-d good or d-d bad!'.[39]

The battle of the Somme remains one of the most controversial military endeavours of modern times. Long considered an unmitigated disaster, a senseless slaughter of the innocent at the hands of incompetent generals whose only plan was an unimaginative, unceasing, grinding attritional warfare, the Somme has been revisited periodically by historians anxious to reassess the evidence and apply new perspectives.[40] Most recently, William Philpott in his *Bloody Victory: The Sacrifice of the Somme* has offered a revisionist interpretation, in which the Somme — for all the scale of its horror and destruction — was the fundamental tipping point in the Great War. Alongside the stout French defence of Verdun, the British Empire on the Somme had challenged and at length undone the intrinsic superiority of the German Army, so obvious in the opening months of the war, and had set the Allies on the inexorable if bloody road to victory in November 1918. In this view, the war of attrition was not a pointless squandering of men and resources without aim, but a necessary prerequisite in the titanic struggle between massively equipped opponents, a sacrifice which made possible the final 'decisive blow' of which Douglas Haig — the British Empire's military commander-in-chief — never lost sight as the ultimate goal.[41]

As Philpott makes clear, the road to victory could never be straightforward or easy, and innumerable hard and painful lessons were learned on the Somme. 'The theorists of the offensive . . . stressed the élan and morale of the infantry',[42] he explains, and in the early days of the Somme this theoretical view predominated among the high command, with undue faith placed on the dash and verve of the infantryman in the face of artillery and the machine gun.

The catastrophic first day of the Somme, with its vast casualties, evidenced the shortcomings of this conviction, and as a new attritional doctrine developed, so it was increasingly understood that 'the artillery conquered and the infantry occupied'.[43] Moreover, in occupying enemy ground, the infantry wedded initiative and intellect to élan, learning to apply new tactical skills (such as mopping up pockets of resistance, or outflanking isolated machine-gun posts). It also learned to work alongside engineers and how to participate in 'all arms' operations, where tanks, aircraft, artillery, mines and other offensive components would combine in overwhelming force.[44] Significantly, as Philpott makes plain, the Australians – who in the early months of the Somme suffered inordinately from belief (including their own) in their dash and élan – went on to become supreme practitioners of 'all arms' operations, in the process acquiring a reputation for unsurpassed battlefield skills and for their tactical superiority over the Germans.[45]

Fromelles

On 19 July 1916, nearly three weeks after the battle of the Somme had commenced, the first Australian troops were committed to the offensive. This was to be a feint by the 5th Division at Fromelles, an attack designed to divert German troops away from the main focus of the battle. The British 61st Division was also involved in the assault, the combined force placed under the command of Lieutenant-General Sir Richard Haking. Haking already enjoyed a reputation as something of a bully and, like many of his contemporaries, was unswerving in his commitment to the offensive and to élan as the deciding factor in battle. 'There is one rule which can never be departed from', he insisted, 'and which alone will lead to success, and that is always to push forward, always to attack'.[46] But from the beginning, the omens were not good. Of the twelve battalions of the Australian 5th Division, six had been in the front line at Fromelles for only two days when they received their orders for the forthcoming operation, and the remaining six had not yet even arrived. Engineering and artillery arrangements were visibly incomplete, and there were other shortcomings in the battle plan.

In particular, as Peter Pedersen has observed, military doctrine laid great emphasis on the dangers inherent in 'inter-divisional boundaries' – the dividing lines between one division and another at the front – where co-ordination might easily break down under the pressure of battle. For this reason, the doctrine declared, boundaries should not be located at critical points. Yet this is precisely what Haking had arranged at Fromelles, where the strategically important Sugarloaf – a vital objective for the 61st Division – lay just beyond the inter-divisional boundary between the British and the Australians. Moreover, the British 61st Division was itself woefully ill-prepared for battle, undermanned and poorly equipped, its confidence badly dented by the hammering it had taken during the terrifying raids it had been required to mount in the month since it had arrived in France. By contrast, the battle-hardened Bavarians who held the German line opposite were well prepared, with a network of concrete machine-gun posts and flame-throwers, the defending troops held safely in rear positions back from the front line itself. Confident of their impregnability, the Bavarians allowed their support trench to fill with stagnant water.[47]

Observing that the Sugarloaf objective lay 420 yards across open ground, Brigadier-General Harold 'Pompey' Elliott, commander of the 5th Division's 15th Brigade, expressed grave misgivings about the enterprise. But his superior, Major-General James McCay, another Australian, was anxious for his division to see action and enthusiastically endorsed the plan. As new to the Western Front as his men, McCay had no experience of warfare in this environment, and was disliked by the troops under his command as harsh and unbending, and unwilling to listen to advice. But, like Haking, he believed in élan and the power of the offensive, and was proud that his division – the last of the Australians to arrive in France – would be the first to be in real action.[48]

In the event, the offensive was delayed by bad weather, and by the time the attack took place on 19 July, the Bavarians were well aware of what was in store, and had planned accordingly. The Allied barrage had battered the German front line from 11am until 6 p.m., and then, in the evening light of a glorious summer's day, the British and Australians advanced at last. The British were swiftly brushed aside by the Bavarians. The Australians attacked with all the dash expected of them, but they too were cut down, wave after wave succumbing to the relentless German fire. Those who made it to the German lines found themselves knee-deep in mud, as water poured in from a main drainage ditch breached and clogged by artillery fire, and were soon bogged down, making easy targets for the remorseless enemy. In the early hours of the next morning the Bavarians began their counterattack, and soon after first light on 20 July an Allied withdrawal was authorised. The Australians stumbled back to their lines as best they could, many shot down as they leapt from shell hole to shell hole. In all, the 5th Division had incurred 5,333 casualties that day – almost a quarter of all the Australian losses at Gallipoli – and the Division was finished as a fighting force for the immediate future. The British 61st Division had lost fewer men, 1,547 in all, and the word among the Australian survivors was that the British had let them down again, just as they had at Gallipoli (see p. 115).[49]

Subsequently classified as an 'action' rather than a 'battle' in its own right, Fromelles (or Fleurbaix, as it was then often known, confusingly) disappeared swiftly from public view, subsumed in the wider 'battle of the Somme' and overshadowed by the even more costly attack at Pozières only a few days later.

26. Anxious moments for the Australians before 'hopping the bags' at Fromelles
on 19 July 1916 – of the soldiers shown here only three survived the action,
and they were wounded.

In this way, the true enormity of Fromelles was hidden from public scrutiny,
the scale of the losses and the inadequacy of the military planning not fully
appreciated until long after the war was over.[50] On northern Yorke Peninsula,
the local press, bewildered by the vastness of the fast-moving events to which
it was so suddenly exposed, failed to distinguish Fromelles from the bigger
picture. 'The Pozières battle is the first pitched engagement in which they
[the Australians] have taken part in France', the *Yorke's Peninsula Advertiser*
reported incorrectly on 28 July 1916.[51] Later, in October, when the *People's*

Weekly published part of Richard Ritter's letter to his sister at Moonta Mines, the newspaper did not realise that it was describing the battle of Fromelles through the eyes of the 5th Division's ill-fated 32nd Battalion:

> I have been in action and our Coy had rather a bad time. The boys were game enough, but there were not many who came back. I think I had a bit of luck in being amongst the fortunate ones. We were out of our trenches and got across no-man's-land alright. Personally, I did not expect to get back. It was a terrible experience. I do not want to spend another such night. The Germans turned water into the trenches and it was up to our waists deep. Then, they used gas and liquid fire on us. Some of the boys got badly burnt and others suffered from shell shock. It is pitiable to hear them cry and see them jump when a gun is discharged. I lost all my mates.[52]

In the closing weeks of July 1916 and into the August, bad-news telegrams began to arrive in droves on Yorke Peninsula, just as they had done at the height of Gallipoli. Hidden among the many bearing ill tidings from Pozières and its aftermath, was notice that Private Richard Hugh Quintrell of the 32nd Battalion had been posted as missing. The *People's Weekly*, reporting the details, hoped that he had been taken prisoner, and would 'turn up safely after the war', but the truth was that Richard Quintrell was already dead, having fallen in the attack on Fromelles.[53] A year later, a court of inquiry was held in the field in France. A soldier in the same Company as Richard gave evidence to the effect that: 'Quintrell's brother, J[ohn] Quintrell who was in the same Coy (D) wrote to his sweetheart in Australia that Quintrell was killed at Armentières in July'. The witness added that 'I did not see the casualty myself and can give no particulars. His brother reported it to me'. The witness also admitted that he did not know the name or address of the former sweetheart. Nonetheless, the court of inquiry was satisfied by his evidence and declared that Richard Quintrell had indeed been 'killed in action'.[54]

The Australian Red Cross, meanwhile, had made its own enquiries. It noted that there was 'No trace Germany' (Richard Quintrell had not been taken prisoner), and at the war's end came the definitive evidence that settled the matter once and for all. On the day after the Armistice was signed, one Sergeant C.F. Lewis reported that at Fromelles he had observed Quintrell 'running from one part of the trench occupied to a shell hole when a burst of machine gun fire caught him, and he dropped, apparently killed. This occurred about 7.30 a.m. 20th July 1916'. A month or so later, Lewis added to his evidence: 'He [Quintrell] belonged to my Platoon, No. 5, B. Coy, and at about 7 a.m. on the 20th he ran across an open space and was caught by a burst of machine gun fire. He was killed instantly and fell alongside me. It was near Fleurbaix when the Germans had counter attacked'.[55]

Notwithstanding the (slightly ambiguous) evidence, it is unclear whether Richard Quintrell's brother John had also fought at Fromelles, his service record showing him as not having joined the 32nd from the Training Battalion until the end of July. Nonetheless, it was not long before he too was in action, where he was wounded slightly on 23 November 1916 and rather more seriously a fortnight later, when he was buried alive by an explosion. Despite his pre-war occupation as a miner, John Quintrell was so unnerved by the experience that he lost the power of speech and never spoke again. Evacuated to hospital in England, his health continued to deteriorate, and at length he was deemed to be unfit for further service. A medical report explained that he had been 'wounded in several places' but that the injuries were 'all superficial'. However, he 'was buried in a shell explosion and suffered afterwards from shell shock and aphonia. Phonation never returned even under electric treatment'. Additionally, the report said, John Quintrell 'sleeps and eats poorly', is 'very costive' (constipated), and suffers from a 'heaving cardiac' as well as 'general debility'. It was decided to return John to Australia but, alas, he never made it home, dying en route from 'inflammation of the liver' in the transport ship *Euripides* on 1 September 1917. He was buried at sea.[56]

As the *People's Weekly* explained, John's widowed mother, Mary Ann Quintrell, had been 'anxiously looking forward to his home-coming with no small amount of pleasure'.[57] Sadly, another son, Clarence, had been reported killed at Mouquet Farm on 16 August 1916, and, with Richard still missing, John Quintrell was the only one of her boys that Mary Ann could be certain was still alive.[58] Indeed, as she awaited patiently John's imminent arrival in Australia, she heard the distressing news that the court of inquiry in France had now deemed missing Richard to have been killed in action. The Rev. Pemberton had visited Mary Ann's cottage on Moonta Mines on Monday 10 September 1917 to break the news. Two days later, on the Wednesday, Pemberton was back unexpectedly, knocking on Mary Ann's door to tell her that the war had now claimed her third son, John, who would not be coming home after all, his body committed to the deep somewhere in the vastness of the ocean. As the *People's Weekly* put it, the 'residents of the district, as well as the widowed mother . . . were stunned at the news', and in the community 'the deepest sympathy went out to the bereaved ones who have suffered so heavily during the past couple of years'.[59]

This was the mothers' 'sacrifice' that John Verran and the others had applauded so heartily. Yet Mary Ann Quintrell bore her losses stoically, as she and the community had been taught to do, and as everyone expected, maintaining a quiet dignity, secure in the knowledge that each of her fallen sons was the epitome of manliness, and proud that they had died in the service of Moonta and the Empire. In November 1921 she wrote to the Base Records Office in Melbourne, thanking the authorities for forwarding the Memorial

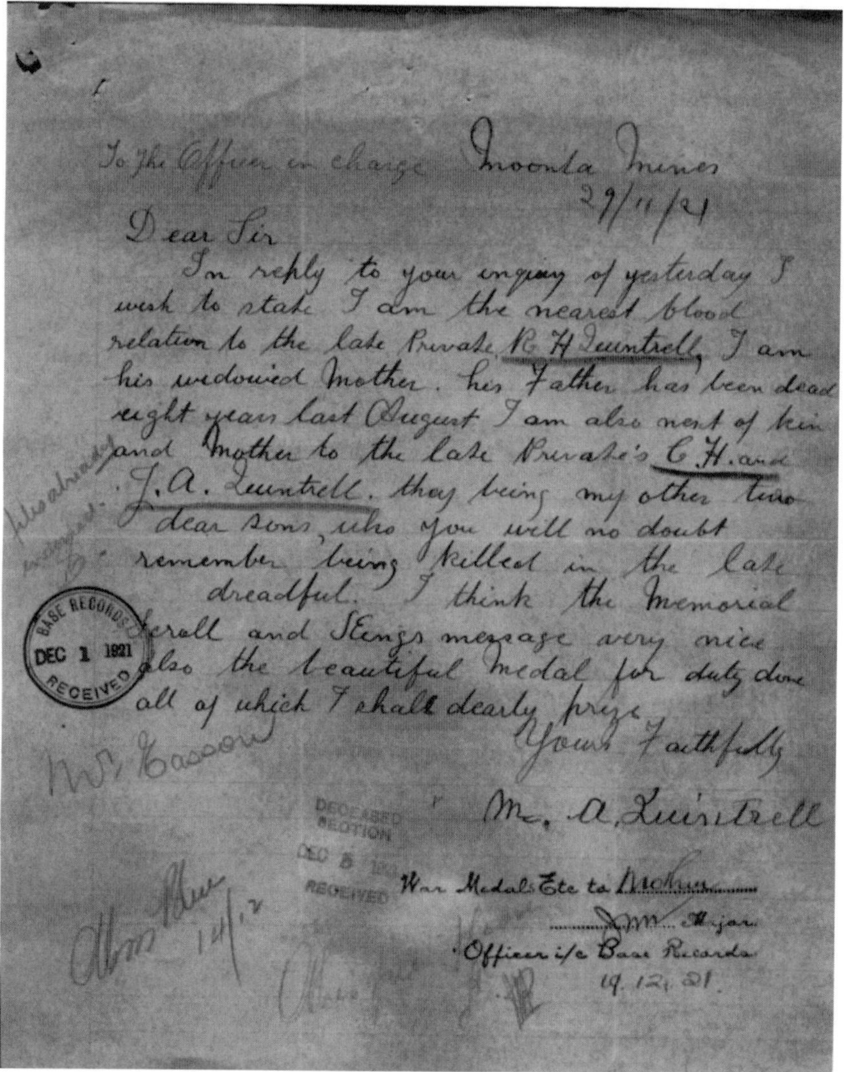

27.   The letter from Mary Ann Quintrell to the Base Records Office, reminding the military authorities that she had lost three sons in the Great War but expressing enormous pride in 'the Memorial Scroll and Kings message ... also the beautiful medal for duty done all of which I shall dearly prize'.

Scroll and Plaque for Richard Hugh Quintrell, the son killed at Fromelles. She confirmed, as requested, that she was 'the nearest blood relative' to Richard, her husband having been 'dead eight years last August'. And, she added, 'I am also next of kin and Mother to the late Privates C.H. and J.A. Quintrell, they being my other two dear sons, who you will no doubt remember being killed

28.   Private Clarence Rhody Swan Hoffman, one of the Kio boys who fell at Fromelles.

in the late dreadful [war]. I think the Memorial Scroll and Kings message are very nice', she said, 'also the beautiful medal [plaque] for duty done all of which I shall dearly prize'.[60]

Of course, Mary Quintrell was not the only mother. Private Clarence Rhody [*sic*] Swan Hoffman, a saddler from Moonta, was another of those who fell at Fromelles. Born at Moonta in 1894, Clarence was the son of Rody Schwan and Sarah Elizabeth Hoffman, both presumably of German descent. They never married. Like many Moonta miners, Rody Schwan went to the Kalgoorlie goldfields in the 1890s, where unfortunately he was killed by a lightening strike. Sarah later married another, becoming 'Mrs Briggs' and moving down to Adelaide. Clarence joined the 32nd Battalion, and was killed, it later transpired, during the initial assault on the German lines at Fromelles on 19 July 1916. At first listed as missing, he was later confirmed as killed in action, with the German authorities returning his identity disc — taken from his body before burial in a mass grave at Pheasant's Wood, near Fromelles.[61]

Meanwhile Sarah, Clarence Hoffman's mother, had been patiently awaiting news of her son's fate. Eventually, in April 1917, she wrote to the Base Records Office in Melbourne. She penned a 'few lines asking if you could give me a little information concerning my son ... he was reported missing in July & in December reported killed'. As she tried to explain: 'It is very hard for a Mother to take for granted she has lost her son just on the word of a cable. Could you let me know if they found him or his Dis[c] and if I am entitled to any private articles'. As she concluded, 'I feel very anxious & would be

29.   Australian dead at Fromelles dumped onto light railway trucks by the Germans for burial in mass graves behind the lines.

grateful to you if you could let me know anything at all about him'.[62] The Base Records Office replied politely that it had no further details about her son's fate. Eventually, she received his identity disc, together with a notebook, papers, letters and photographs also returned by the Germans. But she never knew that, after the battle, Clarence Hoffman's lifeless body had been dumped on a light railway truck by the enemy, whence it was taken to the mass grave dug behind the German lines and interred with other Australian and British troops who had fallen at Fromelles.

Pozières

In the early hours of 23 July 1916, just four days after Fromelles, the Australian 1st Division went into action at Pozières. Unlike Fromelles, a feint conducted away from the main focus of the battle, the village of Pozières was a critical strategic objective, key to unlocking the capture of Thiepval, itself a significant prize in the unfolding struggle on the Somme. Indeed, when Thiepval eventually fell to the Allies on 27 September 1916, the impact on German morale was devastating, contributing to the gradual erosion of the enemy's self-confident sense of martial superiority.[63] In contrast to earlier British attempts to seize Pozières, the initial Australian assault was successful, taking its objectives and resisting the inevitable counterattack; so much so that by 6.30 a.m. the Anzacs were already celebrating. They smoked

German cigars liberated from the enemy, posed for photographers in captured *pickelhaube* spiked helmets, and searched for souvenirs in the German trenches or relaxed in the sun.[64] However, the enemy also recognised the strategic significance of Pozières, and had no intention of ceding this vital strong point to the Australians without a prolonged fight. Fresh German troops were moved in, and the Australians holding the captured positions were subjected to sustained bombardment of unimaginable proportions. Amidst this continuing holocaust, the 2nd and 4th Divisions were also thrown into the battle. When they were relieved in early September, six weeks and some 23,000 casualties later, the Australians victoriously held the crest at Pozières, opening the door to Thiepval, although they had not succeeded in securing their subsequent objective – Mouquet Farm.

'If you Anzacs can take and hold Pozières, we'll believe all we've heard about you', quipped one British Tommy as the Australians had gone into line.[65] When they came out, their ordeal over, the Australians had indeed lived up to – perhaps even enhanced – their reputation for dash and verve. But they were not yet the 'fine instrument' of warfare (as Sir James Edmonds, the British official historian called them) that they became in 1918, and, no less than Fromelles, Pozières was a baptism of fire in which many lessons were learned the hard way.[66] The high casualty rate, perhaps, reflected the tactical naivety of both officers and men, as well as the ferocity of the battle and the intensity of the artillery barrages endured by the Australians. As at Fromelles, there was also the sheer unfamiliarity with the battlefield environment of the Western Front. The War Diary of the 'famous 10th' Battalion, for example, reported 'the greatest difficulty in getting up trench on a/c of the number of dead & wounded men who were lying therein', testament to the intensity of the struggle at Pozières but also to problems of tactical mobility, as was the impact of poison gas shells, which made 'it necessary to put on anti gas helmets which caused some delay in advance'. Likewise, the Diary noted 'a shortage of sand bags & an inadequate number of stretchers and stretcher bearers to cope with the large number of casualties which was suffered'.[67]

In contrast to the public invisibility of Fromelles, Australians at home were soon made aware of Pozières, of the great battle that had taken place there, and of the high casualty rates sustained by the Anzacs. A few days after the action had commenced, the *Yorke's Peninsula Advertiser*, quoting the opinion of the New York *Tribune*, informed readers proudly that now 'the Australians are recognised as the most dashing of all British troops'.[68] A fortnight later, as further news from Pozières filtered through to the community, the indefatigable Harry Gunter delivered 'a stirring patriotic address on "British Ideals" ... justice, freedom, righteousness', contrasting these with the barbarity of the 'Hunnish hordes' and 'Prussian militarism'. In Germany, Gunter said, 'the citizen existed for the State; while with us the country existed for the people'. R.J. Maddaford, sharing the stage with Gunter at this Cross Roads send-off, echoed the new mantra, emphasising 'the dash and valour of the Australian soldiers, who were classed with the best of the Empire's fighters'.[69] Yet even as this renewed sense of pride was being articulated so robustly, so the accumulated evidence of those July and August days told a somewhat different story; of resignation, stoicism and loss, and of a community suffering a further bout of sadness and bereavement – behind closed doors but also, increasingly, in the public arena too. It was like the aftermath of Lone Pine, but perhaps more so because of the terrible sense of *déjà vu* – they had seen it all before.

There was, for the example, the sad news that Private Joseph Keen, a former Moonta miner and veteran of the 10th Battalion at Gallipoli, had fallen at Pozières. The *People's Weekly* reported that he had been killed on 21 July, on the eve of battle, but his service documents recorded the date of his demise as 25 July 1916.[70] There was also an eyewitness account from William Pomeroy, another Gallipoli veteran, who had fought in the same action. 'Just a few lines to let you know I am still well and safe after the great charge we made', he wrote to his parents from Pozières: 'I dare say by now you have heard of our great victory and the wonderful fight we put up'. He continued: 'I have been in the [Lewis] gun section for about a month now . . . I went into action with the gun and had a few narrow escapes. We can all shake hands with ourselves in getting out so lucky'. But others were less fortunate, he added, and 'Poor Joe Keen was killed, so if you see his mother tell her from me that he fought until he fell with exhaustion, and as he fell he was hit by a sniper and died the death of a gallant soldier'.[71]

The Revd Harry Gunter had broken the awful news to Joseph Keen's mother, Fanny, calling at her cottage on Moonta Mines in the now all too familiar pattern, handing her the telegram that had just arrived at the Post Office.[72] But, thereafter, as was so often the case, there was only silence, with no further word as to where and how Joseph had died, and where his body had been interred. Not knowing was intolerable, and on 30 November 1916 – some four months after her son's death – Fanny Keen wrote to the military authorities to seek clarification. 'I have heard nothing since I received the cable', she said, and, struggling to compose her thoughts as she tried to imagine her son's fate, admitted that 'I hardly know what it was'. She yearned, she explained, 'to have . . . full particulars of were [sic] he was buried and how'. The emotion was palpable: '[I] feel it deeply to have had no particulars yet', she added.[73] The Base Records Office replied, in usual fashion, to the effect that there were no other details to hand, although in due course Fanny Keen did receive the few items of Joseph's personal belongings sent home from France: his identity disc, some letters, some coins, a scarf, a wallet, a notebook, five photographs, two brushes, and some cards.

30. Jubilant Australians sport the German caps and *pickelhaube* spiked helmets captured at Pozières – the subsequent German barrage dampened their enthusiasm.

Like most on northern Yorke Peninsula, Joseph Keen was a Methodist by upbringing. His death notice in the *People's Weekly*, with its attempt to make sense of both his short life (he was only 22 years and 10 months when he was killed) and the final sacrifice that he had made, echoed Methodism's central tenets – its commitment to don 'the whole armour of God' in the struggle against worldly evil, and the insistence upon viewing death as the ultimate triumph. As Charles Wesley had put it: 'Rejoice for a brother deceased, Our loss is his infinite gain'.[74] Or, as the death notice expressed it:

> He rose responsive to his country's call,
> And gave his life, his best, his all.
> He died that all he loved might live,
> And man his mission might achieve.
> He died for those he held most dear,
> He died to save the world from fear;
> For faith and liberty and truth,
> He offered up his stalwart youth.
> He fell that peace might come again
> Throughout the tortured world, and reign.
> What are our crosses? – Footsteps to heaven.
> What are our losses? – Eternal gain.[75]

'Quite a gloom fell over the community'

William Pomeroy put a brave face on the battle at Pozières, as 'manliness' demanded, and the *People's Weekly* was more than happy to publish this positive gloss. 'I am pleased to say we captured the place [Pozières]', he wrote, 'it was one of the strongest of the German positions. That makes it all the more gallant achievement for the Australians'. He reckoned that now 'it looks pretty bad for the Huns', predicting (mistakenly) that 'if a man can keep his napper up for the next three months, I think we ought to see home for Christmas'. Musing again on the great battle, he confessed that 'I am glad I was in the charge. It was a real ding-dong go ... I can assure you I accounted for a few and Lee [Pomeroy] for hundreds ... They used all sorts of shells on us, and as we were going into the firing line they gave us a shower of gas shells'.[76]

The intensity of the enemy barrage was something that those who had fought at Pozières would never forget. Writing later in the year from Belgium to a friend at Moonta, Lance-Corporal Richard Daw explained that he had just come out of the firing line after nine consecutive days in the trenches. It had been tough going, he said, but: 'Let me tell you it's a home here compared to Pozières ... you might not believe me when I tell you that at Pozières there were more shells fired in a day than bullets here'.[77] And there were a great many casualties too. Along with Joseph Keen, there were other Kio boys who had fallen in the initial assault and on subsequent days. The *People's Weekly* reported 'a number of Moonta men taking a prominent part in the attack which drove back the Germans in France towards the end of July', and proceeded to list some of those killed in action or wounded or missing.[78] Private John James Williams, for example, had been posted as missing on 25 July 1916. Later confirmed as wounded in action, he succumbed eventually to his injuries; already a widower, he left a seven-year old son to mourn his passing.[79] Similarly, Edwin 'Teddy' Smith, another Moonta boy, was reported to have died of his wounds, and so was Corporal Brian Humphries. Stanley Andrews, from Moonta Mines, was one of those killed in action, and so too was Fred Willard, author of the diary (with its vivid descriptions of training in Egypt) later returned to Australia with his personal effects.[80] Fred had been a member of the Independent Order of Rechabites, and, as in so many similar cases, the friendly society was soon writing to the military authorities, seeking confirmation of death so that insurance claims might be paid. Years later, in 1929, 'exhumation work in the vicinity of Pozières' discovered Fred Willard's body, and it was duly re-interred in a nearby Imperial War Graves Commission cemetery.[81]

The *People's Weekly* intimated that 'rumours were in circulation yesterday regarding other casualties', while the 'flag at the Institute has been flying half-mast in honour of the fallen brave'.[82] At Sunnyvale, south of Moonta, came

31.   Richard Daw (*left*), from Moonta, who survived Pozières but was later wounded in action in 1918.

the tragic news that Private Albert William Sandford had been killed on 25th July. He had been at the dawn landing at Gallipoli, and was twice wounded before his death in battle at Pozières. But he was a committed Methodist, it was reported, and like 'others who left this district, conviction impelled him, and no mad military passion, or love of violence'.[83] Other bulletins arrived, and the *People's Weekly* was forced to admit that the 'fighting in France is taking rather a heavy toll of our Moonta lads'.[84] Especially shocking was the news that Richard 'Dick' Shields, the likeable larrikin who had wept for William Brokenshire and tended his grave at Gallipoli, was among the dead at Pozières. Well known across the Peninsula, Dick Shields was remembered each year thereafter in the 'In Memoriam' columns of the local press:

> No loving mother's gentle hand
> To wipe the death-dews from his brow;
> No token of love in that far-off land
> To mark the spot where he sleepeth now.[85]

And:

> When the flags are o'er the roadways,
> When the troops are marching home,

> When the sisters lean to bless them,
> And the mothers to caress them,
> O God, have pity for the watching ones,
> Whose boys will never return.[86]

Equally popular at home was Private Percy Beaglehole. He too died near Pozières, and when the news reached Moonta 'quite a gloom fell over the community, for young Beaglehole was well known and respected throughout the town and suburbs'.[87] By now the action in France had moved from the Pozières crest to neighbouring Mouquet Farm, and the latest spate of casualties – including, probably, Dick Shields and Percy Beaglehole, both of whom were hit on 16 August – was largely the result of the (unsuccessful) push to secure this further German stronghold. Among the others who fell then were George Vercoe, author of the eloquent if sentimental descriptions of country life along the Somme, and Private V. MacDonald from Wallaroo, who was awarded the Distinguished Conduct Medal posthumously: 'he threw his great coat over a bomb, and held it down until the bomb exploded, thereby probably saving several casualties'.[88]

Clarence Quintrell, one of the three sons that Mary Ann Quintrell lost in the Great War, was also reported killed in action on 16 August 1916, although several eyewitness accounts insisted that he had died a few days earlier, on the 12th. Scribbled in pencil across his service documents was the note 'Buried at Moquet [sic] Farm'.[89] One eyewitness explained that 'I knew Quintrell well ... We called him "Quint"'. He went on: 'On August 12th we were going from Pozières to attack Mouquet Farm. I saw him in a shell hole dead as I went by'. A second witness added: 'We saw his dead body at Pozières on Aug. 12th. He had been blown up by a shell, up near the front line. It was impossible to bury it on account of the heavy shelling'. A third account reported that Quintrell was 'killed by a shell on Aug 12 1916. He was caught in a barrage, and blown to pieces, so that it would be quite impossible for him to be buried'.[90] Nonetheless, Quintrell's remains were collected and interred in an 'isolated grave', as his service documents put it, only later being re-interred in Courcellette British Cemetery.

'Moonta mourns, Moonta hopes, Moonta works'

In time, eyewitness accounts of the struggle for Mouquet Farm reached the Peninsula press. Private Alfred Cross wrote to his father at Cross Roads on 22 August 1916. 'I have been in the firing line and out again', he explained: 'I was one of the lucky ones to come out without a scratch'. The battle 'was like going into hell', he said, and 'I heard Percy Beaglehole was being brought down on a stretcher wounded when a shell burst and killed him'. Alfred was 'sorry that it should happen so. I got to know him very well, and found him to be a nice fellow'. He also admitted that 'I had a narrow escape myself through being knocked over by a big shell. I was knocked quite silly for a couple of days'. The battlefield was now 'a scene of utter desolation', he added, and the 'country where we are fighting is bombed about terribly. Nice little villages have been levelled to the ground'.[91]

Through such accounts, the community became aware gradually of the nature of warfare on the Western Front, of its similarities to the fighting at Gallipoli but, most of all, its differences. The huge destructive scale of industrial conflict on the Somme – with its massive artillery bombardments, the obliteration of buildings and features in the landscape, the titanic effort (not least in terms of human life) required to reach, let alone capture, objectives, eventually became clear. All this the Peninsula population began to understand, although it was difficult for individuals to piece together the complex jigsaw-puzzle picture. Casualty telegrams gave few details of locations, and the military authorities were intentionally vague in releasing further information, not wanting to disclose facts that might aid the enemy. Fromelles had been all but invisible to those at home, and, similarly, for observers on the Peninsula homefront the capture of Pozières crest moved imperceptibly into the assault on Mouquet Farm, sometimes with confusing effect. For the soldiers at the battlefront, the big picture could be equally bewildering, and letters home – including those passed on for publication – could be erroneous or awry. Soldiers were exposed to the wishful thinking of their superiors, and, like their families and friends at home, were likewise susceptible to extravagant propaganda claims designed to exaggerate Allied successes. Additionally, in exposing their souls to friends and family and the wider community, they often chose their words carefully, mindful of the expectations of those waiting at home.

Sometimes the soldiers, in their letters home, presented snapshots – true at the moment of their composition – that were soon hopelessly out of date, even misleading or wrong by the time they reached home. Such was that penned by Signaller T. Allen to his wife at Moonta Mines on 4 September 1916. In his letter he trumpeted the capture of Mouquet Farm, which news was then duly reported in the local press. 'We have just come out of the trenches after having a pretty crook time of it', he wrote, but it was 'nothing to compare the time we gave Fritz'. Indeed: 'we gained a great victory over the enemy, capturing one of his greatest strongholds and taking many prisoners'. As Signaller Allen explained, his unit had gone 'into the trenches at 12 o'clock on Saturday night, September 2, and worked all night digging ourselves in under heavy shell and shrapnel fire'. On discovering their presence, the Germans bombarded them steadily for eight hours 'but there was no shifting our boys. The same night our lads hopped over and captured one of their best

32.   Australian stretcher-bearers, under the Red Cross flag, bring the wounded
down from Mouquet Farm.

strongholds, called Moquet [*sic*] farm, and two lines of trenches the other side of it'. Inevitably, 'Fritz counter attacked, but to his great surprise got driven back again with heavy losses'. There 'wasn't a budge in our boys', reported Allen proudly, and he estimated that they had captured between 400 and 500 prisoners on the night of the attack. The Australians were up against the Prussian Guards, he said, an elite regiment and 'the flower of the German army'. Yet many of them were only too glad to surrender. 'Mercy, comrade, we no want to fight', they cried, throwing up their hands. But 'You can bet', said Allen darkly, 'that we are getting a little of our own back now'.[92]

In fact, although the attack on Mouquet Farm on 2 and 3 September 1916 was initially successful, just as Signaller Allen had described, the Australians were at length driven back by the ferocious counterattack. It was to be their last crack at this difficult objective, for on 5 September the 4th Division was relieved by the Canadian Corps, then moving to join the rest of 1 ANZAC on the Ypres Salient.[93] At home on northern Yorke Peninsula, news of the fighting at Pozières and Mouquet Farm continued to arrive until late in the year, with details of casualties still trickling through weeks and months after the events. There were joyous homecomings for those invalided out of the army, such as the safe return of Lance-Corporal Wilkinson to Moonta Bay in early December, when 'a large crowd of the general public' turned out to cheer 'the young soldier, who limped slightly'.[94] The community was also uplifted by news of decorations for bravery. Private [Presto] John Nankivell, 'an old Cross Roads boy', for example, won the Military Medal for his conduct at Fromelles on 20 July 1916, when he was severely wounded (and eventually discharged), the award featuring in the *London Gazette* on 21 September and filtering through eventually to the *People's Weekly* on 4 November.[95] Likewise, there was a boost to morale at Wallaroo when it was reported that Private Isaac McLean had also been awarded the Military Medal. His chums had heard that the decoration was in recognition of his 'playing the mouth organ whilst going over the top at Pozières'. But the full citation explained that he was 'playing a mouth organ during the advance over No Man's Land. Attacked party of 1 officer and 8 men with bombs, killed the officer, wounded and took prisoner the remainder'.[96]

In the aftermath of the Somme battles, there was a noticeable change of mood on the homefront. The patriotic rhetoric remained, as did the extravagant farewelling of new recruits and the loud applause for daring exploits committed on the field of battle. But there was also a more cautious, even more critical, commentary on the war and its conduct, muted at first but more vocal as 1916 wore on. As early as May, the *People's Weekly* correspondent at tiny Sunnyvale remarked, with a hint of mild subversion, perhaps, that 'Of those who have volunteered from this part, it may be said that they have done so by force of conviction, and not through love of war'. More controversially, the same anonymous correspondent also noted that a 'lot of people are blaming the German Emperor for all the present trouble. If that is so', he opined, 'it is time monarchical systems were at an end'. Whether this included constitutional monarchies was not clear. But this 'latest folly [the war] put[s] all the freaks of democracy in the shade'.[97] Later, towards the end of September 1916, the Sunnyvale correspondent reported the departure of Private Clarence Lamshed, another new recruit destined for the front. It had not been possible, 'owing to circumstances', to organise a 'farewell social'. But Lamshed's 'many friends in this district ... admire his spirit of bravery and self-sacrifice', the report insisted, while all 'wish him a brief, pleasant season of service and a safe return home'.[98]

Not exactly tongue-in-cheek, and presumably not meant to be ironic, the Sunnyvale commentary nonetheless gently probed the 'spirit of bravery and self-sacrifice', and, in hoping for 'a brief, pleasant season of service', looked forward to the satisfactory conclusion of hostilities with a minimum of violence and loss of life and in the shortest possible time — a sharp contrast to the way in which the war had been conducted in recent months. Even Councillor Sweeney, the confirmed Imperialist, began to adopt a different tone. Farwelling Private J. Crago at Cross Roads in November 1916, he compared 'the advantages we have of living in Australia' to those obtaining elsewhere, 'even in England', introducing an element of Australian nationalism that rested now on an assumed superiority over Britain, echoing those criticisms (see Chapter Five) of 'Blighty' and the British Tommies increasingly expressed by many Anzacs. Moreover, Sweeney emphasised that 'Everything in Australia was voluntary, and we should do homage to those who had gone, and honour those who will not return.'[99]

Central to the voluntary principle was recruitment to the Australian armed forces. In contrast to Britain, where Conscription was introduced during January1916 to try to meet soaring manpower demands, Australia remained resolutely committed to the voluntary principle. Indeed, the Anzacs were proud that they were a volunteer army, and as Conscription in Britain pushed increasing numbers of unwilling and unsuited men into uniform, so Australian pride in their own status was enhanced. As we have seen, first at Gallipoli and then in France, Peninsula soldiers had written in scathing terms about those 'shirkers' who had failed to join them at the front, their letters forming an important part of the recruiting drive at home. However, after the Somme, such overt attacks became less common, soldiers at the front increasingly unwilling to coerce others into 'volunteering' against their will. As we shall see (Chapter Five), such an attitude informed the Conscription debate as it had emerged in Australia, with northern Yorke Peninsula becoming firmly 'anti-Conscriptionist' in character, the region voting 'No' to Conscription in the Australia-wide referenda on the subject on 28 October 1916 and 20 December 1917. But as we shall also see, the Conscription controversy was deeply divisive on northern Yorke Peninsula, as it was elsewhere in Australia, undermining that unity of purpose and community cohesion that local newspapers, politicians and religious leaders had striven to create and project. Yet there were those who continued to insist on regional solidarity, asserting as ever the Peninsula's distinctive identity and sense of place. 'Moonta mourns, Moonta hopes, Moonta works', exclaimed the mayor, William Cowling, in December 1916, advocating a kind of 'business as usual' attitude, a stoicism and determination that would allow the community to continue to pull together despite its differences. Put bluntly, he said, 'Moonta wants to remain a British community, and therefore, as far as Moonta is concerned, the Empire must not fall'.[100]

CHAPTER FIVE

'I'm fed up with England now'

Blighty

'English people were the best in the world to soldiers'.[1] This was the firm opinion of Trooper A.J. Smith, a Light Horseman from Moonta, who had been evacuated from Gallipoli suffering from dysentery. By the eve of his departure from the front, he reported, he had lost some 12 lbs in weight and could no longer walk, such was the level of his disability. However, shipped to England, he soon found himself in hospital in Bristol, where he was nursed back to health by a medical staff attentive to his every need. 'Soldiers in England', he said, 'lack nothing'. Indeed, discharged from hospital on 20 October 1915, he had been examined by a military doctor in London who had instructed him to proceed directly to a convalescent home in Epsom, Surrey, for one month's recuperation. This was the kind of military order that Australian soldiers did not mind obeying, and for Smith there was the added bonus that, on release from Epsom, he had been invited by 'a great [aristocratic?] lady in Bristol' to spend his Christmas leave with her.[2]

In all, the several months that Trooper Smith spent in England had transformed him from a dangerously ill soldier at his lowest ebb into a fully recovered, fully rested fighting man fit to rejoin his unit. The comforts of leafy Surrey and female companionship in the West Country had restored his spirit as well as body, and soon he was back in the Middle East (where, alas, he was killed in an enemy aircraft bombing raid in Palestine in July 1918).[3] England had been wonderful, and he had been keen for his relations and friends back on Yorke Peninsula to appreciate just how kind the English were, and how splendid were the conveniences and accoutrements of English civilisation after the privations of Gallipoli.

Trooper Smith's experiences, and his sense of gratitude to England and the welcoming English, were by no means atypical. For a great many Australians, England – and other parts of the United Kingdom – was a retreat of healing and recuperation, especially for the wounded and sick in body and mind, and also a place which offered many entertainments and diversions for those enjoying the freedom of leave. As Australia's principal theatre of war had moved from the Dardenelles to France and Belgium, so England and the UK featured increasingly as the routine destination for Australians proceeding on leave, whether short or extended. For British servicemen and women, of course, this was also the routine, and for those British troops in the trenches of the Western Front there was the knowledge – sometimes reassuring, sometimes tantalising – that 'Blighty' and the comforts of home were but a short journey away.

For the great majority of Australians, by contrast, unless they were lucky enough to be awarded an extended furlough, or were repatriated as invalids or no longer fit for service, or were posted back on official duty, there was little hope of seeing home until hostilities were at an end. Indeed, many had quietly given up thinking of their return to Australia, and were resigned instead to a contingent existence in which they might – or might not – one day go home.[4] In such circumstances, England and the UK assumed great significance as a home-from-home. Many Australians, of course, had been born in the British Isles, and even if they had emigrated as small children, they still nurtured fond memories and half-memories and stories of the old country. In any case, most Australians had relations in various parts of the UK, and leave or recuperation was an opportunity to look up kith and kin and to renew fading family links. Although Australians often ruffled feathers – wittingly or unwittingly – with their cheeky informality, their lack of deference and their willingness to laugh at humbug and posturing appealed secretly to many in socially repressed and class-conscious Britain. Australian soldiers were also attractive to women – generally taller and better built than their British counterparts, and bronzed (at least until exposure to the European winter), their colonial slouch hats a mark of the studied indifference that amused British girls. They were also better paid than their British opposite numbers, and knew how to show a young lady a good time.[5]

'Not much love between the Tommies and Colonials'

Eventually, such distinctions began to rankle in Britain, with Australians acquiring a reputation for rowdiness and indiscipline, and British servicemen increasingly envious of Australian rates of pay and Aussie successes with local women. To the average British soldier, who had to make do on a modest shilling a day, the Australians were now just 'fuckin' five bobbers'.[6] Such reactions often bewildered Australians, disconcerted by a perceived hostility they could not understand, a hurt they had not expected to encounter in the seat of their Empire. But for some Australian servicemen, there was already a keen sense of antipathy between the Anzacs and the British. Private Melville Pethick, 'a Moonta boy', wrote home in January 1916 from Monte Video

Camp at Weymouth in Dorset, where his unit (the 10th) was then based, explaining that 'There is not much love between the Tommies [British troops] and Colonials here'. Indeed, he added, there had 'been many a battle with them, and the authorities have had to shift the Tommies away from these parts on that account'.[7]

At first, Pethick conceded, the Australians – many, like him, veterans of Gallipoli, where he had been wounded and suffered from shell-shock and dysentery – had enjoyed being in Blighty. 'We've all had a good time here in England while it lasted', he admitted, and 'I understand most of the boys have got through £100 each during their furlough, and most of them have drawn all their back pay'.[8] Indeed, although he did not say so publicly, Pethick had himself run out of money, and had wired his father at Moonta Mines to ask him to draw £10 from his account at the Commonwealth Bank and then wire the amount back to him in England as soon as possible. At a loss how to achieve this, Pethick senior had written to the Base Records Office in Melbourne, asking for advice. In reply, a staff officer explained wearily that the Office could not effect the transfer itself but that all Pethick's father had to do was to present himself with the authorising telegram at a branch of the Commonwealth Bank, and that the arrangement would then be made, free of charge.[9] Many had spent their money on women, Pethick suggested, and 'a good many have been married over here'. Whatever the bad blood between the Aussies and Tommies, the hostility did not extend to the female sex. 'Talk about girls', Pethick exclaimed, 'that's about all that is left here now'.[10] Perhaps he was referring to the absence of British menfolk, so many of them now in the Forces, or possibly it was the lack of mail ('I haven't received a paper or parcel since I've been here'), or maybe he viewed women as the last form of entertainment, when all other types of amusement had been exhausted.

Either way, when Melville Pethick moved from Abbey Wood Camp near Bristol to rejoin his unit at Weymouth in early January 1916, he knew that the fun was over. 'I'll tell you some tales when I get back', he promised a friend at Moonta: 'I've got some real good ones, too. Should you ever meet Jack Smith again, ask him how he spent Xmas – he'll keep you laughing for a week'. But for now, although Dorset was a 'rather pretty spot', there was merely the prospect of more training, more drill, more discipline, and endless duties of one sort or another before deployment overseas. 'We are to be issued with full equipment to-morrow', he noted, 'so that looks like business again soon'. The rumour was that they would shortly be on their way to Egypt once more (in fact their destination turned out to be France), Pethick observing that 'I won't be sorry to get back there', although 'I feel a bit fishy about having to cross the Mediterranean Sea again, as enemy submarines have been pretty active there of late'. But it would make a welcome change from the

33.   Australian soldiers in camp at Weymouth in Dorset, England.

monotony of guard and picket duty – 'I'm on picket tonight in the town of Weymouth' – and in any case, he said, 'I'm about fed up with England now – it's getting too cold here for me'.[11]

Pethick was right to be worried about the ill effects of the English winter – he soon went down with double-pneumonia – but his ambivalence towards England and the English was not only a matter of the climate, or the surfeit of tempting girls, or his shortage of cash and dearth of letters from home, or even the rigours of military camp life. Instead, as he freely admitted, 'What had turned us against them was through our boys getting cut up at Gallipoli through the Tommies refusing to reinforce them'.[12] Here Pethick was repeating an opinion that was commonplace among Australians at the time, a sense of betrayal (and a story of indolence and cowardice) that coloured the relationship between Australian and British servicemen throughout the Great War, and which has continued to influence the judgement of British and, especially, Australian historians down to our own era. It was an opinion that encouraged Australians to put away their rose-tinted spectacles, through which hitherto they had viewed the old country and the heart of Empire, and to see Britain, with it is increasingly apparent failings (not least military ones) through the eyes of a more sceptical Australian nationalism. It was an opinion that fed the Anzac myth – the Australians had shown themselves made of sterner stuff than the hesitant British – and for the Anzacs themselves it helped to explain why, as in the failure of the faint-hearted in Australia to enlist, they had not acquired the military critical mass necessary to finally drive the Turks from Gallipoli. It was, moreover, an opinion that was reinforced shortly by the experiences and disillusionments of the Western Front, from the horrors of Fromelles and Pozières in 1916 to the momentous events of 1918 when the Australians (and Canadians) proved themselves, in the estimation of their contemporaries, the shock troops of the British Empire.[13]

The particular event at Gallipoli to which Pethick alluded – 'the Tommies refusing to reinforce them' – was the landing at Suvla Bay, north of Anzac Cove, on 6 August 1915 by the British 10th and 11th Divisions as part of General Hamilton's 'big push' to defeat the Turks.[14] The initial objective of this amphibious operation was the capture of the bay area itself, with the aim of consolidating it as a base from which future operations could be launched, after the Anzacs had captured the Sari Bair ridge. But the ridge was never captured, and as the Australians and New Zealanders fought and died at Lone Pine, The Nek and the assault on Chunuk Bair, so word reached them that the newly arrived British were merely brewing tea on the beach at Suvla Bay.[15] The contrast between the sacrifice of Lone Pine and the alleged tea-party at Suvla was just too much to bear, and the Anzacs vented their fury at the British they imagined to be at that moment lolling about the beach and bathing, instead of joining the great effort against the Turk. It was a contrast that appeared to confirm existing fears about the hesitancy and indecision of British military leadership, and the lack of initiative and drive among the common British soldiery. In fact, the British had not been expected to support the Anzac assaults of 6 August, it was never part of the plan, and in any case their landing at Suvla Bay was no picnic – navigational errors had deposited them at the wrong location, while heat exhaustion, lack of water, and stiff resistance from Turkish defenders had frustrated their attempts at early consolidation.[16] But the damage had been done, and the Tommies were diminished thereafter in Anzac eyes.

Indeed, such was this diminution that the burgeoning Anzac myth had the effect of almost writing the British out of the Gallipoli campaign, as far as the Australians were concerned, or at least reducing their significance. Much was made of the successful Australian evacuation on 18 and 19 December 1915 but it was often forgotten that the British remained at their Cape Helles bridgehead until the New Year of 1916. The British had found themselves in an impossibly dangerous position. Their four divisions were hopelessly outnumbered by the twenty-one available to their Turkish opponents. If the British stayed, the probability was that at some point they would simply be overrun, and pushed back into the sea. But if they tried to creep away, as the Anzacs had done, it was highly unlikely that the Turks would be fooled a second time. And yet, just before Christmas 1915, the decision was made to evacuate. As before at Anzac Cove, groups of men stole away at night, with the aim of completing the withdrawal by 9 January 1916. By 7 January the Helles bridgehead was down to just 19,000 men, and it was at that moment that the Turks chose to attack. A massive artillery barrage, the heaviest of the whole campaign, preceded the infantry assault. The Turks then moved forward but were met with such a concentration of firepower from the British lines that they soon crumbled, their leaders now convinced – despite evidence to the contrary – that the British were there to stay. In fact, the British continued with their evacuation, and it was concluded amidst the high drama of strong winds and rising seas that held-up the final departure almost to the moment when the delayed-fuse explosives blew up spectacularly the ammunition dumps left behind.[17] It was an evacuation as heroic and as successful as that from Anzac Cove, yet somehow it seemed to feature less prominently in the story of Gallipoli. As one Tommy complained, he was 'much annoyed at the prominence that is given to the Australians who are the most boastful men in the old & new worlds . . . it's all Australia & makes one quite sick'.[18] The antipathy that Melville Pethick had expressed at Weymouth was, it seems, mutual – for some, at least.

'Cornwall, near England'

As the contrasting experiences of Trooper Smith and Private Pethick showed, an Australian's opinion of England depended not only on the interplay of British and Australian prejudices encountered but on the particular situation in which a soldier found himself. Leave – even recuperation – could be delightful but life in military camps, especially in bleak windswept locations such as the Dorset heathlands or Salisbury Plain, could be drab and uncomfortable, not least in winter. Yet England was not Britain, and Britain itself was only one constituent territory of the United Kingdom. Beyond England, the United Kingdom at large offered Australians, especially those on leave or recuperation, a diversity of geography and history that made them as much tourists in the British Isles as they had been among the pyramids and mosques of Egypt. Besides, for many Australians, their family roots lay not in England itself but in Ireland, Scotland or Wales.[19] On northern Yorke Peninsula, there was an additional dimension, for Kio boys knew that Cornwall was not really part of England; it was instead, as local lore demanded and their regional newspapers insisted, 'Cornwall, near England'.[20]

In 1927, in an article on Cornish emigration in a booklet published in Truro, Cornwall, to celebrate 'Cornwall Education Week', Harry Pascoe wrote of the enduring links between Cornwall and Australia, recalling the Great War years 'when scores of Australian khaki clad soldiers sought out remote corners of the County to visit for the first and last time the homes of their fathers'.[21] There were khaki clad soldiers too from New Zealand, Canada, South Africa and, later in the war, America, and for those of Cornish-descent of whatever nationality serving in France or Belgium there was the enticing prospect of a sojourn in Cornwall. Tom Whetter, for example, born at Gorran on the south Cornish coast, had emigrated to Canada early in the Great War, and joined-up there. In France, Tom chanced upon Fred Whetter, from Lorneville in Ontario, also serving in the Canadian Army, whose family had emigrated from Lostwithiel many years before. Together, the Whetter cousins decided to visit Cornwall at the next opportunity, where Tom might show Fred the sights and introduce him to family members. But alas it was not to be for Fred Whetter was one of the many Canadians who died taking Vimy Ridge in April 1917.[22]

Yet there were many more who were able to seek out the 'remote corners' of Cornwall, as Pascoe had described the far-flung Cornish mining villages and fishing coves, and among their number was Private Leigh Treweek Lennell, the Moonta boy who had been badly injured at Lone Pine (see pp. 70–1). Melville Pethick, writing home from Weymouth, had noted that among his colleagues at Monte Video Camp was Arthur Trenwith, a former Wallaroo miner who hailed from Moonta Road in south Kadina.[23] 'Art Trenwith, of Kadina, is in this hut with me', Pethick explained, 'and he tells me that L[eigh] Lennell is coming out this way tomorrow. He lost an arm in the Lone Pine charge, and I expect he will be returning home soon'.[24] Lennell's mother had received a wire in early October 1915 from the Base Records Office to say that her son had embarked for England (from Malta, where had been in hospital) on 17 September.[25] A few weeks later she heard from Lennell himself, in her excitement passing on the letter to the *People's Weekly* so that all in the community might share in the good news of her son's recovery. The newspaper marvelled that 'the letter is written by Private Lennell himself, and he has done an excellent job with his left hand', as before the amputation he had been right-handed. In the letter, Lennell explained that he was now in the Fulham Military Hospital in London, and expected to have an artificial arm fitted shortly. 'I am in excellent health', he wrote reassuringly, 'and my arm has healed up splendidly'. It was 'hard luck losing my arm, especially the right', he conceded. But most of his mates had been killed at Lone Pine, he said, and 'one has to be thankful if he gets out of this war alive'.[26]

Lennell added that he did not yet know when he would be returned to Australia but, echoing the effusive words of Trooper Smith, explained that in England 'we are having the time of our lives. It is indeed a change after the Dardenelles'. The 'people simply idolise our boys and take us for motor rides all over the country', he added: 'I have visited many beautiful spots, and have been to some wealthy people's places for tea'. Moreover, at the hospital he had had a 'stroke of good luck', as he put it, in bumping into 'a Kadina boy whom I know really well. His name is Art Trenwith'. As Lennell went on to recount, he had met Art by coincidence at Gallipoli, and here again in London they had been reunited by fate: 'It was just like being home again to meet someone I knew so well'.[27] It was wonderful to be feted by the well-to-do in England, with their smart motorcars and lavish afternoon teas. But better still was the company of old friends from home.

'Exactly like the Cornish at Moonta'

Some weeks later, Leigh Lennell was once more writing home to Moonta, this time from a convalescent home in Putney, where 'I am being well cared for, and am having a jolly time'. He admitted, guiltily, that at 'times I think it is worth losing a limb for ... they can't do enough for me'; although, he added, his artificial limb 'is not much use'. Lennell also reported that 'I expect to spend a week in Cornwall shortly with the Matron of this home, Miss K.M. Cosgrave', adding swiftly that he would be chaperoned throughout: 'Art Trenwith is going also'. [28] Soon, he was writing from the Tywarnhayle Hotel, Perranporth, on the north coast of Cornwall, describing what for he and Art Trenwith had become something of a rite of passage, a pilgrimage of sorts. It was an intense experience where, in the manner Harry Pascoe was to describe, they made the detailed acquaintance of their parents' homeland, and discovered the multiplicity of family and cultural links that still tied Cornwall to old Kio.

'You will see by the address that I am down with the Cousin Jacks', Lennell wrote: 'It is perfectly lovely here, and just like home again'. As he went on to explain, 'The people talk exactly like the Cornish at Moonta ... and as soon as the people knew we were Australians and of Cornish descent, they crowded around us and talked for hours'. They were 'making us Cousin Jack pasties', he said, another reminder of Yorke Peninsula, and were anxious to introduce them to all the places of interest across Cornwall. He listed the locations they had visited already or were soon to see – Redruth, the Lizard, Land's End, Truro, Penzance, Carbis Bay, St Ives, Newquay, Bedruthan Caves, the St Agnes tin mines – 'in fact every place down here'. The sense of affinity with local people was overwhelming. 'I feel sure some of them must have relatives in Moonta', he thought: 'Such names as Polkinghorne, Pengilly, Polgreen, Penberthy, are all old folk here'. Moreover, their dialect and accent was familiar: 'They all say, "How art 'e getting on, ma son", and "Es, boy, es" ... we can understand them and talk like them'. [29]

A few days later, Lennell wrote from the Land's End Hotel. 'While at Penzance a very peculiar thing happened', he said: 'We were in a shop buying some south-wester hats and were talking to a young man, who said he came from South Australia. When asked what part, he said "Moonta Mines"'.[30] Lennell then went on to recount a story which, in its coincidences and with its revelations of unexpected intimacies and connections, stood as a metaphor for the paradoxical situation in which he and Art Trenwith found themselves. Australians from half-a-world away, Anzacs who had participated in the momentous nation-building events of Gallipoli, here they were in Cornwall experiencing – even rekindling – a symbiotic relationship which confirmed the particularist regional identity of their part of Australia. There was no doubt that they were Australians, but for them old Kio remained a special place, a salient part of their individual and collective identities. It was, moreover, a paradox that was made plain to the community of northern Yorke Peninsula, through the publication of the Lennell correspondence in the *People's Weekly*, whose readership shared in the adventures of the two Peninsula boys in distant Cornwall. As Lennell explained, having exchanged introductions with the young man from Moonta Mines, he and Art Trenwith were invited to visit 'the next shop and see his people'.[31] He went on:

> I did, and who do you think they were? Mr and Mrs Rowe and family, who lived just by Truer's shaft and close to Penberthy's. We were all delighted to see each other. I was in the same class at school as the daughter, Pearl. We had a long talk and they gave me some 'People's Weeklies'. I also met a Miss Penberthy, related to Moonta folks by the same name. Messrs Rowe and Penberthy are partners in a grocery business. They enquired of all their old Moonta friends . . . I shall be very sorry to leave here.[32]

'The bombs burst around us and he was missing'

Leigh Lennell arrived back at Moonta in early May 1916, met from the train by representatives of the Town Council and the Soldiers' Aid League.[33] A sizeable crowd had also gathered, and Lennell was cheered as he was driven by motorcar to his home in East Moonta, where flags were flying and a line of bunting hung across the road.[34] The following Saturday, he was guest of honour at a reception at the Moonta Mines Pavilion, where the band played 'See the Conquering Hero Comes' and the usual fulsome speeches were made by local dignitaries. Likewise, Lennell received a hero's welcome at a social at Agery church, organised by the Soldiers' Aid League, where he was presented with a purse of money.[35] It was a sweet homecoming, made sweeter still on 28 November that year when Leigh Lennell married Violet May Anderson of Broken Hill. The *People's Weekly*, reporting the marriage ceremony, observed that a noteworthy coincidence was that both bridegroom and best man had lost their right arms at Gallipoli.[36] As Lennell himself had admitted, with some embarrassment, the loss of his limb had been a blessing in disguise, delivering him alive from the terrors of the war.

Not surprisingly, Art Trenwith, Lennell's long-time pal, could not attend the wedding in distant Australia. After their Cornish sojourn, he had returned to camp at Weymouth, and from there was deployed to France, first to Etaples and then to the front near Bapaume, where he found himself in February 1917. As the *Official History* of the war observed, by the middle of that month the long frost that had impeded operations in the vicinity had ended: 'the last traces of snow were disappearing; rain was falling'.[37] The morning of 17 February broke with slight mist and drizzle, and visibility was poor. Trenwith was busy bringing bombs up to the front line near Switch Trench in preparation for raiding, now that the weather was becoming more favourable, but alas the Germans were active too. Surprised by the enemy, Trenwith was caught off guard and killed. His mother Elizabeth, back in Kadina, was told that her son had been shot cleanly through the head.[38] But witnesses to Trenwith's death thought otherwise. One soldier explained: 'He was with me on a party carrying up bombs to the front line at Swiss [*sic*] Trench ... The Germans started bombing us and he was blown up'. The witness continued: 'I saw him in the party as the bombs burst around us and he was missing after we got back to reserves. He was blown up without doubt but I did not see his body'.[39]

For poor Elizabeth Trenwith, the news of her son's demise was followed by the surprising revelation that, despite Art's declaration to the contrary on enlistment, she was not actually his next-of-kin. Rather, it transpired, next-of-kin was a little girl called Dorothy Mary Jones, then aged about three or four, who was cared for by her grandmother in Gawler, north of Adelaide. Young Dorothy, as the military record put it discreetly, was the 'Child (ex-nuptial)' of Art Trenwith and one Annie May Jones, now Mrs Wasley. Dorothy was, therefore, entitled to a pension of 20 shillings fortnightly (to be paid to her grandmother), and later became the recipient of both her late father's war medals and memorial plaque and scroll. Elizabeth Trenwith was asked formally if he wished to object to this arrangement, but was too ill to form an opinion.[40]

Fate had dealt unkindly with Elizabeth Trenwith. But it had not treated Leigh Lennell's mother entirely fairly, either. For all the joy of Leigh's safe homecoming and subsequent marriage, there remained the nagging anxiety as to the whereabouts and welfare of his elder brother, Fred Lennell. Mrs Lennell had received a letter from Fred dated 22 June 1916, written at Perham Down, one of the many military camps on Salisbury Plain, in England. As Joseph Treweek, her brother, later reported to the Base Records Office in Melbourne: 'We have written to this address repeatedly and also cabled, but we can get no further news'.[41] The Office reminded them to write to the generic address for soldiers serving abroad, citing official number and unit, but even the correct protocol did not elicit a reply from Fred. Months went by, and then Mrs Lennell was informed by the Military that Fred had been admitted to the Voluntary Aid Detachment Hospital at Exeter on 28 February 1917, suffering from severe nephritis, a disease of the kidneys. There

34. Switch Trench, on the Somme, where Arthur Aubrey Trenwith from Kadina
was killed in action on 17 February 1917.

was a further note in the May to say that he had now been discharged from
hospital.[42] But the silence continued. It was not clear whether Fred was again
ill, or was at large in England, or perhaps had been posted to France.

In June 1918 the Military Pay Office in Adelaide wrote to the Base Records
Office on Mrs Lennell's behalf. 'I have a complaint here from Mrs Lennell',
the clerk explained, 'who states that she has not received any letters from
her son No. 4511 Private F.J. Lennell 10th Battalion since July 1916. She had
a parcel of letters returned to her about twelve months ago, marked "not

with this Unit" . . . this is causing the mother great anxiety'. The following month, the secretary of the South Australian Recruiting Office also wrote to the Base Records Office on Mrs Lennell's behalf. 'The mother of the above soldier has not heard anything concerning her son since notice of discharge from hospital, Exeter on 4/5/17 and now receives word of an overdrawn account of £60 and allotment ceased'. Things appeared to have gone from bad to worse, with Fred apparently in debt, even to the extent of cancelling his mother's allowance. And then, in early August 1918, came the distressing news that Fred Lennell was suffering from 'gunshot wound right foot, severe', and had been admitted to the 1st Southern General Hospital in Birmingham, where over subsequent weeks he gradually recovered.[43] Strangely, the great silence, and other irregularities, were never explained – at least not in official documentation – but when Fred Lennell finally left England for Australia in early 1919 for demobilisation, there seemed now to be an air of forgiveness. At last, in late March, the prodigal son (if that he what he was) arrived home, to be welcomed unreservedly by the East Moonta Soldiers' Aid League, just as his brother had been, with a reception held in his honour in the Moonta Mines Pavilion.[44]

'The places you used to speak of when Roy and I were boys'

As the entwined but very different experiences of the Lennell and Trenwith families demonstrated, Blighty continued to mean many things to many people. Blighty might be a place of deliverance and redemption, or perhaps of illness and anonymity, or even the precious lull before the dreadful storm. The 'tyranny of distance', the phrase made famous by Geoffrey Blainey, was as apt a description in this context as in any other area of Australian history.[45] The surreal contrasts of Britain – high tea with the gentry, or picket duty in provincial towns on wintry nights – resonated equally at home, where friends and relations struggled sometimes to make sense of the multiplicity of messages they received (or did not receive). The reading public in Moonta and environs read together in the local press the cosy and reassuring missives from Cornwall – a welcoming and familiar home-from-home, as they were encouraged to believe – but all the while, despite the brave public faces, individuals behind closed doors suffered agonies of uncertainty that could be as traumatic as those experienced when their loved ones were in action at the front.

Of course, individual dramas were played out again and again as the United Kingdom continued to exercise its several roles – as hospital for the seriously ill or severely wounded, as playground for those on leave or recuperation, or as an inhospitable landscape of endless military camps where troops were made ready for their inevitable deployment to the front in France or Belgium. The boundaries between these several roles were often blurred, as the Lennell and Trenwith cases showed, and for many Australian soldiers there were repeated sojourns in Britain, often in different guises. In this way, the amazing wonderland of first acquaintance might turn after several visits to the realm of perpetually grey skies and irritating social stuffiness. Gallipoli veterans continued to nurture their Suvla 'tea-party' grievance, an ill feeling towards the Tommies perpetuated by those Australians who had endured the slaughter of Fromelles and Pozières and witnessed the retreat of British troops in the face of the German spring offensive in 1918.

And often, as we have seen, the Tommies reciprocated, informing a broader antipathy towards the Anzacs that Australians sometimes encountered in Britain. As William Beach Thomas, a British war correspondent on the Western Front, explained, official encouragement by the British military authorities to emphasise the contribution of the Australians and Canadians, led sometimes to the unfortunate 'impression that the whole burden of fighting was on the shoulders of the overseas troops'.[46] Likewise, as the London *Daily Mail* complained, the 'reticence of the British military censorship' to mention the exploits of English units, while 'recording the deeds of the Scottish, Irish, Canadian and Australian regiments', played into German hands. German propaganda was able to insinuate that 'English troops are so rarely referred to because they never do anything. England's part in the war ... is to make profit and to drive others to fight'.[47] It was nonsense, of course, but it fuelled English resentment at the limelight shone on their Celtic and Colonial cousins. Paradoxically, irritated Australians often objected that their feats of arms were reported in the UK press as merely 'British' victories.[48]

As new recruits came forward in Australia, so further waves of Australian troops arrived in Britain, perpetuating those several roles that Blighty played, and beginning afresh each time the processes of familiarisation. For soldiers from northern Yorke Peninsula, Cornwall continued to exercise its particular fascination. Bert Grummet, for example, whose ancestors hailed from the Harz mountains in Germany, was as good a 'Kio boy' as any other – his father had published the well known collection of Moonta's Cornish carols in 1893 – and shared the general enthusiasm for things Cornish.[49] He had been in hospital at Stratford-upon-Avon, where he soaked up that locality's literary and historical atmosphere, and had then proceeded on leave to Cornwall. 'I am enjoying furlough in lovely Cornwall', he reported on a postcard to the *People's Weekly* in June 1918. He had admired Stratford, he admitted, 'which also is lovely, but quite a different kind of beauty to Cornwall'.[50] Earlier, in 1916, Lloyd Pollard, a private in the 11th Field Ambulance, had written to his parents at Moonta Mines. 'At last I can write to you about my trip through dear old Cornwall', he said, 'the places you used to speak of when Roy and I were boys ... we used to hear dad and grandfather speak of the places I had

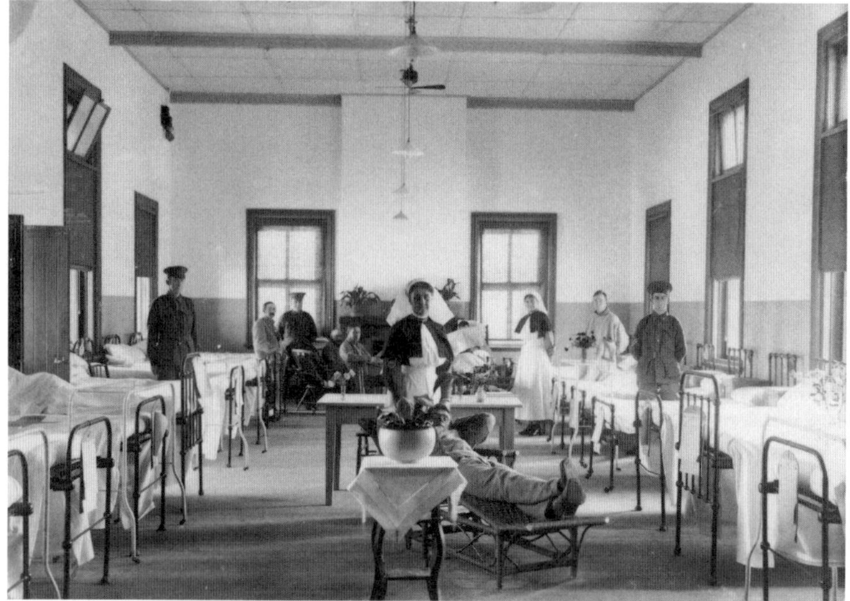

35.   The military hospital at Keswick, near Adelaide, where Lloyd Pollard died of spinal disease in April 1919.

the pleasure to see'. Pollard enthused about holding 'my first conversation with a Cornishman in his native country . . . It was grand to hear the Cornish dialect'.[51] But all good things come to an end, and Pollard was shortly posted to France. There, unfortunately, he met with a serious accident. Some heard that he had injured himself while assisting in the construction of a hospital.[52] Others said that he had 'ricked his back' while bringing in the wounded under fire at Armentières, 'and, it being the second coldest winter in France for nearly 50 years, it affected his spine so much that he never recovered'.[53]

An X-ray and medical report diagnosed caries of the spine, which was attributed to 'exposure and infection', and Lloyd Pollard was sent to England for treatment. At the hospital in Epsom the doctors despaired of his condition. He suffered pain in the 'lumber region of back on slightest movement', it was reported, and it seemed unlikely that he would improve.[54] Yet Pollard remained in up-beat mood, writing cheery letters home in which he avoided mention of his dismal situation. His brother Roy detected that all was not well. Roy had also been in England with the Australian forces – in camp at Weymouth and then in hospital with pleurisy at Dartford – and subsequently in September 1916 was seriously wounded in France, being invalided back to Australia thereafter.[55] Roy Pollard knew the score, and wrote to the Base Records Office for a precise description of his brother's ailment. His parents were 'very anxious concerning him', Roy explained: 'He writes cheerful letters but is very reserved concerning his injuries. I do hope, sir, you could give us the true facts'.[56] The answer came back that Lloyd Pollard was suffering from spinal disease. Little could be done for him, and he was duly repatriated to Australia. There, he was confined to his bed for two years and four months, sixteen of those months in the military hospital at Keswick, near Adelaide, before expiring on 14 April 1919.[57] 'Lloyd Pollard passed away last Monday night', wrote W.H. Harvey to his son Leonard in England, awaiting return to Australia and demobilisation: 'he must have been a great sufferer, but he was most cheerful with it all'.[58]

'England will do me'

Despite the abundance of all they had heard and read, suffering was the least thing on the minds of eager new recruits arriving in Britain from Australia. This had been as true for Lloyd Pollard when he had first set foot in England as it was for any other newcomer. Before his pilgrimage to Cornwall, and ahead of that fateful posting to France, Lloyd Pollard had been enraptured by all he had found and experienced. He wrote at length to his parents at Moonta Mines, and the *People's Weekly* was proud to publish such fulsome reports on 'the old country'. Writing from Larkhill, on Salisbury Plain, in July 1916, he explained how he and the other Australians had arrived in Plymouth Sound, going ashore in launches. He had espied the Hoe, he said, 'where Sir Francis Drake was playing bowls when the Spanish Armada was sighted', and on landing at Devonport the 'first thing I had to eat was three good pasties, on the wharf – boys selling them for 3*d*. each'. It was as good as being in Cornwall, especially as he 'could see a piece of Cornwall just over the River Tamar, which divides Cornwall from Devonshire'.[59] But there was no time to linger, for trains were waiting to take the newly arrived troops to their training camps on Salisbury Plain. As Pollard observed:

> Of course, we were anxious to see the trains which can do 60 miles an hour, and we were gratified. The London South-Western Railway was to take us to camp, and we had a rather slow ride, which, however, was in our favour, as it gave us a good chance to view the passing scenes. The Great Western is the flyer here. They are lovely engines, and are spick and span, as if got up for imperial inspection. This place is full of railways; one runs under a bridge, and another over it. So there is no stop here.[60]

The railway journey provided a grandstand spectacle of Plymouth, the first English city that Lloyd Pollard had ever seen, and he was duly impressed, if a little bewildered by the teeming multitudes that appeared to inhabit the tightly arranged housing. 'I have often wondered how so many people could be packed into this small island', he admitted, but 'now I understand'.[61] He added:

> We passed rather high up over Devonport, so had a good view of the town. The houses are joined to each other for the length of a street; a wall seems to divide these houses in half from end to end. One family lives on one side, another crowd the other, so you can imagine how many live in one little street. These streets run back tier after tier, there must be millions of houses in this spot, and all with slate roofs.[62]

As the journey progressed, Pollard continued to be spellbound by this familiar yet alien landscape, one he knew intimately from geography and history books but have never set eyes on before. 'I couldn't believe they had hedges to divide up these lovely fields', he exclaimed: 'The hedges are all shapes, colours, sizes, uphill and down dale for miles and miles, and the fields are green with different kinds of vegetables'. He noticed women at work in the fields – 'and, in fact, at every occupation ... the men having gone to the front' – and, as the train wound its way through the counties of Devon, Somerset, Dorset and Wiltshire, so the 'passing scenes were indeed lovely to behold'. He noticed the pretty villages, each with its ancient parish church, and observed 'ruins of old castles'. At 'a town called Exeter' the train paused for a while, and Pollard was touched when the 'Mayoress gave us a bottle of tea and a bun each, with a little card saying from whom it came'. Eventually, at seven o'clock in the evening, the Australians arrived at Amesbury, with the prospect of a four-mile march into camp. Larkhill, Pollard explained, was just one component of a vast military infrastructure centred on Salisbury. 'You cannot imagine how extensive this camp is', he reported: 'It is said they could accommodate two million men on these plains'.[63] But despite this all-enveloping military environment, the surrounding villages remained unsullied. Again, he was enchanted:

> The nearest village is that of Amesbury and some of the homes are over 200 years old. You have seen the style, I guess – with thatched roofs, all two storeys high, but very low, with little windows overlooking the street. It is a quaint little village. All the windows have their flowers, mostly geraniums. In the streets the old village pump, made of wood, was too much for us, so we pumped a good drink each. This place is full of chalk and flint. Most of the walls have flint in them. One of the most interesting and ancient sights was an old Abbey, which dates back well over a thousand years. The vicar's wife is nearly always there to explain the meaning of all the relics.[64]

36. The Mayoress of Exeter greets Australian troops as their train pauses
at Exeter Queen Street station in Devon, England. As Lloyd Pollard explained:
the 'Mayoress gave us a bottle of tea and bun each, with a little card saying from
whom it came'.

Pollard's fascination with antiquity and architecture extended to the
locality's literary associations. Drawing upon the reservoir of his childhood
education, he remembered once more the words of Longfellow's verse: '"The
old village blacksmith's"' chestnut tree stands not far from here', he said,
'where "By the fierce red glow of this fire bright, The strokes of his hammer
rung"'. As he mused: 'Just fancy learning these lines at Moonta Mines,
and then coming to England and seeing the spot that gave Longfellow his
wonderful inspiration!'.[65] Likewise, Pollard was enthralled to learn that 'the
Druid Temple' of Stonehenge was so close by, and there was also the exciting
prospect of a trip to London, that mecca for all Australians in Britain. A
return ticket from Salisbury was only seven shillings, he said, and in 'London
we go everywhere free, so I will buzz around'.[66]

The July of 1916 was warm and sunny in England, adding to that sense of
rural idyll that Lloyd Pollard had experienced so powerfully on arrival. He had
little inkling then of the horror that was at that very moment unfolding on
the Somme, where old school chums from Moonta Mines were laying down
their lives for the Empire, and could not have foretold his own fate in France
only a few months hence. He could not begin to imagine the biting cold of
winter on Salisbury Plain, when the wooden camp huts seemed impervious
to the icy draughts and when water froze in the taps. The daily routine of
duties and drills, and punishments for those who erred, had not yet begun to

irk, and so far he had not encountered the ill feelings and jealousies that some disgruntled Tommies harboured towards their Australian cousins. Instead, Lloyd Pollard saw only beauty in this strange but welcoming land, and felt privileged to be at last in that heart of Empire that he had learned so much about as a boy. As he put it: 'England will do me'.[67]

'Plenty of Kio boys'

Gilbert Roy Oats was another Moonta soldier based at Larkhill camp during 1916. He wrote home in the October 'to let you know that I am still at Lark Hill [*sic*] and enjoying myself', although complaining that 'it is getting very cold here'. The 43rd Battalion A.I.F., of which he was a member, 'is well represented by Moonta boys', he said. C Company alone sported fourteen, and there were various others in other companies. As he remarked, 'when we get together we often talk about Moonta and the times we had there; but when we get back we will be able to talk about Lark Hill'. It was a telling insight into the camaraderie that existed between these soldiers who had grown up together in Australia, were now training in the same units in England, and would shortly share the dangers and privations of the front. Oats had heard that they were to go to France next month – 'we have been issued with rifles and bayonets' – and he expected to 'do our bit for King and Country'.[68]

In fact, they embarked at Southampton in late November, bound for France as Oats had anticipated. A stretcher-bearer, Gilbert Oats found himself in the thick of the action. He was slightly wounded in the following June, although able to continue at his post, and was again wounded in action in July 1917 – this time somewhat more seriously; a gunshot wound to the arm, a 'Blighty one' that would not incapacitate but would require evacuation to England for treatment and recuperation. Eventually discharged from hospital, Oats found himself in camp at Dinton on Salisbury Plain. By now, the novelty of camp life had long since worn off, and Oats – like increasing numbers of Australians – decided to award himself impromptu leave. Accordingly, he was adjudged Absent Without Leave from 3.30 a.m. on 13 October 1917 to 3.30 p.m. on 15 October, for which misdemeanour he was fined five days' pay. He was soon back in France, where he was wounded for a third time in May 1918, and again fourthly and far more seriously when he was shot in the back while stretcher-bearing under fire in August 1918. This last earned Gilbert Oats another trip to England – to the Bath War Hospital – and his discharge from the army as medically unfit. It also earned him the Military Medal.[69] As his citation explained, on 22 August 1918 his company's position east of Bray-sur-Somme had been shelled heavily and continuously for three hours. 'During the whole of that period', the citation continued, 'Pte Oats who is a stretcher bearer continued to dress the wounded and remove them to the aid post. He worked without shelter of any kind and at great personal risk'. This was only one of many occasions, it was reported, where 'Pte Oats has in similar capacity shown an utter disregard of danger and a noble spirit of devotion to duty'.[70]

Despite the austere conditions in the training camps in England, especially during winter, rest periods therein were often welcomed as a respite from the travails of trench warfare. In March 1917 Richard ('Lee') Pomeroy wrote home to Yorke Peninsula from Salisbury Plain. 'Am having the time of my life just now', he reported enthusiastically: 'Am in England on a rest, which I wanted very much'. He had been seven-and-a-half months in France, he said, 'where Fritz aims iron foundries at one', and 'I have had some very lively times there'. He had met 'plenty of Kio boys' during his adventures, he added, but was 'sorry to hear that so many boys have fallen'. Lee had also managed to visit his brother William while in England: 'he was badly knocked about, and I think it will be some time before he is fit again'.[71] In fact, William Pomeroy had been wounded in action in France on 1 October 1916, with gunshot wounds to the head, left hand, right leg and right thigh. Thus 'knocked about', he was evacuated to England for treatment at the London General Hospital. He recovered gradually but, as his brother Lee intimated, his health remained poor – in August 1917, for example, he was admitted to 2nd Birmingham War Hospital, suffering from scabies. Yet amid the bad news there were glimmers of hope – the visit from Lee but also the relationship he had struck up with a woman he had met in London.[72]

William Pomeroy married Rosamond Gridley in Kensington, London, in February 1919, shortly before his repatriation to Australia.[73] William duly returned to Moonta, accompanied by his spouse. Such 'English brides', as they were dubbed in the local press, became a familiar part of the social landscape as the war drew to a close and servicemen returned home. In August 1919, for example, Oscar Nankivell arrived back in Moonta with his wife, Margaret Bailey, whom he had married at Grantham in Lincolnshire in the February.[74] It is difficult to know what the newly-arrived women thought of their adopted home, or how they were received by the extended families of which they were now so suddenly a part. But, publicly at least, they were given a cordial reception and were embraced by the community. At a 'very large gathering' (as it was reported) at the Moonta Institute Hall in September 1919, for example, organised by the Moonta Soldiers' Aid Society to support returning servicemen, the Mayor 'extended a welcome to the English brides (Mesdames Tippet and Goldsworthy), which was acknowledged by their husbands'.[75] It was not recorded what the brides themselves had to say, and these women seem strangely silent in the historic record. Perhaps they 'knew their place'; as newcomers and as women submissive to their husbands' wills and opinions.

37.   'English wives' and their babies, bound for Australia in the *SS Borda* in 1919
to join their husbands and new families.

'Obscene language in the presence of an NCO'

For soldiers on leave or convalescence in the UK, or for those posted to camps such as Larkhill on Salisbury Plain or Monte Video at Weymouth, the allure of women was often irresistible — especially after the trials of active service at the front. Most of the marriages contracted between the Australians and local girls were love matches, no doubt, although among those 'English brides' there was inevitably a sprinkling of those who had 'had to get married', to use the euphemism then prevalent. At any rate, there were the usual unintended pregnancies, the product often of brief moments of passion taken roughly and readily as opportunities presented themselves. Alfred James Angove, from Cross Roads, for example, managed to get his English girlfriend 'into trouble' (to use that other contemporary euphemism) during his time at Wilton House, near Salisbury, recovering from injuries.[76]

The yearning for female favours also spawned two perennial misdemeanours: the contracting (and spreading) of venereal disease, and the recourse to Absence Without Leave. The former had long been the scourge of military towns in the United Kingdom, and as early as 1864 the Contagious Disease Act had attempted to contain venereal disease (VD) in localities such as

Aldershot in England and the Curragh in Ireland, making medical inspection and treatment compulsory.[77] But the proliferation of military camps and huge explosion of uniformed personnel during the Great War made control of VD an increasingly uphill battle. VD was reckoned to be the biggest threat to military efficiency in the home commands of the United Kingdom, with the Australians and New Zealanders the worst offenders. It was estimated at the time that the rate of Australian and New Zealand troops admitted for treatment for VD was 128 and 130 per 1,000 respectively, compared to just 24 per 1,000 for British soldiers.[78] Failure to declare VD was a punishable offence under military law, and thus service documents are full of the details of those unfortunates who had no choice but to own up and seek treatment, sometimes repeatedly so. Jake Roach, for example, feted at home as the first Moonta boy to enlist, was just one of many to succumb to 'VD(S)' – syphilis – as it was recorded in his documents, seeking medical assistance for the complaint a fortnight or so after the Armistice in November 1918.[79] Plainly, he had celebrated too well the end of hostilities.

Jake Roach, like many of his compatriots, had also had a taste for Absence Without Leave. In Egypt after the Gallipoli evacuation, he was awarded 168 hours' field punishment for being absent from parade, with a simultaneous sentence of 168 hours' detention for 'using insubordinate language to his superior officer'.[80] Later, in Weymouth in October 1917, he was reduced to the rank of Private and fined four days' pay for being AWOL for three days. A more persistent offender was Frank Harwood, from Kadina. He too acquired the AWOL habit in Egypt in the aftermath of Gallipoli. From there he was posted to England, where in camp at Rollestone in Wiltshire he went Absent Without Leave on three separate occasions between August and December 1916, earning a formal Admonishment and forfeiting a total of twenty-seven days' pay. On active service in France during 1917, there were further instances of unauthorised absence before his return to England in October of that year, suffering from haematuria cystitis, for which illness he spent more than two months in the Bath War Hospital. Recovering, in January 1918 he headed for the bright lights of London, where he promptly went AWOL for two days. He was also accused of 'masquerading as a Corporal' in the capital, and for these two 'crimes' (as they were recorded on his service documents), Harwood was fined seventeen days' pay. There were further 'crimes'. In camp at Littlemoor, near Weymouth, he went missing on the morning of 4 February 1918 but was 'apprehended at Yeovil' at noon the same day by the military authorities. Again at Littlemoor, Harwood was fined one day's pay in July 1918 for 'Absenting himself from duty as Depot Bugler'. He had reported late to the Guard Room but by that time his duty had already fallen to another soldier, and the damage had been done. Evidently, he was not enjoying his spell at Weymouth – later in the month he was reprimanded for 'using obscene language in the presence of an N[on] C[ommissioned] O[fficer]' – and, alas, it was perhaps in those damp and misty Dorset climes that Frank Harwood contracted the 'Epidymitis (probably T.B.)' for which he was declared medically unfit for further service and repatriated to Australia in 1919.[81]

'Frock coated gentlemen and officers of the English Army'

Although, as the above suggests, it is possible to identify trends and themes, as well as to sketch the often-contrasting experiences of Kio boys in the United Kingdom, it is difficult to generalise. However, something of the diverse complexity of this experience as lived by one individual is glimpsed in the series of letters and diaries of Signaller Lance Corporal Leonard John Harvey.[82] Born at Moonta, Leonard Harvey was the son of Hon. William Humphrey Harvey, a former moulder at the Moonta mine workshops who was secretary of the Moonta Miners' Association from 1897 to 1915, when he was elected as a Labor member of the South Australian Parliament.[83] Leonard corresponded with his father on a variety of subjects, including political issues and the Conscription controversy (see Chapter Six), and his letters are full of insights into life at the front (see Chapters Four and Seven) and in Blighty, as he invariably called it. He found himself in Blighty on several occasions – in the summer and autumn of 1916 before deployment to France, in the summer of 1918 at Burdon Military Hospital in Weymouth (recovering from 'gassing') and at No. 4 Hurdcott Command Depot on Salisbury Plain, and finally in the spring of 1919 while awaiting repatriation to Australia.[84]

Leonard Harvey first arrived in England in July 1917, having landed at Southampton from Le Havre after a lengthy train journey across France from Marseilles. He wrote home from Larkhill camp, near Amesbury. It was 'surprising the number of Moonta lads we have met in the 5 days we have been here', he reported to his father: 'about the first Australians we spoke to were Loyd [sic] Pollard, Jack Emerson, and Dick Penrose'.[85] Like Lloyd Pollard, Harvey enthused over the district's historical and literary associations – he had already been to Stonehenge, he said, and waxed lyrical about Longfellow and Tennyson – and 'I am also anxious to see Scotland'. But he was not uncritical of what he found. 'Fruit is very dear at present, bananas and apples in some case 1½ each. It's a terrible place here for pennies and half pennies. I have not had a 3d. given in change yet'. Harvey also thought English towns and cities extremely overcrowded, writing later about the lack of space that he found so oppressive. 'No harm in having plenty of room around the house', he opined: 'I don't like them too close. Have seen too much of the closeness over here'. But nonetheless London, for all the teeming thousands, was endlessly fascinating. He and 'all the Moonta lads' had spent their short

38.   A group of Australian soldiers enjoy picnic refreshments during a YMCA outing in London in 1918.

leave in the capital, he explained, 'and went to all the places in London that we had time to visit'. They were tourists in uniform, taking in St Paul's, the Tower of London, London Bridge, and Westminster Abbey, as well as having 'a look at the captured mine laying submarine UC5'. It was, he admitted, 'a very small craft, but capable of doing a great deal of damage'. It was a popular attraction on the Thames, but they 'ought to use it against the Huns instead of showing it'.[86]

'The Tube railways are a splendid thing', Harvey added, and the busses were cheap. And there were a great many YMCA huts 'all over London', he said, 'which are worked by woman [sic] who do it voluntary, and they can't do enough for the Australians'.[87] Cups of tea and other refreshments were handed out cheerfully to the eager Anzacs. But the Aussies also aspired to grander things, and, describing an incident that seems now stereotypically Australian, Harvey recounted how:

> Four of us went into a 'Café' to dinner, and found ourselves dining with frock coated gentlemen and officers of the English Army. We were taken very good stock of but I don't know the opinion that was formed. I overheard one lady say that she didn't think we were every-day soldiers at any rate she passed the time of the day to us when she was going out.[88]

Similarly enigmatic were Harvey's comments on class and locality in the metropolis:

> We had a look around Richmond and Rotten Row, where all the heads [upper-class] live, it is a lovely place and a good many fine buildings are to be seen. From Richmond we went to the Eastern part of the city, where a poorer class of people are met with. The smell of the market place is simply terrible, but we didn't stop there too long.[89]

Back at Larkhill, the Kio boys stuck together for companionship. 'This letter is being written with Bert Grummet's pen and Charlie Rose's pad', explained Harvey: 'I am down in their hut'.[90] Len Trembath, another Moontaite, impressed his chums with tales of a German air raid he had witnessed recently during weekend leave in London. 'Lucky beggar', exclaimed an envious Leonard Harvey: 'He said it was a marvellous sight when the Zeppelin fell burning to the ground, the place was lit up to a radius of 14 miles'. Len Trembath had also been to see William Pomeroy in Wandsworth Hospital, in London, Harvey added, and there was news of other Yorke Peninsula soldiers in the vicinity of Larkhill – 'Fred Lennell [is] camped at Perham Downs, 14 miles away, with Percy Olds and the Roach boys . . . Fred was looking well and as fat as a pig'.[91] In late October 1916 Jake Roach came across from France to see his two brothers. 'It was the first leave he had since leaving Egypt', according to Harvey.[92] There was also welcome news from home – 'According to the letters received by the Moonta boys Australia day was celebrated in a good way at Kio'[93] – but there was consternation when the transport *Arabic* was sunk en route from the Antipodes. 'She had our next mail on board', wailed Harvey, 'and some say part of the Christmas mail . . . I'm afraid Linda's wedding cake has landed at the bottom of the Mediterranean'.[94]

Inevitably, however, the war began to cast its long shadow over Salisbury Plain. 'According to talk the Australians have been doing a lot of the heavy fighting', Harvey recorded in August 1916 as news of Pozières and the Somme filtered through, 'and there are some very big casualty lists'.[95] Later, in the October, he reported that William Pomeroy had suffered no fewer than ten shrapnel wounds, 'the worst being in the calf of the leg'. As Harvey added: 'Will Pomeroy told me some good tales of what he saw on the "Somme" but I wouldn't be allowed to put them in here'.[96] Before long it was the turn of the Larkhill chums to join their compatriots at the front. Leonard Harvey wrote to his father on the evening of 22 November 1916. As he put pen to paper, he listened to the strangely moving sound of a military band playing in the distance as a battalion marched out that night on its way to the battlefields of France. Harvey's battalion, the 43rd, was due to march out of camp at 10.00 a.m. on the following Saturday, he explained, adding that 'Events point to our immediate action when we arrive in France'. Every soldier had been issued with two gas helmets, he said, two blankets, one steel helmet, 150 rounds of ammunition, a leather waistcoat, greatcoat, rifle, 'and any little thing he can shove into the corners of his pack besides change of underclothes'.[97] After those happy months in Blighty it seemed like the end of an era, and as if to underscore the change of mood and purpose, the weather broke suddenly of the eve of their departure. There was snow, some three to four inches of it Harvey estimated: 'All hands had a go at snowballing each other, and at making figures of men with it'. As Harvey observed: 'The Pommies here told us that it was very early in the season for snow ... It was just like the old English pictures that we have all seen so often'.[98]

'The doctor ... marked me for "Blighty"'

As Leonard Harvey had anticipated, he was plunged into the thick of it. Involved in numerous stunts in France through the long months of 1917, during which he acquitted himself well and was recommended for officer training, he was also among those Australian units which stood firm against the Germans' great offensive of Spring 1918. As he went on to explain: 'We had been in the trenches for five days ... when old Fritz (Hans & Carl must have assisted) started sending over Gas shells. He continued shelling for 15 hours and most of it through the night'. Harvey continued: 'We had our respirators on, but it is a hard and trying ordeal to wear them for any length of time, consequently the majority of us removed our masks for short periods and were slightly gassed'. In fact, the mustard gas was more malign than Harvey had imagined. It took some six to eight hours for it to take full effect, he acknowledged, and Harvey reported stoically that 'Only my eyes were affected, I was partially blind for 8 hours, and after two or three days I was quite well'.[99] But he was putting on a brave face, and feigned astonishment when it was announced that he was to be evacuated to England for recuperation.[100] Earlier, in February 1917, he had admitted himself envious when he had heard that his pal 'Chook Murdock has gone to "Blighty" with a bullet wound in the back of the knee ... Lucky beggar, in a way, to be out of the danger zone for a few weeks'.[101] Now, unexpectedly, it was Harvey's turn. 'I got a big shock one morning when the doctor came in and marked me for "Blighty"', he wrote from hospital in Weymouth: 'am feeling all right but my card is marked "Shell Gas" and owing to that the doctors won't let me take any risks'.[102]

At Weymouth, Harvey learned from home that Lloyd Pollard's condition had deteriorated – 'Sorry to hear Loyd [sic] Pollard was worse'[103] – and a few weeks later, now at Hurdcott on Salisbury Plain, he received the melancholy news 'that one of the Roach boys has been killed, think it was the youngest' (it was, Doug Roach, killed in action on 5 July 1918).[104] Nonetheless, he was determined to make the best of things as he recuperated. 'Am getting to know London as well as I know Moonta', he boasted in a letter home.[105] He also reported that his mate Jack Pyatt was planning a trip to Camborne, in Cornwall, where Jack had an aunt, and had asked him to tag along too.[106] Earlier, at Larkhill in 1916, Harvey had admitted that 'My brain gets in a whirl when I try to think of the different families and their relation to me'.[107] Perhaps the prospect of meeting all those relations was just too daunting, or maybe they just ran out of time. Either way, the visit was apparently postponed, and, fully recovered now from his bout of 'gassing', Leonard Harvey was shortly posted back to France.

Harvey's third and final sojourn in the UK was in the spring of 1919, when he – like thousands of other Australian soldiers – waited for the order to return home. For many, it was a frustrating and unsettling time, and they grew bored and irritable as the months passed. Shortly after the Armistice in November 1918, General Birdwood had issued a general memorandum to the A.I.F. He foresaw, he said, that 'demobilisation will undoubtedly be difficult and irksome' and that 'great personal restraint will certainly be required'. Australia's name stood high in the world, Birdwood argued, and it was up to them to ensure that this was not besmirched 'owing to any behaviour of ours'. Ships to take Australians home would inevitably be in short supply, and everybody would have to wait their turn. 'Play the game, boys, during this time', Birdwood implored, 'as you have always done, and add still more to the debt of gratitude which will always be acknowledged to you by the Empire and remembered by me as your comrade and commander'.[108]

Australians had a soft spot for 'old Birdie', as he had been known since Gallipoli days, and Leonard Harvey seemed touched by Birdwood's heartfelt plea. He carefully preserved the memorandum, placing it neatly with his personal papers, and did indeed 'play the game' during his remaining time in Blighty. Among other things, he and Jack Pyatt finally made their journey to Cornwall. As Harvey explained in a letter home to Moonta in April 1919, he and Jack were to spend a couple days in London before going 'down to Cornwall, to see a few of "They Cousin Jacks"'.[109] The two Kio boys caught the overnight train from Paddington on 17 April, arriving at Camborne the next morning, where they were met by Mrs Bennett, Jack's aunt. They stayed almost a fortnight and, as Harvey noted in his diary, they made the most of it. There was the customary trip to see Land's End, and visits to Penzance (where they met Dick Rowe, the grocer), St Just, St Ives, Sennen, Mousehole and Helston, the latter preparing for Flora Day on 8 May. They even found time to attend a rugby football match between Cornwall and New Zealand which, Harvey observed without further comment, resulted in a 'Win for NZ'.[110] As he wrote with satisfaction to his father: 'So you can see I have now had a look at the land of "Cousin Jacks" and Pasties'.[111] It was not quite the final act. On 3 May Leonard Harvey was one of the 5,000 Dominion troops who marched triumphantly through London, and on 20th of that month he embarked at Liverpool in the transport *Nestor*, bound at last for home.

'Moonta's little, but she's great'

Leonard Harvey and Jack Pyatt were numbered – like Leigh Lennell, Art Trenwith, Bert Grummet and Lloyd Pollard – among those 'scores of Australian khaki clad soldiers' who had visited Cornwall during the war years. They had sought out relations and places with family associations, on occasions meeting Kio folk who had returned to Cornwall years before, all the while reaffirming the affinity between Cornwall and northern Yorke Peninsula, the basis of the latter's distinctive regional identity. It was also, as Harry Pascoe had intimated, a two-way process, and people in Cornwall were often as moved as their Australian cousins by these renewed contacts and exchanges. George Jose, in particular, a former Moonta miner who had retired to his native Cornwall just after the turn of the century, was inspired to compose his 'Moonta and the Great War', a poem published in 1921, in which he celebrated this rekindling of links and affections. He honoured 'the valiant stand of Moonta, / With her few heroic men', and welcomed Anzac soldiers to his home: 'And I'm proud to pen this tribute – / Moonta's little, but she's great'. He hoped, too, for permanence in this rekindling, and imagined the joyful union of visiting Australians and local girls:

> There'll be many an Australian soldier
>   Linked with some sweet Cornish girl.
> Who could blame them? Not the writer.
>   He would e'er their flag unfurl.
>
> He would throw the rice and slipper,
>   And his joy would ne'er abate,
> And he writes with lasting pleasure –
>   Moonta's little, but she's great.[112]

It was a message that eventually found its way 'down under' (Jose's poem was duly printed in the *People's Weekly*), reinforcing a sentimental sense of intimacy between Cornwall and Kio in the immediate post-war years. Yet there were other forces at play, as we have seen, with attitudes to Blighty often ambivalent, even paradoxical, at times something close to a love-hate relationship, especially as the war wore on. This too was a complexity mirrored at home in Australia, not least on northern Yorke Peninsula, where the Conscription issue (see Chapter Six) had added a new dimension to Australian responses to the war and to the relationship with Britain and Empire. At the same moment that George Jose could laud Moonta's heroic deeds, seeking to perpetuate the intimate embrace of Cornwall and Australia, so there were returning Australian servicemen who were only too happy to sing:

> Take me back to dear old Aussie,
> Put me on the boat for Woolloomooloo;
> Take me over there, drop me anywhere,
> Sydney, Melbourne, Adelaide, for I don't care;
> I just want to see my best girl,
> Cuddling up again we soon will be;
> Oh, Blighty is a failure, take me back to Australia,
> Aussie is the place for me.[113]

As E.M. Andrews concluded in his *The Anzac Illusion*: 'Reactions were intensely personal, depending partly on the man concerned, and partly on experiences'. As Andrews explained: 'At first the men had high expectations of the land they had been taught at home and in school to love. But reality, and the mischances of life, changed many of their views'.[114]

CHAPTER SIX

'Not only Germany's war; it's Rome's war too'

Conscription

On 29–30 March 1916, months before the Somme offensive and with recruiting still running strong as the Australian units reinforced and trained in Egypt, a special Recruiting Train visited northern Yorke Peninsula. Among its passengers was none other than the State Premier of South Australia, Hon. Crawford Vaughan, come to make his plea in person for all eligible males to join up. He was accompanied by Corporal Evans, a veteran of Gallipoli, who, speaking of his own experiences, would cajole the local boys into volunteering – or so it was planned. The train arrived at Wallaroo Mines railway station, outside Kadina, at 9.40 in the morning, with a brass band playing and Boy Scouts forming a guard of honour. The Wallaroo and Moonta Mining and Smelting Company, smarting still, perhaps, from its pre-war association with the German military-industrial complex, had made it clear that it would not frustrate the ambitions of those who wished to volunteer, a fact that H. Lipson Hancock – the general manager – had signalled by his presence at farewell socials. Indeed, employees in the mines and at the smelting works were given time off to attend the Recruiting Train, and to listen to the speeches.[1]

'It's no use, Mr Premier … I can't shift them'

Corporal Evans addressed the assembled mine workers, encouraging them to step forward. But nobody moved. He redoubled his exhortation, and still no-one budged. Expressing his disappointment, Evans confessed himself more surprised by this lack of response than he had been by the Turkish reception at the landing at Gallipoli. And he had a warning for the miners. 'Don't you think it is better to go now, voluntarily', he asked, 'than have a sergeant calling for you with a squad of fixed bayonets?' Would it not be more honourable to enlist as a volunteer, he implied, than to wait until Conscription was introduced, with its inevitable coercion into the armed forces of the reluctant

39.   Corporal Evans, the Gallipoli veteran, and the State Premier – the Hon. Crawford Vaughan – share the rostrum during the visit of the Recruiting Train to Wallaroo Mines on 30 March 1916.

and the cowardly? Exasperated, Corporal Evans turned to Crawford Vaughan. 'It's no use, Mr Premier', he cried, 'I can't shift them!' In the end, a paltry handful of men was recruited during the two-day visit to northern Yorke Peninsula: four at Kadina, two each at Wallaroo and Moonta, four at the small agricultural settlement of Paskeville, ten at outlying Port Wakefield, and none at all at Wallaroo Mines.[2]

However, as Keith Bailey has argued, this reluctance was hardly a measure of the miners' patriotic sentiment. Together, they had already contributed some £12,000 to the various voluntary organisations supporting the troops, along with another £13,000 to the government's War Loan Fund. They had also supported fund-raising activities, such as a Miners' Carnival at Kadina, and had held a charity 'hammer and tap' competition at Kadina showground in which 'pares' (groups) of miners competed against each other to see who could drill six inches into a hard-rock slab in the time allotted. In the evening, the competitors had enjoyed a pasty supper and a lantern slide show of Dolcoath mine in Cornwall.[3]

Instead, the miners' apparent reluctance to enlist during the Recruiting Train visit was the result of a complex interplay of attitudes and emotions. As the scale of the slaughter on the Somme became clear by the autumn of 1916, there was an understandable waning in enthusiasm to enlist. But the

Recruiting Train incident was earlier in the year, before the disillusion and uncertainty of late 1916, when recruitment generally had held steady. Like the mine management, the miners knew that they were making good the damage done to the Allied cause by the supply of Peninsula copper to Germany before the war. But more than that, they understood that now they were making a significant contribution to the Empire's war effort, much of their output going directly to assist munitions production in England. Their employment in the mines and in the smelting works, therefore, was war work as significant – perhaps even more significant, given their own specialist skills and the strategic importance of copper – as that of the soldiers in the trenches. When there had been a call for skilled miners to join-up to engage in tunnelling operations, first at Gallipoli and later on the Western Front, Moonta and Wallaroo men had come forward. But otherwise they were inclined to see their place of duty as the mines themselves. Indeed, there was a tacit understanding between the miners' trade union and the mining company, in which they would work together to maximise output. In this way, industrial dispute was kept to a minimum while the mines were able to press ahead with their developmental work. To be sure, the mine workers benefited from the arrangement – high wages and secure employment – but there could be no sense that this was a cushy number, for the mines remained dangerous places

40.   Patriotic carnival at Kadina in 1916, held to boost the fund-raising efforts of homefront organisations supporting Australian soldiers overseas.

41.   War work – miners deep underground on northern Yorke Peninsula, c.1916.

42.   War work – toiling in the heat of the smelting works at Wallaroo.

in which to work. Only recently, for example, the Barnes brothers – Victor and William – had been killed in separate incidents in Taylor's shaft at the Wallaroo mine, while Edward Phillips had been fatally injured in an accident in nearby Young's shaft.[4]

As Corporal Evans was aware, there was also now vigorous grassroots debate about the possibility of Conscription, of the voluntary principle being abandoned in favour of the compulsory enlistment of eligible males. Despite massive levels of volunteer recruitment, Conscription had been introduced in Britain on 25 January 1916 to meet the insatiable demands for manpower, and, inevitably, there was discussion about whether Australia should follow suit. As trade unionists and social democrats, the mineworkers were intrinsically opposed to governmental coercion of any sort, and instinctively suspicious of any move to undermine voluntarism. The Recruitment Train, then, with none other than the Premier embarked, looked uncomfortably like a step in the direction of coercion. This, perhaps more than anything, explained the mood of those who listened to Corporal Evans, the Premier's mouthpiece, and it was a portent of things to come.

'Betterment Principle' and 'Rainbow System'

W.M. 'Billy' Hughes, the London-born Welshman, had become Labor Prime Minister of Australia in October 1915. Although the Labor Party, like the Moonta and Wallaroo mineworkers, was ideologically suspicious of coercion and thus of Conscription as a device, Hughes himself was an early convert to the view that voluntary recruitment alone would not be enough to meet Australia's military manpower requirements. He had left Australia for London on 15 January 1916, ten days before the introduction of Conscription in Britain, and did not return home until more than six months later. During his time away, Hughes had liaised with the British government and attempted to influence Imperial policy, in the process becoming convinced that Conscription was as necessary for Australia as it had been for Britain (and indeed New Zealand), not least to demonstrate unswerving commitment to the Imperial cause. In Australia, meanwhile, an emergency meeting of prominent inter-State trade unionists had declared 'its undying hostility to conscription of life and labour'.[5] Fear of coercion was by no means confined to the Moonta and Wallaroo miners, and reflected the opinions of workers and grass-roots Labor members and supporters across the country.

News of the exploits at Gallipoli had boosted recruitment in Australia but the Somme had had opposite effect. Enlistment in May 1916 was 10,656 but had dropped to about 6,000 a month during June, July and August, a reflection of 'war weariness', perhaps, and evidence that the reservoir of eligible males was already decreasing. On 30 August 1916, Hughes announced the forthcoming

Referendum, claiming in Parliament that no fewer than 32,500 new recruits were required in September, with a further 16,500 per month thereafter.[6] The Referendum announcement unleashed a torrent of vituperative accusation and counter-accusation across Australia, as cracks in society appeared suddenly in areas that only months before had appeared to reflect cosy consensus or at least tacit understanding and co-operation. Ostensibly cohesive communities were now rent asunder as the argument raged.

On northern Yorke Peninsula the mine company had endeavoured to perpetuate a sense of community solidarity. H. Lipson Hancock, as general manager, had put the mines and smelters on a war footing, and had courted the trade unionists through favourable conditions of employment. Part of this was the so-called 'Betterment Principle', which Hancock had developed in the years after 1912, and which he described in a pamphlet published on the eve of war in 1914.[7] Derived from the company's existing welfare policies, and based in turn on the old Cornish-style 'Club & Doctor' fund established at the mines in their early days, the Betterment Principle was an attempt to codify, modernise and extend welfare provision. It was developed apace during the war years, culminating in an explanatory article 'Welfare Work in the Mining Industry' by Hancock in October 1918, and in an extensive report in the *South Australian Department of Mines Mining Review* for the half-year ended June 1919.[8] The latter noted that 65.59 per cent of the workforce had been employed for a decade or more – a measure of the Wallaroo and Moonta company's success in retaining its labour – and commended the general air of 'tidiness, space, and light' at it plants. At the Wallaroo smelting works, the report noted approvingly, there were baths and changing-houses, and at Wallaroo Mines the company had provided for community use a pavilion, croquet lawns, a hockey pitch, and a bowling green with twelve rinks and 'a good club house'.[9] There was similar provision at Moonta Mines, including a billiards room, recreation hall, rotunda, tennis courts, and children's playgrounds. There was also the company's Club and Medical Fund (as it was now called), to which, for example, married men contributed 1*s.* per week to the Medical Fund and 6*d.* to the Club, while boys earning less than 5*s.* per contributed 3*d.* to both the Medical Fund and the Club. An adult employee unable to attend work through illness could claim 20*s.* per week for up to six months, and 10*s.* per week for a further six months thereafter.

The Betterment Principle mirrored the mutual improvement ethos that underpinned Methodism on northern Yorke Peninsula – yet another aspect of the region's Cornish inheritance – and drew upon an existing sense of community solidarity. H. Lipson Hancock, a staunch Methodist himself, was genuinely committed to mutual improvement but also recognised its importance as a device for perpetuating community cohesion during the war years. In the same way, he sought to deploy religious observance

43. The Methodist 'Rainbow System' in full swing at Moonta Mines as the children of the Beginners' Department enjoy their tea-treat.

as a similar device, mobilising northern Yorke Peninsula's overwhelming Methodist identity as an agent of cohesion and solidarity. Specifically, on becoming Superintendent of the Moonta Mines Methodist Sunday School in 1905, Hancock had determined to revolutionise religious instruction by importing the 'Rainbow System' of Sunday school education developed at the Marion Lawrence School at Toledo, Ohio, in America.[10] In the years before and during the Great War, he strove to make Moonta Mines a model of best practice to be emulated throughout the region and beyond. Indeed, by 1918 no fewer than 7,000 visitors had been welcomed to the Sunday School to view its *modus operandi*, and by that time the 'Rainbow System' had been adopted at other Sunday schools across the Peninsula – at Yelta, Agery, Paskeville, Greens Plains West, and Wallaroo Mines.[11]

The 'Rainbow System' was authoritarian and highly structured, its methodical approach and inherent discipline no doubt attractive to Methodist practitioners during the war years. At Moonta Mines the Sunday school was divided into ten Grades or Departments, ranging from the 'Cradle Roll', for children from infancy to three years, to the 'Home Grade' for those too old or infirm to attend the School itself. Although the emphasis was naturally on the children – there were the Beginners, Kindergarten, Primary, Junior,

Advanced Junior, and Intermediate Grades – there was also a 'Senior Grade' for those from 16 to 23 years old, and an 'Adult Grade' for people aged 23 and upwards.[12] In this way, the Rainbow System was able to reach out and touch the lives of people throughout the community. There were no fewer than twenty-two different committees to administer the system – the 'Prayer and Visitation Committee', the 'Statistical Department Committee', the 'Mothers' Meeting Committee', and so on – while the Rainbow course of instruction itself consisted of a rigorous and unvarying syllabus, commencing with 'Lesson 1: The Bible and how we got it' and culminating in 'Lesson 100: The Call of China'.[13] As H. Lipson Hancock explained in 1919, to ensure the highest of standards it was imperative that every teacher should have a firm grasp 'of the principles that underlie the statements of scripture', while being careful to 'Guard against teaching anything that will not bear the strictest examination'. Any error in instruction or deviation from orthodoxy, he warned, placed scholars 'in danger of moral shipwreck'.[14] Exemplary conduct was also expected of the scholars themselves. As one visitor observed: 'A large card suspended before the superintendent's [Hancock's] desk bore the legend "I am early". A minute or so prior to the opening of the service this was replaced by another bearing the words "I am only just in time"'. And finally, the visitor reported: 'When the service began, a third card appeared announcing "I am late" ... Among the mottoes on the walls, "Study to be quiet" was prominent'.[15] Rigid discipline was also observable in the opening formalities. As Hancock had stipulated in 1916:

> After the removal of hats and cloaks, under supervision, the different sections are formed into line, headed in each case by the leader of the day. The procession, to the accompaniment of music, passes through the Kindergarten room on its way to the main hall for the opening exercises, a junior teacher taking a place after every third scholar. One teacher or helper should be available, if possible, for every three scholars, but at least one for every four or five scholars.[16]

'the heart of a sheep ... the face of a lion'

In this way, Methodism sought to exercise its institutional authority on northern Yorke Peninsula during the war years, providing moral certainty in difficult times. A further mechanism was the *Australian Christian Commonwealth*, a weekly Methodist magazine published in Adelaide but popular on northern Yorke Peninsula where it enjoyed a high circulation (John Verran was among its many subscribers). Its editor during the war, apart from a spell in 1915–16 when he was President of the Methodist Conference in South Australia, was the Revd Octavius Lake. A Welshman, he had been a Bible Christian minister before Methodist union in 1900, and had been active on northern Yorke Peninsula where he claimed affinity and common cause with the Cornish miners and Welsh smelters and their families. He had worked closely with the miners' trade union, for example, in tackling poverty on the Moonta and Wallaroo Mines settlements, in 1877 meeting with the local Relieving Officer for Yorke Peninsula and complaining that the poor laws were 'receiving a most harsh and illiberal interpretation'.[17] Lake was also the spouse of Serena Thorne, the celebrated half-Cornish, half-Devonian, 'girl preacher of North Devon' who had been sent by the Bible Christian Conference to Queensland in 1865, from there making her way to Victoria and then South Australia. She married Lake in 1871, joining him on northern Yorke Peninsula, and died in 1902.[18]

In 1914, on the outbreak of war, Octavius Lake was already seventy-three years old, and had been a widower for more than a decade. He was an elderly man of firm opinions, and was not afraid to voice them or to persuade others of their veracity, using his several leadership roles within the Methodist Church in South Australia to influence its attitudes and policies. From the beginning, the Methodist Church had been convinced that here was a 'just war', and as early as March 1915 the *Australian Christian Commonwealth* had suggested that Conscription might be necessary, indeed desirable.[19] It was an opinion that commended itself to Octavius Lake, who in December 1915 wrote to support 'the recruiting campaign . . . [for] men who are fit to go forth as soldiers in our nation's defence, and in defence of small nations like Belgium and Servia'.[20] It was also a view articulated by the columnist 'Thelma' – *nom-de-plume* of Louise Steadman – who in her weekly page for young women in the *Australian Christian Commonwealth* urged them to persuade their men friends to join up.[21] By April 1916 Methodist support for the recruiting campaign had hardened into a demand for Conscription, with the firm insistence that the slippery anti-Conscriptionist, seeking now to shirk his responsibilities, 'combines the heart of a sheep with the face of a lion. He mistakes the pleadings of his self-love for the protests of his conscience'.[22] Inevitably, when Hughes announced the Conscription Referendum, the Methodist Church in South Australia – and its voice-piece, the *Australian Christian Commonwealth* – threw its weight behind the 'Yes' campaign.

Octavius Lake took particular aim at the shirkers, composing an ironic 'Anti-Conscriptionist Song' designed to expose their selfishness, weakness and cowardice:

> We don't want to fight,
> But by jingo if we do,
> We'll stay at home and have our fun
> And send the brave Hindoo!

> We don't want to fight,
> Perhaps the Russians do:
> Then let us hire the poorer types
> For just the Russian screw.
>
> Or look to Africa,
> The lusty, large Zulu;
> Let him be trained to fight the Huns
> Instead of me and you.
>
> We're in an awful funk,
> Believe us, friends, 'tis true;
> Before this close conscription call
> We kept it out of view;
>
> But now unless the 'Nos' —
> The rash, red-raggers' crew —
> Can show them how to save their skins,
> What will the Slackers do?
>
> We do not want to fight,
> We are a peaceful crew;
> To races, pubs, and movey shows
> We'll stick, dear pals — like glue.[23]

In railing against 'races, pubs, and movey [*sic*] shows', Lake was wedding the Conscriptionist cause to a particular long-established Nonconformist hostility to betting, alcohol, and self-indulgence in general, characterising shirkers as moral reprobates. His late wife Serena, after all, had been an especially fierce advocate of total abstention and, as Arnold Hunt put it, 'a formidable opponent of the liquor industry'.[24] On northern Yorke Peninsula, Lake's attitude was echoed by other Nonconformist clergy, such as Revd David Morgan, pastor at the Lloyd Memorial Congregational Church at Wallaroo, who 'in strong terms denounced what he regarded as callousness and frivolity among the people'. He insisted that, instead of such slackness, they should strive to 'live worthily', and needed to raise their 'moral standard' if they were to honour and be deserving of the sacrifice made by young soldiers from the district.[25] For those families whose loved ones had been killed at the front, their everyday exposure to those shirkers with whom they existed cheek-by-jowl was irksome, especially as these shirkers continued to enjoy to the full the worldly pleasures now denied to fallen husbands, bothers, sons. As the *In Memoriam* notice for Fred Willard, the Yelta boy killed at Pozières, put it:

He was no coward or shirker,
   He fought for honour's sake;
He fought hard in muddy trenches
   For the pride of Britain's race,
And our darling now lies cold
   In a soldier's grave in France.[26]

Nonconformist hostility to Roman Catholicism also informed the Methodist stance on Conscription. As early as 1911, the *Australian Christian Commonwealth* had detected a malign Romish influence in John Verran's Labor government in South Australia, warning that 'efforts are being made to dominate the Labour Party by the Church of Rome'.[27] Now the dark hand of Rome was perceived in the anti-Conscriptionist movement, where Irish nationalists active in Australia were thought to be undermining the Imperial cause, and perhaps even siding with Germany. In the rising of Easter 1916 and its aftermath, Irish nationalism had achieved its revolutionary moment, shifting from a more or less polite request for Home Rule to an angry demand for complete independence, the United Kingdom state no longer legitimate in many Irish eyes. For an Empire already threatened by a war that was not going well, this was deeply unsettling. In Australia, with its large Irish-Catholic component in the population and in the workforce, especially in the eastern states of Victoria and New South Wales, where there was a strong Irish-Catholic influence in the Labor movement, there seemed a real risk of subversion and unrest. Octavius Lake warned that 'Sinn Feiners are out to establish "The Irish Republic"', although he also took care to ridicule 'the screaming farce of it', and enquired incredulously if anyone could 'imagine the Scotch or the Welsh embarked on such an enterprise'.[28] Later, warming to his theme, Lake asked rhetorically: 'Why do not the Welsh break into rebellion . . . Why are the Welsh so different from the Irish? They are both of Celtic origin'. The answer was simple, he explained: 'Mark the difference between Romanism and the Evangelical faith and then you will know'.[29]

'The fervour against conscription'

Such debate was designed to influence the homefront. On northern Yorke Peninsula, it was assumed by many observers, the strength of Methodism as the dominant religion would be reflected in widespread support for the 'Yes' vote in the coming Referendum. John Verran, the former Labor Premier, was a vocal advocate of Conscription, and in this as in other areas his religious convictions as a Methodist were closely allied to his ideological imperatives as a Labor politician (see pp. 82–3). Despite fears expressed in the *Australian Christian Commonwealth*, Verran's Labor government of 1910–12 had mirrored

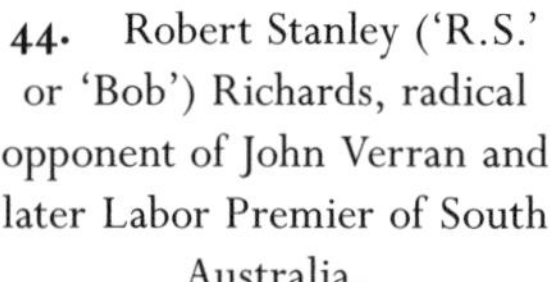

44. Robert Stanley ('R.S.' or 'Bob') Richards, radical opponent of John Verran and later Labor Premier of South Australia.

the strong connection between Methodism and the Labor movement that existed in South Australia.[30] Yet the criticism levelled at Verran's government – that, as in the eastern states, Roman Catholics were attempting to influence Labor policy – prefigured what would become in the years ahead a profound estrangement of Methodism from Labor: in South Australia in general, and on northern Yorke Peninsula in particular.

On Yorke Peninsula, as the Recruiting Train incident had demonstrated, there was already a growing reluctance among the miners and smelters to volunteer for enlistment, an attitude that had everything to do with politics and industrial relations, and almost nothing to do with religion. Moreover, there were now Methodist members of the Labor Party who were campaigning actively for a 'No' vote; not least Robert Stanley [R.S.] Richards, who as recently as April 1916 had shared the rostrum with the likes of Verran and Hancock at recruiting events on the Peninsula, but had now moved firmly into the anti-Conscriptionist camp. When Norman Makin, one of those Labor activists campaigning for a 'No' vote, visited northern Yorke Peninsula he was struck by the strength of local feeling, and could not fail to notice the paradox – an essentially Methodist people expressing widespread opposition to the Methodist Church's declared position on Conscription. Years later, at the grand age of ninety-two, Makin could still recall with some bemusement 'a meeting in the Kadina Town Hall where the fervour against conscription was so strong as to have the flavour of an old-fashioned [Methodist] revival meeting'.[31]

In the referendum on 20 October 1916, South Australia – like Australia as a whole – voted against Conscription: 119,236 (or 57.5 per cent) to 87,924. And, paradoxically, in that part of South Australia where Methodism was strongest, the mining country of northern Yorke Peninsula, the 'No' vote was among the highest recorded: 78 per cent in the Moonta subdivision, 75 per cent in Wallaroo, and 72 per cent in Kadina.[32] For those, like Norman Makin, who had had the opportunity to observe the Conscription controversy on the Peninsula at close quarters, the outcome came as no surprise. Despite the genuine deference afforded Methodist clergy and local preachers, and despite the pervasive cultural and moral influence that Methodism still exerted throughout the district, the strength of the 'No' vote at Moonta, Wallaroo and Kadina revealed the extent to which institutional Methodism had failed to mould local opinion on this critical issue.

This was deeply disappointing for John Verran and other Methodist leaders locally, who had expected the community – including the Labor Party and trade unionists – to be loyal to the Methodist call for Conscription. But the unpalatable reality was, as Arnold Hunt has put it, that 'the church's capacity to influence the thinking of its members on this issue was very limited, and in some areas (such as Moonta) was virtually non-existent'.[33] Moreover, the Labor movement was itself now split on the Conscription issue. Despite the historic and ideological links on northern Yorke Peninsula between Methodism and the United Labor Party, activists here as elsewhere were putting their religious affiliations to one side as they threw their weight behind Labor's increasing hostility to Conscription. For despite Billy Hughes' advocacy of Conscription, echoed in South Australia by the Labor Premier, Crawford Vaughan, Labor supporters were now generally in the anti-Conscriptionist camp.

John Verran may have been dismayed by the 1916 Referendum result on northern Yorke Peninsula. Positively outraged was Jack Scaddan, until recently Labor Premier of Western Australia. Born at Moonta in 1876, Scaddan was passionate about his birthplace, his occupational identity as a hard-rock miner, and his Cornish descent. In 1913, as Premier of Western Australia, he had paid a visit to Cornwall, where he told all who would listen that he was 'of Cornish stock', and that 'in Moonta, South Australia, where he was born, at least 80 percent of the population were Cornish or of Cornish descent'.[34] Proud as he was of being Labor Premier of Western Australia, he was even more proud of his status as a Kio boy, of being Moonta born and bred. He was also a Methodist. Like Billy Hughes, Crawford Vaughan, and John Verran, Jack Scaddan was one of those prominent Labor leaders who had embraced Conscription as a cause, only to find himself hopelessly out of step with the majority of his Party members. He was disappointed by the Referendum results in Australia as a whole, but it was the 'big adverse vote in the Peninsula mining towns' (as the *People's Weekly* put it) that really hurt.[35] Shocked by this betrayal, as he saw it, he launched upon the 'peaceful town of Moonta' what the *Yorkes's Peninsula Advertiser* called 'an unpleasant surprise', sending a telegram to Crawford Vaughan in which he denounced the Peninsula vote. 'I desire officially to notify you', he said, that 'from today I renounce South Australia as my mother State unless Moonta proves to be of true metal'.[36] The formal estrangement remained in place from October 1916 until May 1917 when Scaddan, approving of the outcome in the Federal general election, cabled Crawford Vaughan: 'You may now officially re-enter my acknowledgement of South Australia as my mother State'.[37] Moonta and environs had appeared genuinely taken aback by the strength of Scaddan's attack, but it was a foretaste of what was still to come as well as a measure of Scaddan's rage.

'There will be a big rumpus before it is settled'

For soldiers serving overseas, far removed from the complexity of the domestic debate, there was often puzzlement about the way in which the Conscription campaign had been conducted at home. Individual servicemen varied in their attitude. Some thought that shirkers would be a liability in uniform, others that no-one should be coerced against their will to experience the horrors of the battlefield, and still others that – if the war was to be won – Conscription had now become a necessary evil. Signaller Lance Corporal Leonard Harvey, a Kio boy at Larkhill Camp in England, fell into the latter category. He wrote to his father, W.H. Harvey (a pro-Conscriptionist Labor member of the South Australian Parliament) in August 1916, less than two months before the Referendum, opining that 'going by the paper this morning, conscription seems inevitable in Australia'.[38] Two weeks later Len Harvey reported breezily that: 'We read a lot about Billy Hughes and his [Conscription] policy in the English papers. To all accounts the English think him possible of doing anything'.[39] Less than a month later, however, it appeared that Hughes was not the infallible Welsh wizard after all, and that not only might Conscription fail in Australia but that Labor could be brought down with it. 'Dad', wrote Len Harvey in worried tones after he had heard that the Labor movement in New South Wales had decided to champion the 'No' vote, 'what do you think of the Labour Party in N.S. Wales in connection with Hughes?'. With prescient insight, Len added that '[I] Expect there will be a big split in the Labour movement' across Australia, adding with a palpable sense of frustration that 'Things in that line are not much discussed in the camps'.[40]

But even if the political implications of Labor Party manoeuvring were lost on Len Harvey's fellow soldiers, there was a distinct attitude towards

Conscription emerging in the training camps in England which, according to Harvey, contrasted sharply with that held by the men fighting in the trenches. As he wrote to his father in early November 1916, after the Referendum outcome was known:

> Up to date we have not heard the results of the votes given by the men over there [the Western Front]. However it is rumoured that they voted, strongly, NO. Their reason is that they have seen the firing line, and do not wish their comrades to go through the ordeal. That is not the way we [in camp in England] look at it, we must have every man, not to make new divisions, but to reinforce those at present fighting.[41]

By early December, Len Harvey was himself '"In Billetts" somewhere in France'. But his opinions had not changed. 'According to letters and papers received', he explained to his father, 'the majority of the Moonta population are against conscription. This was shown by one of the meetings J[ohn] V[erran] had there'. He added, caustically: 'I think a few of them must be afraid they will have to come'.[42] Inevitably, the post-Referendum recriminations rumbled on, gaining in intensity, and in January 1917 Harvey reported to his father that 'I have just read the piece in the [Adelaide] Advertiser [newspaper] on the Labor split. Seems as though there will be a big rumpus before it is settled'.[43]

Again, Len Harvey was more right than he could have known. In the aftermath of the Referendum result, Billy Hughes had resigned from the Labor Party, taking four Federal ministers and twenty-six other Federal Labor MPs with him to form a new National Labor Party. In the several States, pro-Conscriptionists followed suit. Len Harvey's father, W.H. Harvey, was one of those in South Australia who went across to the new party, as did John Verran and Crawford Vaughan, and Jack Scaddan in Western Australia. At Moonta, Verran announced the formation of a local branch of the National Labor Party, a direct challenge to the recently formed Moonta Anti-Conscriptionist League, an indication that the solidarity and consensus that H. Lipson Hancock and others had worked so hard to maintain was at last breaking down.[44] At the Federal level, the National Labor Party, with Hughes at the helm, had clung onto power with the backing of the Liberal Party. In February 1917 the two parties merged formally to form the Nationalist Party, with Hughes continuing as Prime Minister, and – with the Labor rump discredited and in disarray – the Nationalists were swept into office in the Federal general election of May 1917. Thereafter, as Dean Jaensch has argued, within the Labor Party 'most of the Protestant influence resigned, leaving the Irish Catholic component with a controlling vote. The party moved to the Left in rhetoric, ideology and policy'.[45]

In South Australia there was also a noticeable move to the left within the Labor Party, exemplified in the increasingly fiery rhetoric of Robert Stanley Richards on northern Yorke Peninsula, but in religious complexion it remained Methodist rather than Roman Catholic – an identity that it would retain after the Great War, and indeed until as late as the 1940s.[46] In the estimation of the Methodist Church, however, all its worst fears had been confirmed by recent events within the Labor movement. Indeed, when the newly elected Nationalist government announced a second Referendum, believing erroneously that victory in the election would translate seamlessly to a 'Yes' vote for Conscription, South Australia's Methodist establishment observed with alarm what it saw as a renewal of the 'Fenian' and 'Popish' undermining of Australia's resolve.

'The venomous snakes of treason'

In the run up to the second Referendum, held on 20 December 1917, all the rhetoric of the previous year was dusted off and deployed once more, in yet more vociferous terms. As Octavius Lake thundered in the pages of the *Australian Christian Commonwealth*, among the many foes confronted by the Empire was the enemy within. 'The venomous snakes of treason lift their heads in many parts of our wide-flung dominion', he insisted, 'but their warmest, most crowded nests are in Ireland and Australia'. It was a theme that Lake would make his own – 'This is not only Germany's war; it is Rome's war also' – he could still exclaim as late as July 1918. But during the 1917 Conscription campaign his particular target was the Irishman Dr Daniel Mannix, who had become Roman Catholic Archbishop of Melbourne in May 1917. Seen by detractors and supporters alike as sympathetic to Sinn Fein, Mannix opposed Conscription, encouraging the Labor Party in its anti-Conscriptionist stance, and seemed cool towards the Empire's cause, only reluctantly condemning German aggression. Mannix also demanded the unswerving respect of Victoria's Catholic population. For the next four decades he would take the salute at the annual St Patrick's Day parade in Melbourne. As Geoffrey Blainey has remarked, Mannix positioned himself at the top of Bourke Street for the march-past 'as if he was the Pope. To a quarter of Victoria he was'.[47]

Across the border in South Australia, Mannix's authority and influence in neighbouring Victoria appeared deeply alarming to the likes of Octavius Lake. He offered his readers clear advice:

> Speak plain at the next Referendum
>   Reply by a thunderous 'Yes!'
> And show Dr Mannix' Sinn Feiners
>   They cannot – yet – answer for us.

> Show those who would hoodwink the workers,
> The manifold pro-German crew,
> That tricks for betraying the soldiers
> Have no inch or quarter with you.[48]

On northern Yorke Peninsula, as in the first Referendum campaign, such rhetoric had only limited impact. Insofar as it had any appeal, it was to the older generation, especially those born in Cornwall, such as John Verran, who strove to preserve the Methodist influence in local politics. The younger generation, more susceptible to an emerging Australian nationalism, and more sensitive to Australian perspectives and Australian agendas, was resistant to institutional Methodism's pro-Conscriptionist stance, and attracted instead by the increasingly militant language of the Labor left. R.S. Richards emerged as champion of this younger generation, and its demand for a more radical politics. Born at Moonta Mines in 1885, Richards was the son of two Cornish emigrants, Richard Richards from Camborne and Mary Jeffery from neighbouring Tuckingmill. Noticeably to the left of Verran and the earlier generation of mineworkers, Richards exercised a ready appeal for the likeminded second generation raised on the Peninsula. There was, for example, Stanley Whitford, born at Moonta in 1878. He was proud to be counted among 'Cousin Jacks from Moonta',[49] he said, and likewise proud to be a Methodist. And yet, as he explained, in the Great War he was 'opposed to conscription because it violated my ideals as a follower of the International Socialist movement'. This was certainly the language of the left. It was also an opinion that placed him at odds with John Verran, who had detected the malevolent influence of the 'the Wobblies' – the International Workers of the World – in the anti-Conscriptionist camp and was the sworn enemy of the 'International Socialist movement'. It was a disagreement that was about to become deeply personal, Whitford condemning Verran as 'robust, good looking, good voiced, but ignorant ... [one] in whom I had no trust ... I placed him among my list of damned old humbugs, and he never reinstated himself in my estimation'.[50]

At the Federal level, Billy Hughes had the task of holding together the new party (in reality still a coalition of disparate interests) and government, and did so by perpetuating the atmosphere of crisis and confrontation. Against the background of increasing numbers of strikes and industrial conflict (sometimes violent) across the country, Hughes took on the trade unions and declared the International Workers of the World illegal, imprisoning over a hundred 'Wobblies' and deporting others.[51] Inevitably, some of this rubbed off on northern Yorke Peninsula, where the old consensus and solidarity had already been dented by the anti-Conscription result of 1916 and the consequent split in the Labor Party locally. The industrial harmony so apparent in the mines after the resumption of production in late 1914 was now a thing of the past, as the mineworkers – increasingly suspicious of vast profits and fat dividends paid to shareholders – sought to construct new patterns of solidarity, this time with other workers beyond the confines of the Peninsula, in opposing the coercive measures of Hughes' government.

To begin with, there was a demand for higher remuneration, led by the Moonta men who had become increasingly dissatisfied with their terms and conditions. In part, this was due to the shift in resources from the Moonta mine to the Wallaroo that had become apparent in recent years, much of the developmental work having been concentrated at the latter. Long accustomed to their presumed superiority over the Wallaroo mineworkers – Moonta had been the more important of the two workings for decades – the Moonta miners felt increasingly marginalised, a sentiment exacerbated when some of their number were required to move across to the Wallaroo mine, where they were accommodated in batching quarters (a boarding house) constructed near Harvey's shaft.[52] The Wallaroo and Moonta company resorted to 'divide and rule', wooing the Wallaroo men and isolating their Moonta counterparts, but the real industrial cleavage in the community that emerged during 1917 was over the proposed merger of the Amalgamated Miners' Association with the Australian Workers' Union (AWU). The younger mineworkers, including R.S. Richards, supported the merger, arguing that it would strengthen the trade union movement across Australia, but the older generation – including John Verran – opposed the proposal and feared that 'We will lose control of industrial matters locally'.[53]

The merger went ahead, with R.S. Richards becoming President of the Moonta branch of the AWU at its foundation. John Verran reacted with characteristic anger, forming an alternative trade union structure, officially the Yorke's Peninsula Miners and Smelters' Association, but known to its opponents locally as the 'Bogus' union. Against the background of the already acrimonious split caused by the Conscription dispute, this new fissure brought recrimination and accusation to even greater heights. The Wallaroo and Moonta company was rumoured to be victimising the militants who had precipitated the AWU merger, while the 'Bogies' (members of Verran's alternative Bogus union) were in turn victimised by the AWU men and ostracised by elements of the local community. Verran, allegedly in cahoots with Hancock and the company, was attacked bitterly for causing so 'much distress in many homes in this district'.[54] But Verran, unrepentant, sneered in reply that the AWU was 'led by Pommies who came out from England to escape conscription'.[55] In this way, the contest locally between the AWU and the Bogies became part of the wider split in the Labor movement over Conscription. Not only had the regional solidarity and cohesion constructed at the outbreak of war broken down, but many of the mineworkers had redefined

45. Trade unionists of the Amalgamated Miners of Australia in the Labor Day
parade at Moonta in 1914.

their sense of occupational identity, less inclined to root it locally and more
willing to claim common cause with workers across Australia.

'Things seem a bit mixed at Kio'

A new mood of industrial militancy became noticeable on the Peninsula,
mirroring the unrest apparent elsewhere in Australia. The Wallaroo and
Moonta company refused to meet AWU representatives to discuss grievances,
and a lengthy nationwide coal strike caused uncertainty at the mines and
smelters as stocks dwindled. When the strike ended, the shortage of coal was
perpetuated by the Seamen's Union, which refused to ship coal supplies. When,
eventually, a vessel laden with coal did arrive at Wallaroo in October 1917, the
local 'wharfies' refused to touch it. Hancock aggravated the confrontational
atmosphere by announcing that operations at the mines would be suspended
forthwith, and it was only with difficulty that the waterside workers were at
last persuaded to unload the precious cargo.[56] Yet, despite these operational
difficulties, the Wallaroo and Moonta company remained hugely profitable.
Turnover was down on the record year of 1916, but production was up, and
annual profits for 1917 stood at £126,736, with a healthy £80,000 paid in
dividends – as the AWU no doubt noted.[57]

The local newspapers, hitherto mechanisms of community solidarity,
found themselves reporting this strife. Moreover, after the announcement in

46.   The jetty at Wallaroo, where in October 1917 'wharfies' refused to unload coal
destined for the mines and smelters.

October 1917 of the impending second Referendum, they became vehicles
for the increasingly bitter debate over Conscription, conducted now with
renewed intensity. Letters, commentaries and advertisements appeared in
the regional press, putting the arguments 'for' and 'against' in often lurid
terms. John Verran had sought to regain the moral high ground for the new
Nationalist Party. 'The civilised world is engaged in the greatest struggle of
all the ages, fighting for Liberty and Democracy against Military Despotism',
explained an advertisement in the *Yorke's Peninsula Advertiser*. Readers were
exhorted to remember the sacrifice made 'by our own brave soldiers – the
men of Gallipoli and Pozières. Remember that the interests of the Empire and
Australia are one. The National[ist] Party stands for Empire, for a decisive
victory'.[58]

Likewise, there was a report in the *Yorke Peninsula Advertiser* on the recent
visit to Moonta Mines and Broken Hill (the latter across the border in New
South Wales, but with numerous links with northern Yorke Peninsula) by the
South Australian State Recruiting Committee. Both localities, it was alleged
censoriously, 'contain a much larger percentage of eligibles than the average
throughout the State'. Moreover, in both areas, 'especially Broken Hill', there
was 'an opposition to recruiting which is political'. Indeed, at Broken Hill 'a
great many persons . . . would not stand during the singing of the National
Anthem'.[59]

In the run up to the December 1917 Referendum, the debate intensified still further. 'A "Yes" vote [for Conscription] on December 20 is for your Empire', claimed one newspaper advertisement, 'A "No" vote is for Germany: your enemy'.[60]

Likewise, it was insisted that those supporting the 'No' vote were:

men who are playing Germany's game in our midst, Sinn Feiners, members of the I.W.W., syndicalists, men of the type responsible for the [coal] strike which paralysed Australia's industries, men responsible for the rebellion in Ireland, the kind of men who, to-day, are in Russia and are offering Germany a separate peace.[61]

There was also the familiar moral persuasion: 'If you turn down the Government's proposal, you not only prove yourself unworthy of freedom, but literally condemn to death the men who are fighting for YOU'.[62] But there was a yet subtler attempt to turn the 'No' voters' argument on its head. 'Electors of Wallaroo, Kadina, and Moonta', exclaimed one pro-Conscriptionist advertisement: 'You are doing Great War Work. Your mines are helping to provide munitions of war'. However, it was explained, 'munitions are useless without men to use them'. But this was not, it was added hastily, an argument for Peninsula men to enlist; far from it: 'Yours is a necessary industry. It must be protected. Your produce is essential. Labor will be exempted to carry on'. Rather, here was an insistence that Conscription was necessary if full use was to be made of the Peninsula's copper output, but with local miners and smelters exempted as reserved occupations: 'Vote YES'.[63]

It was an ingenious argument. But it cut little ice with the committed anti-Conscriptionists, and in any case it was not only the mineworkers who had argued that their work was essential to the war effort. Local farmers had increasingly articulated a similar viewpoint, and there was real fear that Conscription would rob the region of vital agricultural labour. As one newspaper advertisement asked rhetorically: 'One Conscript Equals Five Tons of Wheat. Which Will We Send?'. Or, put another way: 'To equip a transport carrying troops from Australia to Europe means sacrificing tons of dead-weight cargo space for each man carried'. The message, of course, was that support for the anti-Conscriptionist cause was neither unpatriotic nor anti- Empire but embraced the optimum use of Australia's resources to assist the war effort: 'Keep Australia Free. Send Foodstuffs to the Allies. Vote "No"'. Australia did indeed vote 'No', as did northern Yorke Peninsula. The result, predictably, perpetuated local antagonisms, and in the elections to the South Australian State parliament in April 1918 there was something of a sensation when John Verran was defeated in the Wallaroo constituency by R.S. Richards. It marked the ascendancy on the Peninsula of the anti-Conscriptionists, the AWU, and the anti-Hughes Labor Party.

Out of office for the first time since 1901, and with his local power base in tatters, Verran attempted to revive his flagging fortunes by returning to the German question. Early in the war he had urged that Germany be crushed, so that Europe could be cleaned up, 'just as the Cornish people like their general cleaning up at Christmas'. In Parliament in 1916 and 1917 he had introduced Bills designed to disenfranchise South Australia's sizeable German community (both failed narrowly to make their way onto the statute book), with additional proposals to close German schools in the State and to remove 'German JPs'.[64] As he had explained to Parliament: 'It is deplorable to allow those with German blood in their veins to vote in this country. No matter what they cry out, they must have a bias for Germany. I am a Britisher and a Cornishman, and no one can take away my feelings of loyalty to my country'.[65] Now out of Parliament, Verran redoubled his anti-German efforts, finding loyal support in the *Australian Christian Commonwealth* which, in marked contrast to its tolerant attitude to German settlers early in the war, had decided now that every 'German and Austrian among us that from the very first has not given full proof of loyalty should be regarded with vehement distrust'.[66] As Octavius Lake explained in April 1918, it was not merely that the German people had been deceived and 'blindly led by their princes and professors'. Rather, there was something intrinsically evil in the German make-up: 'We are up against all that is ambitious and domineering and treacherous and brutal ... a conspiracy against liberty and justice and human brotherhood'.[67] It was a prejudice that won Verran some friends on the Peninsula: 'Who but a Hun would not say that Mr Verran is one of the most popular legislators of the State',[68] inquired one correspondent to the *People's Weekly*. And it was an opinion to which Verran would return after the war, with some success, but the reality was that after his electoral defeat in April 1918 his political career was all but over.

As before, the fast moving political scene – on the Peninsula, and in Australia as a whole – could be bewildering for those soldiers observing it from afar. Len Harvey, writing to his father from 'France' in March 1917, thought it 'a pity that the political issue in Australia is in such an uproarious condition'. He admitted that 'I don't know what to think of this matter', and wondered if 'it points that Australia has had enough of war and wouldn't mind pulling out'.[69] A month later, Harvey was 'In Belgium', predicting that recruitment would remain difficult on the Peninsula for the foreseeable future: 'It will take a lot to move some the young fellows [in the mines], especially if there has been a good year and wages are good'. He was also dismayed to hear about the demands for higher remuneration: 'Fancy the fellows putting such requests to the Coy. I think they are making a big mistake, especially as everything is at so critical a period'.[70] 'In the Trenches' at the end of April, Harvey observed that 'Things seem a bit mixed at Kio', especially the news that R.S. Richards had broken ranks with John Verran, and was now the leader of the radical left on the Peninsula. 'Didn't expect that of Bob R.', he exclaimed, 'fancy he would get a bit of a knock if he stood [for Parliament] against JV'.[71] It was an issue to which he returned later in the year, writing home from the 2nd Army Signal School in France in October 1917. 'Things must be a little mixed in Moonta', he said again: 'Fancy Bob Richards opposing J. Verran, probably he is after something higher. I should guess he would not have much of a chance to defeat John'.[72]

As the second Referendum approached, Harvey wrote from 'Froggie Land' in November 1917. 'The state of affairs all over Australia at the present time is shocking', he insisted: 'The men that are out on strike don't realise how much they are assisting the Hun . . . especially [the] coal miners and men connected with iron works'. Closer to home, the 'fellows at Wallaroo must be a queer lot', he opined, commenting on the waterside workers' reluctance to unload coal for the mines and smelters: 'expect they are just sympathising with the strikes in other states'. Nonetheless, he thought that common sense would prevail. 'I think eventually the conscription issue will be carried in Australia', he wrote to his father, 'it is quite time the people realised the dire necessity of combining all their efforts to bring about the crushing defeat of Prussianism'.[73] In the trenches, he explained, 'the arguments as a rule get very heated'. But 'I tell them if I had 20 votes they would all go for conscription'. And yet, he recognised that there was another side to the argument, held by many soldiers at the front: 'Another party tells you if he was silly enough to enlist he isn't going to vote to bring another more sensible man'.[74]

By early 1918, however, Len Harvey was expressing exasperation with the turn of events back home – not only the rejection once more of Conscription but also the new militancy at the Yorke Peninsula mines consequent upon the AWU merger. 'What has gone wrong with the peaceful Moonta miners?' he inquired rhetorically: 'The affairs of the union have taken a big turn in the last two years. I can't quite understand Bob Richards . . . I should judge Robert is out to gain a seat in Parliament . . . Mr Verran must be heartily sick of them all from that part'.[75] In low spirits, or at least in sombre mood, Harvey tried to respond to his father's inquiry about the strength of the 'No' vote among the soldiers at the front. 'Dad!' he wrote:

I would like to give you a satisfactory answer to your question re. the reason for so many soldiers voting No, but I'm afraid I can't. A large number, when questioned, said it was immaterial to them which side won, and it wasn't for them to vote yes to bring another man into the war. Others reckoned they were out to crush militarism, and that by voting yes they would be helping to bring militarism to Australia.[76]

Disappointed by the Referendum result, especially on the Peninsula, where Moonta, Wallaroo and Kadina had again rejected Conscription, Len Harvey considered that: 'Perhaps some of the inhabitants of "Kio" will regret later on that they took such a stand as they are taking now'.[77] Equally, he was dismayed to learn the news that he had only recently thought unthinkable – that R.S. Richards had unseated John Verran in the South Australian Parliamentary elections. However, he did not believe that this result pointed to a permanent shift of political fortunes on the Peninsula, and said so. Writing to his mother from Weymouth, England, in June 1918, Harvey agreed that Verran's defeat would be only a temporary reversal, and that at the next election the proper order of things would be restored. 'Yes Mum I agree with you in your statement about Mr Verran', he said: 'I told some of the lads from Kio, that JV may have been beaten this year, but next elections he will give the other chaps a big drop'.[78]

After the war, John Verran did indeed attempt a comeback. He strove to regain the Methodist vote by embracing the anti-alcohol 'prohibitionist' cause, again with the support of the *Australian Christian Commonwealth*, the Great War (as Arnold Hunt has argued) having 'made Methodism a church of total abstainers – for at least a generation'.[79] However, as in the Referenda campaigns, voters on northern Yorke Peninsula were motivated by considerations other than religious affiliation, and John Verran failed to regain his Wallaroo seat in 1921. He likewise failed in 1924, when he contested Wallaroo as a Liberal, and as he drifted further to the political right, so he found himself ever further in the political wilderness. He enjoyed a brief spell in the Federal Senate, from 1927 to 1928, when he was appointed to fill a casual vacancy. But his political career had effectively ended in April 1918; he died in 1932. R.S. Richards, by contrast, continued to represent Wallaroo until his resignation in 1949, and during his long Parliamentary career achieved high office – including the Premiership of South Australia during 1933. Despite the fervent hopes to the contrary of Lance-Corporal Leonard Harvey, viewing events from half-a-world away, the political and industrial climate on northern Yorke Peninsula had changed irrevocably during the war, the threat of Conscription – and the coercion implicit within it – having exposed the conditional nature of regional solidarity. It was a new climate that would contribute dramatically to the further changes wrought in the local society and economy in the years after the Peace of 1919.

CHAPTER SEVEN

'Doing their best for the Empire'
Australia Triumphant

By 1917 and, especially, 1918 – the Year of Victory – the Australians had learned from the mistakes of bloody encounters such as Fromelles and Pozières, the costly élan of such actions replaced gradually by more subtle strategies, culminating (as we shall see) in the tactics of so-called 'peaceful penetration' in what, under Monash, would become effectively a semi-autonomous Australian Army. But it was a long and difficult journey, made via First and Second Bullecourt, Messines, and Third Ypres, and by the end of 1917 Australia's casualties on the Western Front had amounted to some 76,836 for that year – compared to 42,270 in 1916. Yet by the time the Australians played their part in stemming the rapid German advance in the spring of 1918, it was apparent that they had come to deserve their reputation as the shock troops of the British Empire. Increasingly, Monash's carefully planned all-arms actions complemented his soldiers' wealth of experience and tactical superiority, ensuring a prominent place for the Australians in the final Allied Victory later that year.

On northern Yorke Peninsula, as we have seen, the bitterness and divisions of the 1916 Conscription campaign were replicated with even greater animosity in the Referendum of 1917. Likewise, for many Peninsula soldiers on leave or recuperating in Britain, familiarity with Blighty– after initial enrapture – had often bred contempt, or at least disappointment. It was a disappointment conveyed sometimes in letters written home, and which on occasions surfaced in the regional press, surprising those who had not expected to read criticism of the seat of Empire but adding to the mood of uncertainty that had become apparent during 1916. Inevitably, these varying experiences and impressions coalesced to further shape an emergent Australian nationalism, often paradoxical in its attitude to Britain and Empire, and which fuelled heated debates in the Peninsula press over local political allegiances and trade union affiliation. Yet, in the community and in the press, there were those – for the usual multiplicity of reasons – who considered it imperative to keep faith with the region's soldiers at the front, and to gloss over the deep divisions that had become apparent with a new veneer of cohesion and solidarity.

'The jaws of death and the very mouth of hell'

Welcoming home a clutch of local boys in February 1918 – those repatriated as no longer fit for active service, through sickness, gassing or wounds – Moonta's new Mayor, Robert Learmond, emphasised that the community was united in its applause for the soldiers 'who had been away doing their best for the Empire'.[1] Others agreed. The soldiers' 'noble work on behalf of the Empire would never be forgotten by their friends here', it was insisted, while the whole region was humbled by the sombre knowledge that 'these broken and scarred warriors' had 'come back from the jaws of death and the very mouth of hell'.[2] Against the background of the deep divisions that had become apparent on the Peninsula during 1916 and 1917, the community solidarity implicit in local war work performed by women became even more important. Men might quarrel about politics or industrial matters. But, while they squabbled, their womenfolk were constant in their efforts in organisations such as the 'Moonta Mines Knitting and Trench Comforts League', continuing to provide much needed personal items for soldiers at the front while keeping up appearances at home, especially at farewells or homecomings where they provided sumptuous suppers and a welcoming female presence.[3] The 'Girls Knitting Class' at Moonta continued its good work too, as in August 1917 when it presented 'a parcel of woollen comforts' to a departing soldier, Lance-Corporal F.H. Robinson, with the 'Misses Jean Roach, Mollie Trathen, Dorrie Reed, and Laurel Pascoe' providing appropriate musical entertainment.[4]

Women on the whole were happy to play this role, at least on Yorke Peninsula – nurturers rather than warriors – but there were those who sought yet more active engagement, opportunities to apply their skills more directly to the war effort. In June 1917, for example, it was reported that Sister Elsie McMartin (Matron-in-charge) and Nurse Daisy Farrow, both of Wallaroo Hospital, had 'enlisted for active service, and will be leaving shortly'.[5] A week later, it was likewise reported that Nurse Mary Ferry from Moonta had become the town's 'first local lady to be accepted for active service at the front'.[6] In volunteering, these women exhibited a level of courage and commitment that could not fail to impress, but often Australian nurses found their deployments overseas deeply frustrating. They served in France, Belgium, Greece, Egypt, India and elsewhere, but were often poorly managed and poorly equipped with inadequate or inappropriate allocations of medical instruments and supplies. That Australian nurses –unlike their New Zealand

47.   Robert Learmond, local grocer and Mayor of Moonta, whose patriotic rhetoric attempted to heal the deep divisions in the community caused by the Conscription issue and the subsequent splits in the Labor movement.

and Canadian counterparts – held no military rank until 1916 contributed to their marginalisation, as did the lack of a formal command structure.[7]

In the case of these three Peninsula women, Elsie McMartin, who had trained at Wallaroo Hospital, was eventually prevented from serving with the Australian Imperial Force, on account of her 'lameness'. But she was accepted for civilian service in Western Australia in December 1918 when she 'Volunteered to nurse influenza', responding to the epidemic that was already reaching global proportions.[8] Daisy Farrow, meanwhile, 38 years old when she enlisted, was posted to India, where she served in military hospitals in Bombay and later Gharial (where she was promoted to Sister), returning to her native Wallaroo in January 1920 following demobilisation.[9] Mary Ferry, who had worked in the Children's Hospital in North Adelaide for three years before joining up, was 27 years of age when she volunteered, with 'clear complexion, blue eyes, fair hair'. Like other women joining the Army Nursing Service, Mary was required to declare that 'I will serve in accordance with the undermentioned terms with the Australian Imperial Force as a Nurse, and agree to obey all lawful commands whilst on active service'. She went first to Suez, and from there to Salonika, where in September 1918 she herself became a victim of the influenza that was sweeping the globe. Confined to hospital, she suffered 'disabling boils and debility', and was formally discharged from active service in the December and repatriated to Australia.[10]

War, it seemed, was equally as capable of dealing with women volunteers in unexpected and pitiless ways as it was in meting out random injury or sickness – or worse – to soldiers at the front. After their huge efforts on the Somme, Australian units had been posted for a time to 'quieter' sectors, 1 ANZAC finding itself relocated to the Ypres Salient in Belgium. It was from here, in November 1916, that Lance-Corporal Richard Daw, from Moonta, wrote to relatives to observe with some relief that 'it's a home here compared to Pozières', commenting on the relative lightness of the artillery and machine-gun exchanges compared to what he and others had endured on the Somme a few months before.[11]

Private Les Bishop, writing to his sister at Moonta on 10 September 1916, drew a similar contrast. Now in the relative calm of Ypres, where he was pleased to find that the 'Belgian people speak our language more fluently than the French', he was glad of the opportunity to reflect quietly on all that he had gone through at Pozières. 'I have been in the thick of the fight', he admitted, and the 'last time we went over was on my birthday' – 23 August 1916, the first day of the assault on Pozières. 'When the enemy spotted us coming', he wrote, 'I lay in a shell hole for fully four hours, with shells bursting all round'. Eventually, Bishop explained, 'things got fairly quiet', and he 'crawled over the rough, broken ground to see where the rest of the boys were'. He found one 'in an old German dug-out' and, pausing for a moment, remembered that the day was his birthday. Now, just a few weeks later at Ypres, Les Bishop relived the experience in his mind, going over again the details of that terrible battle. He recalled keenly that: 'While you are under shell fire it is not too bad, but after its is over there is a kind of reaction, and you feel yourself going, and it is then that you have to pull yourself together'. Such was the nature of shellshock, or post-traumatic stress disorder, as it was labelled much later. 'To a certain extent one gets used to the shells', added Bishop, 'but often one gets smothered in dirt . . . big drops of dirt drop on your shrapnel helmet'. Indeed: 'many of our chaps can thank their steel helmets for safeguarding their lives. I have seen some nice dents in their helmets, and but for them the wearers would have been finished'.[12]

'While I am writing this', he continued, 'the boys are practising bombing', a relatively leisurely pastime after the desperate reality of hand-to-hand warfare experienced only recently at Pozières.[13] But grateful as he was to have survived Pozières, Les Bishop's trials were not yet over. After Ypres, a perhaps over-exuberant period of leave in England resulted in a dose of gonorrhoea (together with an outbreak of scabies), and on return to the front he was 'gassed, severe', resulting in hospitalisation in UK, the military authorities taking care to inform his anxious mother at Kadina of his progress towards recovery. Back at the front once more, he was wounded in September 1918, and shortly thereafter repatriated to Australia, where he settled at Lochiel, east of Kadina.[14] Having cheated death at Pozières, he had survived the war. He died in July 1959, aged 68, survived by his wife Elsie who lived to the grand old age of 97 before expiring in October 1990.

'Lark Hill Lancers'

For the soldiers of 1 ANZAC the Ypres sojourn had been something of a welcome break. But all too soon they were ordered back into France, taking over the Allied front line between Flers and Gueudecourt from 21 October 1916. The scene here was one of utter devastation, of mud and corpses, and lack of drinking water and no hot food to speak of. Trench foot was endemic. During the November there were several costly attempts to take an adjacent section of the German line at a place called the Maze, and in these and subsequent actions Peninsula men lost their lives or were injured. In the first of these attacks, on 5 November 1916, Joseph Lanyon – a nephew of Sam Sampson of Moonta Mines – was killed in action, his body interred 450 yards NNW of Gueudecourt.[15] Private Clarence Swann Padman, serving in the 8th Machine Gun Company was killed on 29 November, and likewise buried near Gueudecourt. His death was reported with much regret on Yorke Peninsula, for he 'was very popular here'.[16] A teacher at Moonta school, he was also active in the Methodist Young People's Union and superintendent of the Junior Grade at Moonta Methodist Sunday School, where an enlarged photograph of him was subsequently unveiled in the assembly hall in his honour and memory.[17]

Also popular in the community was Sapper William Verran, youngest son of Catherine and the late Henry Verran of East Moonta, who was wounded in action on 14 December 1916, and died the same day in the 14th Australian Field Ambulance.[18] Verran's chum, Sapper K.H. Mackinlay, wrote to his late friend's mother, Catherine Verran, to offer his condolences. 'Having been a comrade of your late son for the past two months', he wrote on 17 December, 'I am writing to convey to you my deepest sympathy in your sad bereavement. During the time I was associated with your son', Mackinlay continued, 'I found him straight, honest and every inch a man'. He explained that Verran's mortal wound was caused by shrapnel and that, although medical aid was procured at once, 'he died while on the way to the clearing station. The only consolation I can give you is that he suffered very little pain. We buried him where he fell, and have erected a suitable cross, with inscription over his grave'.[19] Later, William Verran's sister Ada wrote to the military authorities 'on behalf of my widowed Mother', requesting a death certificate as 'My Mother has been informed by The [friendly society] Lodge of which Her late Son was a Member that She cannot receive payment due, without a Certificate of Death'. The authorities duly obliged, and in addition Catherine

Verran was awarded a state pension of £2 per fortnight, William having been unmarried, and she a widow.[20] Such was the day-to-day minutiae of the war as it affected the homefront; the routine reports in the local press, always with something positive to say about individual casualties, and the behind the scenes correspondence – often intimate and painful – in sorting out the affairs of the deceased and the bereaved.

In November 1916 the Australian units on the Western Front were joined by the 3rd Division. Unlike earlier units, it had gone directly from Australia to England, where it trained relentlessly on Salisbury Plain in the most realistic of conditions, perfecting new operational tactics that would stand its soldiers in good stead when at last they met the enemy. Apt to be smiled on patronisingly as 'Lark Hill Lancers' – a reference to Larkhill camp on Salisbury Plain – by veterans of Gallipoli and Pozières, the fact was that the 3rd Division was far better trained than earlier Australian units.[21] Major-General John Monash, who took command, thought there was 'a certain air about the men' of the 3rd Division: 'They all have a mature, independent, hard and active look, the outstanding characteristic being intelligence'.[22] Among such men was Signaller Lance Corporal Leonard Harvey, the 43rd Battalion of which he was a member being part of 11th Brigade, 3rd Division. Others included Jack Pyatt, Reuben 'Charlie' Rose, Fred Davey, Peter Sampson, William Shorter, Richard 'Dick' Trembath, William 'Len' Trembath, Gilbert Oats, William 'Billy' Abbott, Lloyd Pollard, Eustice 'Glynn' Pethick – all those Kio boys who had been farewelled in the pavilion at Moonta Mines Recreation Grounds back in April 1916 (see p. 80).

Like other Australian soldiers, Len Harvey found rural France enchanting, and tried his best to communicate with the family with which he was billeted, aided by a useful phrasebook he had acquired. 'You would have a good laugh if you could see me trying hold a conversation with some of the French people', he admitted to his father in a letter home in early December 1916 from 'Somewhere in France'.[23] But he was struck by the cold and the wet (the winter of 1916–17 was to prove the severest in France for forty years). 'Am writing this in the kitchen of the house at which we are billetted [*sic*]', he said, 'nice and warm alongside the fire. Had a little snow yesterday, just enough to make things a little colder'. Indeed: 'We can't get away from our billett without walking through 18 inches of water. Talk about cold feet, never dreamt one's feet could get so cold'.[24]

Len Harvey was anxious, after all his training, 'to have a go at the Germans'.[25] He did not have to wait long. 'I went into the trenches for a few hours on Christmas Eve', he reported to his father, 'we were a fatigue party. Only a few shells flying about'.[26] A week later, on 5 January, he could add that at 'last the 43rd has been in action'. As he explained: 'We went in on the 29 of last month [December 1916], a day before my birthday. German shells were not a very nice birthday gift'.[27] He was in the trenches for six days, and had now come out for six days' rest:

> My job in the line is an operator at the Coy. H.Q; there are 3 Pts and 1 corporal. We have a shell proof dug out to sleep and work in, but it is in a bad position about 200 yards behind the firing line, just where all the shells land. The place leaked like a sieve, and we used to bale it out morning noon and night.[28]

His company had only suffered three casualties so far, he reported, and after 'about the first three days, one gets used to the bursting shells, and seem to take no notice of them'. But he regretted the impact of artillery fire on the local landscape and buildings: 'Beautiful big churches, absolutely ruined. It seems as though the spires of churches offer a target for Fritz'. For now, all 'the Moonta lads are well', he added, 'and don't seem to be any the worse for their first encounter'.[29]

Things were about to get rougher, however, and a fortnight later Len wrote home to complain: 'Have only been out of the trenches for a few hours, feeling rather tired and dirty, otherwise all right'. This time the routine had been 'five days rest and then seven days in, and they were days. First it rained, then it snowed, then it rained and snowed, and the frost was terrible'. Additionally, 'Fritz landed a couple of shells close to our dug out, the old place shook and [I] felt "shaky"'.[30] Another fortnight or so passed, and then on 5 February 1917 Len Harvey was involved in the action which won Len Trembath his Military Medal (see p 85). As he explained: 'Len Trembath has been complimented by the O[fficer] C[ommanding] for the fine way he acted, and the coolness he displayed, while the enemy were playing machine gun fire on our scouts'. Seeing that one of the scouts (Private Edgecombe) had been hit, Trembath had gone onto the parapet with his Lewis gun, drawing the fire on himself, and allowing the wounded man to be rescued: 'all the time he was there enemy bullets were tearing the sandbags around him, how he didn't get hit is hard to say'. Subsequently, 'Jake Roach bound the man's wounds. Peter Sampson, Bill Shorter, Charlie Rose and myself were in the line at the time. Moonta was well represented . . . all the Kio lads are in No. 9 platoon'.[31]

Later in the month, Len Harvey was involved in another action, a raid on German lines. 'Luckily I had practically the best job in the party', he explained to his father, 'my position was on our own parapet, receiving signals from the party in "No Man's Land"'.[32] He went on:

> The poor lads got into Fritz's trench alright, but just before the time was up Fritz shelled his own trench and thus gave our fellows a bad time, inflicting a good many casualties. All the wounded and killed were got

back to our parapet, which was a great feat considering the rough time they had been given. . . . [Lieutenant] Wally Price was wounded and has gone to Blighty. His men thought the world of him. A better officer it will be hard to find . . . It was the first raid the B[attalio]n has made and it has undoubtedly made a good name for all concerned . . . Up to date there has not been a single casualty among the Moonta lads, and I hope there never will be . . . All the Kio boys are well.[33]

Intriguingly, Len Harvey had not been impressed by the enemy's performance in the few months he had been at the front. 'I think Fritz has had enough of war', he confided to his father, 'and in my opinion, this spring will bring with it a lot more fighting, but also a termination of the war'.[34] It was wishful thinking, of course, yet Harvey recognised that the enemy's unrestricted submarine warfare would probably bring America into the war, adding immeasurable weight to the Allied effort. 'Germany is a deceiving and cunning nation', he wrote, 'probably she will get all the world to go to war against her and then give in with the excuse that she cannot fight the whole world. Her submarine methods are fiendish, and no doubt she will stick to her word as regards sinking all ships at night'.[35] It was an interesting, and in its way prescient, insight. As Monash had observed, his men in the 3rd Division had been trained to think tactically, 'the outstanding characteristic being intelligence'.

'The Bullecourt push'

The events of March 1917, when the Germans made their famous retreat to the heavily defended Hindenburg Line, appeared at first to support Leonard Harvey's thesis, evidence enough that the enemy had lost the initiative and that the attritional strategy on the Somme had worked.[36] The Australians had been preparing to attack the Maze once more. But, unexpectedly, the Germans began their withdrawal towards Bapaume on 23 February. All along the Australian line, the Germans pulled back, abandoning even Bapaume (where they left numerous booby traps to ensnare the unwary). Among those killed in the furious pursuit of the enemy was Private Ernest 'Snowy' Reynolds from Wallaroo Mines, who fell in an assault on 2 March 1917, leaving his widowed mother Lily for whom he had been 'the sole support'.[37] Reynolds was buried where he fell: 'Just N.E. of Warlencourt, Eaucourt. 2½ mls S.W. of Bapaume, France'.[38] Emboldened by the German retreat, British commanders hoped to breach the Hindenburg Line in the Bullecourt sector, providing Haig with his long-cherished opportunity for a cavalry breakthrough.10 April 1917 was fixed for what became known as First Bullecourt, which would include the 4th Australian Division, only

48. The makeshift battlefield grave of Ernest Elmer 'Snowy' Reynolds, from Wallaroo Mines, which he shared with his fallen colleague Horace Pottinger. 'Snowy' Reynolds was killed in action near Bapaume on 2 March 1917, as the Germans retreated to the Hindenburg Line. Although its position was recorded roughly in his service documents, Reynolds' grave could not be relocated after the Armistice and was considered lost.

recently worked-up to a pitch of tactical and fighting efficiency after six weeks training at Albert.

It was, however, a hasty and ill-conceived battle plan — much of the failing down to General Hubert Gough, under whose command the 4th Division fell — and the apparently innovative scheme to involve tanks in the assault was a disaster. The idea was that the twelve tanks allocated to the battle would crush the German wire (obviating the need for artillery) ahead of the infantry, confounding the enemy and ensuring success. But the Mark II tanks earmarked for the attack were worn-out, under-armed and under-armoured, and slow. Moreover, on 10 April the weather had taken a turn for the worse,

49.   Australian Tunnellers work by candlelight beneath Flanders' fields, 1917.

with driving snow blizzards blinding the tanks as they tried to make their way towards the start line. Amid scenes of chaos, the assault was postponed to the next day. But 11 April proved equally chaotic, and only three tanks had turned up by the time the attack was due to commence. They were so slow that, instead of leading the infantry, they often lagged behind – with inevitable effect – and the Australians were routed. Among the losses was Private Harold Hall, from Kadina, 'taken prisoner in the Bullecourt push', as it was reported, who was subsequently interned in Germany. Hall had fought at Gallipoli and at Pozières (where he was wounded) but he was still only nineteen years of age when he died in captivity – of 'sickness' – on 17 September 1917.[39]

Despite the element of high farce in the operation, the Australians had nonetheless breached and held the Hindenburg Line, albeit briefly, a remarkable tribute to their fighting skill amidst the chaos of the battle plan. As William Philpott has observed, Anzac troops had 'renewed confidence in their martial skill, which had been so badly undermined at Pozières. Come the spring the Australian infantry were shaping up to be audacious trench fighters'.[40] Thereafter, 'the revivified 1 Anzac Corps – trained, re-equipped and shining – would commence its ascent to the pinnacle of battlefield skill and reputation'.[41] The Germans, meanwhile, had decided that attack was the best form of defence against the Australians, on 15 April 1917 throwing a formidable force of some 16,000 men against the 4,000 defending Anzacs. But the Australians, remembering their training, defended in depth, holding their lines and repulsing the enemy assaults. A fortnight later, on 3 May – Second Bullecourt – the Australians retaliated, taking advantage of the suddenly opportune spring weather. But the Germans were well prepared, and the assault soon descended into bloody attack and counter-attack. However, when it was all over, the Anzacs had captured – and continued to hold – parts of the Hindenburg Line near Bullecourt. Moreover, after a final Allied effort to take the rest of Bullecourt on 12 May, the Germans tacitly admitted defeat and withdrew to new positions in that sector, behind the Hindenburg Line. It was an Australian victory.

Flushed with success, the Australians felt confident about future engagements. The 3rd Division, with Monash in charge, was under the overall command of General Sir Herbert Plumer – part of 'Daddy Plumer's Army', as the Australians called it – and were soon in action at Messines Ridge. Australians and New Zealanders had served with Plumer in the Boer War, and they admired his leadership qualities, his reputation in the Antipodes a further boost to their confidence and renewed optimism. A preparatory operation in advance of Third Ypres, the Messines Ridge battle rested on the work of the 1st Australian Tunnelling Company, which had burrowed deep down through the sticky clay beneath the Ypres Salient to prepare two large groups of mines under enemy positions – Hill 60 and the so-called 'Caterpillar'. Together, the three companies of the Australian Tunnelling Corps had first arrived on the Western Front in May 1916 where, as Peter Barton and colleagues have observed, their comprehensive reinforcement of the Allies' mining effort was 'a great shot in the arm for the British moles who had been hard at work underground for over a year'.[42] Among their number was Sapper Percy Quintrell, a Moonta miner, nearly twenty-five years of age when he joined up in April 1916. By March 1917 he was serving with the Australians near Bullecourt. In trouble for being 'in an Estaminet during prohibited hours' and giving 'a false name to the Provost Corporal' (for which offences he was fined seven days' pay and given fourteen days' field punishment), Quintrell was wounded on the first day of Second Bullecourt (gun-shot wound, right leg) but sufficiently recovered to be in the firing line on the eve of Third Ypres, where he was 'gassed' on 28 July 1917.[43]

'They got mercy … they got hell!'

Professional miners like Percy Quintrell formed the backbone of the Australian tunnelling companies. Hill 60 at Messines was the first major project entrusted to them. They needed all their experience and expertise for the dangerous and nerve-wracking task, not least in detecting and neutralising German countermining. But, by nightfall on 6 June 1917, the day before the date set for detonating the mines, their work was complete. 'Gentlemen, we may not make history tomorrow', commented Plumer, 'but we shall certainly change the geography'.[44] At 3.10 a.m. on 7 June, the Australians blew their mines. The blast was heard in London and the shock waves felt across south-east England, as many thousands of Germans were blown sky-high. Alongside British and New Zealand units, the Australians of II ANZAC rose from their trenches to assault what was left of the enemy lines. Reorganised by Monash in the light of Canadian experience, each Australian platoon was now 'a complete and independent tactical unit', consisting of a bombing section (equipped with hand grenades), a Lewis machine-gun section, and two rifle sections (including a number of rifle bombardiers).[45] Individuals in a platoon were also taught other men's jobs (a Lewis gunner knew how to bomb, for example), allowing flexibility and encouraging initiative when under fire or suffering casualties. Sure of their tactical training, the Australians advanced with confidence, encountering only sporadic and half-hearted opposition, and secured their objectives. It was another victory.

Among the Australians attacking that day was Private Richard 'Dick' Trembath, one of those Moonta boys who had been farewelled with Leonard Harvey in April 1916. On 17 June, ten days after the assault, Dick Trembath found time to pen a letter to his parents. 'We have been unable to write lately on account of preparing for the advance', he explained, 'which is now practically finished and turned out to be a great success'. He added: 'We are now having a rest after a strenuous go at Fritz, which absolutely outclassed him, both in fighting hand-to-hand and in artillery duels. There is no doubt Fritz played his cards alright; but he forgot one thing and that there's a joker in the pack, and I really think the Australians are the joker'. Proud of his fellow Australians and their accomplishments, Trembath could only wish that there were 'a few [more] of the Moonta boys over here to see the real life, the hardships, and the outcome of war when an advance is on. I bet a lot of them would stop and have a go at Fritz and fight a lot better than us'. And yet, as he admitted: 'To describe war is a very hard thing, and one cannot write everything concerning it without at times seeing your pals, and good pals at that, dead and wounded lying close to you'.[46] Continuing, he added:

Before the push started at Messines we were carrying all material and food to our front line, which was a bad a job as one would wish to get. Talk about shells – they would fall around you thickly; but we only had to think of our pals up the line waiting for food, and it would take a barrage of shells thicker than rain to stop us. A number of our chaps got hit before we started to advance, but those left fought harder and better when they knew they had to have revenge for those who were unfortunate.[47]

Revenge was a bittersweet emotion, and, as he wrote, Dick Trembath remembered with a chuckle the censor's phrase 'Somewhere in France', used routinely in correspondence, records and communications to disguise the exact location of individuals and units on the Western Front:

> Well, it is easy to see who is winning when you have a look at both our lines and the enemy's. Ours are knocked about a bit, but all you can see of Fritz's lines are shell holes and dugouts knocked almost to sand. Talk about superior shells and men; he's not in the same street. Before our division hopped the bags a number of mines were blown, which meant severe losses to the enemy. One under Messines hill [60], caused Fritz's dugouts to collapse and buried a great number of Germans. We learnt from a prisoner that one dugout alone at that time contained 600 men. Where they are now is a hard thing to say, but I have some idea they are 'Somewhere in France'.[48]

Alive to the sobering horrors of war, which he had experienced to the full, Dick Trembath – with his desire for revenge – was not yet immune from the bloodlust that could sometimes overtake the individual soldier in the heat of battle. It was an emotion that Trembath readily admitted, and in describing his preoccupation with revenge, he imagined Australian volunteers – battle-hardened, tactically and materially superior, warriors by nature – exacting a terrible vengeance on behalf of the poor British conscripts who in earlier contests had been shown no quarter by the barbarous Huns:

> When our men were advancing the Germans rushed out with their hands up, calling their usual cry – 'Mercy, comrades'. They got mercy too; they got hell! What could they expect? When their artillery was superior in quality, overwhelming in numbers, did they give our English Tommies mercy? No, they simply wiped them out. Did the Tommies hold their hands up and cry for mercy? No, they fought to the last man, as a soldier should do, and now why should they be spared?[49]

Trembath explained how the Australians had been required to 'advance again after the first push', and how they had encountered hordes of fleeing Germans, who ran for their lives: 'a few stopped, but they soon got fixed [with bayonets]'. Anticipating, perhaps, that his letter might well find its way into the local press on Yorke Peninsula (by now a common occurrence), he confessed that such lurid tales might not appeal to 'some of the deep thinkers' at home. But such 'thinkers' did not know what it was like to be in a battle, to be confronted with a vast sea of countless Germans in their field grey uniforms and coalscuttle helmets, and to experience the ultimate fear of kill or be killed: 'if they would only see the enemy lines after an advance and wonder where all the Germans came from'. And in any case, he added, not all those Germans who had surrendered at Messines had been killed. Some, especially the wounded, had been ushered back towards the Australian lines, where they 'get treated as we do; but perhaps they have to wait a little longer, as our own men come first'.[50]

Looking to the future, Dick Trembath felt that Messines had been a turning point. 'There is only one way to bring this world and this war to a peaceful ending', he opined, 'and that is to absolutely crush Germany, and, if in our power, which it absolutely is, we will do it and do it well'. Moreover, he added, the 'Germans are absolutely fed up with the war and want to finish, but the heads [military top brass and political leaders] cannot surrender after what they have said. However, it must come sooner or later'. Reflecting for a moment on those unfortunate Germans 'coming to our lines, giving themselves up', Trembath observed that such deserters could not 'get ... back behind our lines quick enough', and that as prisoners of war they were extremely helpful and 'cannot do enough for us'. Contemptuous as he was of these broken Huns, he could not help feel pity for one Bavarian deserter who had swum across a river to reach the Australian positions. As the Bavarian wandered about behind the lines, Dick Trembath 'spotted him and halted him. He never heard me, but my revolver soon told him where we were, and he stopped all of a sudden'.[51] As Trembath explained:

> I did not shoot him, but shot in front of him, because I thought him deaf and he had not any firearms, so we had a bit of pity on him and took him prisoner. This was the first prisoner I had taken, and I think the first one taken in the battalion. This poor devil was absolutely beaten and came back to surrender and complained about our shelling. This is what we want, as it is only what Fritz gave us, being returned with a big percentage of interest.[52]

'Fritz got a good haul of Kio lads'

Leonard Harvey, signaller in the 43rd, had been out of the line when the mines were blown at Hill 60 and the Caterpillar. 'While I was away the capture of Messines took place', he said, 'and our lads were in it'. They had had 'a hard time' as 'the enemy's bombardment [sic] were very heavy, and some of them had a miraculous escape from death and injury ... It seems funny that not one of the 12 Kio lads [in the Battalion] were touched and I hope it will continue that way'.[53] A few weeks later, on 12 July 1917, he reported that both he and Jim Roach (one of the Kio lads) had been 'slightly wounded, remaining on duty', a portent perhaps of things to come. As he explained, there had been a break in telephone communication, and he and Jim were detailed to lay several yards of new wire. It was 10 o'clock in the morning, and broad daylight. 'I jumped out of the trench with the wire on my shoulder', Harvey wrote: 'Jim waited for me to get a few yards ahead and then he got out and followed in my track'. Immediately, they were spotted by the enemy. Jim Roach 'had taken only three steps when a bullet hissed by and dug into the ground a few yards ahead of me. We had been shot at by a sniper, who aimed at me. The bullet passed through Jim's tunic, trousers and field dressing, just enough to sear the flesh and break the skin near the hip bone'. As Harvey mused: 'A narrow escape no doubt'. As for his own wound: 'I was hit by a piece of shrapnel, which luckily had come a good distance and had lost all its force. It broke the skin and made a big bruise just below the right shoulder blade'.[54]

Alas, far worse was to follow. The 31 July 1917 had been earmarked by Haig for the start of the Allies' new major offensive, Third Ypres, designed to attack from the Ypres Salient with the aim of clearing the enemy from Passchendaele Ridge, thus enabling (it was hoped) the liberation of the Belgian Channel ports from German occupation. As part of the general assault, II ANZAC was to launch a diversionary attack against German positions at Warneton, south of Ypres, close to Messines. Len Harvey was in the thick of it, writing to his father a few days after the action. He explained that 'our battalion participated in a very hard stunt, which entailed some casualties'. As he put it, 'I regret to say that the Kio representatives suffered heavily. Out of thirteen there now remains four, Charlie Rose, Percy Rodda, Jim Roach and self'. Among the fallen was 'Poor Dick Trembath' – author of the recent vivid description of the battle at Hill 60 – and 'Bill Pollard and Bill Abbott . . . fine fellows the three of them'. Additionally, 'Len Trembath, Will Shorter, Bert Oats, Peter Sampson, Jack Pyatt, Doug Roach and [?] were all wounded but I don't think any serious wounds'.[55] But soon after, 'word came through that Will Shorter had died of wounds in hospital'. As Harvey added, 'Shorter's was a case of pure hard luck, he held on to his post all day and half the way through the night, and he was nearly back to camp when a piece of stray shell hit him below the knee'. The soldiers who had carried Shorter to the dressing station reported that he had suffered a 'Blighty' – a wound that was not life threatening but which would necessitate treatment in England – and so 'when news of his death came, it was a big shock'.[56]

Privately, in his diary, Leonard Harvey also reflected on the consequences of that terrible day:

Tuesday. 12 midday. Waiting for Bn. to reach jump off trench. 3.50a.m. Zero hour. Bn. just arrived in time. No. 6, 7 & 8 strong point captured, and men started to consolidate. Our Coy. suffered heavy casualties.
Len Trembath – wounded

Pete Sampson – wounded
Jack Pyatt – wounded
Dick Trembath – killed
Billy Abbott – killed
Doug Roach – wounded
Will Shorter – killed D[ied] of W[ounds]
8.30 p.m. Huns counter-attacked No. 7 Post and drove our men out.
12.30 p.m. Our men re-counter attacked and firmly established themselves
in No. 7 Pn.[57]

Suddenly bereft, with his little tight-knit group of Kio boys torn asunder, Len Harvey went in search of his wounded compatriots. Relieved from his duties by signallers from the 41st Battalion, he went first to 'Bailleul to try to find some of the boys, no luck, they had all gone through the Steenwerck hospital'.[58] The following day, 2 August 1917, Harvey was assigned to the battalion burial party. As he recorded in his diary: 'Thursday. 3 a.m. Left camp for trenches, with Bn pioneers to bury 43rd dead. Not a very nice job. Buried Dick Trembath in hole between No. 8 post and front line. 12 men in same hole. Dick on extreme right facing Warneton. Trenches in awful condition'.[59]

The appalling state of the trenches was due in part to the incessant rain that had accompanied the assault, and before long Third Ypres – or Passchendaele, as it became known – had become literally and impossibly bogged down, the military engineers helpless in the face of miles and miles of mud and water. Len Harvey suffered in these conditions, as did every other soldier, Allied and enemy, but it was the sudden loss of his close friends that he felt most keenly. Looking for pals, he went off to find the 27th Battalion, where he discovered 'Harry Chappell [sic] and several Kadina and Wallaroo lads'.[60] Delighted, he wrote to his father: 'met a few Kio lads . . . had a yarn with a few Wallaroo & Kadina lads I know'.[61] There was also the good news that Len Trembath was recuperating well in hospital in Birmingham. But such positive reports were more than tempered by the continuing flow of melancholy events. 'Young Herby Bray from X [Cross] Roads joined the Bn. while I was away', Harvey wrote to his father, 'and he was killed shortly afterwards'.[62] Likewise, he said, he had come across 'young Pedler of X Roads', a member of the 32nd Battalion and 'a good friend of Tom Gibbs' and his wife Hetty at Moonta. But, pleasant as it was to meet 'young Pedler', there was yet more bad news. Pedler explained that he had been in bombing party sent out to relieve a group of which Tom Gibbs was a member. 'Just as Pedler got out of the trench a shell landed a few yards away', wrote Harvey, and 'he heard a moan and went to investigate'. Alas, 'unfortunately poor Tom was the one who was hit, he had half his head blown off'. They put Tom's shattered body

50.   Australian soldiers fix bayonets in the forward area trenches near Zonnebeke,
in the Ypres sector, September 1917.

on a stretcher and carried him to the nearest dressing station, where he died. As Harvey observed, the 'trenches were in such a bad state that it took ten men to carry him down'.[63]

Like Len Trembath, Private Peter Sampson — another of Len Harvey's mates — was in hospital in Birmingham, recovering from wounds received on 31 July 1917. From there he wrote to a friend at Moonta Mines: 'No doubt you have heard about a few of us getting wounded, including Len Trembath, Dug [sic] Roach, Bert Oats, and Jack Pyatt, so you see Fritz got a good haul of Kio lads'. Continuing, Sampson tried to convey something 'of my experiences on the morning of July 31st. At five to 4 in the morning', he explained, 'we went over the top, and I had not gone more than 100 yards when Fritz threw one of his iron foundries at me, and stopped me in the thigh', producing a gash some ten inches long and five inches wide. Jack Pyatt had been hit at the same time, 'so we made for the nearest shell-hole, where had to remain for six hours, and, needless to say, they were the worst six hours I have spent in my life'. Eventually, Sampson and Pyatt decided to crawl forward to the captured positions, 'where our boys were digging in'. They made it but the ordeal 'knocked us out'. One of the soldiers, recognising the severity of Sampson's wound, 'offered to carry me back to our old front lines ... He pinned some white rag on his arm and away we went, and, to give Fritz his credit, he did not snipe at us'. From the front line, Sampson was taken by stretcher-bearers to a dressing station, and from there was conveyed to the military hospital at Boulogne, where he underwent an immediate operation. Later, he crossed the Channel to Dover, and was taken to Birmingham, where 'I will be ... for a few months'.[64]

'The mining towns of Yorke's Peninsula have been hit hard of late'

Echoing the assessments of Leonard Harvey and Peter Sampson, the *People's Weekly* in November 1917 reviewed the recent months of fighting at Ypres. 'The mining towns of Yorke's Peninsula have been hit hard of late', it opined, furnishing a thumbnail summary from the latest casualty lists. Private Percy Champion of Kadina had been killed on 6 October, it reported, his mother's only son, and Sergeant-Farrier William Whitbread of the same town – who had enlisted back in September 1914 – had fallen on 9 November. Andrew Darmody of Wallaroo Mines had been wounded in action, as had Corporal William J. Mitchell, from near Kadina. Hurtle McKee, from Wallaroo, had been gassed. Private Charles Miller from Maitland, further down the Peninsula, had been killed. Private Oscar Nankivell of Cross Roads was

51.   Seymour Jacka Thomas, from Moonta, 10th Battalion A.I.F., killed in action aged twenty-one on 8 October 1917 on the eve of the 'famous 10th's' disastrous assault on Celtic Wood, Passchendaele.

among the wounded, as was Fred Maddern of East Moonta. And so the list went on.[65]

There was particular sorrow at the death of Seymour Jacka Thomas, from Moonta, son of J.H. 'Johnnie' Thomas, the Peninsula's well-known musician and composer. Farewelled in June the previous year, Private Thomas had spent Christmas 1916 in England, and had been ill in hospital in France for much of 1917. Reaching the Ypres front in the September, he at last rejoined his unit (the 'famous 10th') but was killed in action soon after, on 8 October 1917, a few weeks short of his twenty-second birthday.[66] Back on the Peninsula, the Star of Moonta Lodge of the United Ancient Order of Druids held a memorial service in All Saints church on 2 December in honour of Seymour Thomas and the other five of its brethren – Percy Beaglehole, George Vercoe, William Verran, William Shorter, and Herby Bray – who had also given their lives. The 'Dead March in Saul' was played at the close, and the 'The Last Post' sounded.[67]

Seymour Thomas' death had occurred on the eve of the renewed assault by II ANZAC on the German lines at Passchendaele, the last and perhaps most horrific of the attacks at Third Ypres in which I and II ANZAC had participated, and in which so many Peninsula soldiers had become casualties. The assault on 9 October 1917 – in which a raid by the 10th Battalion, Thomas's unit, on Celtic Wood resulted in the loss of 71 of its 85-strong raiding party – was a disaster, quickly bogged down in the mire, just as other attacks had been. Men drowned in the mud, and stretcher-bearers took hours to cover just a few hundred yards as they struggled to get the wounded back to dressing stations.[68] But, as Leonard Harvey reported to his father on 18 November, there were glimmers of good or at least positive news, such as the award of the Military Medal to Jim Roach 'for gallantry in the last stunt'. Genuinely pleased for his pal, Harvey added that: 'The O[fficer] C[ommanding] of our Company Capt. E.C. Colliver (related in some way to the people next door [at Moonta]) has just been to congratulate him', such was the boost that the news had given to the hard-pressed troops.[69] Roach had won his distinction on 5 November 1917, five days before the Canadians – with Australians in support – finally took Passchendaele, awarded for carrying despatches under the heaviest of fire, a daunting task he had performed three times over. He was decorated in the field by General Birdwood, and sent the medal ribbon home to his mother Clara at Moonta as a keepsake.[70] Another of Harvey's Kio mates, Harry Chappel, had also won the Military Medal after continuous service in France and Belgium – at 'Flers, Warlencourt, Lagnicourt, Sullecourt, Polygon Wood, and Zonnebeke', as the *People's Weekly* put it: 'It was in the last named battle, in September last, that he won the coveted medal'.[71]

For wives and mothers on the Peninsula, as always, the period of renewed

52.   An 18-pounder gun of the Australian Field Artillery dug in among the ruins of
an old factory near Zonnebeke, Ypres sector, October 1917.

fighting had heightened anxieties. Extensive press reports, detailing the fallen
and the wounded and the feats of the decorated on the battlefield, combined
with events at home such as the Star of Moonta Lodge memorial service, to
create a sombre public mood in which families lived in constant fear of the
clergyman at the gate. When Leonard Harvey had written to report the death
of Tom Gibbs, he had thought of poor Hetty, Tom's widow, and the impact
of the awful news, asking his father, W.H. Harvey, to use his discretion
in showing her the letter, with its graphic description of Tom's demise. A
parliamentarian of some distinction and experience, W.H. Harvey MP also
used his discretion and influence to help the mother of another of his son's
late pals, Richard 'Dick' Trembath. He wrote to the Base Records Office in
Melbourne, on behalf of Margaret Trembath and her family in September
1917, 'to see if it is possible to have his Kit Bag and any other belongings
returned to them at Moonta Mines'. There was no sign of a kit-bag but other
incidental personal effects — two balaclavas, three Testaments, two pairs
of mittens, three pairs of socks, two periscopes, one religious book, some
photographs, and a woollen scarf — were eventually sent home. Margaret
was also granted a pension of 20 shillings per fortnight. Yet she yearned for
other possessions that she knew her son Dick had taken to the war, and she
herself wrote to the military authorities in July 1919 to complain that 'I never

received my boy's pay book nor the other things that were taken from his dead body', adding that 'there was several papers I know I should have received . . . I should be glad to have them if it was possible they would be priceless to me'. Such was a mother's angst. But the Base Records Office replied tersely that it had in its possession 'no other personal effects other than packages forwarded on 4/1/18 and 10/7/18'.[72] Such was the nature of war.

'The Hun is going to make a big effort this year'

After the morale-boosting successes of Second Bullecourt and Messines, the floundering and slaughter of Third Ypres had dampened Australian spirits. Casualties continued to mount – such as Percy Sutton from Wallaroo and William Perry from Cross Roads, both sappers in the 2nd Tunnelling Corps and both gassed, although each lived to tell the tale.[73] Some, like Leonard Harvey, now saw no prospect of an early Allied victory. The Americans had entered the war but the Russians had made their peace with the Germans, allowing the release of massive German reinforcements for the Western Front. Prescient as ever, Len Harvey mused that the 'spring will be on us shortly, then I think we will see some big battles'.[74] As he explained, writing

53. Sapper William James Perry, 1st Reinforcements, No. 5 Tunnelling Company, from Cross Roads near Moonta, who survived being 'gassed' in action in March 1918 and later returned safely to Australia.

home in February 1918: 'The papers say the Hun is going to make a big effort this year. He has more men and more guns from the Eastern front, which is a splendid asset to his chance of breaking through on the Western front'.[75] Indeed, the Germans recognised all too keenly that they needed to take swift advantage of their newfound superiority in troops and materiel, now that the Russians were out of the war, and had to act quickly before the arrival of the Americans changed the balance of forces in the Allies' favour. Accordingly, at 4.40 a.m. on 21 March 1918 the Germans launched their spectacular 'Spring Offensive', masterminded by their commander Ludendorff, and two days later the enemy had opened a breach in the British lines some forty miles wide. Soon the Germans were threatening Amiens, and with it the road to Paris. A defence line was thrown up to protect the town, and on 25 March the Australian 3rd and 4th Divisions, along with the New Zealanders, were sent hastily to help plug the gap in the British lines and halt the assault on Amiens.

In fierce fighting around Villers-Bretonneux and Dernancourt, the Australians managed to hold the Germans. Len Harvey noted in his diary entry for 27 and 28 March 1918 that he and the 43rd had been moved in to directly oppose the German advance: 'Wednesday & Thursday. Arrived at DOLLENS 3am. and taken in motor buses to FRESCHVILLIERS. Left packs at BONNAY and marched to position on ridge halfway between AMIENS and ALBERT'. Surveying the new enemy positions, he added: 'Hun occupying ridge 1,000 yards in front. Looks to be digging in'.[76] On Saturday afternoon, 30 March, the inevitable German assault began. 'Hun attacked at 1.30 p.m.', Len Harvey wrote in his diary, '1st wave advanced 300 yards and then repulsed'.[77] The next day, he reported: 'Shell landed on dugout. Killed 4 and wounded several. Very narrow escapes'.[78] Suffering now from trench foot, Harvey was sent behind the lines for treatment, where he had time to reflect on the pace of recent events and to pen a letter home. 'Old Fritz has given us a big blow on the Western front', he admitted to his father on 9 April 1918. But, sensing that the enemy was already in danger of losing the initiative, of becoming a spent force with nothing left in reserve, he added wryly: 'our time will come later'.[79]

By the end of the month, Len Harvey had rejoined his battalion and was, according to his diary, 'Living in trenches on hill outside BONNAY overlooking River Ancre and not far from where R[iver] SOMME meets ANCRE'.[80] By then Villers-Bretonneux, lost briefly to the enemy on 24 April, had been retaken by Australian and British troops, as the Allies struggled to check the German offensive. Ludendorff was not finished yet, and in a series of further massive attacks struck at the Allies during May. Writing home on 16 May 1918, Len Harvey observed that the current spate of fine, warm weather was 'just right for old Fritz to push on with his offensive'. As he

54.   Overnight on 25–26 May 1918, Leonard Harvey and several of his mates in the 43rd Battalion were 'gassed' in a fierce enemy barrage. Here, on the following day, gassed Australians await medical attention at the dressing station at White Chateau, near Villers-Bretonneux.

added, 'to date things don't look like being cleared up this year. Not very cheering what I write but it is no use saying the war is going to end within a couple of months when in my mind I think it is going to last this year out'.[81] By 20 May, Harvey and the 43rd Battalion were in the reserve trenches near Villers-Bretonneux, with the French in front and North African troops on their right flank.[82] Overnight, on 25 and 26 May, Harvey's unit was subjected to fifteen hours of continuous shelling, and, as he explained in a letter home a few days later, he and several mates were 'slightly gassed', an injury serious enough to warrant his evacuation to England for treatment and recuperation (see p. 135).[83] He was out of the conflict for the moment, and when he arrived back on the Western Front a few months later, the fortunes of war had changed dramatically – just as he had forecast. The war might not be over immediately but, as Harvey had foreseen, the German spring offensive was already running out of steam.

There was not, however, a corresponding lull in the lengthening list of Kio casualties, which grew steadily as before. On 28 May 1918 Sergeant-Major Richard Ritter, a veteran of Fromelles (see p. 96), died of wounds received in the recent fighting, leaving behind elderly parents at East Moonta and a wife and three children in Adelaide.[84] Later, in early July, the 'people of Moonta

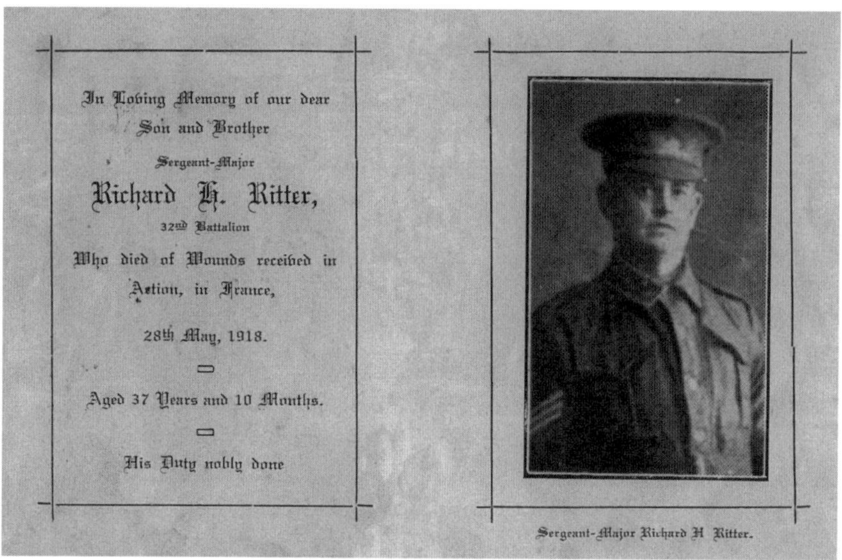

55.   Sergeant-Major Richard Ritter, veteran of Fromelles, who died of his wounds
on 28 May 1918.

sustained another shock', as the *People's Weekly* put it, when 'the sad news came through' that Private Doug Roach had died of wounds on 5th of that month.[85] Only twenty-one years of age, Doug was the younger brother of Jim Roach – who had recently won the Military Medal – and Jake, who had served since Gallipoli days. A further casualty was Wilfred Pedler of Cross Roads, like Doug Roach another of Len Harvey's mates, who was reported to be suffering from 'multiple gunshot wounds, dangerous'.[86] Private Kingsley Luscombe of Kadina was killed in action on 4 July. Samuel Hocking from Wallaroo had died on the battlefield a few years earlier, on 28 June. His 'loved one, Lillian Childs', placed a notice in the *People's Weekly*:

> He fought a great fight in the trenches,
> In response to our dear nation's call;
> Australia is proud of our hero,
> He was only a Private – that's all.[87]

'Peaceful penetration'

By the end of May 1918, John Monash had assumed command of the entire Australian Corps (comprising all five Australian divisions), which had been created in November 1917, initially under Birdwood. Monash's appointment completed the 'Australianisation' of the A.I.F. on the Western Front, enhancing its corporate identity as an Australian army under the leadership now of an Australian-born General. His first operation as Corps Commander was the capture of the Hamel spur on 4 July 1918 (when Kingsley Luscombe was killed and Doug Roach mortally wounded), a brilliantly planned and skilfully executed 'all arms' offensive in which the close co-ordination of infantry, artillery, tanks and aircraft proved too much for the enemy. Those who remembered the Bullecourt fiasco had been dubious about the efficacy of tanks, but this time the vehicles in question were the new Mark Vs, altogether superior to earlier versions, with Monash keen to make use of the latest battlefield technologies. Alongside the commitment to 'all arms' action, Monash encouraged the stealth tactics of 'aggressive patrolling' and 'peaceful penetration', activities at which the Australians had become adept. 'Peaceful penetration' was an ironic play on words, borrowed from the phrase used by the Germans before the war to describe their penetration of the Australian economy – not least, as Kio boys knew, domination of the Australian copper industry.[88]

Here, then, was another kind of revenge, as the Australians patrolled aggressively, usually at night and in small groups, killing the unwary or taking them back as prisoners for questioning, probing defences, and capturing territory. The bayonet was often the preferred weapon in such encounters, and by now the Australians had perfected its tactical use in the so-called 'throat jab', where the bayonet was thrust upwards under an enemy's chin and directly into his spinal chord, killing him – or so it was said – instantly, painlessly and silently.[89] But other weapons had their place in 'peaceful penetration' too, notably the portable and highly versatile Lewis light machine gun, whose use the Australians had also perfected. Corporal Percy Olds, for example, from Moonta, won the Military Medal for his actions between 10 and 12 August 1918 when, according to the official citation, he had 'displayed great bravery and initiative in handling his Lewis gun. He repeatedly stalked the enemy machine guns and shot down their crews from short range'.[90]

The victory at Hamel was evidence that the tide had been checked, and was an important boost to Allied morale as well as to the reputation of the Australian Corps. It helped pave the way for the great Allied counter-offensive, which commenced on 8 August 1918 and culminated in Germany's unconditional surrender on 11 November that year. As the Australians themselves were (and are) quick to acknowledge, Monash and the Australian Corps played a significant role in this final push to Victory.[91] On 8 August they and the Canadians spearheaded the Allied attack at Amiens, the Australians taking some 8,000 German prisoners in the first nine hours of the operation, for the loss of 2,450 men.[92] Over the next few months, the Australians remained in the vanguard on the Western Front. One British Territorial (part-time Reservist) unit, the Penryn No. 3 Works Company of the Cornwall Fortress Royal Engineers, found itself sapping for the Australians at Amiens and later, at the end of August, during the capture of the strategically significant Mont St Quentin.[93] One of these Cornish Tommies, Sapper (later Lieutenant) Cecil Williams, was so impressed by these 'Diggers' – as the Australians were now universally known – that throughout his life thereafter he purchased and smoked *Digger* pipe tobacco in their perpetual honour.[94]

But if the reputation – and admiration – of the Australians appeared now to rest solely on their exploits on the Western Front, this should not obscure their contribution towards final victory in other theatres of the Great War. After Gallipoli, as we have seen, Egypt continued as an important training and concentration area for Australian troops, some of whom also participated in defence of the Suez Canal. Moreover, the Australian Light Horse had remained in the Middle East for the duration of the war. In 1916 it had participated in the ejection of the Turks from Sinai, and during November and December of 1917, under General Edmund Allenby, assisted in the capture of Gaza and Jerusalem. The following year the Light Horse was active in the occupation of Lebanon and Syria, forcing Turkey to sue for peace on 30 October 1918.[95] The total number of deaths in these actions was 1,394, a tiny fraction compared to the huge accumulated losses of the Western Front, but the actions themselves were often epic – in the imagined Anzac tradition. The charge of the Australian Light Horse at Beersheba in October 1917 was one such action, as was the triumphal 'Great Ride' into Damascus in September 1918. As Joan Beaumont has argued, in Australia the exploits of the Light Horse in the Middle East fitted neatly into the 'bushman-soldier mythology of Anzac', expert horsemanship combining with skills nurtured in the Outback to ensure not merely survival but triumph in a harsh, unforgiving desert environment.[96]

On northern Yorke Peninsula, there was likewise keen interest in tales of the Light Horse, especially those Kio boys who had found themselves in the Middle Eastern theatres of war. Inevitably, too, there was the usual reportage in the regional press, especially of casualties. Thus, in the *People's Weekly* in May 1917, the death in action of Corporal-Trumpeter Harold Samuels 'in the Palestine war' was recorded. A member of the 9th Australian Light Horse, Samuels hailed from Wallaroo, where his parents still resided, and the newspaper noted with regret that only three weeks before embarking for the Middle East, he had married Violet Bennett of Petersburg. 'Great sympathy is felt for the young widow and parents', it was added.[97] Later in the year, Harold Samuels' father received a letter from Trooper Clive Blight, 'a Kadina boy', which explained that his mate had been killed on 9 April 1917, fighting the Turks in Gaza, falling 'victim to a shrapnel wound in the heart'.[98]

Similarly, there was the melancholy news in May 1918 that Trooper

56.   On 8 August 1918, the first day of the great Allied counter-offensive,
Australians collect German dead for burial in the aftermath of the battle for Amiens.

W.J. Learmouth, also in the 9th Light Horse, an East Moonta boy, had died
in Palestine, apparently as a result of fracturing his skull in an accident,
presumably falling from his horse.[99] A third death was that of Trooper
A.J. Smith, from Moonta, the same Trooper Smith who had enjoyed an
uproarious time in England a few years before (see p. 111). Captain Joseph
Best, his company commander, wrote from 'Jordan Valley, Palestine' to
Smith's parents on 17 July 1918 to explain the circumstances of their son's
death, and to offer condolences. 'On Sunday, July 14, at 5 in the morning',
he wrote, 'we were bombed by enemy planes'. He continued: 'Your boy was
wounded in the leg high up, and was taken back immediately. He was in
good spirits, but died later eight miles south of us at the receiving station'.
Enclosing a map to show the location, 'on the road to Jerusalem', Captain Best
added that 'I went down and buried him that night at the Anzac Receiving
Station Cemetery. He was a good lad, and very popular with his mates'.[100]
Ten days before the Turks sued for peace, there was a further death – Trooper
Roy Francis, from Ballarat Row, Moonta Mines – who succumbed on 'the
Palestine front' to 'malarial fever'.[101]

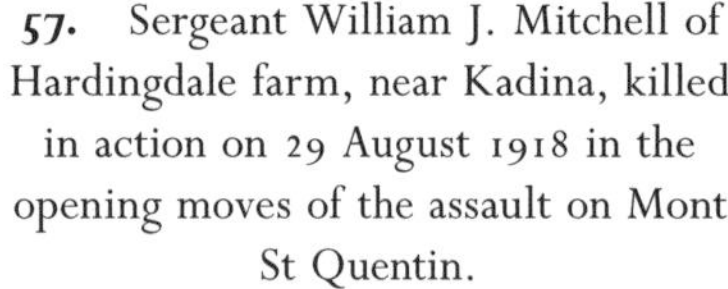

57. Sergeant William J. Mitchell of Hardingdale farm, near Kadina, killed in action on 29 August 1918 in the opening moves of the assault on Mont St Quentin.

'Nearer, my God, to thee'

Meanwhile, back on the Western Front, the Australians capitalised on their remarkable advances after 8 August 1918, the 'Black Day' of the German Army as Ludendorff had termed it. Charlie Rose, another of Leonard Harvey's Kio mates, was killed on 26 August as they pursued the retreating enemy (see pp. 84–9), and on 29 of that month Sergeant William J. Mitchell of Hardingdale farm, near Kadina, was likewise killed in action, less than a year since he had been wounded.[102] This was during the first moves of the audacious attack on Mont St Quentin and subsequent advance to Péronne and beyond. The Germans, shaken badly, retreated to the Hindenburg Line, which was to be the next target for the Australian Corps. The initial attack was touch and go, with the still inexperienced Americans faltering as they attempted to support the Australian advance. Nonetheless, by 30 September 1918 Len Harvey could note confidently in his diary: '11th Bde mopping up Hindenburg line at BONY and QUENNEMONT'.[103]

Len Harvey also described the assault in a letter to his father. 'Was unable to write last Sunday (29) owing to being in the attack on the Hindenburg line', he explained: 'The Americans were over first, and it was all planned for the Australians to leapfrog the Yanks later on in the day'. It did not go

58.   The elaborate cross marking William J. Mitchell's grave.

quite as planned but, generously, Harvey reported that 'In nearly all cases the Yanks reached their objectives and our fellows went through them and did good work'. However, 'Owing to unforeseen difficulties the Yanks in front of us were held up, and when our fellows arrived they had to set to work and help them. There was a lot of heavy fighting, but in the end our fellows got the Hun out of his first line defences'. When it was all over, Leonard Harvey surveyed the extraordinary fortifications of the Hindenburg Line, amazed and disbelieving. 'When one stands in the vicinity of the Hindenburg line', he wrote, 'and sees the rows of barbed wire, yards in depth and four and five feet in height, he wonders how anything human managed to get through'.[104]

Tired as they were, the Australians were proud of their achievements, and of their leader, John Monash. When Len Harvey heard that a politician had asked in the South Australian Parliament 'If it was true that the G.O.C. [General Officer Commanding] of the A.I.F. was a German Jew', he was furious.[105] But Harvey was also looking to the future, recognising now that the war must surely come to an end soon. 'I am trying to get into a school for motor mechanics', he explained in a letter home: 'I have been thinking seriously of late what occupation I am going to follow when I return to Australia. It is pretty certain to me that I will not be content to sit at a desk and do clerical work'. Knowing that it would be some weeks before his letter

59.   Australian infantry in action at Mont St Quentin, 1 September 1918.

reached Moonta, he added – in Cornish idiom – a premature 'Appy noo near to ee all'.[106]

The war was indeed almost over. At home the regional press had tired of reprinting long verbatim extracts from 'letters from the front', reflecting perhaps the impatience of its readership for the conflict to be at an end. There were exceptions. Brevet-Major A.R. Clayton, for example, had written to his brother at Moonta, the local doctor, explaining how a shell fragment had caught his little finger, and how living in dugouts near a lake meant that 'as the shells explode in it fish are killed and one can often find a few on the edges of the lake to eat'.[107] But there were no longer tales of daring-do, and even the farewell parties seemed muted affairs compared to earlier occasions, which had been reported extravagantly at great length. Homecomings were reported joyously – as when Len Trembath was feted by the Moonta Mines Male Voice Choir at a welcome home social in late July 1918 – but for the most part now war reporting was restricted to the publishing of casualties.[108] Even as the war entered its final weeks, the lists continued. Harry Brokenshire, for instance, whose brother Bill had died at Gallipoli, was listed as killed in action in the *People's Weekly* edition for 12 October 1918, as was Percy Polglase on 26 October.[109]

The final collapse came quickly. The Austrians and the Turks had sued for peace in October. The German High Seas Fleet had mutinied, and the Kaiser

60. Hundreds of people gather outside the Institute at Wallaroo on 11 November 1918, waiting for news of the Armistice. Unofficial word came through in the late evening but many people waited at the Institute until, just after midnight, formal confirmation arrived.

abdicated on 9 November. At 11 o'clock in the morning on 11 November 1918 the Armistice was signed, signalling Germany's defeat and the end of the fighting. Leonard Harvey, writing a few days before, had forecast 'that 1919 will not see any hostilities'.[110] On 13 November, reflecting on the momentous events of recent days, he wrote home to his parents. 'I think you learnt the good tidings as soon as we did', he said: 'Nothing was announced officially to the men. The French people had their flags out a day and a half before we received the papers with the news of the signing of the armistice'. It was all very low-key, almost an anticlimax. 'Probably the "heads" thought the troops would get too excited' if more had been made of the German surrender, mused Len Harvey.[111]

On northern Yorke Peninsula, the news had indeed arrived swiftly. At Wallaroo anxious crowds gathered outside the Institute, waiting for an announcement, and at 9.30 in the evening on 11 November word came through that the war was over. Immediately, the steam whistles were sounded at the Moonta and Wallaroo mines, and bells were rung throughout the district. Youngsters appeared on the streets of the three towns, beating empty kerosene drums and riding their bicycles up and down, trailing strings of tin cans. On Tuesday all businesses were closed, and at Moonta community singing was led by the Moonta Mines Male Voice Choir. At 2.30 that afternoon, the combined bands of the district led a parade through the town. The crowds, in joyful relief, sang 'Nearer, my God, to thee'.[112]

'Returning with the scars of deadly conflict'

Aftermath

Relief was perhaps the dominant emotion in the days after the Armistice had been announced. There was justifiable pride in Australia's feat of arms, and in its contribution to the Empire's cause and to the Allies' victory, as well as satisfaction at the support given at every level by the people of northern Yorke Peninsula – in the mines and smelters, and on the farms, in the homes and churches, by local councils, and by the myriad regional organisations that had emerged to further the war effort. But, most of all, there was relief that it was all over.

Yet for many it was not over. As the *People's Weekly* observed ruefully on 16 November 1918, less than a week since the Armistice had been signed, 'notification of the death of a soldier at the front is sad news at any time, but coming during the closing scenes of the war seems to increase the feelings of sadness'.[1] The editor was thinking especially of Sapper Charles Bodinner, killed in an air raid in the last days of the war, notice of whose demise had reached Moonta on Saturday 9 November, a matter of hours before the guns fell silent. Bodinner's widow and two daughters were left stricken by grief, therefore, as their neighbours celebrated news of the Armistice. For James Symons and his wife, celebration turned abruptly to anxiety, as word came through on Wednesday 13th that their son Parker, serving in 'the flying squadron', had been reported missing in action. The next day, Thursday, Mrs N. Walters heard that her brother, Corporal C.W. Richards, had been gassed at the front and was by now in Hospital in Bristol. And so the war went on, or so it seemed.[2] Nearly a year later, there was 'Quite a gloom . . . cast over the town', it was reported, when news came through to Moonta that Private W. Ellery had died of bronchial pneumonia in hospital in London.[3]

61.   The flags of the victorious Allies decorate the Wallaroo Mines Methodist
Sunday school tea-treat, late 1918.

'Returning home … with honors thick upon him'

However, there was also great excitement at the prospect of the safe return of
many servicemen from overseas, some of whom had been away for years. In
the final months of the conflict, a war weariness had descended on northern
Yorke Peninsula, with war reporting restricted largely to casualty lists, brief
notices of farewells, and only occasionally news of a spirited homecoming.
When Len Trembath had arrived back in July 1918, his reception 'provided
one of the most enthusiastic and happy gatherings that Moonta has known
for a considerable period', a most welcome change of mood, but overall
the pervasive air of gloom survived into early 1919.[4] Only then did local
communities allow themselves the luxury of unrestrained joy. When Sergeant
Stan Anderson returned home during February, for example, his arrival 'was
the signal for the gathering of a good crowd at the railway station'. As the
People's Weekly explained, the 'career of this young military medallist in France
and Flanders had been watched with interest by the people of Moonta'; not
only his immediate family and friends but the whole community: 'the shops
were decorated for the occasion and two flags were flown from the Institute
… Sgt Anderson was heartily cheered as he stepped on to the carriage
platform'. Yet even here the homecoming was tinged with sadness, for
Anderson had lost an eye and suffered a fractured hip during his three long
years of service. The *People's Weekly* put a brave face on it: 'although bearing
the scars of battle upon his body, he was returning home to his widowed
mother with honors thick upon him'.[5]

However, there was more to Stan Anderson's homecoming than was immediately apparent. A month after his safe return from 'the din of battle and the dangers and privations', he was afforded a 'military wedding' (as the press dubbed it), held at Moonta Methodist church and with a reception in the nearby lecture hall. The church was decorated with the flags of the victorious Allies and arches of greenery, with a military guard of honour – under the command of Len Trembath – at the door to salute Stan Anderson and his bride, Beatrice Victoria Lukey. After the editorial restraint of recent years, when to dwell too long on possibly self-indulgent detail might be deemed inappropriate or offensive, the *People's Weekly* could not contain itself. The bride had 'made a pretty picture' as she entered the church on her father's arm, the newspaper reported breathlessly. 'She was robed in a costume of crepe-de-chene', it added admiringly, 'with silver trimmings, and a court train trimmed in swansdown tulle. She also wore a veil and orange blossoms, and carried a handsome bouquet of white flowers'. As for the bridesmaid (Beatrice's cousin, Elma), she 'was dressed in white ninon, trimmed in fine lace, and wore a black pan velvet hat'. When the ceremony was complete, the happy couple and guests adjourned to the neighbouring lecture hall, which was decked out in blue and purple, the colours of Stan Anderson's 50th Battalion: 'The usual toasts were honoured, after which general merry-making was indulged in'.[6] It was something like a return to normality, albeit with a strong military flavour and conducted in the shadow of the erstwhile war.

The return of a large body of servicemen from half-a-world away, it was acknowledged, was a huge logistical and administrative task. As the *People's Weekly* observed in early July 1919, the 'repatriation of Australian soldiers who have played their part – and right manfully, too – in the great war, is being effected with all possible speed'. As the paper explained: 'Transports are arriving in the wake of each other, and some 59 have been reported as being due to arrive during the present month. Each week Moonta boys are returning home'.[7] Some of the troops in France or on leave in England grew restive, as Birdwood had feared (see p. 136), and at the final Australian march past before the King in London on a chilly 25 April 1919 many refused to make the respectful 'eyes right' when ordered to do so.[8] When George V cast his gaze upon the Australians, one of them shouted out: 'How's it for a loan of your overcoat, King'.[9] But many made the best of it, indulging in a spot of tourism in Britain while they had the chance, waiting for their turn to go home. For the troops in France over Christmas 1918 and into the Near Year, it was a frustrating time – the war was over, and yet there was no prospect of being with their loved ones during the festive season, or even for months yet. Small irritants rankled, as Leonard Harvey noted in his diary. On Christmas Day, for example, Harvey's Company had held their dinner in a marquee erected at the top of the village, a place called Le Frauley. The Battalion had

62.   Coming home! Australian soldiers line the decks of a troopship as it docks at Outer Harbour, Port Adelaide, in 1919.

helped itself to a number of large concrete slabs, found in the village, to assist in setting up the big tent and its cooking range. The local Mayor, when he learnt of the removal, was furious. He stormed down to the 43rd Battalion to complain, and 'tried to stop the cooking of turkeys'.[10] Needless to say, the Australians gave him short shrift. But it was a silly intervention that they could have done without.

Len Harvey eventually arrived home at Moonta on the afternoon of Wednesday 2 July 1919, having sailed from Liverpool in the transport *Nestor* on 20 May.[11] He was 'met at the station by a large assemblage, and received a right royal welcome' – three cheers, the National Anthem, speeches by local dignitaries, and a cavalcade of motor cars through the streets to deliver him to his home. That evening, he and other recently returned servicemen were accorded a rousing welcome home at the Institute Hall. 'The building was literally packed with residents from all parts of the district', it was reported, 'while many stood outside the doors unable to gain admittance'. Indeed, 'everything was characterised with the greatest enthusiasm from start to finish'.[12] It was an auspicious gathering of returnees:

Cpl Jake Roach, Anzac, first Moonta boy to enlist with the A.I.F. (4 years).

63.   Anxious relations await their returning loved ones.

Seaman Wm. Reynolds, first Moonta lad to enlist in the Australian navy
    (2 years).
Sgt J[ack] Pyatt (3 years)
Lance Cpl Len. Harvey (3 years).
Trooper Claude Major (2½ years).
Signaller J[im] B. Roach, M.M. (3 years).
Pte T.G. Cliff (3 years).
Gunner A.L. Champion (3 years).
Gunner R.S.T. Smith (4 years).
Sgt W. Woods (4 years).
Trooper Semmens (3 years and 9 months).
Cpl McInerney (3 years).[13]

As the Mayor remarked in his address, it 'was somewhat singular that
Sgt Pyatt, Sgt J.B. Roach M.M., and Lance-Cpl Harvey were farewelled
together, sailed together, and together were being welcomed that night'. They
had fought together too, and now people from across the Peninsula 'were
delighted that they had been spared to return to home and mother'.[14]

'But a mother's part is a broken heart, / And a burden of lonely years'

Unfortunately, one of those unable to attend the welcome home was Clara Roach, mother of the surviving Roach boys – Jake and Jim – who were being feted with their mates. Discreetly, it was explained that 'Mrs Roach had been a great patriotic worker from the commencement of the war until she took to her bed'.[15] Quite what accounted for this retreat into introspection and depression was not made clear. But it was in all probability the death of her third son Doug in July 1918 (see p. 186) that had been the final straw for Clara. She had lived with the war since the earliest days – the unofficial suffix 'Anzac' appended to Jake's name indicated that he had participated in the initial 'dawn landing' at Gallipoli – and each of her three boys had had narrow escapes during their long years of service. Doug himself had been wounded on the first day of Third Ypres, nearly a year before his fatal wound in 1918. For Clara, who had busied herself in war work to keep anxiety at bay, it had, perhaps, suddenly become all too much. She was not alone, of course, and it was inevitable that, for those whose sons and husbands and brothers who would not be coming back, the constant stream of returnees and attendant celebrations was a perpetual reminder of their grief. The *In Memoriam* notices in the local press were the means by which the bereaved sought to express their sorrow amidst the prevailing atmosphere of joyous return. In April 1919, the sister and bother-in-law of Lance-Corporal A.C. Pascoe, 43rd Battalion, who had died of wounds in France two years previously, composed their remembrance:

> When we see the boys returning,
> Our hearts they throb with pain,
> To think that you're not there, dear Albert,
> And will never come back again.
>
> Could we have raised your dying head,
> Or heard your last farewell,
> The blow would not have been so hard
> For us, who loved you well.[16]

Likewise, the grieving mother of Lance-Sergeant Abraham Thomas, who had been killed in France two years before, inserted her sad composition in October 1919:

> Could I, his mother, have clasped his hand,
> The son we loved so well,

> Or kissed his brow when death was near,
> And whispered 'My son, farewell'!
>
> I seem to see his dear, sweet face,
> Through a mist of falling tears;
> But a mother's part is a broken heart,
> And a burden of lonely years.[17]

Other relations added:

> We pictured your safe returning,
> We longed to clasp your hands;
> But God has postponed our meeting,
> It will be in a better land.[18]

The returned servicemen themselves were aware of their status as lucky survivors, and sometimes discomforted by the fact. When Private Lloyd Pollard, who had injured his spine while stretcher-bearing under fire (see p. 124), died at the Keswick military hospital in Adelaide in April 1919, he was accorded a military funeral at Moonta, with returned soldiers acting as pall bearers, paying their respects to a fallen colleague who had suffered greatly.[19] Indeed, through local branches of the Returned Sailors' and Soldiers' Imperial League [RSSIL], first formed in 1916, returned servicemen took an increasing interest in the affairs of the community, assisting in organising the rush of homecoming receptions but also helping to support the returnees – especially those injured in mind and body – and the bereaved. In this way, they accepted and expressed their responsibilities as returnees.

But they also sought to protect and promote the interests of returned servicemen more generally, and Anzac Day – 25 April each year – was to prove the principal vehicle for the continued assertion of their place in the community, long after the homecoming receptions were over. For now, however, the homecomings remained an important forum for the RSSIL. In June 1919, for example, a welcome home gathering was an opportunity for ex-Sergeant-Major Matthews to speak 'at considerable length' on the role of the League, and to warn of the manifold 'difficulties with which returned soldiers were faced'. There were 330,000 former servicemen out of work in London, he said, and closer to home in Adelaide there were 'also many without employment'. Additionally, with prescient insight, Matthews foresaw looming economic difficulties in Australia, which could only make things worse for the returnees. In neighbouring Victoria, he observed, the Bryant & May match factory had closed down recently, with the loss of up to 900 jobs, because people preferred cheaper 'Jap brands', and 'this was the state of affairs they [returnees] were coming home to'. He had even heard workers, he said, jealous of their own jobs, exclaim pejoratively 'Here comes a returned soldier', a measure of the suspicion with which returnees were now regarded in certain civilian circles.[20]

'Incapacitated for any manual labour'

During 1919 the homecomings continued unabated. Among the returnees now were prisoners of war from Germany, sent initially to England for repatriation to Australia. The lists of liberated prisoners, it was reported, included several from northern Yorke Peninsula: Sergeant W. Woods of Moonta Mines, Lance-Corporal S.C. Barnard (Moonta Bay), and Privates C. Cloak (Moonta), E.S. Stevens (Wallaroo Mines), G.C. Jacob, W.H. Knuckey, F.H. Stevenson, C. Whiting, and W. Porter (the latter all of Kadina).[21] Some, like Private Cloak, who had been in captivity at the Prisoner of War camp at Stendal in Saxony-Anhalt for two years and four months (where Private Leslie Woon, from Wallaroo, was also an inmate), no doubt bore psychological as well as physical symptoms of their long periods of incarceration.[22] Indeed, when one commentator spoke of local men 'returning with the scars of deadly conflict', he was thinking of injuries mental as well as bodily.[23] Missing limbs were now a common sight in the three Peninsula mining towns and their rural hinterland, and remained so for many years. In December 1933, for example, it was reported that F.V. Olifent, now of Perth, had arrived at Moonta to spend Christmas with his parents: 'he served in the war, and besides being gassed, had the misfortune to lose a leg'.[24] Earlier, when Privates Jasper Porker and W. Curnow returned to Sunnyvale in June 1919, it was noted that both 'men are war scarred', the former with a fractured knee and the latter with an injury to the throat.[25]

Likewise, in the same month, when Private J. Medlin, now of Orroroo in South Australia's 'far north', came to stay with his brother at Moonta, it was reported sympathetically in the press that he had 'received internal injuries in the battle of the Somme', and in consequence was now 'incapacitated for any manual labour'.[26] Earlier, when Roy Pollard had been invalided home to Moonta, efforts were made to give him his old job back (on the staff of the local branch of the National Bank), the *People's Weekly* opining that 'Moonta has reason to be proud of her brave lads ... and should be well pleased to find that room has been found for Mr Pollard so near home'.[27] It was an early example of successful rehabilitation that, alas, could not always be replicated as economic conditions worsened and the number of returnees grew. Even the sound of body, as Sergeant-Major Matthews had anticipated, could experience difficulty in finding a position. 'A Returned Soldier, aged 25 years, desires to learn farming on up-to-date lines', explained one newspaper advertisement in

64. This group of thirty-three Allied Prisoners of War at Stendal POW camp in Germany (where Privates C. Cloak from Moonta and Leslie Woon of Wallaroo were incarcerated) contains at least one Australian, as his slouch hat indicates.

June 1920: 'will accept 12/6 per week and keep. Good education; sober and industrious. Apply Miss M. Prisk, Moonta'.[28]

Some returned servicemen, like James Donlon of Wallaroo, exhibited strange behaviour which others put down to the ill effects of war. In May of 1919, Donlon had met Amy Maude Hendry of Moonta, and they swiftly formed a close relationship. Soon he was going down to Moonta three or four times a week to 'walk out' with Miss Hendry, and subsequently they became engaged to be married, with the date set for 27 September that year. James and Amy met the vicar of All Saints, Moonta, to discuss arrangements, a licence was obtained, and invitations sent out. However, on 16 September James Donlon disappeared suddenly from Yorke Peninsula and never returned. Subsequently, it transpired that he had married another women in Adelaide. Moreover, he insisted later that there had been no betrothal, and, furthermore, when it was suggested that he owed Amy Hendry some recompense for what had happened, he protested that he was 'a returned soldier and out of work'. Indeed, he added, he 'had no money nor property – not even a home of his own', and that to pay Miss Hendry anything at all 'would only do his young wife an injury'. The matter went to court, at Moonta, where it was found that, instead of being penniless, since his return James Donlon had worked at the British mill in Wallaroo for 14s. per day. The court also heard that Amy Hendry had suffered the indignity and expense of placing advertisements in the press to explain that the wedding had been 'postponed'. Needless to say, the Bench took a dim view of Donlon's duplicity, whatever its cause, and, despite his plea that he was a returned soldier deserving of sympathy, the magistrates decided that he 'was the kind of blackguard that ought to be made an example of'.[29] He was fined a total of £102 4s. 6d., an extremely large sum. Plainly, not all homecomings had a happy ending.

Some, indeed, seemed sadly ironic, such as the fate of 29 year-old Sapper Percy Quintrell from Cross Roads. A member of the 3rd Australian Tunnelling Company, he had used his mining skills to good effect in the tense underground warfare of the Western Front, and had seen considerable action during his three years service, including the unpleasant experience of being gassed.[30] He had arrived back home on Wednesday 25 June 1919, and was met 'with a few words of welcome and congratulation' at Moonta station by R.S. Richards MP.[31] Less than six months later, Quintrell suffered a minor domestic accident. As he opened a bottle, it burst and cut his hand badly; enough for him to seek medical treatment. All seemed to be going well until lockjaw (tetanus) set in, and he was removed to Wallaroo hospital, where he died subsequently of 'blood poisoning'.[32] A further irony of sorts was that, only a few months earlier, Percy Quintrell's mother had been thrilled to learn that her nephew, Captain Arnold Santo Waters, had been awarded the Victoria Cross for his actions on 4 November 1918, when supervising under heavy fire the completion of a bridge across the Olse-Sambre Canal in France.[33]

Influenza added to the travails of the region, as returnees and locals succumbed to the epidemic that had swept much of the world, the mobility of vast armies in the closing months of the war and its aftermath having contributed to its spread. In August 1918, the *Yorke's Peninsula Advertiser* had reckoned that locally 'in most houses one or more of the family are laid aside through sickness', which seemed a fair estimate.[34] The epidemic, with peaks and troughs, lasted for about a year, and by the end of 1919 it was more or less over, coinciding with the fall-off in homecomings. The 'last welcome home social' at Sunnyvale was held in January 1920, a consciously elaborate affair designed to round off the cycle of such events.[35] By early May, however, there was only a 'fair attendance' at a homecoming at Moonta Mines for some of the final returnees, evidence perhaps that such gatherings had by now lost their novelty, and with it something of their significance.[36]

'A new brotherhood'

Having found its voice at the homecomings, the RSSIL moved on to other arenas, as we shall see, but for John Verran the dwindling of welcome home socials after 1919 deprived him of an important political platform. Having lost his Parliamentary seat in April 1918, Verran had looked for new opportunities to perpetuate his political influence in the region. A familiar figure at farewell events in earlier years, when he had spoken robustly in support of the Empire's war aims and had condemned the enemy in the most lurid terms, he now turned his attention to the homecomings. Speaking at a public welcome for a large group of returned soldiers in March 1919, for example, Verran embraced the returnees as 'the gentlemen of Australia' – who were neither 'those who stayed at home nor the wealthy folk' – a swipe at the shirkers and erstwhile anti-Conscriptionists, as well as a reminder that his sympathies remained with ordinary working people.[37]

However, even as he extended his formal welcome to the returnees, so Verran warned that 'they had come from one conflict to another'. On northern Yorke Peninsula and across Australia as a whole, strikes and industrial disputes had disrupted the economy and posed a threat to society. Indeed, 'Australia was as near hell today as it could be', he insisted, 'with the influence of the I.W.W. [International Workers of the World – the 'Wobblies'] and the spirit of Bolshevism abroad'. It was the duty of the returnees, Verran suggested, to help eradicate this malaise. 'These things ought to be run out of Australia', he said, 'and they were looking to the returned men to assist in wiping them out'. It was a political call to arms, in which Verran envisaged 'a new brotherhood' of returned servicemen who would 'stand together and dictate their demands to Australia'. This brotherhood would bring 'new aspirations to Australia', and 'must make itself felt throughout the length and breadth of the land'. Still smarting from his electoral defeat, Verran reminded the returnees that in their absence 'he had been dropped out of political life'. Part of the conspiracy against him, he revealed, had been the state's German community and its sympathisers. 'While the soldiers were dealing with the Germans overseas', he explained, 'he had been endeavouring to deal with them at home, and when he was defeated as a politician they held an early prayer-meeting to thank God for it'.[38]

Embittered in defeat and politically marginalised, not least in and by the Labor movement on northern Yorke Peninsula, Verran had identified the returned servicemen as a new constituency to which he might appeal. The RSSIL had already made its presence felt in the community, and was ready to speak out on a range of issues that affected the returnees. By aligning his rhetoric with the concerns of the RSSIL, Verran calculated that he could make political common cause. It was a theme that he was to develop further, at another homecoming in June 1919 advising the newly returned soldiers 'to associate themselves with the R.S.&S. Imperial League ... to establish a new brotherhood which could never have been conceived of before the war'. On the same occasion, he explained that the apparent undue delay in the signing of the Peace Treaty at Versailles was due to the heroic steadfastness of the Australian Prime Minister, W.H. 'Billy' Hughes, for whom he had the highest regard. 'That gentleman believed that a number of the islands of the

Pacific rightly belonged to Australia', said Verran in agreement, 'and had been fighting, almost single-handedly, to secure them to the Commonwealth'.[39] In fact, the British government, anxious to encourage the Japanese as allies during the war, had led Japan to expect certain Pacific territories as a reward for co-operation, a prospect that thoroughly alarmed the Australian government, while separately the United States had laid claim to the Solomon Islands. At Versailles, David Lloyd George, the British Prime Minister, found himself in direct confrontation with Billy Hughes, with observers bemused as the two leaders 'descended to abusing each other in Welsh'.[40]

In the end a compromise was struck, with Australia receiving a number of territories − including German New Guinea − as 'mandates' rather than new colonies *per se*. In supporting Hughes' intransigence, John Verran was continuing to align himself with the erstwhile Labor leader who had advocated Conscription, just as he had himself, and whom he had followed into the Nationalist camp. It was a trajectory of which Verran was proud, despite his own electoral defeat, and in claiming close affinity with Billy Hughes remembered that the latter had been popular among Australian troops in France and Britain.[41] Verran hoped, no doubt, that he would inherit this popularity among the returnees. Emulating Hughes, he ridiculed the efforts of President Woodrow Wilson at Versailles, exclaiming that the American leader's high-minded principles would make no greater contribution to global peace than the 'German Bolsheviks' would to 'the settlement of the industrial troubles of the world'. Indeed, Verran considered that under the Versailles Treaty 'Germany should pay the penalty for her crimes ... bring Germany to her knees'. It was important to keep Germany subdued in the future, he added: 'If they gave Germany a chance she would crawl back to her former methods'.[42] Verran's virulent ant-German stance extended to the management of soldier-settler schemes, where returning soldiers where allocated land − often in unpromising locations − on which to start farms, a government initiative to tackle the problem of returnee employment. Verran, speaking at yet another homecoming, in August 1919, objected to 'German' returned servicemen − those of German descent − being given the same opportunities as other Australian soldiers. 'He protested against Germans being allowed to enter into competition with [other] returned soldiers in securing such land', it was reported: 'Many of these Germans retained the grin of their Kaiser when they bested the returned men'.[43]

In the end, as we have seen (p. 162), John Verran's comeback attempt came to little. However, in advocating a brotherhood of returned servicemen, he had tapped into a potentially rich vein of political sentiment, one increasingly associated with the conservative right − the direction in which he was now himself heading firmly. It was a sentiment, for example, that appealed to Brigadier-General Raymond Leane, a stalwart of the Cornish Association of South Australia, the much-decorated returned soldier who had fought at Gallipoli and been badly wounded at Third Ypres. In 1920 Leane was appointed Police Commissioner of South Australia. Associated with the extreme-right Citizens League movement, in 1928 Leane recruited League members among the 3,000 Special Constables raised to crush the Port Adelaide 'wharfie' strike, and through the Depression years he clamped down hard on what he imagined were Communist-inspired demonstrations by the unemployed. Likewise, another potential Verran ally was Sir William Sowden, born of Cornish parentage in the Victorian goldfields in 1858, who as a boy had lived briefly at Kapunda (as had Verran) before settling at Moonta in 1874, where he became a reporter on the staff of the *Yorke's Peninsula Advertiser*. By 1881 he had joined the *South Australian Register*, which he went on to edit, and which became mouthpiece for his pro-Conscriptionist views during the Great War. Sowden became the first President of the RSSIL in South Australia, and over subsequent years moved firmly to the political right, confiding to a friend in Cornwall that 'My firm intention is to advocate the abolition of Parliament' and expressing the view that the unemployed 'are learning lessons in thrift and prudence which they ought to have taken to heart years ago ... things might have been still blacker than they are'.[44] Yet, despite their common ground with Verran, their returned servicemen credentials, and their Cornish connections with northern Yorke Peninsula, neither Leane nor Sowden sought to tap into the vein that Verran had identified. Indeed, an attempt to form an extreme right-wing movement at Moonta during the Depression years came to nought. Political events on the Peninsula had by then taken a different turn, as we shall see below.

'A lasting monument to the memory of our heroic dead'

As the homecomings dwindled, so thoughts turned to the memorialisation of the region's dead. The South Australian State Trophy Committee had the task of allocating captured war trophies to settlements across the state. Moonta and Kadina, with their sizeable populations, were earmarked for German field guns and limbers, while tiny Port Victoria, further down the Peninsula, had to make do with a machine gun.[45] Local committees appointed trustees to take charge of the trophies, and to ensure their appropriate siting and maintenance.[46] At Moonta, the captured field gun arrived in June 1921 and, under the direction of the local RSSIL branch, was placed in the Memorial Park gardens.[47] A month later a similar gun, captured in Palestine, arrived at Kadina. Meanwhile, plans for permanent war memorials were coming to fruition. In September 1919, a deputation from the Moonta RSSIL – led by Len Trembath, Henry Banfield and J.W. Gill – had met Moonta Town Council to outline their proposals. Initially, the RSSIL and Town Council did not

65.   The unveiling of Moonta's War Memorial, 27 November 1920.

quite see eye to eye, the League mindful of its responsibility to the memory of the fallen, the Council of its democratic accountability to the electorate.[48] There was, perhaps, some jostling for position, a power struggle of sorts as the Councillors defended their traditional role against the RSSIL's assertion of its newfound authority.

Be that as it may, debates about funding, location, size and style were at last resolved, and on 27 November 1920 'a lasting monument to the memory of our heroic dead' was unveiled at Moonta. Unseasonal rain kept the crowds away but nonetheless there was a parade by 'cadets, returned soldiers, and rejects' (the latter being volunteers deemed unfit for military service) under the charge of Sergeant-Major Matthews. The recently formed Soldiers' Female Relatives' Association provided refreshments for those who had braved the inclement weather: 'Pasties, Mesdames Sampson, Dunstan and Sleep; ice cream, Mrs Burnell; cool drinks, Mrs Keen; tea, Mesdames Marshall and Luscombe; scones, Mesdames Wearne and Davey; sandwiches, Mrs Andrewartha; cake, Mrs Maddaford'.[49]

'O God, our help' played the band before the memorial's unveiling, followed by an 'impressive address' by Revd H. Woolnough, the RSSIL's state President. Wreaths were laid, the names of the fallen read out, and the 'Last Post' sounded. Most significant perhaps was the choice of anthem to accompany the unveiling, 'The Song of Australia', already regarded by many South Australians as their unofficial national song. Indeed, on northern Yorke Peninsula it had a particular resonance, for its author – Caroline Carleton – had lived at Matta House at Kadina until her death in 1874, and was buried at Wallaroo.[50] The choice of anthem, then, was distinctly national – if not nationalist – with a strong state and regional dimension that emphasised its relevance locally. In press reports of the unveiling, there was no mention of 'God Save the King', although 'The Song of Australia' did acknowledge the country's elevated position within the British Empire, with a deferential nod towards the old country. It was an anthem that evoked the boundless expanses of the Australian continent, and the wide, dazzling bright-blue summer sky:

> There is a land where summer skies
> Are gleaming with a thousand dyes,
> Blending in witching harmonies, in harmonies:
> And grassy knoll, and forest height,
> Are flushing in the rosy light,
> And all above in azure bright –
> Australia!

It was also an anthem, especially relevant in South Australia and on Yorke Peninsula, that paid tribute to the country's extraordinary mineral wealth:

> There is a land where treasures shine
> Deep in the dark unfathomed mine,
> For worshippers at Mammon's shrine,
> Where gold lies hid, and rubies gleam,
> And fabled wealth no more doth seem
> The idle fancy of a dream –
> Australia!

And it was an anthem that celebrated the freedom and pride of Australia, with its own flag to fly and its superior status within the Empire. It was a sentiment tailor-made for post-Great War Australia:

> There is land where, floating free,
> From mountain top to girdling sea,
> A proud flag waves exultingly,
> And freedom's sons the banner bear,
> No shackled slave can breathe the air,
> Fairest of Britain's daughters fair –
> Australia![51]

A return to normality?

Yet post-war Australia, if not exactly the 'hell' that John Verran had depicted, was hardly the romantic idyll of the 'The Song of Australia' – especially on northern Yorke Peninsula. In June 1919 the Versailles Treaty had at last been signed, and the Australian government announced two days of celebration – Sunday 6 July for religious observance and thanksgiving, and a secular 'Peace Day' on Saturday 19 July for community activities. On the latter day, each schoolchild in Moonta, Wallaroo and Kadina was presented with a Cornish pasty.[52] The choice of fare was highly significant. It was a choice suggestive of regional cultural unity and distinctiveness, drawing on the district's Cornish origins, and promoted a sense of regional solidarity in the aftermath of war. Moreover, it was a gesture that, in looking to the future, placed great store on what had gone before, an act of faith which anticipated that life on northern Yorke Peninsula would return shortly to its pre-war normality. Fundamental to this normality were the mines and smelters that had produced prosperity before and during the conflict, supporting the economic, social and cultural fabric of the regional community. The Cornish pasty was symbolic of this regional identity, and an icon of regional stability and self-confidence.

However, even as the schoolchildren munched their Peace Day pasties, so reality on the Peninsula had begun to diverge from the comforting symbolism that the choice of fare implied. To begin with, any sense of regional solidarity had been undermined by the Conscription issue and Referenda, together with the attendant splits in the Labor movement locally and nationally. Additionally, the return during 1919 of scores of servicemen had prompted worries as to how these former soldiers would be found jobs and reintegrated into the community. But the major problem facing the district was the future of the mines themselves. By the end of 1918 it was evident to all who cared to see that the 'good times' were over, perhaps permanently.[53] Profit for the year had declined by almost half, compared to 1917 levels, although – as the local trade unionists no doubt observed – shareholders had still received £80,000 in dividends. In August 1918, anticipating the end of the war, the British government had terminated its contract for Yorke Peninsula copper, a grim foretaste of what lay ahead. Timely intervention by the Prime Minister, Billy Hughes, secured an extension until the end of the year but the writing was already on the wall.[54]

The reality was that the mines and smelters of northern Yorke Peninsula had prospered as part of a war economy – before August 1914 as part of Germany's 'peaceful penetration' in quest of raw materials to fuel the expansion of its military-industrial complex, and thereafter in support of the British Empire's war effort. On 1 January 1919, the Wallaroo and Moonta Mining and Smelting Company took the unpopular but perhaps inevitable decision to reduce wages.

66. Peace Procession at Moonta, probably on 'Peace Day', Saturday 19 July 1919.

The Moonta men, still smarting from their perceived loss of status attendant upon the relative decline of their mine compared to the Wallaroo, took particular exception, a meeting of 400 miners protesting that the Company was sitting on £250,000 of accumulated war profits.[55] Meanwhile, the price of copper on the international market had dropped alarmingly, while costs of production at Moonta and Wallaroo continued to climb.

As Keith Bailey has observed, this was an 'impossible position', with the cost of producing one ton of local copper now an extraordinary £20 above its market price.[56] In March 1919 activity at the mines was curtailed severely, coming to a complete stop on 15 April, with a renewed coal strike in New South Wales ensuring that Moonta and Wallaroo would lie idle throughout the winter months. The stoppage coincided with the rush of returned servicemen, and many who had expected to get their old jobs back – like James Roberts, an employee in the pay office at the Wallaroo mine before going off to war – were disappointed.[57] The arrival of a ship laden with coal at Wallaroo in early September signalled a return to production at the mines, but there was a further period of inactivity from January to March 1920, with coal shortages again being part of the problem. The continuing depression of international copper prices precipitated another closedown over Christmas 1920, with the mines lying idle once more from January through to August 1921. The Australian Workers Union (AWU) approached the Company several times during this period, seeking negotiations with a view to re-opening the mines. But the management was resistant to talks, explaining that the shortage of coal made a resumption of operations quite impossible at present. Inevitably, industrial relations were set to take a marked turn for the worst.[58]

R.S. Richards, the local MP who had ousted John Verran and masterminded the AWU merger (see pp. 156–9), supported the AWU in its approaches to the Company and in its desire to negotiate a return to work on existing pay and conditions. Verran, meanwhile, with the support of his Bogus union, insisted that the men would happily accept a further wage cut, if this was what was required to get the mines working again. Here was a return to the internecine industrial warfare of earlier years: the personal feud between John Verran and R.S. Richards, and the continuing struggle for legitimacy between the AWU and the Bogies. Verran and the Bogies came close to a deal with the management, but the AWU was determined that any return to work would be on its terms alone. Verran had made many enemies in the community. Yet there were those, such as 'Old Cornishman' who put pen to paper in August 1921, who complained loudly about the blocking tactics of the AWU militants and welcomed Verran's pragmatic attempts to re-open the mines.[59] In the event, work was at last resumed on 22 August 1921. But the resumption was short-lived. The price of copper fell to £65 per ton in January 1922, and then down to £58 in the February. Production costs now stood at £88 per ton, and so once more operations were suspended, the mines remaining closed from 15 February until the August.[60] Then, in a further attempt to reduce costs, the Moonta and Wallaroo Company announced that in future the jackhammer rock drills used underground would be manned by one miner only rather than the customary two. The AWU scheduled a meeting at Kadina to discuss the matter but before it was convened two miners at Moonta were sent 'to grass' for refusing to adopt the new working practice.[61] This precipitated a walkout by workers at both Moonta and Wallaroo, a short but bitter strike in which R.S. Richards issued his passionate call-to-arms and final denunciation of Verran and the Bogies, a leaflet that was circulated urgently throughout the district:

> Starvation may drive us back into the Mines; man's inhumanity to man may make countless thousands continue to mourn; but, whatever the result, we will never forget those men who aided the oppressor, we will never forget those men who played us false, and when the Time comes to show our contempt for them, we will do so in no uncertain manner. In the meantime:

> We will speak out, we will be heard, though all earth's system
> crack;
> We will not bate one single word or take a letter back,

For the cause that lacks assistance, 'gainst the wrongs that need
                                                    resist resistance,
For the future in the distance, and the good that we can do.

>   R.S. Richards MP
>   North Moonta.[62]

The dispute went to Arbitration and a compromise was struck, with a
return to work on 7 November 1922. Prompted by R.S. Richards, the South
Australian government undertook a local geological survey with the aim of
assisting future development work at the mines. But by now the reality was
that there was no future. Some exploratory work continued at the Wallaroo
mine during 1923 but on the afternoon of 23 October 1923, the National Bank
foreclosed on the Wallaroo and Moonta Mining and Smelting Company.[63] Far
from the return to normality that the celebrants of Peace Day in 1919 had
sought so earnestly, here was the final act in the post-war disintegration of the
industry that had underpinned northern Yorke Peninsula's regional identity
and so much of its economy.[64] Old Kio would never be the same again.
Indeed, after the mines went formally into liquidation in November 1923,
the wholesale dismantling and disposal of the plant and infrastructure had
a profound impact on the local environment, fondly remembered buildings
on the skyline felled overnight and derelict (and dangerous) wastelands left
in their wake. For the returned servicemen, so recently exposed to the
destruction and tortured landscapes of the Western Front, this was a dreadful
irony: not only the disappearance of jobs to which they might have aspired,
but also the violent disruption of a hitherto familiar topography.

'Their orgy of destruction'

Some of those returned servicemen, at least, found temporary employment
amidst the dismantling of the mines, assisting in the demolition of buildings
and plant and the marshalling of miscellaneous assets for sale.[65] Designed to
offset the Company's losses, the dismantled infrastructure – even recovered
bricks and stones – was sold off, with an auction catalogue of machinery
and stores compiled which, in its extraordinary comprehensiveness, included
everything from Cornish pump engines, Cornish boilers, railway locomotives,
blast furnaces and travelling cranes, to miners' helmets and emery cloth.[66]
Even as late as 1932 the process of demolition was continuing, when the
chimney stack at the old Matta mine was dynamited and Elder's engine house
at the Wallaroo mine was dismantled. Fred Botterill of Kadina, a former
miner, expressed his sorrow at this continuing destruction. 'It is rather a
pity that we cannot have one or two landmarks left', he complained: 'They

67.   Salvaged material collected for sale at the Wallaroo mine, following closure in
November 1923.

[the Company] are not content without they tear down everything they can.
When the mine was going its was dividends for shareholders – now, when she
is done, they try to see how much wreckage they can leave about the place'.[67]
Another critic was Graham Jenkin, who shared Botterill's misgivings. He
too regretted that nothing was 'preserved as a memorial to the thousands of
people who had made such a mighty contribution to this state and nation'. As
he put it: 'Nothing was left ... The capitalists, in their orgy of destruction,
got their money'.[68] In fact, several of the old Cornish engine houses did
survive, too solid and therefore too expensive to demolish and recycle, left
abandoned amid the derelict landscape. In a way they were memorials, but
not yet comparable to those that marked the fallen of the Great War.

Traumatic for the community as a whole, returnees as well as others,
the closure and subsequent dismantling of the mines was a prelude to the
departure of much of the younger element of the population. During the first
twelve months since closure, more than 500 adults had quit the district, and
a choir of unemployed miners had already won popular attention in Adelaide,
with its repertoire of Methodist hymns and Cornish carols.[69] Subsequently,
others left for Broken Hill and Kalgoorlie – both traditional destinations for
Peninsula folk – and some went to Port Pirie and Whyalla, industrial centres
within South Australia. Many cottages were left abandoned, especially on the
old mineral leases at Moonta Mines and Wallaroo Mines where they were
simply pulled down. 'Whole suburbs, which happened to be built on the

68. Oswald Pryor's cartoon 'Scatterin' The Bal' (dismantling the mine) is designed to be humorous but there is no escaping the sense of bewilderment and powerlessness experienced by his onlookers as they witness the wholesale destruction of their environment.

mineral leases', Jenkin complained, 'were flattened so that the stone in the cottage walls and the galvanized iron roofs could be sold as rubble or scrap'.[70] Overall, it was estimated, more than 3,000 people left northern Yorke Peninsula in the decade after 1923, some 85 per cent of these from the mineral leases. The Royal Geological Society of Australia detected a 'strong defeatist attitude' at Wallaroo in the inter-war period, a mood which it contrasted with the stubbornness of the mineral lease dwellers. Even 'when the source of employment was removed', the Society reported, 'the population [at Moonta Mines and Wallaroo Mines] proved highly resistant to migration. While many left, hundreds clung on, eking out a bare living by casual labour on farms, docks and grain depots until entitled to old age or incapacity pensions'.[71]

Some of the returned servicemen, invalided home during the war, already had their incapacity pensions. But for others the desperate shortage of local employment opportunities meant that they joined the exodus of young people from the region, leaving behind 'a high proportion of aged and infirm', as it was reported.[72] Some were enticed to the copper mines of Bougainville; others went to a brief reworking of the old Preamimma mine, near Callington.[73] A few tried their luck in 'one-man shows', prospecting alone or in small groups amidst the abandoned mines of northern Yorke Peninsula. Fossickers, as they were known, scavenged among the waste dumps at the New Cornwall and Wandilta mines, near Kadina, searching for minerals, and in 1936 there was a short lived attempt to re-open the New Cornwall. The Poona mine, near Moonta, was worked intermittently for a few years after 1923, and in the mid-1930s the old Doora and Duryea mines were opened briefly for prospecting work. Groups of unemployed men, with the familiar local names – Nankivell, Anderson, Trenwith, Harvey – scoured the old Wallaroo mine property for signs of untouched ore. The Wild Dog Mine, east of Yelta, was one 'show' that enjoyed relative success. First opened in 1918, it was employing ten men by 1922 and lingered until late 1930.[74]

During 1924 a Moonta Copper Recovery Co. had purchased the cementation works at the mine, employing twenty-four men and working intermittently during the 1920s and 1930s. Likewise, a Moonta Prospecting Syndicate was formed to rework the south-eastern portion of the Moonta leases. It worked steadily until 1929 when, as copper prices rose, R.S. Richards – by now Minister of Mines in the South Australian government – was able to arrange a state subsidy to support the Syndicate and other groups of 'tributers' working on their own account. Richards also negotiated short-term financial assistance from the Federal government, the combined effect of his efforts being to keep the Syndicate in operation more or less continuously until it was wound up in 1939. Although none of these schemes was ultimately successful, it was argued that they had been worthwhile, creating jobs for men who would otherwise have been unemployed or forced to leave the Peninsula. As Richards himself

69. The cementation works at the Moonta mine, purchased in 1924 by the Moonta
Copper Recovery Co.

had observed, the subsidies were 'the most practicable way to relieve the
serious unemployment' in the district, especially given 'the interest and
willingness displayed by the employees'.[75]

Yet all this was exceptionally small beer compared to the glory days of
Moonta and Wallaroo. Only a tiny handful of men was able to find sustained
employment among the fossickers, tributers and syndicalists, hardly enough
to stem the continuing exodus of the young and healthy. The community
also suffered in sometimes unexpected ways. Local sporting organisations,
for example, that had looked forward to the reinvigorating influence of
athletes returning from the war, found instead that their ranks diminished
alarmingly as key players left to find work elsewhere. The Federal Rovers
Football Club, at Kadina, struggled on until 1926 when, reluctantly, it was
disbanded. Musical groups faced similar problems – the Federal Brass Band
collapsed soon after the mines were closed, followed shortly by the renowned
Wallaroo Mines Orchestra.[76] Where there was hope, was in the continued
development of northern Yorke Peninsula as an agricultural region. By now
recovered from the drought of the early war years, local farmers were able
to absorb some of the returned servicemen into their workforce. Kadina
emerged as the largest and strongest of three erstwhile mining towns, and
became a regional centre serving an extensive agricultural district that
ranged from southern Yorke Peninsula to Balaclava in the east and Crystal
Brook in the north. Wallaroo weathered the closure of the copper smelters,
its sulphuric acid plant surviving as an important destination for Broken Hill

70.   A changing regional economy – stacking wheat at Moonta railway station, c.1930s.

zinc concentrates, its port an increasingly important outlet for the region's agricultural produce. Only Moonta found it difficult to adjust, settling down as a dormitory town for its two more active neighbours.[77]

The rapid and bewildering demise of the Yorke Peninsula mines was, as we have seen, a direct result of the Great War. This was the supreme irony for the returning servicemen, who had looked forward to their homecoming amidst the familiar sights of the three towns and their hinterlands, and had anticipated an easy return to old jobs or the acquisition of new in what they thought to be a still booming regional economy. Some, like Leonard Harvey, had been alarmed by news of the deep divisions revealed by the Conscription controversy, and by evidence of mounting industrial tensions at the mines. Yet even Len Harvey was unprepared for the swift demise of the Peninsula mines, and, like other returned soldiers, was met not by the reassuring noise and bustle of prosperity but rather long spells of unsettling silence, culminating in collapse. Worse still, perhaps, was the violent transformation of the mighty industrial infrastructure they had known so well into a blasted and blighted landscape, not unlike the battlefields they had so recently endured. For the 'boys from old Kio', who at the battlefront had so resolutely displayed their regional solidarity and local patriotism, it was a return – if not to hell – then to a homefront environment that none of them could possibly have imagined when they marched away to war.

'The Hub of the Universe?'

'A veteran of the 1914–1918 war had a story to tell of Moonta patriotism', wrote Oswald Pryor in his light-hearted but telling local history *Australia's Little Cornwall*, first published in 1962:

> One evening I was drinking in an estaminet in France with a cobber, Billy Bray from Moonta. He was small in size but big in heart, and Moonta was his theme song. Some liquid had been spilt on the table, and when the waitress came to take our order Billy said: 'Mamzelle you compree the world?' as he drew a circle with a wet finger. She said that she did. 'Then', said Billy, dabbing a finger in the centre of the circle, 'this is where I come from – Moonta'.[1]

As Pryor observed: 'To thousands of people like Billy Bray, Moonta was the hub of the universe'.[2] He might have added that the apocryphal Billy Bray also typified Kio boys at the front. So obviously Australian – a 'cobber' – he was nonetheless deeply rooted in the region of his birth, northern Yorke Peninsula, a regional identity signified by his so obviously Cornish name and expressed in the excessive claims made for the significance of his hometown, Moonta. During those war years, as the copper-mining economy of Yorke Peninsula boomed in response to the Empire's demand for this strategic metal, such pride in place seemed more than justified. But, as we have seen, beneath the veneer of regional solidarity, those years also spawned deep divisions within the community – not least over the Conscription issue – splits which soldiers at the front became aware of but slowly and found deeply disturbing. Moreover, as demand slumped dramatically at the war's end, so the mines and smelters of Moonta, Wallaroo and Kadina were plunged into crisis, struggling from one temporary closure to the next until they were abandoned for good in 1923. The divisions of the war years were perpetuated in the bitter industrial climate that characterised the death throes of the mines. Returned soldiers, arriving home at last, found a community still riven with ideological suspicions, and an economy apparently in tatters. There were forlorn attempts to revive the mining corpse – the Moonta cementation works, for example, and the efforts of various tribute parties and syndicates – but their impact was limited. Many had to look beyond the Peninsula for work. But the Returned Sailors' and Soldiers' Imperial League (RSSIL), mindful of its comrades' sacrifice and the mourning omnipresent in the community, took the lead in local Commemoration – administering war trophies, erecting war memorials, organising Anzac Day events – and in so doing became a voice of authority in the locality.

In many ways, during the Great War the people of northern Yorke Peninsula had been encouraged to think of themselves first and foremost as Australians. The exploits of the A.I.F., from the dawn landing at Gallipoli to the impressive performance of Monash's corps, had underscored this sense of Australianess. But so too had events in Australia itself. Local mineworkers, for example, had begun to see their interests, loyalties and occupational identities in Australia-wide rather then merely Peninsula contexts, notably in the merger with the Australian Workers Union. Taken together, the salience of this consolidating Australian identity, and the at least partial disintegration of the social and economic fabric of northern Yorke Peninsula consequent upon the Peace, might have heralded the demise of regional distinctiveness. Even Moonta, so long assured of its privileged status within the Peninsula, had diminished in relative importance during the war, when resources were shifted heavily to the Wallaroo mine, a decline that became absolute after 1919 when Kadina assumed the mantle of leading township in the district.

In such circumstances, the notion of old Kio did indeed begin to fade away. The phrase, commonplace throughout the Great War, started to fall from general use, although never forgotten and still retained affectionately in private use in many families. No longer in the public domain, Kio had retreated into this private sphere, a suitable name for a family boat, or dog, or holiday shack. Nonetheless, the wider regional identity proved surprisingly robust in the face of social and economic change. R.S. Richards, the left-wing agitator who had replaced John Verran as local MP, continued to represent the Wallaroo constituency in the South Australian parliament until 1949, and was briefly state Premier during 1933. In this lengthy career he personified and led the continuing influence of the Peninsula's political tradition in the affairs of the state's Labor Party. As John Lonie noted in his analysis of the Australian Labor Party in South Australia in the inter-war years: 'By the 1930s, the ALP itself did not mirror, in its hierarchy, the changes that had taken place in the composition of the workforce . . . especially since the end of World War I'. Instead, 'its composition and ideology reflected the social situation of the 1890s. Of note was the still very strong Methodist flavour

71. The 'Cousin Jacks' who took Thomas Wood underground at the Moonta
Extended Mine, c.1930–31.

which derived in the first place from the mine workers of Burra and Wallaroo who were of Cornish stock'.[3] Despite the sudden abandonment of the Yorke Peninsula mines and the dispersal of the workforce, the distinctive political legacy had remained.

When the English travel writer Thomas Wood visited northern Yorke Peninsula in the early 1930s, he was also struck by the region's enduring distinctiveness. He found it 'as British as can be' but 'distinct and clannish'. At its heart was 'Moonta, where the Cousin Jacks . . . still eat Cornish pasties and Cornish cream', and where 'every other man you meet talks copper, and licks his chops against the day when it will fetch its price again'.[4] These were the years when various syndicates were trying their luck on the old mineral leases. 'Two families working together had just sunk a new shaft', Wood explained: 'I wanted to go down? Good-O! said a chorus of Cousin Jacks; and down we went'. He was also intrigued by the recycling of old motor vehicles at the cementation works, where 'Moontanians with strong Cornish accents smash them to bits, spread them out in troughs, pump Mine water over them for a month or two, clean the troughs out, and send for more cars'.[5]

In a lightness-of-touch style of a type later made famous by Oswald Pryor, Thomas Wood had anticipated the post-industrial re-invention of northern Yorke Peninsula as 'Australia's Little Cornwall'. 'Pure Cornwall; except for the gorse and the bluebells', was his conclusion, and in this imagining of Moonta and environs he prefigured the heritage tourism constructions of the post-Second World War era.[6] But for now it was enough to note the survival of a distinct regional identity, readily observable to outsiders, in the difficult aftermath of the Great War.

Joan Beaumont, in her discussion of the impact of the Great War upon Australia, has pondered the debate between those who consider the conflict to have been a major agent of change, and others who stress the continuity between the pre- and post-war worlds, where the war merely accelerated existing trends. Wisely, Beaumont steers a middle course between the two, noting examples to support both hypotheses.[7] In the case of northern Yorke Peninsula, it is clear that the Great War accounted for both the boom times and subsequent bust in the regional mining economy, with returned soldiers coming home to a region in turmoil. In none of the victorious Allied countries was there 'a land fit for heroes' in the 1920s and 1930s, and for those soldiers who had trumpeted the charms of old Kio there was a particular poignancy, even irony, in their homecoming. Yet northern Yorke Peninsula shared in the new myths of nationhood forged by war, and, despite the reverses it suffered, continued to assert a powerful regional identity. War memorials at Moonta, Wallaroo and Kadina – and at other settlements across the Peninsula – were also testament to an enduring memory of those who had gone from the community to fight in distant lands, many never to return.

Today, as the Peninsula celebrates its Cornish mining past, it also continues to commemorate and memorialise the fallen of the Great War. Not far, perhaps, from where the old 'Kio' signpost stood a century or more ago, now stands the lovingly refurbished war trophy, the captured German field-gun first presented to Moonta in 1921. Located in its especially constructed display housing, the gun was rededicated in a public ceremony in February 2007, a striking memorial that catches the eye of all who enter Moonta from the Kadina road, evidence of a sombre pride that still suffuses the community in the early twenty-first century.

Notes

Chapter 1. 'A different war': The regional experience

1. Brian Cooper, *The Quintrells of Moonta Mines in the Great War: Richard Hugh Quintrell – 32ⁿᵈ Btn; Clarence Horace Quintrell – 50ᵗʰ Btn; John Adolfus[sic] Quintrell – 32ⁿᵈ Btn* (Mount Gambier, 2003), p. i.

2. Cooper, *The Quintrells of Moonta Mines*, p. i.

3. Annette Becker, *Les Monuments aux Morts* (Paris, 1989); I am grateful to Martin Thomas for drawing Becker's work to my attention.

4. Cooper, *The Quintrells of Moonta Mines*, appendix 1.

5. See, for example, Jay Winter, *Sites of Memory, Sites of Mourning: The Great War in European Cultural History* (Cambridge, 1995); Jay Winter, Geoffrey Parker, and Mary R. Habeck (eds), *The Great War and the Twentieth Century* (New Haven, 2000); Dan Todman, *The Great War: Myth and Memory* (London, 2005), Jay Winter and Antoine Prost, *The Great War in History: Debates and Controversies, 1914 to the Present* (Cambridge, 2005). For Australian perspectives, see Joy Damousi, *The Labour of Loss: Mourning, Memory and Wartime Bereavement in Australia* (Cambridge, 1997) and Bart Ziino, *A Distant Greif: Australians, War Graves and the Great War* (Fremantle, 2007).

6. See Paul Fussell, *The Great War and Modern Memory* (Oxford, 1975, repub. 2000).

7. Daphne du Maurier, *Gerald: A Portrait* (London, 1934, repub. 2006), pp. 133, 135, 165.

8. A.J.P. Taylor, *The First World War: An Illustrated History* (London, 1963, repub. 1982), p. 287.

9. Gary Sheffield, *Forgotten Victory: The First World War – Myths and Realities* (London, 2002); William Philpott, *Bloody Victory: The Sacrifice on the Somme* (London, 2009); see also Paddy Griffith (ed.), *British Fighting Methods in the Great War* (London, 1996) and Gary Sheffield, *The Chief: Douglas Haig and the British Army* (London, 2011).

10. Mark David Sheftall, *Altered Memories of the Great War: Divergent Narratives of Britain, Australia, New Zealand and Canada* (London, 2009), p. 185.

11. Sheftall, *Altered Memories of the Great War*, p. 184.

12. Jean Beaumont (ed.), *Australia's War, 1914–18* (St Leonards (NSW), 1995), p. 149.

13. K.S. Inglis, 'The Anzac Tradition', *Meanjin Quarterly*, March 1965; E.M. Andrews, *The Anzac Illusion: Anglo-Australian Relations during World War I* (Cambridge, 1993); Christopher Pugsley, *The ANZAC Experience* (Auckland, 2004).

14. Patricia Grimshaw, Marilyn Lake, Ann McGrath and Marian Quartly, *Creating a Nation, 1788–1900* (Ringwood (Vic.), 1994), p. 218; Robin Gerster, *Big-Noting: The Heroic Theme in Australian War Writing* (Melbourne, 1987).

15. John Hirst, *Sense and Nonsense in Australian History* (Melbourne, 2006), p. 233.

16. Martin Crotty, '25 April 1915. Australian Troops Land at Gallipoli: Trial, Trauma and the "Birth of a Nation"', in Martin Crotty and David Andrew Roberts (eds), *Turning Points in Australian History* (Sydney, 2009), p. 102.

17. John McQuilton, *Rural Australia and the Great War: From Tarrawingee to Tangambalanga* (Melbourne, 2001), p. 219; see also Bruce Scates, *Return to Gallipoli: Walking Battlefields of the Great War* (Cambridge, 2006).

18. Beaumont (ed.), *Australia's War, 1914–18*, p. 175; Bill Gammage, *The Broken Years: Australian Soldiers in the Great War* (Canberra, 1974, repub. London, 1975).

19. Neville Meaney, 'Britishness and Australia: Some Reflections', in Carl Bridge and Kent Fedorowich (eds), *The British World: Diaspora, Culture and Identity* (London, 2003), p. 121; see also Stuart Ward, *Australia and the British Embrace: The Demise of the Imperial Ideal* (Melbourne, 2001).

20. See Philip Payton, *Making Moonta: The Invention of Australia's Little Cornwall* (Exeter, 2007).

21. See Patrick Lindsay, *Fromelles* (Prahan (Vic.), 2008).

22. *Yorke Peninsula Country Times*, 8 July 2008.

23. *Hill Gazette* (Western Australia), 30 June 2009.

24. Michael McKernan, *The Australian People and the Great War* (Melbourne, 1980); McQuilton, *Rural Australia and the Great War*.

25. Bobbie Oliver, *War and Peace in Western Australia: The Social and Political Impact of the Great War* (Fremantle, 1995).

26. Raymond Evans, *Loyalty and Disloyalty: Social Conflict on the Queensland Homefront* (St Lucia, 1987), p. 2; see also Dan Coward, 'The Impact of War on New South Wales: Some Aspects of Social and Political History', unpub. Ph.D. thesis, Australian National University, 1974; Marilyn Lake, *A Divided Society: Tasmania during World War I* (Melbourne, 1975); Marilyn Lake, *The Limits of Hope: Soldier Settlement in Victoria, 1915–1926* (Melbourne, 1987).

27. McQuilton, *Rural Australia and the Great War*, p. 2.

28. Alistair Thomson, *Anzac Memories: Living with the Legend* (Oxford, 1994), p. 118–19.

29. See Carl Johnson and Andrew Barnes (eds), *Jacka's Mob: A Narrative of the Great War by Edgar John Rule* (Prahan (Vic.), 1999).

30. J.G. Fuller, *Troop Morale and Popular Culture in the British and Dominion Armies 1914–1918* (Oxford, 2006), p. 160.

31. Moonta *People's Weekly*, 29 September 1916.

32. Lyn Macdonald, *Somme* (London, 1983), p. 36.

33. Fuller, *Troop Morale and Popular Culture*, p. 42.

34. Fuller, *Troop Morale and Popular Culture*, p. 43.

Chapter 2. 'To make Australia's name glorious': Kio goes to war

1. I am grateful to Liz Coole and the late Jim Harbison for explaining the hitherto obscure origins of the term 'Kio'.

2. This 'Cousin Jack humour' was exemplified in the cartoons of Oswald Pryor; see Oswald Pryor, *Cornish Pasty* (Adelaide, 1961) and Oswald Pryor, *Cousin Jacks and Jennys* (Adelaide, 1966).

3. Oswald Pryor, *Australia's Little Cornwall* (Adelaide, 1962).

4. Payton, *Making Moonta*, chapter 1.

5. *People's Weekly*, 21 July 1945.

6. *People's Weekly*, 12 August 1899, 23 November 1940.

7. *People's Weekly*, 28 September 1935.

8. *People's Weekly*, 31 March 1906.

9. *People's Weekly*, 4 May 1907, 27 July 1907.

10. I am indebted to Elizabeth Harris for this information.

11. Pers. comm. (email), Liz Coole to Philip Payton, 6 May 2008.

12. See Payton, *Making Moonta*, pp. 28–31.

13. *People's Weekly*, 10 November 1906.

14. Payton, *Making Moonta*, chapter 4.

15. *People's Weekly*, 17 July 1915.

16. W.G. Spence, *Australia's Awakening: Thirty years in the Life of an Australian Agitator* (Sydney, 1909), p. 27.

17. Arnold Hunt, *This Side of Heaven: A History of Methodism in South Australia* (Adelaide, 1985), p. 117.

18. Payton, *Making Moonta*, chapter 4.

19. R. Norris, 'Economic Influences on the 1898 South Australian Federation Referendum', in A.W. Martin, *Essays in Australian Federation* (Melbourne, 1969), p. 150.

20. Payton, *Making Moonta*, pp. 181–2.

21. Jan Lokan, 'From Cornish Miner to Farmer in Nineteenth-Century South Australia: A Case Study', in Philip Payton (ed.), *Cornish Studies: Sixteen* (Exeter, 2008), pp. 48–77.

22. See Philip Payton, *The Cornish Farmer in Australia* (Redruth, 1987), pp. 91–2.

23. *Observer* (Adelaide), 9 July 1870.

24. *Yorke's Peninsula Advertiser*, 2 May 1873.

25. *Yorke's Peninsula Advertiser*, 22 May 1874; 13 June 1876.

26. *Yorke's Peninsula Advertiser*, 1 January 1878.

27. Philip Payton, 'The Cornish in South Australia: Their Influence and Experience from Immigration to Assimilation, 1836–1936', unpub. Ph.D. thesis, University of Adelaide, 1978, pp. 331–3.

28. Payton, *Making Moonta*, p. 61.

29. May Vivienne, *Sunny South Australia* (Adelaide, 1908), p. 263.

30. Payton, *Making Moonta*, especially chapters 1 and 2.

31. Norris, 'Economic Influences', p. 150.

32. Gavin Souter, *Lion and Kangaroo: The Initiation of Australia* (Melbourne, 1976; new edn 2000), pp. 57–8.

33. Geoffrey Blainey, *A Shorter History of Australia* (Milsons Point (NSW), 1994; new edn 2000); Phillip Knightly, *Australia: Biography of a Nation* (London, 2000), p. 58;

Wilfred Prest, Kerrie Round and Carol Fort (eds), *The Wakefield Companion to South Australian History* (Adelaide, 2001), pp. 77–8; P.A. Howell, *South Australia and Federation* (Adelaide, 2002), p. 213.

34. From Monty Grover (1870–1943), 'I Killed a Man at Graspan: The Tale of a Returned Australian Continenter Done in Verse', in John Laird (ed.), *The Australian Experience of War* (London, 1988), pp. 31–2.

35. *People's Weekly*, 8 February 1900.

36. *People's Weekly*, 20 January 1900.

37. *People's Weekly*, 7 April 1900.

38. Blainey, *A Shorter History of Australia*, pp. 152–3; Joan Beaumont, 'Australia's War', in Beaumont (ed.), *Australia's War 1914–18*, pp. 3–4; David Stevens, '1900–1913: The Genesis of the Australian Navy', in David Stevens (ed.), *The Royal Australian Navy: A History* (South Melbourne, 2001, repub. 2006), pp. 13–27.

39. *Yorke's Peninsula Advertiser*, 3 October 1913.

40. Marnie Haig-Muir, 'The Economy at War', in Beaumont (ed.), *Australia's War 1914–18*, p. 107.

41. Keith Bailey, *James Boor's Bonanza: A History of Wallaroo Mines, South Australia* (Kadina, 2002), p. 134.

42. These models remain at the Moonta School of Mines, now a museum and research centre under the aegis of the National Trust of South Australia, Moonta Branch.

43. Pam Maclean, 'War and Australian Society', in Beaumont (ed.), *Australia's War 1914–18*, p. 64.

44. *People's Weekly*, 10 January 1914.

45. David Steven, '1914–18: World War One', in Stevens (ed.), *The Royal Australian Navy*, pp. 33–6.

46. For an insight into the complexity of British opinion, see Stuart Dalley, 'The Response of Cornwall to the Outbreak of the First World War', in Philip Payton (ed.), *Cornish Studies: Eleven* (Exeter, 2003), pp. 85–109, and Catriona Pennell, *A Kingdom United: Popular Responses to the Outbreak of the First World War in Britain and Ireland* (Oxford, 2012).

47. *People's Weekly*, 25 March 1916.

48. *Australian Christian Commonwealth*, 11 September 1915. Bound copies of the *Australian Christian Commonwealth*, sporting John Verran's signature, were located at the Parkin-Wesley College in Adelaide in the mid-1970s.

49. *Yorke's Peninsula Advertiser*, 4 December 1914.

50. *Yorke's Peninsula Advertiser*, 8 January 1915.

51. *Yorke's Peninsula Advertiser*, 16 October 1914.

52. *Australian Christian Commonwealth*, 9 August 1914.

53. *Australian Christian Commonwealth*, 9 August 1914.

54. Liz Coole, Jim Harbison, Judith Hayde and Rosemary Gray, *Moonta Cemetery: A Walk through the Lives of the Pioneers from 'Australia's Little Cornwall'* (Moonta, 2009), pp. 12, 14, 65, and 92.

55. *People's Weekly*, 8 August 1914; 20 November 1915.

56. *People's Weekly*, 7 October 1916.

57. *Kadina and Wallaroo Times*, 13 January 1915.

58. *People's Weekly*, 8 August 1914.

59. Maclean, 'War and Australian Society', pp. 102–3

60. Bailey, *James Boor's Bonanza*, pp. 134–7.

61. *Yorke's Peninsula Advertiser*, 27 November 1914.
62. Haig-Muir, 'The Economy at War', p. 103.
63. *South Australian Register*, 4 August 1914.
64. Payton, *Making Moonta*, p. 181.
65. Bailey, *James Boor's Bonanza*, p. 136.
66. *Yorke's Peninsula Advertiser*, 16 April 1915.
67. Bailey, *James Boor's Bonanza*, p. 138; *Kadina and Wallaroo Times*, 3 July 1915.
68. *People's Weekly*, 5 September 1914.
69. *Yorke's Peninsula Advertiser*, 6 November 1914.
70. *Yorke's Peninsula Advertiser*, 26 March 1915.
71. *Yorke's Peninsula Advertiser*, 24 December 1914.
72. *People's Weekly*, 19 September 1914.
73. *People's Weekly*, 10 July 1915; National Archives of Australia (NAA) B2455/8071183 William Linton Rowett.
74. *People's Weekly*, 19 December 1914.
75. NAA B2455/8013596 James Merrifield.
76. NAA B2455/3489789 Oliver Leopold Davey.
77. *People's Weekly*, 1 December 1915.
78. NAA B2455/2489789 Oliver Leopold Davey.
79. *People's* Weekly, 29 May 1915.
80. NAA B2455/7365456 Ross Blyth Jacob.
81. NAA B2455/7365448 Kenneth Grant Jacob.
82. NAA B2455/5823123 H.S. Holthouse.
83. Gammage, *The Broken Years*, pp. 10–11.
84. Alec H. Chisholm, *Selected verse of C.J. Dennis* (Sydney, 1950), p. 45.
85. Peter Barton, Peter Doyle and Johan Vanderwalle, *Beneath Flanders Fields: The Tunnellers' War, 1914–18* (Staplehurst, 2004), pp. 72–4.
86. *Kadina and Wallaroo Times*, 23 October 1915.
87. *People's Weekly*, 6 May 1916, 15 July 1916, 16 November 1918.
88. *People's Weekly*, 19 May 1917, 11 August 1917, 13 October 1917, 21 June 1919, 28 June 1919, 12 July 1919, 26 July 1919; NAA B2455/8025040 Stanley Quintrell; NAA B2455/8025038 Percy Quintrell.
89. *People's Weekly*, 12 December 1914.
90. *People's Weekly*, 6 February 1914.
91. *People's Weekly*, 6 February 1915.
92. *People's Weekly*, 27 February 1915.
93. Gammage, *The Broken Years*, p. 26.
94. NAA B2455/3128325 Percy Brokenshire.
95. NAA B3455/1975495 Charles Anderson.
96. *Yorke's Peninsula Advertiser*, 7 May 1915.
97. *Yorke's Peninsula Advertiser*, 29 January 1915.
98. *People's Weekly*, 25 September 1914.
99. Robin Neillands, *The Old Contemptibles: The British Expeditionary Force, 1914* (London, 2004), pp. 281, 290, 304.
100. *People's Weekly*, 9 January 1915.
101. *People's Weekly*, 16 January 1915.
102. *Kadina and Wallaroo Times*, 27 March 1915.
103. Gammage, *The Broken Years*, p.39.

104. Noel Carthew, *Voices from the Trenches: Letters to Home* (Frenchs Forest (NSW), 2002), p. 87.

105. *Kadina and Wallaroo Times*, 27 March 1915.

106. *People's Weekly*, 5 June 1915.

107. *Corryong Courier*, 13 August 1914; cited in McQuilton, *Rural Australia and the Great War*, p.20.

108. Jillian Durance, *Still Going Strong: The Story of the Moyarra Honor Roll* (Moyarra, 2006), p. 9.

109. *West Australian*, 6 August 1914; see Oliver, *War and Peace in Western Australia*, pp. 27–60.

Chapter 3. 'Our motto is "dig on, dig ever": Gallipoli

1. *Yorke's Peninsula Advertiser*, 7 May 1915.

2. *People's Weekly*, 16 December 1893.

3. Anon., *The Barrier Silver and Tin Fields in 1888* (Adelaide, 1888, repub. 1970), p. 5.

4. *Burra Record*, 23 March 1892.

5. *People's Weekly*, 9 January 1915.

6. *People's Weekly*, 9 January 1915.

7. *People's Weekly*, 9 January 1915.

8. *People's Weekly*, 9 January 1915.

9. Brian Kennedy, *Silver, Sin and Sixpenny Ale: A Social History of Broken Hill, 1883–1921* (Melbourne, 1978), p. 130.

10. *People's Weekly*, 9 January 1915.

11. *People's Weekly*, 9 January 1915.

12. Kennedy, *Silver, Sin and Sixpenny Ale*, p. 131.

13. *People's Weekly*, 11 September 1915.

14. *People's Weekly*, 8 April 1916.

15. *People's Weekly*, 8 April 1916.

16. *Yorke's Peninsula Advertiser*, 10 September 1915.

17. Beaumont, 'Australia's War', p. 10.

18. Robert Kearney, *Silent Voices: The Story of the 10th Battalion AIF in Australia, Egypt, Gallipoli, France and Belgium during the Great War 1914–1918* (Sydney, 2005), pp. 69–71.

19. David Lowe, 'The Anzac Legend', in Beaumont (ed.), *Australia's War 1914–18*, p. 150.

20. *Argus*, 8 May 1915.

21. *Yorke's Peninsula Advertiser*, 7 May 1915.

22. *Yorke's Peninsula Advertiser*, 2 July 1915.

23. *Kadina and Wallaroo Times*, 23 June 1915.

24. *People's Weekly*, 15 May 1915.

25. *People's Weekly*, 26 June 1915.

26. NAA B2455/3041671 Leslie Ernest Barlow.

27. *People's Weekly*, 29 May 1915.

28. NAA B2455/3541656 Arthur Thomas Elphick.

29. *People's Weekly*, 18 June 1915.

30. NAA B2455/8015555 Melville Pethick.

31. *People's Weekly*, 26 June 1915; *Yorke's Peninsula Advertiser*, 2 July 1915.

32. Nigel Steel and Peter Hart, *Defeat at Gallipoli* (London, 1994), p. 172.

33. NAA B2455/3047551 David Ballantyne.

34. *People's Weekly*, 26 June 1915.

35. NAA B2455/1797570 Harry Cecil Brown; Australian War Memorial (AWM), Australian Red Cross Society Wounded and Missing Enquiry files, 1914–18 War, (ARCSWME files) IDRL/0428, 110 Sergeant Harry Cecil Brown, 10th Battalion.

36. NAA B3455/4736522 Lee Bray Nankivell.

37. *People's Weekly*, 10 July 1915.

38. *People's Weekly*, 17 July 1915.

39. NAA B2455/8070300 Fred Raymond.

40. *People's Weekly*, 17 July 1915.

41. NAA B2455/8019367 Richard Leopard Pomeroy.

42. *People's Weekly*, 17 July 1915.

43. *Yorke's Peninsula Advertiser*, 9 July 1915.

44. *Yorke's Peninsula Advertiser*, 9 July 1915.

45. *Yorke's Peninsula Advertiser*, 9 July 1915.

46. Cecil B.L. Lock, *The Fighting 10th: A South Australian Centenary Souvenir of the 10th Battalion, AIF, 1914–19* (Adelaide, 1936), p. 235.

47. Gammage, *The Broken Years*, p. 56; Steel and Hart, *Defeat at Gallipoli*, p. 63; Kearney, *Silent Voices*, p. 86–7.

48. Cited in Peter Pedersen, *The Anzacs: Gallipoli to the Western Front* (Camberwell (Vic.), 2007), p. 57.

49. NAA B2455/8016334 Roy Pickering.

50. NAA B2455/3048009 Henry Charles Banfield.

51. *Yorke's Peninsula Advertiser*, 27 August 1915.

52. *Yorke's Peninsula Advertiser*, 20 August 1915.

53. *Yorke's Peninsula Advertiser*, 27 August 1915.

54. *People's Weekly*, 28 August 1915.

55. *People's Weekly*, 28 August 1915.

56. *People's Weekly*, 28 August 1915.

57. *Yorke's Peninsula Advertiser*, 3 September 1915.

58. *People's Weekly*, 28 August 1915.

59. *People's Weekly*, 28 August 1915.

60. *People's Weekly*, 28 August 1915.

61. *People's Weekly*, 18 September, 1915, 24 September 1915.

62. *People's Weekly*, 1 December 1915.

63. *People's Weekly*, 21 August 1915.

64. *People's Weekly*, 21 August 1921.

65. *Kadina and Wallaroo Times*, 9 November 1915; *Yorke's Peninsula Advertiser*, 16 July 1915.

66. *Yorke's Peninsula Advertiser*, 16 July 1915; *People's Weekly*, 27 November 1915.

67. *Kadina and Wallaroo Times*, 9 November 1915; *Yorke's Peninsula Advertiser*, 16 July 1915; *People's Weekly*, 11 September 1915, 2 October 1915, 6 November 1915, 27 November 1915, 1 December 1915.

68. *People's Weeksly*, 1 December 1915.

69. *Yorke's Peninsula Advertiser*, 15 October, 1915; Reg Chapman, *Badges of the Childrens/ Schools Patriotic Funds: South Australia* (Balaclava (S.A.), 2000), pp. 1–4

70. *Yorke's Peninsula Advertiser*, 11 February 1916.

71. NAA B2455/8098856 Frederick Teo.

72. McQuilton, *Rural Australia and the Great War*, p. 101.

73. *Yorke's Peninsula Advertiser*, 6 August 1915.

74. *Yorke's Peninsula Advertiser*, 10 September 1915.

75. *Yorke's Peninsula Advertiser*, 10 September 1915.

76. *People's Weekly*, 31 December 1915.

77. Steel and Hart, *Defeat at Gallipoli*, p. 174

78. *People's Weekly*, 14 August 1915.

79. *People's Weekly*, 21 August 1915.

80. *People's Weekly*, 28 August 1915.

81. *London Gazette*, 1 June 1915; NAA B884/6330047 Joseph Cook Weatherill.

82. *People's Weekly*, 24 September 1915.

83. Steel and Hart, *Defeat at Gallipoli*, p. 230; L.A. Carlyon, *Gallipoli* (Sydney, 2001), p. 435.

84. Carlyon, *Gallipoli*, p. 447.

85. *People's Weekly*, 4 September 1915; see also *Yorke's Peninsula Advertiser*, 3 September 1915.

86. *People's Weekly*, 18 September 1915.

87. *People's Weekly*, 28 August 1915.

88. *People's Weekly*, 9 October 1915, 23 October 1915.

89. NAA B2455/3128351 William James Brokenshire.

90. *People's Weekly*, 20 November 1915.

91. *People's Weekly*, 9 October 1915.

92. NAA B2455/3128351 William James Brokenshire.

93. *People's Weekly*, 6 November 1915.

94. NAA B2455/8198155 Leigh Treweek Lennell.

95. NAA B2455/8198155 Leigh Treweek Lennell.

96. *People's Weekly*, 9 October 1915.

97. NAA B2455/8198155 Leigh Treweek Lennell.

98. *Yorke's Peninsula Advertiser*, 19 November 1915.

99. *Kadina and Wallaroo Times*, 16 October 1915; *People's Weekly*, 9 October 1915.

100. *People's Weekly*, 1 December 1915.

101. *Kadina and Wallaroo Times*, 13 November 1915.

102. NAA B2455/4738519 Frank Norman Harwood.

103. *People's Weekly*, 9 October 1915.

104. *People's Weekly*, 9 October 1915.

105. *People's Weekly*, 9 October 1915.

106. *People's Weekly*, 20 November 1915.

107. *People's Weekly*, 31 December 1915.

108. *People's Weekly*, 31 December 1915.

109. *People's Weekly*, 11 September 1915.

110. *People's Weekly*, 20 November 1915.

111. *People's Weekly*, 24 September 1915.

112. *People's Weekly*, 20 November 1915.

113. NAA B2455/8033143 Jacob Roach.

114. *People's Weekly*, 13 November 1915.

115. *People's Weekly*, 9 October 1915.

116. *People's Weekly*, 11 December 1915.

117. *People's Weekly*, 20 November 1915.

118. *People's Weekly*, 20 November 1915.
119. *People's Weekly*, 1 December 1915.
120. *People's Weekly*, 6 November 1915.
121. *People's Weekly*, 13 November 1915.
122. *People's Weekly*, 24 July 1915.
123. *People's Weekly*, 23 October 1915.
124. *People's Weekly*, 11 December 1915.
125. *Kadina and Wallaroo Times*, 22 December 1915.

Chapter 4. 'Mothers, Manliness and Moonta': The Somme

1. *People's Weekly*, 22 January 1916, 19 February 1916, 4 March 1916.
2. *Yorke's Peninsula Advertiser*, 28 April 1916.
3. National Trust of South Australia, Moonta Branch Archives (NTSAMBA), '"In the Best of Health and Spirits": The Letters and Diaries of Signaller Lance Corporal Leonard John Harvey No. 1029 of the 43rd Battalion A.I.F. to his Parents and Family in South Australia during the First World War when he served Overseas in England and France between 1916 and 1919', unpub. MS compiled by Rob and Carol Howard, Elizabeth M. Scott, Diana Kay Arula, and John Campbell Harvey, n.d.; Letters dated 5 August 1917, 12 August 1917; Diary entries 31 July 1917, 1 August 1917, 2 August 1917.
4. NAA B2455/4735734 Leonard John Harvey; NAA B2455/8022790 John Pyatt; NAA B2455/3017060 William Townsend Abbott; NAA 2455/8036906 Reuben Charles Rose; NAA B2455/3489528; NAA B2455/3489528 Frederick Davey; NAA B2455/8074734 Peter Bramwell Sampson; NAA B2455/8082840 William George Addison Shorter; NAA B2455/8393969 Richard Douglas Trembath; NAA 2455/9393977 William Thomas [Leonard] Trembath; NAA B2455/8005089 Gilbert Roy Oats; NAA 2455/8019308 Lloyd Ewart Pollard; NAA B2455/8015554 Eustice Glynn Todd Pethick.
5. *Yorke's Peninsula Advertiser*, 28 April 1916.
6. *People's Weekly*, 25 March 1916.
7. *People's Weekly*, 1 April 1916.
8. *People's* Weekly, 18 August 1917.
9. *People's Weekly*, 25 March 1916.
10. *People's Weekly*, 25 March 1916.
11. *People's Weekly*, 8 April 1916.
12. NAA B2455/8399010 Frederick Gordon Verran.
13. South Australian Archives (SAA) D3627(L), Addendum, Impressions of Moonta by Sir Lennon Raws.
14. *People's Weekly*, 29 April 1916.
15. *People's Weekly*, 29 April 1916.
16. *People's Weekly*, 29 April 1916.
17. *People's Weekly*, 29 April 1916.
18. *People's Weekly*, 15 June 1918.
19. *People's Weekly*, 12 May 1917; NAA B2455/9393977 William Thomas [Leonard] Trembath; *London Gazette*, 23 March 1917; *Commonwealth of Australia Gazette*, 21 August 1917.
20. *People's Weekly*, 14 September 1918.

21. *People's Weekly*, 29 April 1916.

22. *Kadina and Wallaroo Times*, 7 June 1911; *Yorke's Peninsula Advertiser*, 9 June 1911; *People's Weekly*, 16 June 1934.

23. The flag has survived, but not the letters, carefully preserved by the Moonta Branch of the National Trust of South Australia.

24. Les Carlyon, *The Great War* (Sydney, 2006), p. 663.

25. NAA B2455/8036906 Reuben Charles Rose.

26. NAA B2455/8036906 Reuben Charles Rose; *Commonwealth of Australia Gazette*, 23 May 1919.

27. NAA B2455/8036906 Reuben Charles Rose.

28. *People's Weekly*, 21 September 1918.

29. *People's Weekly*, 21 September 1918.

30. *People's Weekly*, 4 January 1919.

31. *People's Weekly*, 15 February 1919.

32. *People's Weekly*, 8 April 1916.

33. NAA B2455/3468211 Albert Fleetwood Cross.

34. NAA B2455/8388822 Frederick Willard.

35. *People's Weekly*, 28 July 1917.

36. *People's Weekly*, 3 June 1916.

37. *People's Weekly*, 16 September 1916.

38. *People's Weekly*, 16 September 1916.

39. *People's Weekly*, 16 September 1916.

40. See, for example, chapter XII 'Anti-Myth: The True Texture of the Somme', in John Terraine, *The Smoke and the Fire: Myths and Anti-Myths of War 1861–1945* (London, 1980, repub. 1992), pp. 111–26.

41. Philpott, *Bloody Victory*.

42. Philpott, *Bloody Victory*, p. 20.

43. Philpott, *Bloody Victory*, p. 114.

44. Philpott, *Bloody Victory*, p. 265.

45. Philpott, *Bloody Victory*, p. 422, 426, 457.

46. Cited in Peter Pedersen, *The Anzacs: Gallipoli to the Western Front* (Camberwell (Vic.), 2007), p. 125.

47. Pedersen, *The Anzacs*, pp. 125–7.

48. Pedersen, *The Anzacs*, p. 127.

49. Pedersen, *The Anzacs*, p. 124–43; see also Beaumont, 'Australia's War', pp. 16–17.

50. Lindsay, *Fromelles*.

51. *Yorke's Peninsula Advertiser*, 28 July 1916.

52. *People's Weekly*, 28 October 1916.

53. *People's Weekly*, 2 September 1916.

54. NAA B2455/8025039 Richard Hugh Quintrell

55. AWM, ARCSWME files/3885 Private Clarence Horace Quintrell, 50th Battalion.

56. NAA B2455/83025035 John Adolphus Quintrell.

57. *People's Weekly*, 22 September 1917.

58. NAA B2455/8025031 Clarence Horace Quintrell.

59. *People's Weekly*, 22 September 1917.

60. NAA B2455/8025039 Richard Hugh Quintrell.

61. NAA B2455/5283805 Clarence Rhody Swan Hoffman; AWM, ARCSWME files/2050 Private Clarence Rhody Swan Hoffman, 32nd Battalion.

62. NAA B2455/5283805 Clarence Rhody Swan Hoffman.

63. Philpott, *Bloody Victory*, p. 337.

64. Pedersen, *The Anzacs*, p. 153.

65. Pedersen, *The Anzacs*, p. 147.

66. Richard Holmes, *Tommy: The British Soldier on the Western Front 1914–1918* (London, 2004), p. 180; G.D. Sheffield, 'The Australians at Pozières: Command and Control on the Somme, 1916', in David French and Brian Holden Reid (ed.), *The British General Staff: Reform Innovations c.1890–1939* (London, 2002).

67. AWM, AWM4/Australian Imperial Force unit war diaries, 1914–18 War/Infantry/ 23/27/9/ 10ᵗʰ Infantry Battalion, July 1916.

68. *Yorke's Peninsula Advertiser*, 28 July 1916.

69. *People's Weekly*, 12 August 1916.

70. *People's Weekly*, 19 August 1916; NAA B2455/7368729 Joseph Keen.

71. *People's Weekly*, 29 September 1916.

72. *People's Weekly*, 12 August 1916.

73. NAA B2455/7368729 Joseph Keen.

74. See Hunt, *This Side of Heaven*, pp. 173–4.

75. *People's Weekly*, 26 August 1916.

76. *People's Weekly*, 29 September 1916.

77. *Yorke's Peninsula Advertiser*, 17 November 1916.

78. *People's Weekly*, 9 September 1916.

79. *People's Weekly*, 9 September 1916, 16 September 1916; NAA B3455/1809469 John James Williams.

80. *People's Weekly*, 9 September 1916.

81. NAA B2455/8388822 Frederick Willard.

82. *People's Weekly*, 9 September 1916.

83. *People's Weekly*, 2 September 1916.

84. *People's Weekly*, 16 September 1916.

85. *People's Weekly*, 18 August 1917.

86. *People's Weekly*, 17 August 1917.

87. *People's Weekly*, 16 September 1917; NAA B2455/3060492 Percy Beaglehole.

88. *People's Weekly*, 29 September 1916.

89. NAA B2455/3060492 Clarence Horace Quintrell.

90. AWM, ARCSWME files/3886 Private Clarence Horace Quintrell, 50ᵗʰ Battalion.

91. *People's Weekly*, 28 October 1916.

92. *People's Weekly*, 18 November 1916.

93. Pederson, *The Anzacs*, p. 171.

94. *People's Weekly*, 9 December 1916.

95. NAA B2455/4736521 Presto John Nankivell; *London Gazette*, 21 September 1916; *Commonwealth of Australia Gazette*, 14 December 1916; *People's Weekly*, 4 November 1916.

96. NAA B2455/1953256 Isaac Leonard McLean; *London Gazette*, 21 September 1916; *Commonwealth of Australia Gazette*, 14 December 1916; *People's Weekly*, 21 October 1916.

97. *People's Weekly*, 20 May 1916.

98. *People's Weekly*, 29 September 1916.

99. *People's Weekly*, 9 December 1916.

100. *Yorke's Peninsula Advertiser*, 1 December 1916.

Chapter 5. 'I'm fed up with England now': Blighty

1. *People's Weekly*, 1 December 1915.
2. *People's Weekly*, 1 December 1915.
3. *People's Weekly*, 21 September 1918.
4. Pedersen, *The Anzacs*, p. 108.
5. Andrews, *The Anzac Illusion*, pp. 179–89.
6. Fuller, *Troop Morale and Popular Culture*, p. 76.
7. *People's Weekly*, 11 March 1916.
8. *People's Weekly*, 11 March 1916.
9. NAA B2455/8015555 Melville Pethick.
10. *People's Weekly*, 11 March 1916.
11. *People's Weekly*, 11 March 1916.
12. *People's Weekly*, 11 March 1916.
13. Carlyon, *The Great War*, p. 665.
14. Robin Prior, 'The Suvla Bay Tea-Party: A Reassessment', *Journal of the Australian War Memorial*, no. 7, 1985, pp. 25–34.
15. Gammage, *The Broken Years*, p. 75.
16. Beaumont, 'Australia's War', p. 14.
17. Alan Moorhead, *Gallipoli* (London, 1956, new edn 1974), pp. 324–30.
18. Steel and Hart, *Defeat at Gallipoli*, p. 417.
19. See, for example, Jeff Kildea, *Anzacs and Ireland* (Cork, 2007), especially chapter 4.
20. Early examples include *Wallaroo Times*, 30 May 1868; *Yorke's Peninsula Advertiser*, 22 May 1874, 15 September 1876.
21. Harry Pascoe, 'Cornishmen and Emigration: The Adventurous Cornish Miner', in Arthur Quiller-Couch (ed.), *Cornwall Education Week Handbook* (Truro, 1927), p. 145.
22. Philip Payton, *The Cornish Overseas: A History of Cornwall's Great Emigration* (Fowey, 2005), pp. 390–1.
23. NAA B2455/8394022 Arthur Aubrey Trenwith
24. *People's Weekly*, 11 March 1916.
25. *People's Weekly*, 2 October 1915.
26. *People's Weekly*, 20 November 1915.
27. *People's Weekly*, 20 November 1915.
28. *People's Weekly*, 15 April 1916.
29. *People's Weekly*, 15 April 1916.
30. *People's Weekly*, 15 April 1916.
31. *People's Weekly*, 15 April 1916.
32. *People's Weekly*, 15 April 1916.
33. *People's Weekly*, 6 May 1916.
34. *People's Weekly*, 13 May 1916.
35. *People's Weekly*, 20 May 1916.
36. *People's Weekly*, 13 January 1917.
37. Charles Bean, *The Official History of Australia in the Great War of 1914–1918, Vol. IV, The Australian Imperial Force in France, 1917* (St Lucia, 11th edn 1941), p. 40.
38. *People's Weekly*, 17 March 1917.

39. AWM, ARCSWME files/1DRL/0428 1822 Private Arthur Aubrey Trenwith, 10th Battalion.

40. NAA B2455/8394022 Arthur Aubrey Trenwith.

41. NAA B2455/8198154 Fred Jeram Lennell.

42. *People's Weekly*, 17 March 1917.

43. NAA B2455/8198154 Fred Jeram Lennell.

44. *People's Weekly*, 15 February 1919, 5 April 1919.

45. Geoffrey Blainey, *The Tyranny of Distance: How Distance Shaped Australia's History* (Melbourne, 1966).

46. William Beach Thomas, *With the British on the Somme* (London, 1917), p. 123; see also Martin J. Farrar, *News From the Front: War Correspondents on the Western Front 1914–18* (Stroud, 1998), p. 172.

47. *Daily Mail*, 10 September 1917.

48. Andrews, *The Anzac Illusion*, p. 138.

49. Philip Payton, *Cornish Carols from Australia* (Redruth, 1984).

50. *People's Weekly*, 24 August 1918.

51. *People's Weekly*, 6 January 1917.

52. *People's Weekly*, 18 April 1919.

53. *People's Weekly*, 26 April 1919.

54. NAA B2455/8019308 Lloyd Ewart Pollard.

55. NAA B2455/ 8019318 Roy Percival Pollard.

56. NAA B2455/8019308 Lloyd Ewart Pollard.

57. *People's Weekly*, 26 April 1919.

58. NTSAMBA: 'The Letters and Diaries', Letter, 19 April 1919.

59. *People's Weekly*, 16 September 1916.

60. *People's Weekly*, 16 September 1916.

61. *People's Weekly*, 16 September 1916.

62. *People's Weekly*, 16 September 1916.

63. *People's Weekly*, 16 September 1916.

64. *People's Weekly*, 16 September 1916.

65. *People's Weekly*, 16 September 1916.

66. *People's Weekly*, 16 September 1916.

67. *People's Weekly*, 16 September 1916.

68. *People's Weekly*, 23 December 1916.

69. NAA B2455/8005089 Gilbert Roy Oats.

70. NAA B2455/8005089 Gilbert Roy Oats; *London Gazette*, 17 June 1919; *Commonwealth of Australia Gazette*, 10 October 1919.

71. *People's Weekly*, 12 May 1917.

72. NAA B2455/8019373 William Albert Pomeroy.

73. NAA B2455/8019373 William Albert Pomeroy.

74. NAA B2455/7990826 Oscar Nankivell; *People's Weekly*, 16 August 1919.

75. *People's Weekly*, 20 September 1919.

76. Information from Liz Coole, Moonta School of Mines; for a history of the Angove family see Wendy Angove, *Growing the Angove Puzzle Tree* (n.p.: 2006)

77. Holmes, *The British Soldier*, p. 117.

78. Holmes, *The British Soldier*, p. 483.

79. *People's Weekly*, 28 June 1919; NAA B2455/8033143 Jacob Roach.

80. NAA B2455/8033143 Jacob Roach.

81. NAA B2455/4738519 Frank Norman Harwood

82. NAA B2455/4735734 Leonard John Harvey; NTSAMBA: 'The Letters and Diaries of Signaller Lance Corporal Leonard John Harvey'.

83. Howard Coxon, John Playford and Robert Reid, *Biographical Register of the South Australian Parliament 1857–1957* (Adelaide, 1985), p. 101; (Adelaide) *Advertiser*, 7 November 1935.

84. NAA B2455/8019308 Leonard John Harvey.

85. NTSAMBA: 'The Letters and Diaries', Letters, 25 July 1916; 31 July 1916 (received 18 September 1916).

86. NTSAMBA: 'The Letters and Diaries', Letter, 11 August 1916 (received 22 September 1916); Letter, 2 May 1919.

87. NTSAMBA: 'The Letters and Diaries', Letter, 11 August 1916 (received 22 September 1916).

88. NTSAMBA: 'The Letters and Diaries', Letter, 11 August 1916 (received 22 September 1916).

89. NTSAMBA: 'The Letters and Diaries', Letter, 11 August 1916 (received 22 September 1916).

90. NTSAMBA: 'The Letters and Diaries', Letter, 28 August 1916.

91. NTSAMBA: 'The Letters and Diaries', Letter, 5 September 1916.

92. NTSAMBA: 'The Letters and Diaries', Letter, 26 October 1916.

93. NTSAMBA: 'The Letters and Diaries', Letter, 16 September 1916.

94. NTSAMBA: 'The Letters and Diaries', Letter, 5 November 1916.

95. NTSAMBA: 'The Letters and Diaries', Letter, 27 August 1916.

96. NTSAMBA: 'The Letters and Diaries', Letter, 26 October 1916.

97. NTSAMBA: 'The Letters and Diaries', Letter, 22 November 1916.

98. NTSAMBA: 'The Letters and Diaries', Letter, 22 November 1916.

99. NTSAMBA: 'The Letters and Diaries', Letter, 31 May 1916.

100. NTSAMBA: 'The Letters and Diaries', Letter, 11 June 1918.

101. NTSAMBA: 'The Letters and Diaries', Letter, 2 February 1917.

102. NTSAMBA: 'The Letters and Diaries', Letter, 11 June 1918.

103. NTSAMBA: 'The Letters and Diaries', Letter, 22 June 1918.

104. NTSAMBA: 'The Letters and Diaries', Letter, 28 July 1918.

105. NTSAMBA: 'The Letters and Diaries', Letter, 13 July 1918.

106. NTSAMBA: 'The Letters and Diaries', Letter, 19 August 1918.

107. NTSAMBA: 'The Letters and Diaries', Letter, 26 October 1916.

108. NTSAMBA: 'The Letters and Diaries'; Memorandum: General Birdwood, 'In the Field, 14 November 1918', *To the Officers, Non-Commissioned Officers and Men of the Australian Imperial Force*.

109. NTSAMBA: 'The Letters and Diaries', Letter, 9 April 1919.

110. NTSAMBA: 'The Letters and Diaries', Diary entries, 17 April 1919, 18 April 1919, 21 April 1919, 22 April 1919, 23 April 1919, 25 April 1919, 26 April 1919, 26 April 1919.

111. NTSAMBA: 'The Letters and Diaries', Letter, 2 May 1919.

112. *People's Weekly*, 21 August 1921.

113. Max Arthur, *When this Bloody War is Over: Soldiers' Songs of the First World War* (London, 2001), p. 105; Graham Seal (ed.), *Echoes of Anzac: The Voices of Australians at War* (Melbourne, 2005), pp. 208–9.

114. Andrews, *The Anzac Illusion*, p. 181.

Chapter 6. 'Not only Germany's war; it's Rome's war too': Conscription

1. Bailey, *James Boor's Bonanza*, pp. 140–1.

2. Bailey, *James Boor's Bonanza*, p. 141.

3. Bailey, *James Boor's Bonanza*, p. 141.

4. Bailey, *James Boor's Bonanza*, pp. 138–9.

5. Cited in Joan Beaumont, 'The Politics of a Divided Society', in Beaumont (ed.), *Australia's War 1914–18*, p. 44.

6. L.L. Robson, *Australia and the Great War* (Melbourne, 1969), p. 15.

7. H. Lipson Hancock, *The Wallaroo and Moonta Mines* (Wallaroo Mines, 1914).

8. H. Lipson Hancock, 'Welfare Work in the Mining Industry', *Australian Chemical Engineering and Mining Review*, October 1918; *South Australian Department of Mines Mining Review*, Half Year Ended June 1919.

9. *South Australian Department of Mines Mining Review*, Half Year Ended June 1919, pp. 53–4.

10. H. Lipson Hancock and William Shaw, *A Sunday School of Today* (Adelaide, 1912).

11. H. Lipson Hancock and William R. Penhall, *The Missionary Spirit in Sunday School Work* (Adelaide, 1918).

12. H. Lipson Hancock, *Modern Methods in Sunday School Work* (Adelaide, 1916), p. 20.

13. H. Lipson Hancock, *A Digest of Reports: Read at the Half-Yearly Meeting of Officers and Teachers of the Above School, August 18th 1913, with other Recent Records* (Moonta Mines, 1914).

14. H. Lipson Hancock, *The Rainbow Course of Bible Study* (Adelaide, 1919), p. 7.

15. Hancock, *A Digest of Reports*, p. 98.

16. Hancock, *Modern Methods in Sunday School Work*, pp. 20–1.

17. *Yorke's Peninsula Advertiser*, 18 May 1877.

18. Hunt, *This Side of Heaven*, p. 129.

19. A.D. Hunt, *Methodism Militant: Attitudes to the Great War* (Adelaide, 1975), p. 11.

20. *Australian Christian Commonwealth*, 3 December 1915.

21. Hunt, *This Side of Heaven*, p. 285.

22. *Australian Christian Commonwealth*, 7 April 1916.

23. *Australian Christian Commonwealth*, 27 October 1916.

24. Hunt, *This Side of Heaven*, p. 129.

25. *People's Weekly*, 17 March 1917.

26. *People's Weekly*, 4 August 1917.

27. *Australian Christian Commonwealth*, 1 November 1911.

28. *Australian Christian Commonwealth*, 5 May 1916.

29. *Australian Christian Commonwealth*, 26 May 1916.

30. Payton, *Making Moonta*, pp. 171–7.

31. Hunt, *This Side of Heaven*, p. 290.

32. Hunt, *This Side of Heaven*, p. 291.

33. Hunt, *This Side of Heaven*, p. 291.

34. *Kadina and Wallaroo Times*, 2 April 1913.

35. *People's Weekly*, 19 May 1917.

36. *Yorke's Peninsula Advertiser*, 18 May 1917.

37. *Yorke's Peninsula Advertiser*, 18 May 1917; *People's Weekly*, 19 May 1917.

38. NTSAMBA: 'Letters and Diaries', Letter, 27 August 1916.

39. NTSAMBA: 'Letters and Diaries', Letter, 10 September 1916.

40. NTSAMBA: 'Letters and Diaries', Letter, 1 October 1916.

41. NTSAMBA: 'Letters and Diaries', Letter, 5 November 1916.

42. NTSAMBA: 'Letters and Diaries', Letter, 4 December 1916.

43. NTSAMBA: 'Letters and Diaries', Letter, 5 January 1917.

44. *People's Weekly*, 21 October 1916, 21 April 1917.

45. Dean Jaensch, *The Politics of Australia* (Melbourne, 2nd edn 1997), p. 225.

46. Donald J. Hopgood, 'A Psephological Examination of the South Australian Labor Party from World War One to the Depression', unpub. Ph.D. thesis, Flinders University of South Australia, 1973; John Lonie, 'Conservatism and Class in South Australia during the Depression Years 1924–1934', unpub. MA thesis, University of Adelaide, 1973.

47. Geoffrey Blainey, *A History of Victoria* (Melbourne, 2006), p. 157.

48. *Australian Christian Commonwealth*, 23 November 1917.

49. SAA D3627(L), Stanley Whitford, 'An Autobiography', unpub. MS., 1956, p. 352.

50. SAA D3627(L), pp. 478, 401, 399.

51. Beaumont (ed.), *Australia's War 1914–18*, p. 51.

52. Bailey, *James Boor's Bonanza*, p. 141.

53. *People's Weekly*, 15 September 1917.

54. *People's Weekly*, 5 April 1918.

55. *People's Weekly*, 18 June 1921.

56. Bailey, *James Boor's Bonanza*, pp. 145–6.

57. Bailey, *James Boor's Bonanza*, p. 146.

58. *Yorke's Peninsula Advertiser*, 27 April 1917.

59. *Yorke's Peninsula Advertiser*, 11 May 1917.

60. *Yorke's Peninsula Advertiser*, 30 November 1917.

61. *Yorke's Peninsula Advertiser*, 14 December 1917.

62. *Yorke's Peninsula Advertiser*, 14 December 1917.

63. *Yorke's Peninsula Advertiser*, 14 December 1917.

64. *Yorke's Peninsula Advertiser*, 1 September 1916.

65. *South Australian Parliamentary Debates*, 30 August 1916, p. 1095.

66. *Australian Christian Commonwealth*, 12 October 1917.

67. *Australian Christian Commonwealth*, 12 April 1918.

68. *People's Weekly*, 18 August 1917.

69. NTSAMBA: 'Letters and Diaries', Letter, 13 March 1917.

70. NTSAMBA: 'Letters and Diaries', Letter, 11 April 1917.

71. NTSAMBA: 'Letters and Diaries', Letter, 25 April 1917.

72. NTSAMBA: 'Letters and Diaries', Letter, 1 October 1917.

73. NTSAMBA: 'Letters and Diaries', Letter, 18 November 1917.

74. NTSAMBA: 'Letters and Diaries', Letter, 27 November 1917.

75. NTSAMBA: 'Letters and Diaries', Letter, 21 January 1918.

76. NTSAMBA: 'Letters and Diaries', Letter, 25 March 1918.

77. NTSAMBA: 'Letters and Diaries', Letter, 26 February 1918.

78. NTSAMBA: 'Letters and Diaries', Letter, 22 June 1918.

79. Hunt, *Methodism Militant*, p. 31.

Chapter 7. 'Doing their best for the Empire': Australia Triumphant

1. *People's Weekly*, 23 February 1918.
2. *People's Weekly*, 23 February 1918.
3. *People's Weekly*, 23 February 1918.
4. *People's Weekly*, 1 September 1917.
5. *People's Weekly*, 9 June 1917.
6. *People's Weekly*, 16 June 1917.
7. Pam Maclean, 'War and Australian Society', in Beaumont (ed.), *Australia's War, 1914–18*, pp. 76–7.
8. NAA B2455/1956006 Elsie McMartin.
9. NAA B2455/3549536 Daisy Clara Hotham Farrow.
10. NAA B2455/3554392 Mary Franceska Ferry.
11. *Yorke's Peninsula Advertiser*, 17 November 1916.
12. *People's Weekly*, 18 November 1916.
13. *People's weekly*, 18 November 1916.
14. NAA B2455/3085150 Edward Leslie Bishop.
15. *People's Weekly*, 16 December 1916; NAA B2544/7379673 Joseph James Lanyon.
16. *People's Weekly*, 23 December 1916.
17. *People's Weekly*, 13 January 1917; NAA B2455/8003824 Clarence Swann Padman.
18. *People's Weekly*, 6 January 1917.
19. *People's Weekly*, 10 March 1917.
20. NAA B2455/8399016 William Richard Verran.
21. Pedersen, *The Anzacs*, pp. 222–3.
22. Cited in Pedersen, *The Anzacs*, p. 222.
23. NTSAMBA: 'Letters and Diaries', Letter, 4 December 1916.
24. NTSAMBA: 'Letters and Diaries', Letter, 13 December 1916.
25. NTSAMBA: 'Letters and Diaries', Letter, 4 December 1916.
26. NTSAMBA: 'Letters and Diaries', Letter, 28 December 1916.
27. NTSAMBA: 'Letters and Diaries', Letter, 5 January 1917.
28. NTSAMBA: 'Letters and Diaries', Letter, 5 January 1917.
29. NTSAMBA: 'Letters and Diaries', Letter, 5 January 1917.
30. NTSAMBA: 'Letters and Diaries', Letter, 17 January 1917.
31. NTSAMBA: 'Letters and Diaries', Letter, 10 February 1917.
32. NTSAMBA: 'Letters and Diaries', Letter, 24 February 1917.
33. NTSAMBA: 'Letters and Diaries', Letter, 24 February 1917.
34. NTSAMBA: 'Letters and Diaries', Letter, 2 February 1917.
35. NTSAMBA: 'Letters and Diaries', Letter, 10 February 1917.
36. Philpott, *Bloody Victory*, pp. 379–90.
37. *People's Weekly*, 6 April 1917.
38. NAA B2455/8031237 Ernest Elmer Reynolds.
39. *People's Weekly*, 19 January 1918.
40. Philpott, *Bloody Victory*, p. 422.
41. Philpott, *Bloody Victory*, p. 426.
42. Barton, Doyle and Vandewalle, *Beneath Flanders Fields*, p. 72.
43. NAA B2455 Percy Quintrell
44. Cited in Pedersen, *The Anzacs*, p. 224.
45. Pedersen, *The Anzacs*, p. 228.

46. *People's Weekly*, 20 October 1917.

47. *People's Weekly*, 20 October 1917.

48. *People's Weekly*, 20 October 1917.

49. *People's Weekly*, 20 October 1917.

50. *People's Weekly*, 20 October 1917.

51. *People's Weekly*, 20 October 1917.

52. *People's Weekly*, 20 October 1917.

53. NTSAMBA: 'Letters and Diaries', Letter, 17 June 1917

54. NTSAMBA: 'Letters and Diaries', Letter, 12 July 1917.

55. NTSAMBA: 'Letters and Diaries', Letter, 5 August 1917.

56. NTSAMBA: 'Letters and Diaries', Letter, 12 August 1917.

57. NTSAMBA: 'Letters and Diaries', Diary entry, 31 July 1917.

58. NTSAMBA: 'Letters and Diaries', Diary entry, 1 August 1917.

59. NTSAMBA: 'Letters and Diaries', Diary entry, 2 August 1917.

60. NTSAMBA: 'Letters and Diaries', Diary entry, 18 November 1917.

61. NTSAMBA: 'Letters and Diaries', Letter, 18 November 1917.

62. NTSAMBA: 'Letters and Diaries', Letter, 24 October 1917.

63. NTSAMBA: 'Letters and Diaries', Letter, 18 November 1917.

64. *People's Weekly*, 20 October 1917.

65. *People's Weekly*, 24 November 1917.

66. *People's Weekly*, 10 November 1917; NAA B2455/3002359 Seymour Jacka Thomas.

67. *People's Weekly*, 1 December 1917.

68. Pedersen, *The Anzacs*, pp. 263–7.

69. NTSAMBA: 'Letters and Diaries', Letter, 18 November 1917.

70. *People's Weekly*, 2 February 1918; *London Gazette*, 4 February 1918; *Commonwealth of Australia Gazette*, 27 June 1918.

71. *People's Weekly*, 9 February 1918; NAA B2455/3235112 John Henry Chappel.

72. NAA B2455/8393969 Richard Douglas Trembath.

73. NAA B2455/8097351 Percy Sutton; NAA B2455/8014385 William James Perry.

74. NTSAMBA: 'Letters and Diaries', Letter, 18 February 1918.

75. NTSAMBA: 'Letters and Diaries', Letter, 18 February 1918.

76. NTSAMBA: 'Letters and Diaries', Diary entry, 27 and 28 March 1918.

77. NTSAMBA: 'Letters and Diaries', Diary entry, 30 March 1918.

78. NTSAMBA: 'Letters and Diaries', Diary entry, 31 March 1918.

79. NTSAMBA: 'Letters and Diaries', Letter, 9 April 1918.

80. NTSAMBA: 'Letters and Diaries', Diary entry, 27 April 1918.

81. NTSAMBA: 'Letters and Diaries', Letter, 16 May 1918.

82. NTSAMBA: 'Letters and Diaries', Diary entries 20 May 1918 and 22 May 1918.

83. NTSAMBA: 'Letters and Diaries', Letter, 31 May 1918.

84. *People's Weekly*, 15 June 1918.

85. *People's Weekly*, 13 July 1918; NAA B2455/8032839 Douglas Peter Roach.

86. *People's Weekly*, 13 July 1918.

87. *People's Weekly*, 20 July 1918.

88. Malcolm Brown, *1918: Year of Victory* (London, 1998), pp. 179–82.

89. Pedersen, *The Anzacs*, p. 341.

90. *People's Weekly*, 6 September 1919.

91. See Roland Perry, *Monash: The Outsider who won a War* (Sydney, 2007).

92. Beaumont (ed.), *Australia's War, 1914–18*, pp. 25–6.

93. C.J.H. Mead, *Cornwall's Royal Engineers: A History of the Regiment from its Formation up to the Early Part of the Second World War* (Plymouth, 1947); Payton, *The Cornish Overseas*, p. 390.

94. Cecil Williams was the author's grandfather.

95. Beaumont (ed.), *Australia's War, 1914–18*, p. 26.

96. Beaumont (ed.), *Australia's War, 1914–18*, p. 27.

97. *People's Weekly*, 5 May 1917.

98. *People's Weekly*, 8 September 1917.

99. *People's Weekly*, 4 May 1918.

100. *People's Weekly*, 21 September 1918.

101. *People's Weekly*, 26 October 1918.

102. *People's Weekly*, 21 September 1918.

103. NTSAMBA: 'Letters and Diaries', Diary entry, 30 September 1918.

104. NTSAMBA: 'Letters and Diaries', Letter, 7 October 1918.

105. NTSAMBA: 'Letters and Diaries', Letter, 15 October 1918.

106. NTSAMBA: 'Letters and Diaries', Letter, 29 October 1918.

107. *People's Weekly*, 29 June 1918.

108. *People's Weekly*, 27 July 1918.

109. *People's Weekly*, 12 October 1918; 26 October 1918.

110. NTSAMBA: 'Letters and Diaries', 4 November 1918.

111. NTSAMBA: 'Letters and Diaries', 13 November 1918.

112. *Yorke's Peninsula Advertiser*, 16 November 1918.

Chapter 8. 'Returning with the scars of deadly conflict': Aftermath

1. *People's Weekly*, 16 November 1918.

2. *People's Weekly*, 16 November 1918.

3. *People's Weekly*, 18 October 1919.

4. *People's Weekly*, 27 July 1918.

5. *People's Weekly*, 15 February 1919; see also *People's Weekly*, 30 November 1918.

6. *People's Weekly*, 22 March 1919.

7. *People's Weekly*, 5 July 1919.

8. Andrews, *The Anzac Illusion*, p. 186.

9. E.P.F. Lynch (ed. Will Davies), *Somme Mud: The Experiences of an Infantryman in France, 1916–1919* (London, 2006), p. 399.

10. NTSAMBA: 'Letters and Diaries', Diary entries for 24 December 1918 and 25 December 1918.

11. NAA B2455/4735734 Leonard John Harvey.

12. *People's Weekly*, 5 July 1919.

13. *People's Weekly*, 5 July 1919.

14. *People's Weekly*, 5 July 1919.

15. *People's Weekly*, 5 July 1919.

16. *People's Weekly*, 26 April 1919. Not all possessed the gift of poetic composition, of course, and such memorial rhymes were available 'off the shelf', although frequently altered to meet personal needs.

17. *People's Weekly*, 11 October 1919.

18. *People's Weekly*, 11 October 1919.

19. *People's Weekly*, 18 April 1919.

20. *People's Weekly*, 14 June 1919.

21. *People's Weekly*, 15 February 1919.

22. *People's Weekly*, 14 June 1919; NAA B2455/3442933 Leslie George Woon.

23. *People's Weekly*, 29 March 1919.

24. *People's Weekly*, 23 December 1933.

25. *People's Weekly*, 25 January 1919.

26. *People's Weekly*, 7 June 1919.

27. *People's Weekly*, 30 June 1917.

28. *People's Weekly*, 19 June 1920.

29. *People's Weekly*, 21 February 1920.

30. NAA B2455/8025038 Percy Quintrell.

31. *People's Weekly*, 28 June 1919.

32. *People's Weekly*, 13 December 1919, 20 December 1919.

33. *People's Weekly*, 10 May 1919.

34. *Yorke's Peninsula Advertiser*, 2 August 1918.

35. *People's Weekly*, 31 January 1920.

36. *People's Weekly*, 8 May 1920.

37. *People's Weekly*, 29 March 1919.

38. *People's Weekly*, 29 March 1919.

39. *People's Weekly*, 14 June 1919.

40. Andrews, *The Anzac Illusion*, p. 208.

41. Beaumont (ed.), *Australia's War, 1914–18*, p. 107.

42. *People's Weekly*, 14 June 1919.

43. *People's Weekly*, 16 August 1919.

44. Correspondence between William Sowden and Fernley O. Pascoe of Camborne, Cornwall, dated 7 February 1931 and December 1931. See Payton, 'The Cornish in South Australia'.

45. Rhoda Heinrich, *Wide Sails and Wheat Stacks: A History of Port Victoria and the Hundred of Wauraltee* (Port Victoria, 1976), p. 59.

46. *People's Weekly*, 21 August 1920.

47. *People's Weekly*, 11 June 1921.

48. *People's Weekly*, 13 September 1919.

49. *People's Weekly*, 4 December 1920.

50. *People's Weekly*, 4 December 1920.

51. Of course, when Caroline Carleton first penned this verse, the 'proud flag' was the Union Flag. By 1920, however, those singing the 'The Song of Australia' might as easily imagine Australia's national flag – with its own evocation of the wide southern sky.

52. *People's Weekly*, 19 July 1919.

53. Bailey, *James Boor's Bonanza*, p. 155.

54. Bailey, *James Boor's Bonanza*, p. 147.

55. Bailey, *James Boor's Bonanza*, p. 155.

56. Bailey, *James Boor's Bonanza*, p. 155.

57. Bailey, *James Boor's Bonanza*, p. 156.

58. Bailey, *James Boor's Bonanza*, p. 160.

59. *People's Weekly*, 6 August 1921.

60. Bailey, *James Boor's Bonanza*, p. 162.

61. Bailey, *James Boor's Bonanza*, p. 170.

62. SAA, D5341(T), Peter Thomas, *Scrapbook Relating to Kapunda, Burra, Wallaroo, and Moonta Mines;* Pamphlet issued by R.S. Richards MP.

63. Bailey, *James Boor's Bonanza*, p. 172.

64. SAA RN218, *Notes on the Reasons for the Decline and Closure of the Wallaroo and Moonta Mines, 1919–23.*

65. *People's Weekly*, 31 March 1925.

66. National Trust of South Australia, Kadina Branch Archive, *Wallaroo and Moonta Mining and Smelting Co. Ltd. (in liquidation): Catalogue of Machinery, Plant and Stores for Sale.*

67. Cited in Bailey, *James Boor's Bonanza*, p. 175.

68. Graham Jenkin, *Calling Me Home: The Romance of South Australia in Story and Song* (Adelaide, 1989), p. 147.

69. *People's Weekly*, 18 March 1919.

70. Jenkin, *Calling Me Home*, p. 147.

71. K.W. Thomson, 'The Changes in Function of Former Mining Settlements: The Wallaroo Copper Belt', *Proceedings of the Royal Geological Society of Australia, South Australian Branch*, 56 (1955), p. 57.

72. Thomson, 'The Changes in Function', p. 57.

73. *People's Weekly*, 25 May 1935, 14 June 1924.

74. For details of mining and prospecting activity on northern Yorke Peninsula between 1924 and 1939, see the *South Australian Department of Mines Mining Review*, published half yearly.

75. *South Australian Department of Mines Mining Review*, Half Year Ended 1931.

76. Bailey, *James Boor's Bonanza*, p. 177.

77. Thomson, 'The Changes in Function', pp. 50–7.

Epilogue: 'The Hub of the Universe?'

1. Pryor, *Australia's Little Cornwall*, pp. 148–9.

2. Pryor, *Australia's Little Cornwall*, p. 149.

3. John Lonie, 'Conservatism and Class in South Australia during the Depression Years, 1924–1934', unpub. MA thesis, University of Adelaide, 1973, p. 173; see also Philip Payton, '"Vote Labor, and Rid South Australia of a Danger to the Purity of Our Race": The Cornish Radical Tradition in South Australia, 1900–1939', in Philip Payton (ed.), *Cornish Studies: Nine* (Exeter, 2001), pp. 173–203.

4. Thomas Wood, *Cobbers* (London, 1934; repub. Oxford, 1961), p. 142.

5. Wood, *Cobbers*, p. 142.

6. Wood, *Cobbers*, p. 142; see also Payton, *Making Moonta*, especially chapters 6 and 7.

7. Beaumont (ed.), *Australia's War, 1914–18*, pp. xviii–xix.

Index

Abdullah, Mullah, 47
Adelaide, 14, 18, 20, 21, 26, 29, 31, 37, 47, 57, 58, 71, 99, 120, 121, 125, 138, 165, 184, 201, 203, 214
Adelaide, Port, 71, 207
Adelaide, University of, xiv
Adelaide Cheer-Up Society, 58, 59, 61
Adelaide Hills, 27, 57
Aden, 57
Afghanistan; Afghan, 47, 48
Africa; African, 185
Agery, 30, 62, 119, 145
Albany, 43
Albert, 171, 184
Aldershot, 131
Alexandria, 49, 50, 56, 58
Allenby, General Edmund, 188
Amalgamated Miners Association of Australia, 18, 28, 29, 156
America; Americans (*q.v.* United States of America), 10, 15, 24, 48, 116, 170, 183, 184, 190–1
Amesbury, 126, 132
Amiens, 184, 187
Anderson family, 216
Anderson, Violet may, 119
Andrewartha family, 208
Andrewartha, Ilene, 63–4
Anglicans; Anglicanism, 9
Anzac Cove (*q.v.* Gallipoli), xiv, 35, 49, 50, 53, 55, 60, 66, 69, 77, 115, 116
Anzac Day, xiii–xiv, xv, 6, 201, 220
Anzac myth/tradition, xiv, 4, 21, 56, 76, 114, 188
Anzacs (*q.v.* Military units), xiv, 4, 32, 35, 49, 55, 57, 66, 67, 68, 72, 76, 77, 79,

100, 101, 110, 112, 114, 115, 119, 123, 133, 137, 173, 200
Ardrossan, 39
Armentières, 85, 96, 124
Arthurton, 30
Asia; Asian, 49
Ashmead-Bartlett, Ellis, 49
Australia, National Archives of, xvi, 11
Australia Day, 65
Australian National University, xv–xvi
Australian Red Cross, 62, 96
Australian Red Cross Society Wounded and Missing Enquiry Bureau, 11
Australian War Memorial, xvi
Australian Workers' Union, 156, 157, 159, 161, 211–13, 220
Austria; Austrians; Austria-Hungary, 47, 48, 160, 192

Bailey, Margaret, 129
Bailleul, 178
Balaclava, 217
Baluchistan, 47
Banfield, Olive, 57
Bapaume, 86, 120, 170
Barnes, Victor, 143
Barnes, William, 143
Barossa Valley, 21, 27
Barunga, 79
Barunga Gap, 9
Base Records Office, Melbourne, 53, 70, 86, 87, 97, 99, 100, 102, 113, 117, 120, 122, 124, 182–3
Bath, 128, 131
Bathbridge, 38
Bean, C.E.W, 4

Bedruthan, 118
Beersheba, 188
Belgium; Belgians, 25, 26, 30, 39, 80, 112,
116, 123, 160, 164, 166, 177, 181
Belgian Relief Fund, 30
Bennett, Brigadier-General H.G., 34
Bennett, Violet, 188
Bible Christians (q.v. Methodists;
Methodism, q.v. Primitive Methodists,
q.v. Wesleyans), 17, 146
Birdwood, Lieutenant-General Sir William,
57, 75, 136, 181, 186, 197
Birmingham, 30, 122, 129, 178, 179, 180
Bishop, Elsie, 167
Black Sea, 48
Blake, Father, 50
Blighty, (q.v. Britain; British, q.v. British Isles,
q.v. England; q.v. United Kingdom),
112, 113, 122, 123, 128, 132, 125, 136,
163, 170, 177
Boer War; Boers, 21, 22, 23, 25, 32, 35, 52,
173
Bogies (q.v. Yorke's Peninsula Miners and
Smelters' Association), 156, 212
Bolshevism, 205, 206
Bombay, 165
Botterill, Fred, 213–14
Bougainville, 216
Boulder City, 15, 43, 85
Boulogne, 89, 180
Bray-sur-Somme, 128
Briggs, Sarah Elizabeth (q.v. Hoffman, Sarah
Elizabeth), 99
Bristol, 38, 111, 195
Britain; British (q.v. Blighty; q.v. British Isles,
q.v. United Kingdom), 3, 4, 6, 7, 12,
15, 21, 22, 23, 24, 25, 26, 27, 30, 39,
43, 48, 49, 56, 71, 92, 94, 97, 100,
101, 110, 113, 114, 115, 116, 122, 123,
125, 128, 138, 143, 160, 163, 170, 173,
174, 175, 184, 203, 206, 210, 221
British Australian Studies Association, xvii
British Empire, 2, 6, 12, 21, 22, 23, 24, 25,
26, 29, 35, 39, 41, 42, 44, 46, 50, 56,
59, 60, 66, 76, 77, 83, 92, 102, 110,
114, 127, 138, 141, 143, 149, 154,
158, 159, 163, 164, 195, 209, 210,
219
British Isles (q.v. Blighty, q.v. Britain; British,
q.v. United Kingdom), 35, 112
British World, 6, 10, 21

Broken Hill, 45–7, 48, 119, 158, 214, 217
Brokenshire, Catherine 'Kate', 68, 70
Buckingham Palace, 39
Bullecourt (First and Second), 12, 163,
170–3
Burnell family, 208
Bute, 79

Cairo, 39, 40, 41, 47, 48, 56, 59, 63, 64, 70
Callington (Australia), 216
Camborne, 136, 155
Canada; Canadians, 4, 10, 115, 116, 117, 123,
164, 174, 181, 187
Canberra, xv, xvi
Cape Helles, 49, 115
Carbis Bay, 118
Carleton, Caroline, 209
Catholics, Roman; Catholicism, 9, 48, 50,
149, 150, 153, 154
Celtic Wood, 181
Channel, the, 177, 189
Childs, Lillian, 186
China; Chinese, 24, 76
Churchill, Winston, 48
Citizens League, 207
Cocos Islands, 25
Colombo, 57
Comley, Ethel, 38
Congregationalists, 148
Conscription crisis, 7, 29, 43, 82, 84, 110,
132, 138, 139, 143–4, 147–56, 163,
205, 206, 207, 210, 218
Constantinople, 48, 56, 76, 78
Coolgardie, 43
Cornwall; Cornish (q.v. Cousin Jack; Cousin
Jacks; Cousin Jennys), xvi, 3, 6, 9, 12,
13, 14, 15, 16, 17, 18, 19, 23, 36, 46,
65, 66, 75, 77, 116–17, 118–19, 122,
123, 124, 125, 135, 137, 138, 144, 147,
151, 155, 160, 188, 192, 207, 210, 213,
214, 219, 221, 222
Cornish Association of Broken Hill, 46
Cornish Association of South Australia,
206–7
Courtney's Post (q.v. Gallipoli), 66
Cousin Jack; Cousin Jacks; Cousin Jennys
(q.v. Cornwall; Cornish), 13, 15, 18,
23, 118, 136, 137, 155, 221
Cowell, 79
Cowling, Richard, 66
Cowling, William, 81, 82, 110

Cross Roads (*q.v.* Moonta), 30, 36, 37, 50, 53, 63, 67, 68, 73, 76, 83, 84, 102, 106, 109, 130, 178, 180, 183, 186, 204
Crystal Brook, 217
Cunliffe, 30
Curragh, the, 131

Damascus, 188
Dardenelles, 48, 49, 50, 52, 57, 68, 76, 78, 112
Dartford, 124
Davey family, 208
Degenhardt, Edgar (*q.v.* Russell, Edgar), 27
Dennis, C.J., 36
Dernancourt, 184
Devonport, 125, 126
Devon(shire), 125, 126, 147
Dodd, H. Pennerley, 70–1
Dorset, 113, 116, 126, 132
Dover, 180
du Maurier, Daphne, 3
Dunstan family, 208
Dunstan, Emily, 85

Eaucourt, 170
Edmonds, Sir James, 101
Egypt; Egyptians, 11, 12, 31, 33, 39, 40, 41, 45, 47, 49, 54, 59, 60, 64, 70, 79, 89, 90, 91, 104, 113, 116, 131, 139, 164, 188
El Faw peninsula (*q.v.* Iraq), xiv
Elliott, Brigadier-General Harold 'Pompey', 94
Elphick, Sarah Jane, 50, 52
England; English, (*q.v.* Blighty), 3, 10, 11, 12, 30, 32, 33, 38, 55, 71, 80, 83, 85, 89, 97, 110, 111, 112, 113, 114, 116, 117, 120, 121, 122, 123, 125, 127, 128, 129, 130, 131, 132, 133, 134, 141, 152, 153, 166, 174, 175, 177, 181, 185, 189, 197, 202
'English brides', 129–30
Epsom, Surrey, 111, 124
Etaples, 35, 38, 119
Europe; European, 19, 26, 27, 39, 41, 48, 89, 91, 159, 160
Exeter, 120, 126
Exeter, University of, xvi
Eyre Peninsula, 61, 79

Federal Brass Band, Kadina, 217
Federal Rovers Football Club, Kadina, 217

Fishponds, Bristol, 38
Flanders, 12, 35, 54, 80
Flers, 167, 181
Fleubaix, 94
France; French, xiii, 2, 11, 12, 23, 25, 35, 36, 37, 48, 49, 50, 53, 57, 65, 72, 76, 79, 80, 83, 85, 89, 90, 91, 92, 94, 95, 96, 97, 105, 110, 112, 113, 116, 119, 121, 122, 124, 125, 127, 128, 131, 132, 134, 135, 136, 160, 161, 164, 166, 168, 175, 181, 185, 193, 196, 197, 200, 204, 206, 219
Fromelles (*q.v.* Fleurbaix, 94; *q.v.* Pozières; *q.v.* Somme, Battle of), 7, 12, 93–100, 115, 123, 163, 185

Gallipoli (*q.v.* Anzac Cove, *q.v.* Courtney's Post, *q.v.* Quinn's Post, *q.v.* Lone Pine, *q.v.* Shrapnel Gully, *q.v.* Third [Gun] Ridge, *q.v.* Second Ridge, *q.v.* Suvla Bay), *q.v.* Victoria Gully), xiv, 4, 11, 12, 21, 27, 31, 32, 33, 35, 36, 39, 43, 49, 50, 52, 53, 54, 57–60, 62, 65, 67–9, 71, 72, 75–8, 79, 94, 96, 102, 105, 107, 110, 111, 113, 115, 116, 117, 119, 123, 131, 139, 141, 143, 158, 168, 172, 186, 188, 192, 200, 207
Gawler, 120
Gaza, 188
George V, King, 197
Germany; German, xiii, 2, 9, 12, 21, 22, 23, 24, 25, 26, 27, 28, 34, 40, 47, 48, 72, 76, 83, 85, 86, 89, 92, 93, 96, 99, 100, 101, 104, 106, 107, 109, 120, 123, 135, 139, 141, 149, 154, 159, 160, 166, 168, 170, 171, 172, 173, 175–6, 177, 183, 184, 185, 187, 190, 191, 192, 193, 202, 205, 206, 210, 222
Gharial, 165
Ghezireh, 54
Gibbs, Hetty, 178, 182
Gippsland, South, 43
Goldsworthy family, 129
Gorran, 117
Gough, General Sir Hubert, 171
Goyder, George, 19
Grantham, 129
Greece, 164
Green's Plains, 20, 145
Gridley, Rosamond, 129
Gueudecourt, 167

Gunter, H.A. 'Harry', 80, 81, 82, 83, 101, 102

Hahndorf, 27
Haig, Field Marshall Sir Douglas, 92, 177
Haking, Lieutenant-General Sir Richard, 93
Hamel, 86, 187
Hamilton, General Sir Ian, 57, 67, 71, 72, 75, 115
Hamley Flat (*q.v.* Moonta Mines), 39
Hancock, Henry Richard, 18
Hancock, Henry Lipson, 18, 27, 62, 83, 84, 139, 144–6, 153, 157
Hanover, 40
Harvey family, 216
Harvey, William Humphrey, 50, 125, 132, 152, 153, 182
Harwood, Harry, 72
Harz mountains, 123
Hayes, William Henry, 83
Hazebrouck, 34
Heliopolis, 40, 89
Helston, 136
Hendry, Amy Maude, 203
Highlanders (*q.v.* Scotland; Scottish), 10
Hindenburg Line, 170, 172, 173, 190, 191
History SA (*q.v.* South Australia, History Trust of), xvii
Hoffman, Sarah Elizabeth (*q.v.* Briggs, Sarah Elizabeth), 99
Hughes, W.H. 'Billy', 28, 29, 143, 147, 151, 152, 153, 155, 156, 159, 205–6, 210
Hull, University of, xvi
Hummocks, 20

India; Indians, 30, 39, 47, 48, 49, 164, 165
International Workers of the World (*q.v.* Wobblies), 155, 159, 205
Iraq (*q.v.* El Faw peninsula), xiv
Ireland; Irish, 10, 116, 123, 131, 149, 153, 154, 159
Islam; Islamic, 47, 48

Japan; Japanese, 23, 24, 206
Jeffery, Mary, 155
Jenkin, Graham, 214–16
Jerusalem, 188, 189
Jew; Jewish, 191
Johannesburg, 23
Jones, Annie May, 120
Jones, Dorothy Mary, 120

Jordan Valley, 189
Jose, George, 137–8

Kadina, 9, 13, 16, 20, 30, 32, 33, 34, 35, 40, 45, 50, 63, 72, 77, 79, 117, 120, 139, 140, 150, 151, 159, 162, 166, 167, 172, 178, 180, 186, 188, 190, 202, 207, 209, 210, 212, 213, 216, 217, 219, 220, 222
Kadina Young Men's Club, 63
Kalgoorlie, 43, 99, 214
Kapunda, 207
Keen family, 208
Keen, Fanny, 102
Kensington, 129
'Kernewek Lowender' Cornish festival, xv
Keswick, 71, 125, 201
Kings College London, Menzies Centre for Australian Studies, xvi
Kingston, Charles Cameron, 22
Kio (*q.v.* Moonta), 9, 11, 12, 13, 14, 15, 16, 17, 18, 20, 21, 37, 39, 43, 45, 49, 54, 56, 58, 75, 77, 80, 83, 90, 104, 116, 118, 119, 123, 129, 132, 134, 137, 151, 152, 160, 162, 168, 169, 170, 176, 177, 178, 179, 181, 185, 187, 188, 190, 213, 218, 219, 220, 222
Kitchener's Army, 10

Labor Party (*q.v.* United Labor Party), 9, 21, 28, 29, 132, 143, 149–55, 156, 210, 220
Lagincourt, 181
Lake, Octavius, 146–8, 154, 160
Lancashire, 10
Land's End, 118, 136
Lathlean, Porter, 63
Learmond, Robert, 164
Leane, Brigadier-General Raymond, 206–7
Lebanon, 188
Le Frauley, 197
Le Havre, 132
Lemnos, 49, 55, 57, 60
Lennell, Mrs E., 70, 71, 117, 120–22
Liberal Party, 153
Lincolnshire, 129
Liverpool, 198
Lizard, The, 118
Lloyd George, David, 206
Lochiel, 166
London, 111, 117, 123, 127, 129, 131, 132–4, 136, 195, 197

Lone Pine, Battle of (*q.v.* Gallipoli), 65,
    67–70, 72, 73, 76, 77, 102, 115,
    117
Lostwithiel, 117
Ludendorff, Erich, 35, 86, 184, 190
Lukey, Beatrice Victoria, 197
Luscombe family, 208
Lutherans, 21, 22

Maddaford family, 63, 208
Maddaford, R.J., 102
Mahomet, Gool, 47
Maitland, 79, 180
Makin, Norman, 150–1
Malta, 32, 70, 71, 117
Major, Ephraim jun., 26, 38, 43, 59, 60, 68,
    84
Manchester, 33
Mannix, Daniel, 154
Marseilles, 90, 132
Marshall family, 208
Matta House, 209
McCay, Major-General James, 94
Mediterranean, 48, 49, 113, 134
Melbourne, 53, 86, 97, 99, 113, 120, 138,
    154, 182
Mena, 57
Messines, 12, 163, 173, 174, 175, 177
Methodists; Methodism (*q.v.* Bible
    Christians, *q.v.* Primitive Methodists,
    q.v. Wesleyans), 9, 16, 17, 18, 26, 37,
    48, 63, 65, 80, 81, 82, 83, 84, 85,
    103, 144–7, 149–51, 154, 155, 162,
    167, 197, 214, 220
Middle East, 39, 45, 79, 111, 188
Military units, Boer War and Great War
    Allied:
      I ANZAC Corps, 90, 108, 166, 167, 172,
        181
      II ANZAC Corps, 174, 177, 181
      1st Australian Division, A.I.F., 90, 100
      1st Australian Tunnelling Company,
        A.I.F., 173
      1st Machine Gun Battalion, A.I.F., 54
      2nd Australian Tunnelling Corps, A.I.F.,
        183
      2nd Australian Division, A.I.F., 90, 101
      3rd Australian Division, A.I.F., 168, 170,
        173, 184
      3rd Australian Tunnelling Company,
        A.I.F., 204

3rd Brigade, 1st Australian Division, A.I.F.,
    49, 55
3rd Light Horse, 32
3rd Training Battalion, A.I.F., 33
4th Australian Division, A.I.F., 90, 101,
    108, 170, 171, 184
4th Field Ambulance, A.I.F., 40
5th Australian Division, A.I.F, 92, 94, 96
8th Machine Gun Company, A.I.F., 167
9th Australian Light Horse, A.I.F., 188,
    189
10th Battalion, A.I.F. (the 'famous 10th'),
    33, 49, 50, 55, 57, 59, 69, 101,
    102, 113, 121, 181
10th British Division, 115
11th Brigade, 3rd Australian Division,
    A.I.F., 168, 190
11th British Division, 115
11th Field Ambulance, A.I.F., 80, 123
12th Battalion, A.I.F., 34, 35
14th Battalion, A.I.F., 10
14th Field Ambulance, A.I.F., 167
15th Field Ambulance, A.I.F., 83
16th Field Ambulance, A.I.F., 83
27th Battalion, A.I.F., 178
32nd Battalion, A.I.F., 96, 97, 99, 178
41st Battalion, A.I.F., 178
43rd Battalion, A.I.F., 80, 85, 87, 128,
    168, 184, 185, 198
50th Battalion, A.I.F., 197
61st British Division, 93, 94
'Accrington Pals', 10
Australian Corps, 186, 187, 190
Australian and New Zealand Army Corps,
    xiv, 49
Australian Army Medical Corps, 36
Australian Army Nursing Service, 165
Australian Light Horse, 188
Australian Tunnelling Corps, 36, 37, 173
Bush Veldt Carbineers, 22
Canadian Corps, 108
Duke of Cornwall's Light Infantry, 23
New Zealand Division, 90
Otago Mounted Rifles, 71
Overseas Training Brigade, A.I.F., 32, 97
Pay Corps, A.I.F., 83
Penryn No.3 Works Company, Cornwall
    Fortress Royal Engineers, 187–8
Scots Guards (1st and 2nd Battalions), 29
'Sheffield Pals', 10
South Australian Mounted Rifles, 22

Territorial Army (United Kingdom), xvi, 187–8
Enemy:
Bavarian Reserve Regiments, 94
Prussian Guards, 108
Mines
Australian:
Block 10, 45
Broken Hill Proprietary, 46
Burra Burra, 17, 221
Central (Broken Hill), 47
Doora, 216
Duryea, 216
Hamley, 46, 50
Ivanhoe, 85
Kapunda, 17
Matta, 213
Moonta, 16, 17, 18, 24, 27, 36, 83, 85, 132, 141, 143, 156, 161, 193, 211, 212, 216, 217
New Cornwall, 216
Poona, 216
Preamimma, 216
Wallaroo, 16, 17, 18, 24, 27, 30, 46, 85, 89, 117, 141, 143, 156, 193, 211, 212, 213, 217, 220, 221
Wandilta, 216
Wild Dog Mine, 216
Cornish:
Dolcoath, 140
Monash, Major-General Sir John, 85, 163, 168, 170, 173, 174, 186–7, 220
Mont St Quentin, 86, 188, 190
Moonta (*q.v.* Cross Roads, *q.v.* Kio), xv, xvi, 1, 3, 7, 9, 13, 14, 15, 16, 17, 18, 20, 22, 26, 27, 30, 31, 36, 37, 39, 40, 41, 42, 43, 44, 45, 46, 48, 50, 52, 54, 57, 59, 62, 65, 68, 69, 70, 72, 75, 77, 79, 83, 84, 89, 91, 97, 99, 102, 104, 105, 110, 111, 112, 113, 117, 118, 119, 122, 128, 129, 131, 132, 135, 137, 138, 140, 151, 153, 155, 159, 161, 162, 164, 166, 167, 168, 169, 174, 178, 181, 182, 185, 187, 189, 192, 194, 195, 196, 197, 198, 201, 202, 203, 204, 207, 208, 210, 218, 219, 220, 221, 222
Moonta Athletic Club, 41
Moonta Bay, 16, 108, 202
Moonta Branch, National Trust of South Australia (*q.v.* Kadina Branch, *q.v.* Wallaroo Branch), xvi, 16

Moonta, East, 47, 57, 69, 72, 77, 85, 119, 122, 167, 181, 185
Moonta Miners Association, 132
Moonta Mines (*q.v.* Hamley Flat), 1, 6, 17, 30, 32, 38, 39, 50, 54, 61, 63, 73, 75, 79, 80, 81, 83, 84, 85, 89, 90, 96, 97, 102, 107, 118, 119, 122, 125, 127, 144, 145, 155, 158, 167, 179, 182, 189, 202, 214, 216
Moonta Mines Knitting and Trench Comforts League, 164
Moonta Mines Male Voice Choir, 38, 84, 85, 192, 194
Moonta Mines Soldiers' Aid League/Society, 30, 80, 84, 119, 122, 129
Moonta, North, 30, 213
Moonta Patriotic Committee/League, 12, 30, 44
Moonta Prospecting Syndicate, 216
Moonta Recovery Company cementation works, 216, 220, 221
Moonta School of Mines, xv, 24
Moonta, South, 85
Moonta Tennis Club, 63
Morant, Harry 'Breaker', 22
Morphetville, 57
Mousehole, 136
Mount Barker, 57
Mouquet Farm, 89, 97, 101, 106, 107, 108
Moyarra, 43
Mudros, 49, 50

Nankivell family, 216
Nankivell, Mr and Mrs Elias, 54
National Labor Party, 153
National(ist) Party, 153, 154, 158
Naura, 25
Nek, The, 115
New Guinea (*q.v.* Papua), 23, 25, 206
New Ireland, 26
New South Wales, 8, 28, 45, 149, 152, 158, 211
New Zealand; New Zealanders, xiv, 1, 4, 10, 39, 40, 48, 49, 71, 79, 90, 115, 116, 131, 136, 143, 164, 173, 174, 184
Newquay, 118
Nullarbor, 79

Ontario, 117
Ottoman Empire (*q.v.* Turkey; Turks), 48, 50, 66, 76

Pacific Ocean, 23, 24, 26, 27, 206
Palestine, 111, 188, 189, 207
Papua (*q.v.* New Guinea), 23
Paris, 90, 184
Pascoe, Laurel, 164
Paskeville, 140, 145
Passchendaele (*q.v.* Ypres, Third Battle of),
        177, 181
Pemberton, Revd, 97
Penang, 30
Penberthy family, 119
Penzance, 118, 136
Péronne, 86, 190
Perranporth, 118
Perth (Australia), xiii, 43, 202
Petersburg, 188
Phillips, Edward, 143
Piper, Richard, 46
Plumer, General Sir Herbert, 173, 174
Plymouth, 125
Polygon Wood, 181
Ponsanooth, 23
Port Kembla, 28
Port Pirie, 214
Port Victoria, 207
Port Wakefield, 140
Pozières (*q.v.* Fromelles; *q.v.* Somme, battle
        of the), 4, 12, 57, 89, 90, 94, 95, 96,
        100–6, 108, 108, 115, 123, 134, 148,
        158, 163, 166, 167, 168, 172
Price, Councillor W., 51, 62
Primitive Methodists (*q.v.* Bible Christians;
        Methodists; Methodism; Wesleyans),
        17
Prisk family, 203
Protestants, 48, 153
Prussia, Prussian, 101, 161
Pryor, Oswald, 13, 16, 17, 36
Putney, 118

Queensland, 8, 55, 147
Quinn's Post (*q.v.* Gallipoli), 32, 53, 66
Quintrell née Datson, Mary Ann
        (*q.v.* Quintrell, Clarence Horace;
        q.v. Quintrell, John Adolphus;
        Quintrell, Richard Hugh; Quintrell,
        Stephen), 1, 2–3, 6, 7, 97–9, 106
Quintrell, Stephen, 3

Rabaul, 25
Redruth, 118

Reed, Dorrie, 164
Returned Sailors' and Soldiers' Imperial
        League, 201, 204, 205, 207–8, 220
Richards, Richard, 155
Richards, Robert Stanley, 84, 150, 154,
        155, 156, 159, 161, 162, 204, 212–13,
        216–17, 220
Roach, Clara, 181, 200
Roach, Jean, 164
Rose, Ernest, 85
Rose, Isabella, 85, 86–9
Rose, Reuben snr, 85
Rowe family, 119, 136
Royal Holloway College, University of
        London, xiv
Royal Marines, 3 Commando Brigade, xiv
Royal Naval College, Greenwich, xiv
Royal Navy, xiv, 23, 48, 49
Royal Australian Navy, 24, 25
Rule, Edgar, 10
Russell, Edgar (*q.v.* Degenhardt, Edgar), 27
Russia; Russians, 2, 23, 159, 184

Salisbury Plain, 11, 32, 116, 120, 125, 126,
        127, 128, 129, 130, 132, 135, 168
Salonika, 165
Salvation Army, 57, 58, 61
Sampson family, 208
Sampson, Sam, 167
Scaddan, John, 151–2, 153
Schwan, Rody, 99
Scotland; Scottish (*q.v.* Highlanders), 10, 53,
        85, 91, 115, 123, 132, 149
Second Ridge (*q.v.* Gallipoli), 58, 66
Second World War (*q.v.* World War II), xiii,
        222
Sennen, 136
Servicemen and women
        Abbott, William 'Billy' Townsend, 80,
                168, 177–8
        Allen, T., 107–8
        Anderson, Charles, 37, 38, 39
        Anderson, Stanley 'Stan', 196–7
        Andrews, Stanley, 104
        Angove, Alfred James, 130
        Ballantyne, David, 53
        Banfield, Henry Charles, 57–61, 207
        Barlow, Leslie Ernest, 50
        Barnard, S.C., 202
        Beaglehole, Percy, 106, 181
        Best, Joseph, 189

Bishop, Les, 166
Blight, Clive, 188
Bodinner, Charles, 36, 195
Bowden, Thomas, 67
Bray, Herbert 'Herby', 178, 181
Brokenshire, Harry, 192
Brokenshire, Percy, 37, 38, 39, 69, 70, 76
Brokenshire, William 'Bill', 37, 54, 65, 68–70, 72, 76, 105, 192
Brown, Harry Cecil, 53
Carthew, Fred, 40
Champion, A.L., 199
Champion, Percy, 180
Chappel, Richard Harold 'Harry', 75, 76, 178, 181
Clayton, A.R., 192
Cliff, T.G., 199
Cloak, C., 202
Cock, Joe, 52
Colliver, E.C., 181
Crago, J., 109
Cross, Albert Fleetwood, 89, 106
Curnow, W., 202
Cuttris (Signaller), 71, 72
Davey, Frederick, 80, 168
Davey, Oliver Leopold, 31, 52
Davies, (Private), 75
Daw, Richard, 104, 166
Donlon, James, 204–5
Dowling, Donald, 40, 41
Dunstan, William, 68
Edgecombe, (Private), 169
Ellery, W., 195
Elphick, Arthur Thomas, 50–2
Emerson, Jack, 132
Evans, (Corporal), 139–40, 143
Farrow, Daisy Clara Hotham, 164–5
Ferry, Mary Franceska, 164–5
Francis, Roy, 189
Gibbs, Thomas 'Tom', 178–9, 182
Gill, J.W., 77, 207
Green, Cliff, 47
Green, G. 53
Grummet, Bert, 63, 123, 134, 137
Hall, Harold, 172
Harvey, Leonard John, 80, 125, 132–7, 152–3, 160–2, 168–70, 174, 176–80, 181–2, 183, 184–5, 186, 190–2, 193, 197–9, 218
Harwood, Frank Norman, 72, 131–2
Hocking, Samuel, 186

Hoffman, Clarence Rhody Swan, 7, 99–100
Holthouse, H.S., 31, 35
Humphries, Brian, 104
Jacka, Albert, 66
Jacob, John, 31
Jacob, G.C., 202
Jacob, Kenneth Grant, 31, 34, 35
Jacob, Ross Blyth, 31, 32, 34, 35
Keen, Joseph, 69, 77, 102–3, 104
Kindail, T., 31
Knuckey, W.H., 202
Lanyon, Joseph James, 167
Lamshed, Clarence, 109
Learmouth, W.J., 189
Lennell, Fred Jeram, 120–2, 123, 134
Lennell, Leigh Treweek, 54, 70–1, 117–19, 120, 123, 137
Lewis, C.F., 96
Luscombe, Kingsley, 186, 187
MacDonald, V., 106
Mackinlay, K.H., 167
Maddern, Fred, 181
Major, Claude, 199
Martyn, Alf, 66, 73, 76
Matthews, (Sergeant-Major), 201, 202, 208
Medlin, J., 202
Merrifield, James, 31
McInerney, (Corporal), 199
McKee, Hurtle, 180
McLean, Isaac, 109
McMartin, Elsie, 164–5
Miller, Charles, 180
Mitchell, William J., 180, 190
Murdock, 'Chook', 135
Nankivell, Lee Bray, 53, 54, 68
Nankivell, Oscar, 129, 180–1
Nankivell, Presto John, 109
Oats, Gilbert 'Bert' Roy, 80, 128–9, 168, 177, 179
Olds, Percy, 134, 187
Olifent, F.V., 202
Padman, Clarence Swann, 167
Pascoe, A.C., 200
Pedler, Thomas, 72, 178
Pedler, Wilfred, 186
Penrose, Dick, 132
Perkins, Roy, 68, 69, 70, 72, 73
Perry, William James, 183
Pethick, Eustice Glynn Todd, 80, 168

Pethick, Melville, 52, 112–15, 117
Pickering, Roy, 54–7
Polglase, Percy, 192
Pollard, Lloyd Ewart, 80, 123–8, 132,
    134, 137, 168, 201
Pollard, Roy Percival, 63, 123–5, 202
Pollard, William 'Bill', 177
Pomeroy, Richard 'Lee' Leopard, 37, 54,
    66, 73, 90, 103, 129
Pomeroy, William 'Will' Albert, 37, 41,
    54, 73, 90, 102, 103, 129, 134
Porker, Jasper, 202
Porter, W., 202
Price, Wally, 170
Pyatt, John 'Jack', 80, 87, 136, 168,
    177–8, 179, 199
Quintrell, Clarence Horace 'Quint', 1, 3,
    97, 98, 106
Quintrell, John Adolphus, 1, 3, 96, 97, 98
Quintrell, Percy, 37, 173, 203
Quintrell, Richard Hugh, 1, 3, 7, 96–8
Quintrell, Stanley 'Stan', 37
Raymond, Fred, 54
Reynolds, Ernest Elmer 'Snowy', 170
Reynolds, William, 199
Richards, C.W., 195
Rieken, Hans, 27
Ritter, Richard, 96, 185
Roach, Douglas 'Doug' Peter, 134,
    135–6, 177–8, 179, 186, 187
Roach, Jacob 'Jake', 69, 73, 75, 76, 131,
    134, 169, 186, 198, 200
Roach, James 'Jim', 134, 176–7, 181, 186,
    199, 200
Rodda, Percy, 177
Rogers, Leigh, 63
Roberts, James, 211
Robinson, F.H., 164
Rose, Reuben Charles 'Charlie', 80, 84,
    85–9, 134, 168, 169, 177, 190
Rowett, William Linton, 31
Sampson, Peter Bramwell, 80, 87, 168,
    169, 177–8, 179–80
Samuels, Harold, 188
Sandford, Albert William, 105
Semmens, (Trooper), 199
Shaw, D.G., 31
Shepley, G.W., 31
Shields, Richard 'Dick', 31, 40, 54,
    59–60, 66, 69, 70, 72, 75, 105,
    106

Shorter, William 'Will' George Addison,
    80, 168, 169, 177–8, 181
Smith, A.J., 111, 113, 117, 189
Smith, Edwin 'Teddy', 104, 116
Smith, R.S.T., 199
Simpson; John Kirkpatrick, xiv
Stevens, E.S., 202
Stevenson, F.H., 202
Sutton, Percy, 183
Symons, Parker, 195
Symons, William, 68
Teo, Frederick, 63–4
Thomas, Abraham, 200
Thomas, 'Masher', 75, 77–8
Thomas, Seymour Jacka, 181
Trembath, Richard 'Dick', 80, 168,
    174–6, 177–8, 182–3
Trembath, William Thomas 'Leonard',
    80, 84, 85, 87, 168, 169, 177, 179,
    192, 196, 197, 207
Trenwith, Arthur Aubrey, 117–20, 137
Tubb, Frederick, 68
Vercoe, George, 91–2, 181
Verran, Frederick Gordon, 83
Verran, William Richard, 167–8, 181
Waters, Arnold Santo, 204
Weatherill, Joseph Cook, 66, 73
Whetter, Fred, 117
Whetter, Tom, 117
Whitbread, William, 180
Whiting, C., 202
Wilkinson, (Lance-Corporal), 108
Willard, Frederick, 90, 104, 148
Williams, Cecil, xiv, 188
Williams, John James, 104
Williams, R., 62
Wood, Herbert, 39
Woods, W., 199, 202
Woon, John Dunstan, 73
Woon, Leslie, 202

Ships
  Allied:
  Arabic, 134
  Australcrag, 35
  Australia, 24
  Ayrshire, 52
  Ballarat, 58
  Clan MacGillivray, 57
  Coo-ee, 35
  Dunluce Castle, 70

Euripides, 97
Gascon, 50
Nestor, 137, 198
Prince of Wales, 55, 56
Queen Elizabeth, 57
Sydney, 25
Enemy:
Emden, 25
Ships
Contemporary:
Anzac, xiv
Ark Royal, xiv
Kanimbla, xiv
Shetlands, 1
Shrapnel Gully (*q.v.* Gallipoli), xiv, 53
Sinai, 188
Sinn Fein, 149, 154, 159
Silverton, 46
Sleep family, 208
Soldiers' Female Relative's Association, 208
Solomon Islands, 206
Somerset, 126
Somme, Battle of (*q.v.* Fleurbaix;
     q.v. Fromelles; *q.v.* Mouquet Farm;
     q.v. Pozières), 4, 10, 89, 90, 91, 92.
     93, 94, 100, 109, 127, 134, 139, 140,
     143, 166, 170, 202
Song of Australia, The, 209–10
South Africa; South Africans, 10, 22, 23,
    115
South Australia; South Australian, xv, 3, 12,
    13, 17, 19, 21, 22, 27, 35, 36, 43, 46,
    49, 55, 63, 82, 118, 132, 139, 146,
    147, 150, 151, 152, 154, 159, 162, 191,
    202, 207, 209, 214, 220
South Australia, History Trust of (*q.v.* History
    SA), xvii
South Australia, State Library of, xvi
South Australian Children's Patriotic Fund,
    63
South Australian (Wounded) Soldiers' Fund,
    61, 62
South Australian Recruiting Office and
    Committee, 122, 158
South Australian State Trophy Committee,
    207
Southampton, 128, 132
Sowden, Sir William, 207
St Agnes, 118
St Ives, 118, 136
St Just-in-Penwith, 136

St Patrick's Day, 154
Stendal Prisoner of War camp,
    Saxony-Anhalt, 202
Stocker, W., 72, 75
Stonehenge, 127, 132
Stratford-upon-Avon, 123
Sudan; Soudan, p.48
Suez Canal, 39, 79, 89, 90, 165, 186
Sullecourt, 181
Sunnyvale, 104, 109, 202, 204
Suvla Bay (*q.v.* Gallipoli), 115, 123
Sweeney, Councillor, 59, 81, 109
Switch Trench, 120
Sydney, 53, 71, 138
Symons, James, 195
Syria, 188

Tamar, River, 125
Tasmania, 8, 16, 55
Taylor, A.J.P, 3
Tel-el-Kebir, 31, 90
Temby, Porter, 62
Thiepval, 100, 101
Third (Gun) Ridge (*q.v.* Gallipoli), 56, 57
Tippara, 30
Thomas, J.H. 'Johnnie', 65, 181
Thomas, William Beach, 123
Thorne, Serena, 147, 148
Tickera, 79
Tippet family, 129
Toledo, Ohio, 145
Trathen, Mollie, 164
Tregear, Mary Elsie, 16
Trembath, Margaret, 182–3
Trenwith family, 216
Trenwith, Elizabeth, 120
Treweek, Joseph C., 71, 120
Truro, Cornwall, 116, 118
Tsingtao, 24
Tuckingmill, 155
Turkey; Turks (*q.v.* Ottoman Empire), 2, 4,
    27, 32, 39, 46, 47, 48, 49, 54, 54, 56,
    60, 66, 67, 68, 71, 72, 76, 77, 78, 89,
    114, 115, 116, 139, 188, 192

United Kingdom (*q.v.* Britain, British,
    q.v. British Isles), 111, 112, 116, 122,
    123, 130, 136, 166
United Labor Party (*q.v.* Labor Party), 18, 22,
    84, 151
United States of America (*q.v.* America), 206

Vaughan, Crawford, 139–40, 151, 152, 153
Verdun, 92
Verran, Ada, 167
Verran, Catherine, 167–8
Verran, Henry, 167
Verran, John, 18, 26, 63, 82–3, 97, 146,
        149–51, 153, 155, 156, 158, 159–60,
        161, 162, 204–7, 210, 212, 220
Versailles, Treaty of, 205–6, 210
Victoria; Victorian (Australia), 6, 9, 17, 21,
        43, 66, 68, 147, 149, 154, 201, 207
Victoria, Queen, 13
Victoria Gully (q.v. Gallipoli), 69
Villers-Bretonneux, 184, 185
Vimy Ridge, 117

Wales; Welsh, 10, 116, 143, 146, 147, 149,
        206
Walker, Major-General Harold 'Hookey',
        34
Wallaroo, 9, 14, 16, 20, 30, 31, 45, 50, 53,
        62, 66, 73, 75, 77, 79, 84, 106, 109,
        140, 144, 148, 151, 157, 159, 161,
        162, 164, 165, 178, 180, 183, 186,
        193, 203, 204, 209, 210, 211, 216,
        217, 219, 220, 222
Wallaroo and Moonta Mining and Smelting
        Company, 27, 29, 62, 83, 139, 144,
        156, 157, 210–14
Wallaroo Branch, National Trust of South
        Australia (q.v. Kadina Branch,
        q.v. Moonta Branch), xvi
Wallaroo Mines, 30, 62, 79, 139, 140, 144,
        147, 170, 180, 202, 214, 216
Wallaroo Mines Dramatic Company, 30
Wallaroo Mines Orchestra, 217
Walters, Mrs N., 195
Warlencourt, 170, 181
Warneton, 177, 178
Warren, John, 45
Wearne family, 73, 208
Wedderburn, 66
Weetulta, 30
Wesley, Charles, 103
Wesleyans (q.v. Bible Christians, Primitive
        Methodists, Methodist; Methodism),
        15, 17, 70

West Coast, 79
Western Australia; Western Australian, xiii,
        8, 15, 16, 40, 43, 55, 85, 151, 165
Western Front, 11, 36, 79, 101, 107, 112,
        115, 141, 168, 184, 185, 186, 187, 188,
        190, 204, 213
Weymouth, 11, 38, 113, 114, 116, 117, 119,
        124, 130, 131, 132, 135, 162
White, Frank, 46, 47
Whitford, Stanley, 155
Whyalla, 214
Wiltshire, 126, 131
Wilson, Woodrow, 206
Wobblies (q.v. International Workers of the
        World), 155, 205
World War II, xiii (q.v. Second World War)
Wood, John, 39
Woolnough, H., 208

Yelta, 90, 145, 148, 216
Yelta, North, 73
Yeovil, 131
Young Men's Christian Association, 133
Yorke Peninsula, xv, 3, 6, 7, 9, 11, 12, 13,
        14, 15, 16, 17, 18, 19, 20, 21, 22, 23,
        24, 25, 26, 27, 28, 29, 30, 36, 37, 39,
        40, 41, 43, 44, 45, 46, 47, 49, 50, 53,
        54, 58, 61, 65, 66, 75, 76, 77, 79, 81,
        84, 89, 95, 96, 103, 105, 107, 110,
        111, 116, 118, 119, 123, 129, 134, 137,
        139, 140, 141, 144, 145, 146, 147,
        148, 150, 152, 155, 156, 157, 159,
        160, 161, 162, 163, 164, 165, 167,
        175, 180, 181, 188, 193, 195, 196,
        199, 202, 203, 205, 207, 209, 210,
        214, 216, 217, 218, 219, 220, 221, 222
Yorke's Peninsula Football Association, 30
Yorke's Peninsula Miners and Smelters'
        Association (q.v. Bogies), 156
Yorkshire, 10
Ypres, First Battle of, 39
Ypres, Third Battle of (q.v. Passchendaele),
        12, 80, 85, 163, 173, 177–80, 181,
        200, 207
Ypres Salient, 108, 166, 167, 173, 177, 181

Zonnebeke, 181